THE UNCOMMON LIFE OF

DANNY O'CONNELL

A TALE OF BASEBALL CARDS,
"AVERAGE" HEROES AND
THE TRUE VALUE OF AMERICA'S GAME

bancroft
press

STEVE WIEGAND

The Uncommon Life of Danny O'Connell

Cover & Interior Design: TracyCopesCreative.com
Author Illustration: By Pulitzer Prize-winning cartoonist Jack Ohman.

978-1-61088-633-8 (Hardcover)
978-1-61088-634-5 (Paperback)
978-1-61088-635-2 (Ebook)
978-1-61088-636-9 (PDF Ebook)
978-1-61088-637-6 (Audiobook)

bancroft
press

Published by Bancroft Press
"Books that Enlighten"
(818) 275-3061
4527 Glenwood Avenue
La Crescenta, CA 91214
www.bancroftpress.com
Printed in the United States of America

To all of us who have hit .260 in life ...
and are just fine with it.

TABLE OF CONTENTS

INTRODUCTION,

OR

"WHO IN THE HELL IS DANNY O'CONNELL AND WHY SHOULD WE CARE?"

*"Next to religion, baseball has a greater impact on our American
way of life than any other American institution."*
– American president Herbert C. Hoover

*"Whoever wants to know the heart and mind of America
had better learn baseball."*
– American historian Jacques Barzun

"I always wanted to see my picture on a bubble gum card."
– American baseball player Al "The Bull" Ferrara

I first met Danny O'Connell in the late spring of 1960. It was at the Par Liquor Store, which was part of an unremarkable strip mall, about a half-mile from my unremarkable tract house in an unremarkable San Diego suburb called Serra Mesa.

To launch this book on a reasonably accurate level, I should here point out that I did not actually meet Danny O'Connell at the liquor store. What I encountered was his photographic image, on the front of a 2.5" by 3.5" piece of cardboard. In the color photo, he is holding a baseball bat behind his head and above his right shoulder. He has something of a world-weary look on his handsome, if slightly jowly, face. He is sporting a five o'clock shadow, which judging from most of the other photos I've seen of him apparently began sprouting about ten minutes after he finished shaving each morning. The color photo is flanked on the left by a smaller black-and-white picture of a crouching O'Connell, wearing an infielder's glove on his left hand and a facial expression that suggests the imminent arrival of a bouncing baseball.

On the back of the card, I learned that Danny O'Connell was 31 years old, 5'11" tall, 185 pounds in weight and hailed from Paterson, New Jersey. The card back listed his major league batting statistics, and sported a cartoon of a player sliding into third base and a caption reporting "Danny once hit three triples in one game." It also offered the cheerfully apologetic observation that "although Danny did not see too much action last season, he's still a great man to have around. He is a real seasoned pro on defense and adds stability to the lineup."

I did not like Danny O'Connell. I was not impressed that, at least according to the baseball card writer, he was stable and "a real seasoned pro." I didn't even care that he was wearing the uniform of the San Francisco Giants, which was then, is now, and always will be my favorite major league baseball team. I did not like Danny O'Connell because during the spring and summer of 1960, I saw way too much of him.

I was eight years old, going on nine, tall and skinny, with a shock of unruly curly hair and ears big enough to embarrass a small flying elephant. My parents had only recently begun giving me an allowance of 25 cents per week, and I used much of it to buy baseball cards. I collected them with an avidity I devoted later in life only to avoiding meaningful labor. Once a week I would traverse the half-mile to the liquor store, which at eight-going-on-nine seemed like 10 miles each way, with both directions uphill. I would buy two packs of cards for a nickel each, and spend another dime on a can of BigTime cherry cola. The last nickel invariably became the subject of a mental tug-of-war: spend it on a third pack of cards, or buy one of the maddening multitudes of candy bars taunting me from the store's endless array. I don't recall that last nickel ever accompanying me home.

Outside the store, I would quickly rip open the packs, reflexively stuff a hard pink slab of what I assumed was bubble gum into my mouth, and eagerly thumb through the cards. The dream was to find at least one of my beloved Giants among them.

It was an oft-shattered dream. There were 572 different cards in the complete set, which was manufactured by a Brooklyn-based company called Topps. Of that 572, only 36—or roughly 6.3 percent—featured Giants, and that included the manager, coaches and team card, on the last of which the individuals were so small as to be unrecognizable. The total of 36 Giants did not include the card of Gordon Jones, a Baltimore Orioles pitcher who was depicted wearing a Giants cap. Jones had been traded by the Giants after the 1959 season, and apparently no one at Topps noticed he was still sporting last season's chapeau. My point is that even if you counted Jones as half a Giant, the odds still weren't great I'd see any of my favorite team's players when I pulled off those wax paper wrappings.

But on those rare occasions when I did get a card of someone wearing an SF cap (not counting Gordon Jones), it was invariably No. 192, which bore the likeness of—you guessed it—Danny O'Connell. This was made all the more vexing when I eventually learned O'Connell didn't even play for the Giants in 1960. He was cut in the last days of Spring Training, after the Topps cards had been produced, and spent the season playing for Tacoma, the Giants' Triple-A farm team in the Pacific Coast League.

I was thus piling up card after card of a player who was only masquerading as a big leaguer. So I did not like Danny O'Connell. It took six decades, but I eventually changed my mind.

My re-encounter with Danny O'Connell, again indirectly, came in early 2022, this time in the form of a spate of news stories about a gold-rush-like boom in what had once been a kids' hobby of sports card collecting. Ostensibly sane people were paying staggering sums not only for rare "vintage" cards of icons such as Babe Ruth, but also for untested teenagers who had yet to play a single inning in the major leagues.

A 1909 card featuring Honus Wagner, for example, sold for $6.6 million in August, 2021. Wagner, for the uninitiated, is considered one of the greatest shortstops ever, and was part of the inaugural class in the Baseball Hall of Fame. Five months later, a 2021 card featuring Jasson Dominguez sold at auction for $474,000. At the time, Dominguez was an 18-year-old prospect who had played just 49 games of professional baseball at its lowest level, and not exactly sparkled. Even a 1958 Danny O'Connell card that was graded in "gem mint" condition was being offered on eBay in late 2022 for a hefty $13,125. Seriously.

American free enterprise adroitly adapted to the influx of big bucks into baseball card collecting. A slew of auxiliary cottage industries sprang up to get a piece of the action. As I write this in the fall of 2023, there are companies to appraise your cards' condition; auction your cards; insure your cards, and store your cards in vaults secured by around-the-clock armed guards. Seriously.

Baseball cards, I learned, had become valid components of Wall Street investment portfolios. Investors with shallower pockets could pool their resources with their pals or even strangers and buy a percentage of a particular card or collection. You could also buy a card that exists only as data in a digital blockchain. In March 2022, a 1952 Mickey Mantle NFT—or non-fungible token—sold for $470,000. The proud owner can brag about it, gaze upon it online and with any luck sell it for more than he paid. But he can never ever touch it, flip it or put it in his bicycle spokes to make that neat clicking sound, unless he owns a virtual bicycle.

There were apparently a lot of people with enough money and interest to invest in small pieces of very expensive cardboard. "The industry is at its hottest point in my 40-year history," the founder of a major sports collectibles auction house told *The New York Times*. "It is nearly impossible to keep up with demand from buyers."

This was clearly not the hobby of my distant and largely misspent youth. Back then, baseball card collecting basically consisted of collecting baseball cards. You paid your nickel, opened the pack, tried to chew the gum or else saved it for replacing roof shingles on the tool shed, and did stuff with the cards. For instance, you could spread them on the living room floor and play a game using a marble as a ball and a pencil as a bat. If the marble rolled over a card, it was an out. If not, it was a single, double, triple or homer, depending on how far the marble went.

You could stick them in your bicycle's tire spokes so the wheels made a clicking noise, just like the big kids' bikes, which had real gears and ball-bearing derailleurs. My bike spokes featured cards of which I had doubles, or those bearing the likenesses of the hated Los Angeles Dodgers.

You could gamble with them. One game consisted of betting on whether two cards flipped in the air would both land face-up or face-down, or one of each. The winner got to keep the cards. Another game was to toss the cards Frisbee-like at a wall. The card closest to the wall was the winner, and the card's owner thus entitled to all the other tossed cards.

And you could trade them. I learned a lot about human nature trading baseball cards. One of the kids I traded with, coincidentally enough, was named Danny O'Connell. A nice kid, but hopelessly naïve when it came to trading cards. He would part with a Rocky Colavito, a six-time All-Star who once hit four homers in a single game, for a Rocky Nelson, a zero-time All-Star who once hit five homers in an entire season, on the theory that after all they were both nicknamed Rocky. It was very hard not to take advantage of Danny. Sometimes I didn't.

On the other hand, there was John Shaw. He was a kid from New York who stubbornly insisted Micky Mantle was better than Willie Mays. Despite this character defect, he was one shrewd card trader. His acumen served him well when he grew up and got a chance to trade real people in his role as president of the Los Angeles Rams pro football team.

At no time in my youth did money enter into card transactions, except once. I sold a 1956 Roy Campanella, a Dodger that a relative had given me, to Frankie Till, a kid across the street, for one dollar. He threw in two 1960 Giants: Hobie Landrith, a catcher who was best known for being the first player selected to play for the legendarily bad 1962 New York Mets and for having a cool first name, and Andre Rodgers, a shortstop from the Bahamas who was better at playing cricket than baseball. The Landrith and Rodgers cards are worth maybe $3 each as I write this. Campanella is in the Hall of Fame, and his 1956 card is worth maybe $200 today. Frankie Till went on to earn a doctorate in mathematics and became superintendent of two major U.S. urban school districts. I majored in English and became a newspaper reporter. So, there you go.

In the parlance of baseball card collecting, Landrith, Rodgers and yes, O'Connell, are known as "commons." It means they are players that few people, even ardent fans, remember. In baseball card price guides, they often aren't even listed by name. They are just "commons" for a particular year's set, all fetching the same low price. And they are seldom if ever the subjects of biographies. Baseball biographies are reserved for the sport's luminaries—Aaron and

Gehrig, Koufax and Williams, Cobb and Clemente. But the stories about rampant speculation and fabulous riches in the brave new world of card collecting spurred in me memories of my long-ago quest for Giants cards. I remembered Danny O'Connell. And after a bit of digging into who he was and what he did, I found that "common" and "average" are not necessarily the same thing.

I learned that during his 10-year big league career, Danny O'Connell scored the first run ever in a major league game on the West Coast, and also made the last out ever in a venerable major league stadium on the East Coast. He was the most valuable player for the first big league team he played for, and also the last. He held one team's modern single-season consecutive-game hitting streak for more than 60 years. He still shares a major league record for most triples in one game. And he once played for two different clubs in games that started on the same day.

O'Connell's likeness (on a baseball card) can be found in the collections of the New York Metropolitan Museum of Art. At various times he was his team's best singer, golfer, shuffleboard player, card sharp, pool hustler, comedian and public speaker. And when it came to baseball, he was very, very smart. "He has one attribute that every good ball player must have," said Fred Haney, who managed O'Connell on two different clubs. "He thinks."

As an example, Haney recalled a game against the New York Giants in 1953, when he was manager of the Pittsburgh Pirates and O'Connell was his third baseman. Giants shortstop Alvin Dark was on first base late in the game when Bobby Thomson smacked a sharp single into right field. Dark raced to third ahead of the throw, whereupon Thomson took off for second. With no chance to get Thomson, O'Connell faked a throw then whirled and tagged out Dark, who had taken a step toward home. "You can't fool with that kid," acknowledged Giants manager Leo Durocher, who was not widely known for complimenting anyone, especially opposing players. "He's the kind of player who's always thinking one play ahead."

While thinking might help keep a player in the big leagues for a decade, it doesn't show up in the box scores. Baseball is a numbers game, and to put it charitably, Danny O'Connell's career statistics -- .260 lifetime batting average, .333 on-base percentage, .975 fielding average, 39 homers—were not the stuff of legends. But if there are lots—and lots—of numbers in baseball, there are also lots of ways to look at them.

An axiom often attributed to Mark Twain (née Samuel L. Clemens) is that there are three kinds of falsehoods: lies; damned lies, and statistics. Twain himself rather vaguely attributed the origin of the aphorism to the eminent British statesman Benjamin Disraeli. I choose to stick with Twain, as he was an ardent baseball fan, and Disraeli, insofar as I know, was not. Disraeli might have liked cricket. That should not be allowed to detract from his prominent place in British history.

Evidence of Twain's status as a baseball fan, on the other hand, is abundant. While a resident of Hartford, Connecticut, he often attended games at the town's 2,000-seat ballpark to cheer on the hometown Dark Blues, and sometimes took copious notes about the games on his personal stationery. For one season, Twain/Clemens was even part-owner of the local club.

I digress from my point, which is that no other human endeavor proves the truth of Twain's statement about lies and statistics as much as baseball. Even casual fans are obsessed with various calculations, permutations and formulas that buttress their arguments, based on those numbers alone, about who is a player worthy of one's admiration and who is a bum that should be quickly exiled to the low minors.

"If philately (stamp collecting) attracts perforation counters, and sumo wrestling favors the weighty," observed the eminent evolutionary biologist and self-described baseball nut Stephen Jay Gould, "then baseball is the great magnet for statistical mavens and trivia hounds."

The obsession with statistics in baseball has only gotten more pronounced in recent years. The 21st century onslaught on most of the world by endless combinations of ones and zeroes—the Digital Age—has led in turn to an onslaught of new baseball-related statistics that breed like so many computerized rabbits. There is, for example, a new statistic called "Rdp," which as I understand it measures how well a player does at helping his team score runs by not hitting into double plays. For the record, Danny O'Connell's lifetime

Rdp was 1, which is exactly the same as Hall of Famer Stan Musial and twice as good as those of Hall of Famers Orlando Cepeda, Ernie Banks and Bill Mazeroski, among others.

The fellow I think most responsible for this obsession with esoteric data is Bill James, a statistician, historian and baseball nut who began analyzing and writing about the game while working as a security guard at a pork and beans cannery. James went on to: write more than 20 books; be named in 2006 by *Time* magazine as one of the 100 most influential people in the world; help the Boston Red Sox win four World Series as a senior advisor to the club, and coin the term "Sabermetrics." It's James' name for the science of mathematically scrutinizing everything that happens in and around a baseball game to the point that you seriously consider watching professional lawn bowling or pickle ball instead.

James adapted his term from a group of statistics-obsessed followers of baseball that in 1971 formed a serious, scholarly -- and frankly pretty nerdy -- organization called the Society for American Baseball Research, or SABR. At the risk of being charged with gross hypocrisy for grumping about the intrusion of silly numbers into the game of baseball, I must acknowledge that I am a proud dues-paying SABR member. So there.

All of this leads us back in a perhaps-regrettably convoluted way to Danny O'Connell, and the dismissive designation of him as an "average" player whose baseball cards are worthy only of "common" status. I beg to differ, and here are some statistics to support my position:

- The U.S. Census Bureau reports that there were 1,114,814 male human beings born in America in 1929, one of whom was Danny O'Connell. Of those, according to the *Baseball Almanac*, just 93—or 0.0000834 percent—grew up to play major league baseball. Some of those 93 were hardly in The Show long enough to get their jerseys dirty. Bill Abernathie, for example, pitched two innings for the Cleveland Indians on Sept. 27, 1952, gave up two singles, a triple and a home run, and never appeared in the big leagues again. In fact, only 27 of the 93 (that's a miniscule 0.0000242 percent of all of America's 1929 baby boys) played parts or all of at least 10 years in the majors. Danny O'Connell was one of them.

- According to Baseball-Reference.com, the leading oracle of baseball statistics, 20,272 players made it to the big leagues from the founding of the National League in 1876 through the 2022 season. Of that number, fewer than 10 percent lasted as long in the majors as Danny O'Connell.

- According to Stathead, another sports statistics research website, of the 20,272 major league players from 1876 through 2022, 1,346, or 6.6 percent, compiled at least 1,000 hits in their careers. Danny O'Connell had 1,049 career hits, or more than 93 percent of all big-league ballplayers. Ever.

- Homing in a bit more, between 1950 and 1962, the span encompassing O'Connell's career, 1,926 men played in the big leagues. Of those, only 72, or a paltry 3.7 percent, had more hits than O'Connell's career total.

- And as for his major league record-tying three triples in one game, it's true that through 2022, 43 other players—or 0.00195 percent of all big leaguers -- had also hit three triples in a game. But just two of those hit all of their three-baggers against a Hall of Fame pitcher. O'Connell was one of them. He did it in 1956, against Robin Roberts of the Philadelphia Phillies, who was one of the most dominant pitchers of the era. (The other fellow to hit three triples off a Hall of Famer was Ray Powell, a Boston Braves outfielder. Powell hit his in 1921 against Brooklyn spitballer Burleigh "Old Stubblebeard" Grimes. Neither Powell nor Grimes appears elsewhere in this book.)

There's more. From 1954 to 1958, O'Connell was second three times, third once and fourth once among National League second basemen in fielding percentage, despite persistent suggestions in the press that he was not especially adept at the position. In "Range Factor" (putouts plus assists), he led the league in 1953 at third base and in 1955 at second base. In one season or another during his career, he was in his league's top 10 in singles, doubles, triples, walks, stolen bases, sacrifices and being hit by pitches. And for a guy who neither hit for power nor was particularly fast, he even finished in the top 10 in 1957 in the National League's "Power-Speed#" stats, which factors home runs and stolen bases. (Admittedly, O'Connell's 10th place number was 8.5; Willie Mays' league-leading number was 36.4.)

Having thus proved the appropriateness of Twain's (or Disraeli's) axiom when it comes to the hasty and often misguided designation of some major league ballplayers as "common," I present to you the story of Danny O'Connell, a North New Jersey kid who grew up during the Great Depression and World War II, and for whom life was baseball and baseball was life.

This is also a book that touches on the evolution of baseball cards, from their birth as lures to entice young boys to take up cigarette smoking to their ascension, however transitory it may prove to be, as commodities that at least fiscally rival the artistic masterpieces of Michaelangelo and Monet, artifacts from ancient civilizations, and almost anything they show you on *Antiques Roadshow*.

But it's mostly about the life of a "common" player during what is often referred to—with a great deal of both nostalgia and nonsense—as baseball's "Golden Era." Danny O'Connell's career perfectly mirrored the period, beginning as it did in the year after World War II ended and ending with the expansion years of the early 1960s. It was a time when baseball was still the country's dominant team sport and still truly an American obsession, when even average players were lionized, while performing under an employment system reminiscent of mediaeval serfdom. It was a profession that at its highest level had a total of just 400 jobs each year. Moreover, O'Connell's career coincided precisely with the long-overdue racial integration of the game. As talented African-American players finally got a chance to compete in the National Pastime, competition for major league jobs got that much tougher.

Like other big leaguers, O'Connell made more money than most Americans of his generation. But he also lived with far greater uncertainty about his long-term financial future, and labored—or played if you prefer -- in a profession with a much shorter lifespan than almost any other. He never strayed far from his North Jersey roots, but also lived much of his adult life out of suitcases. His career was marked by an almost unbroken string of bad timing, tough breaks and missed chances. And he died tragically, and far too soon.

Still, for most of his life he got to play a game he loved. "I can't figure a guy not liking to play ball for a living," O'Connell told a sportswriter early in his big-league career. "Maybe after I've been in this game a long, long time I won't love it so much, but the way I look at it now, I can't get too much of it."

So this is a book about a man who had a devoted and loving wife, and four children who all grew up to be good people. It's about a hometown hero in post-war America who for a decade routinely got his name in newspapers across the country, and his visage on pieces of cardboard that brought pleasure to millions of kids.

And maybe it's also about how, if we're lucky, our childhood dreams and aspirations never really die. They just adapt to the real world. At 10, for example, I would gladly have given two fingers of my left hand to see my photo on a major league baseball card. At 72, probably no more than one.

NOTES FOR INTRODUCTION

A 1909 card In early September 2023, Dominguez was called up by the Yankees and got off to a very promising start, hitting four homers in his first eight games, before being seriously injured and projected to miss most or all of the 2024 season. Check back in five years or so to see whether that will justify spending $475,000 for his baseball card.

And there were *The New York Times*, Feb. 18, 2021, p. B7.

"If philately" Stephen Jay Gould, *Full House: The Spread of Excellence from Plato to Darwin*, p. 78.

O'Connell's likeness *Sport Magazine*, Vol. 16, No. 2 (Feb. 1954), p. 64.

As an example, Ibid.

Still, for most *Sport Magazine*, op. cit., p. 67.

CHAPTER 1
"THE LUCK OF THE IRISH"
DANNY'S GAME

On a bright and breezy San Francisco afternoon in mid-April, 1958, Daniel Francis O'Connell III stood 90 feet—and 2,895 miles—from home.

The first distance is easy to explain. O'Connell was perched on third base and aspired to reach the five-sided piece of hard white rubber that constituted home plate. Almost exactly 100 years before this particular afternoon, the Founding Fathers of baseball had decided the proper distance between bases should be 90 feet. So, easy to explain that distance. (If you're interested why they settled on 90 feet, see the notes at the end of the chapter.)

O'Connell had reached third base at an auspicious moment in the annals of baseball. It was his team's first game of the 1958 season, and also happened to be the first official major league game ever played on America's West Coast. To heighten the drama, it was being played by the archest of arch-rivals: the Los Angeles Dodgers, formerly of Brooklyn, and the San Francisco Giants, formerly of upper Manhattan. Leading off the bottom of the third inning of a scoreless tie, O'Connell, the Giants' second baseman, coaxed a walk from Dodger pitcher Don Drysdale. He thus became the first San Francisco Giant in history to reach base safely in a game that counted.

He advanced to second on another walk, and reached third on an infield single by Giants pitcher Ruben Gomez. Now, with the bases loaded and nobody out, O'Connell, along with more than 23,000 other people who had jammed into San Francisco's cozy Seals Stadium, waited anxiously as Jimmy Davenport, the Giants' rookie third baseman, approached the plate. Davenport had already struck out in the first inning against the 6'-5" 210-pound flame-throwing Drysdale, whose career would eventually be capped by entrance into baseball's Valhalla—the Hall of Fame.

That second distance mentioned above, 2,895 miles, is a bit of geographic literary license. Danny O'Connell had been born in, grew up in, and still resided just outside Paterson, New Jersey, a blue-collar town across the Hudson River from New York City. Even with traffic on the George Washington Bridge, Paterson was usually no more than a 30-minute drive from the colorfully named Polo Grounds, which is where the Giants had played their home games for three-quarters of a century. But in 1958, the Giants had moved to San Francisco, and the Dodgers from Brooklyn to Los Angeles.

The move greatly lengthened O'Connell's commute. He had viewed the relatively short drive from Paterson to the Polo Grounds as something of a consolation prize after being traded in the middle of the 1957 season to the Giants from the Milwaukee Braves. He had grown up attending Giants games with his dad. He had had some memorable moments in the venerable—if dilapidated and architecturally-ridiculous-stadium.

"My father would take me to the Polo Grounds about ten or eleven in the morning," he told an interviewer in 1957. "We'd bring our lunch and wait around until the game started. I'd get as much a kick out of watching Mel Ott and Burgess Whitehead and Travis Jackson and all those fellows in practice as in the game." O'Connell told the reporter he still had a foul ball hit by Ott. "It's the only ball I ever caught as a fan." So when he was traded to New York, Danny jokingly put it down to "the luck of the Irish...playing in the Polo Grounds gives me a chance to renew some old acquaintances in the New York area. And it will be nice being close to home. I only hope the Giants stay here."

They didn't. But if anyone was equipped to deal with the vagaries and vicissitudes of professional baseball, it was Danny O'Connell. Since he was six years old, his life's goal was to play baseball. He worked hard at playing. "I don't ever remember him not playing something," his younger sister, Alice O'Connell, recalled. "Even in the dead of winter, Danny would be pestering someone to play catch or shoot baskets."

He began playing baseball professionally at the age of 17. On that afternoon of April 15, 1958, he had reached third base after a dozen years of determination, hard work, and just enough athletic talent to achieve his dream of playing the game he loved at its highest level. But after a bright and promising start, at which various baseball soothsayers predicted looming stardom, his career sputtered, then plateaued. Sometimes it seemed the word "disappointing" appeared so often in front of "O'Connell" in newspaper stories, the casual reader could have been forgiven for thinking it was his first name.

Indeed, there were times when it seemed Danny was destined for disappointment. He lost two seasons to military service just as his big-league career began. He lost a chance to make an All-Star team because the team included a knuckleball pitcher and the manager decided he needed an extra catcher who specialized in corralling the unpredictable pitch. And he had a record-setting hitting streak snapped just one game before being honored by his hometown with a "Danny O'Connell Night"—at the Polo Grounds.

The Giants jersey on his back that afternoon in 1958 was part of the third uniform he had worn since beginning his major league career in 1950, (or fourth if you include the U.S. Army attire he sported for two years.) He was 29, which in the lifespan of a ballplayer was well into middle age. He had a wife and two very young daughters to support. He had a high school diploma, but no demonstrable job skills other than those associated with baseball.

It was true that with an estimated $14,500 contract for the season (about $158,000 in 2024 dollars), he stood to make almost three times what the average American family was earning in 1958. Moreover, Danny's salary had nearly tripled since his first full season in the majors in 1953, while the average American family's income had increased by only 11.7 percent during that five-year period. But most American workers in the 1950s could expect to put in 30 years or more with one employer if they chose and retire with a decent pension. Or they could sell their skills and talents to another company if they wanted.

In contrast, most major league players had a career life expectancy of maybe five years—if they stayed both skilled enough and healthy enough to fend off a constant stream of competitors for their jobs. For example, 66 players, including Danny O'Connell, made their major league debuts in 1950. Of that number, just 18, including Danny O'Connell, lasted in the majors for a decade or more. Twenty-eight lasted fewer than five seasons. Anything short of a 10-year career meant only a modest pension. And in April 1958, Danny still had more than a year to go before he had a decade's time in the majors.

In addition, thanks to a 1922 U.S. Supreme Court decision that appeared to be based more on *Alice in Wonderland* than the United States Constitution, baseball was exempt from the nation's anti-trust laws. Ballplayers were *de facto* indentured servants. The "reserve clause" in every major league contract bound the player to only one team in perpetuity. He could not peddle his services elsewhere, even after his contract expired, while the club could peddle him to any team it pleased at any time. Newspapers routinely referred to players as "chattel," "expendable" "or "trade bait."

"You did what the owners told you," Bob Kuzava, a pitcher whose 10-year career ended in 1957 at the age of 34, recalled. "If you refused to sign a contract, they wouldn't let you come to spring training. They'd say 'Well, stay home. Get a job in a factory.'"

And finally, there was the fact that there were generally only 400 jobs available at any given time in the big leagues. That was considerably fewer than the estimated 1,315,200 public school teaching positions at the time. Statistically speaking, it was much easier to get and hold a job as a second-grade teacher than to get and hold a job as a second baseman for the San Francisco Giants.

"Sometimes the deck seems a little stacked against us (players)," O'Connell acknowledged after the 1957 season to his pal Joe Gootter, the longtime sports editor and columnist for Paterson's *Evening News*. "But you sign a contract, you agree to the terms of the contract...and when you're out there playing, it's the game that counts. You just play hard and worry about the rest of it when the game's over."

Playing hard was Danny's game. He was not a worrier by nature. But he knew he needed to have a good year in 1958. Maybe a very good year. Scoring the first run in the first official major league game on the West Coast before a stadium crammed with new and enthusiastic fans would be a promising start. So Danny O'Connell was itching to get home.

There were times the former Veronica Cecilia Sharkey must have despaired of ever being home again—or knowing where it was likely to be. A petite and strikingly pretty 28-year-old woman who was known to everyone as "Vera" and who since early 1955 had been the wife of Danny O'Connell, she was a North Jersey girl who before marrying Danny had rarely if ever been far from the environs of Paterson. And Vera wasn't the type to yearn for whatever excitement and adventure that came with relocating across a continent. "She never liked the spotlight," recalled the O'Connells' oldest daughter Maureen. "She was just a typical 1950s housewife who kept things going and kept things to herself and sort of rolled with the punches."

In an interview toward the end of Danny's baseball career, Vera estimated "we have had at least 25 different homes during our married life. It all adds up, you know...apartments at spring training camps, apartments in (new) cities, apartments on the road. But living out of a suitcase isn't as bad as it might sound...You soon learn to compromise."

In early February 1958, a New Jersey paper featured Vera watching a beaming Danny pack for the Giants' spring training camp in Mesa, Arizona, while she held their two-month-old daughter Nancy. A bewildered-looking two-year-old Maureen, meanwhile, held her daddy's fielder's glove.

O'Connell explained he would drive the 2,400 miles to Mesa alone, and Vera and the kids would fly down two weeks later. "It's easier for the wife to take a plane than being on the road for four or five days and having to contend with formulas, warming bottles and changing diapers," he explained, although he didn't specify for whom it would be easier—Vera or himself.

Danny actually reported early to camp for what the Giants called "Operation Great Wash." Located at Buckhorn Mineral Wells, a spa of sorts just outside Mesa, the program was set up to give players an additional 10 days of conditioning before the official start of spring training on Feb. 24. The "conditioning" consisted largely of soaking in hot springs-fed baths, sweating in steam rooms, massages, a low-fat diet, golf and lounging by the pool.

"The guys at Mesa—there'll be 12 to 15 of us in all—are some of the older players, or like myself, are a little overstocked in the weight department," Danny told a reporter, choosing to put himself in the too-fat category rather than the too-old group. "I think some of the trouble I have with my back and legs in the spring can be eased," he told another reporter.

Whether it was a result of the baths, the diet or the pool-lounging, it was a good spring for the Giants and O'Connell, even if it began ignominiously—at least for Danny. During the first infield drills, he swallowed his chaw of tobacco and had to be excused for the rest of the day's activities, much to the amusement of his teammates. Then he slumped at the plate, rekindling rumors the

Giants might open the season with someone else at second base.

But Giants manager Bill Rigney somewhat unexpectedly rallied to O'Connell's side. "Danny was jumping at the ball too much last year," Rigney said, "but he's been swinging on solid footing this spring. I think Danny's ready for a great year." In another interview, Rigney praised O'Connell's play at second. "I never really worried about Danny's defense," he said, "and even that has improved...Danny used to make two motions with his hands before throwing. Now he is grabbing and throwing—Right Now! Let's Go! No wasted motion. One full arc."

Public praise from Rigney could be fleeting. Known as "Specs" because he was one of the relatively few big-league players in the '40s and '50s to wear eyeglasses, Rigney had been a Giants infielder for eight seasons. He was better known for his ability as a "bench jockey" than as a player, with a talent (which O'Connell also possessed) for needling the opposition from the dugout to the point of distraction. "Rig is a skinny, wiry man with a lot of nervous energy," a New York writer observed, "and he makes sudden violent gestures when he speaks."

After taking over as manager from the flamboyant Leo "the Lip" Durocher in 1956, Rigney accomplished two sixth-place finishes, and had a reputation for being mercurial in his decisions and overly anxious about the results. "Rigney sweats a lot during a ball game," wrote Cincinnati Reds pitcher Jim Brosnan in *The Long Season*, his groundbreaking journal of a year in the majors. When Rigney visited the mound to remove a pitcher, Brosnan noted, he would rub his hands together, "going through the motions of purging himself of any associated guilt."

Still, Danny must have taken Rigney's encouraging words to heart. By the end of March, he was hitting .352. "Second base was wide open a week ago," the *San Francisco Examiner* reported, "but the way Danny O'Connell has been playing, nobody is going to move him out of there." While that was sweet music to Danny's ears, so was the tune he sang back to the city. "When you have 20,000 or more fans going all out for you, it really makes you better," he said, referring to reports of excellent pre-season ticket sales in San Francisco. "… I think this will be a much better club than we had last season. Everybody is hustling."

O'Connell's optimism was well-founded. The Giants finished their exhibition season with a glittering 14-7 record. "There's something about playing in San Francisco and the change from the East that has the kids pretty souped up," said Rigney, who had grown up in Oakland, across the bay. "It's a new life for us all."

And if Mrs. O'Connell wasn't too excited about going to San Francisco, San Francisco was positively giddy about the looming arrival of Mr. O'Connell and his teammates. An enthusiastic crowd of about a thousand well-wishers met the Giants at the airport when they arrived shortly before 10 p.m. on April 13, at the end of spring training and an exhibition tour through several Midwestern states. The *Examiner* hyperbolized it was "the most vociferous welcome ever accorded a team of athletes in San Francisco."

The widespread buzz created by the Giants' arrival wasn't lost on businesses throughout the region. In Redding, 215 miles north of San Francisco, a clothing store offered customers who bought blue jeans or other "sports clothing" a chance to win transportation and tickets to any of the season's first six games, and threw in "a crisp ten-dollar bill for pocket money." In 1958, that could get a fan six hot dogs, four beers, three bags of peanuts and a book on the Giants (written by a New York sportswriter.) In Stockton, 85 miles southeast of what San Franciscans self-approvingly referred to as "The City," a motel/restaurant offered a $12 package that included a bus ride to any Sunday home game, a chicken box lunch on the bus, a "choice reserved seat" at the game and a prime-rib, lobster or steak dinner upon returning to the motel.

Lest Bay Area women feel left out, the upscale Joseph Magnin clothing store distributed booklets to its female customers that explained the rudiments of baseball and offered advice as to the proper attire in which to attend a game. "It is a common sight to see a (store) window display of Danny O'Connell's smiling Celtic features," a visiting New York writer noted, "surrounded by baseballs, bats and women's apparel."

The pre-season hoopla peaked on April 14, with a ticker-tape parade for the area's new heroes down the city's Montgomery Street. The players rode two to a convertible -- with signs on the sides indicating who they were -- past an estimated 200,000 or so cheering spectators, with the motorcade ending at the Sheraton-Palace Hotel. In the excitement, someone misspelled the name of

Giants team owner Horace Stoneham on his car as "Stoneman." At the hotel, they were applauded by a thousand more fans and listened to an effusively tedious speech by S.F. Mayor George Christopher. They also swapped autographs with Shirley Temple Black, America's Depression-era child movie star who was now married to local business tycoon Charles Black. The former "Little Princess" had served as the parade's honorary queen.

The next day, 23,448 people squeezed into the 23,000-seat Seals Stadium to see the first game against the hated Dodgers. Opened in 1931 as the home of the Pacific Coast League's San Francisco Seals, the downtown park was considered among the best minor-league stadiums in the country. When the Giants' move from New York was confirmed, San Francisco officials spent $75,000 ($790,000 in 2024) to improve its lighting. Someone sensibly thought to replace an outfield sign advertising a funeral home with one pitching wrist watches. They also added several thousand more seats to bring capacity up to 23,000. Even so, it remained the smallest big-league park in terms of seats.

While Seals Stadium had its faults—parking was scarce and the stadium was susceptible to the city's winds and fog—it also had its peculiar charms. "One of the most pleasant aspects," Cincinnati pitcher Jim Brosnan noted, "is the smell. Walking from the hotel to the ballpark, you pass by a bakery, which dispenses the scent of sugary rolls and freshly brown-crusted bread...the visiting clubhouse overlooks the bakery. The window cannot be opened in the clubhouse without causing immediate hunger pains."

Brosnan also noted the visual and olfactory pleasures offered by the Hamm's Brewery adjacent to the park. The brewery featured a huge neon sign in the shape of a mug, which would appear to fill with beer, flash three times, then slowly drain, only to refill a minute later. Brosnan said Hamm's also advertised its presence "by wafting vast clouds of freshly brewed beer over the leftfield grandstand...there's nothing quite like the smell of new beer in the morning after a night in Frisco."

Like a lot of pitchers, Brosnan was not enamored of the park's stiff winds that turned routine fly balls into souvenirs for fans in the left field seats. "The wind frequently prevails," he noted, "even against the most clever and well-executed pitching." When Johnny Antonelli, the Giants' ace left-hander, complained about San Francisco's often-lousy summer weather, the local press proved itself pretty provincial in its sensitivity. The *Chronicle* suggested the Giants hang a pacifier near Antonelli's locker, and the *Examiner* excoriated him for daring to criticize the city's "life-giving summer breeze, the sweet wind that sweeps San Francisco clean each morning."

Those who got there early enough on Opening Day were treated to the always-entertaining spectacle of two politicians making fools of themselves. This involved S.F. Mayor Christopher attempting to throw a ceremonial first pitch to Los Angeles Mayor Norris Poulson, who was standing at home plate with a bat. Christopher's first two pitches went behind Poulson. The third bounced on the plate. Poulson did manage to hit a weak dribbler on the fourth pitch—and promptly ran toward third base instead of first.

When the game finally started, the first pitch was fouled off by Dodgers left fielder Gino Cimoli (a San Francisco native) and eventually ended up behind the bar of a saloon in Caspar, California, about 160 miles north of San Francisco. Cimoli didn't hit it that far; it was caught by a pal of the saloon owner and gifted to him. As for the game, Giants pitcher Gomez tight-roped his way through the first three innings, despite giving up three walks and two singles. The Dodgers' Drysdale, meanwhile, mowed down the first six Giants he faced, none of whom hit the ball out of the infield. Then O'Connell led off the Giants third inning with a walk, followed by another walk and a single that loaded the bases.

Up stepped Jimmy Davenport, the rookie third baseman, who tenta- tively dug a foothold in the batter's box and waited. Nicknamed "Peanuts" (bestowed on him as a tyke by a grandfather), the 24-year-old Davenport hailed from an Alabama cotton mill town he said "wasn't as big as two blocks in San Francisco." He had been a star quarterback at the University of Southern Mississippi and enjoyed a decent three seasons in the minor leagues.

But he hadn't been expected to make the Giants' roster in '58, let alone win the starting third baseman's job. That he had done both was not only a surprise but a testament to the uncertainty of the team's prospects in the coming season. In fact, Davenport was one of three rookies to start the San Francisco Giants' first game. "Coming to San Francisco, a new city," he recalled years later in his syrupy drawl, "they wanted to bring up some young kids to see what they could do."

What Davenport, who in later years was a much-beloved coach (and briefly a remarkably unsuccessful manager) for the Giants, could do on this particular at-bat was hit a long drive to right field. There the Dodgers' Carl Furillo made a leaping catch at the fence, robbing Davenport of extra bases. Still, it was deep enough for Danny O'Connell to trot those 90 feet necessary to score the first run in the history of San Francisco's new team. The Giants went on to an easy 8-0 win. The Dodgers managed only six hits; the Giants' Darryl Spencer and rookie Orlando Cepeda homered; Willie Mays demonstrated two of his signature maneuvers in centerfield by making a basket catch on one flyball and running out from under his hat while chasing down another, and five Giants, including O'Connell, reached base at least twice.

For the moment at least, Danny O'Connell was home.

CHAPTER 1 NOTES

On a bright It's generally agreed among baseball historians that the 90-foot distance between bases was established in 1858, when a group of men representing two dozen clubs in the Northeast met in New York City to formulate a set of rules for the game of "base ball," as it was known then. Under the leadership of Daniel Lucius "Doc" Adams, a Yale-educated physician and the player credited with inventing the position of shortstop, the group decided the linear interval between each of the diamond-shaped infield's four bases would be 90 feet. Previous to this, the distance had been varied and arbitrary. A popular measure was "42 paces," but exactly how far that was depended on whether the pacer was 5'6" or 6'1". It was decided 80 feet was too short to be fair to infielders, who would have little chance to throw out runners at first base. On the other hand, 100 feet would be unfair to batters, even the fleetest of foot. Ninety feet seemed, Goldilocks-like, to be just right. See the eminent baseball historian John Thorn's *Baseball in the Garden of Eden*, pp. 35-36. Thorn's book covers all you will ever need or want to know about the game's origins.

The move greatly lengthened *Arizona Republic*, Feb. 7, 1958, p. 51.

"My father would" *Milwaukee Sentinel*, Aug. 4, 1957, p. 14.

They didn't. But Author's interview of Alice O'Connell, Aug. 5, 2022.

It was true O'Connell's 1958 salary estimate is based on contemporary press reports. Other figures are from the U.S. Bureau of Labor Statistics and the *Monthly Labor Review*, Vol. 83, No. 5 (May, 1960), pp. 491-500.

"You did what" Gene Fehler, *When Baseball Was Still King: Major League Players Remember the 1950s*, p. 165.

And finally, there It may or may not be worth noting here that in 1958, the average major-league player salary was estimated to be about $16,300, or about 3.1 times the average salary of a public-school teacher. In 2022, the average ballplayer salary was $4.41 million, or 68 times the average salary of a teacher. This must say something either about society's misplaced values or how really hard it is to hit a 94-mph slider on the outside corner at the knees.

"Sometimes the deck" *The (Paterson NJ) Evening News*, Oct. 15, 1957, p. 22.

There were times Author's interview of Maureen O'Connell Hurley, April 12, 2022.

In an interview *The (Paterson NJ) Evening News*, May 24, 1963, p. 28.

O'Connell explained *Newark Star-Ledger,* Feb. 7, 1958, p. 22.

"The guys at" *The (Paterson NJ) Evening News*, Feb. 8, 1958, p. 12.

But Giants manager *San Francisco Chronicle*, March 25, 1958, p. 2H; *Paterson (NJ) Evening News*, April 1, 1958, p. 26.

Public praise from *Newsday*, Sept. 18, 1957, p. 113.

Taking over as Jim Brosnan, *The Long Season*, p. 86.

Still, Danny must *San Francisco Examiner,* March 25, 1958, p. 28; *Passaic (NJ) Herald News,* March 5, 1958, p. 27.

O'Connell's optimism Steve Bitker, *The Original San Francisco Giants*, pp. 25-26.

And if Mrs. O'Connell, *San Francisco Examiner*, April 14, 1958, p. 39.

Lest Bay Area *New York Newsday*, April 14, 1958, p. 4.

While Seals Stadium Brosnan, op. cit., p. 83.

Brosnan also noted Ibid.

Like a lot Ibid., p. 82; Brian Murphy, *San Francisco Giants, 50 Years*, p. 34.

When the game *Baseball Digest*, Vol. 17, No. 7, August 1958.

But he hadn't Ed Attanasio interview with Jim Davenport for the Society for American Baseball Research (SABR) Oral History Project, Oct. 1, 2003.

CHAPTER 2
"HIS NICKNAME WAS "THE HEAD""
ROOTS

I t can be stated with only moderate exaggeration that Danny O'Connell's hometown was born because George Washington, Alexander Hamilton and the Marquis de Lafayette decided to have a picnic. There were of course other factors involved. But the picnic was certainly one of them.

It occurred in early July 1778. Two weeks earlier, American and British forces had furiously fought to what was pretty much a draw at the Battle of Monmouth Courthouse in New Jersey, midway between Philadelphia and New York City. But on this particular day, the titanic trio of the American Revolution found themselves at a peaceful spot about 50 miles north of Monmouth, near a Dutch-settled hamlet known as Acquackanonk.

While they noshed on what Hamilton recalled as "a modest repast" of ham, tongue and biscuits, they also drank in the grandeur of a roaring waterfall. The area's original Native American inhabitants, the Lenni Lenape, called it "Totowa," meaning "forced down by the water's weight." To European settlers, it was the much more prosaic "Great Falls." Whatever you called it, it was impressive. The cascade plunged more than 70 feet into a narrow gorge, hurtling hundreds of millions of gallons of the Passaic River each day toward its eventual end in a back bay of New York Harbor.

Fast-forward to 1792. Washington is at the end of his first term as president, and wearily resigned to being unanimously elected to a second term. Lafayette is caught up in the throes of the French Revolution, which would see him spend nearly a decade in prison for trying to find a less bloody and more reasonable path forward for his country. And Hamilton, as America's first Treasury secretary, is recalling the picnic by the waterfall.

Ever the capitalist, Hamilton had recognized the fall's potential as a source of hydro power to operate mills. He was also well aware that 16-year-old

America had to grow up fast when it came to developing an economic foundation not based solely on agriculture. So when his chief assistant came up with a plan called the Society for Establishing Useful Manufactures (S.U.M.), Hamilton enthusiastically embraced the idea.

Under the plan, the federal government would subsidize private interests who would create not just a single wool or cotton mill, but an entire town built around manufacturing. The government would get its money back through various fees and profit-sharing deals; investors would reap handsome profits through consolidation of costs, a concentrated labor pool and centralized supplies of raw materials and equipment; consumers would benefit from lower prices on goods, and America overall would grow fat and happy. Hamilton knew just the place for it—the spot where he, Washington and Lafayette had munched tongue sandwiches in 1778.

Hamilton approved the issuance of government bonds to provide the project with seed money, and helped promote the sale of stock to raise the rest of the startup capital. Then he began bending the ear of New Jersey Gov. William Paterson, an acid-tongued former United States senator who became acquainted with Hamilton while the two of them helped draft the U.S. Constitution. Paterson would later become a justice of the U.S. Supreme Court. The governor agreed to grant the S.U.M. group a town charter near the Great Falls and give S.U.M. monopolistic status in the region. He even threw in a ten-year exemption from paying New Jersey property taxes. In return, S.U.M. directors decided "Paterson" was a good name for the new town.

Historians generally regard the S.U.M. project as America's first attempt at a public-private business enterprise. A financial panic in 1793 - coupled with the pillaging of S.U.M.'s bank accounts by one of its directors, grandiosely expensive design plans and generally inept onsite management—caused the effort to initially founder. The undeniable hydropower provided by the falls, however, was eventually harnessed through construction of a series of canals. By 1815, Paterson had 13 cotton mills, a wire factory, a steel rolling mill and a saw mill. By 1832, the town's population had reached 9,000, four times what it had been in 1820. More than a quarter of the population, including women and children, worked in the mills or mill-supporting businesses such as machine shops. After the Civil War, cotton gave way to silk as Paterson's dominant textile, earning it the nickname "the Silk City."

Other enterprises followed the mills. In 1836, a Connecticut firearms maker showed up and began manufacturing pistols with revolving cylinders. This allowed the gun to be fired multiple times without reloading. A deep national economic slump in 1837 and the inability to land government contracts for his guns forced Samuel Colt to close up shop in Paterson after a year. He returned to Connecticut, where he wound up doing pretty well in the gun business. And as it turned out, the relatively few revolvers he made in Paterson are today among the most coveted firearms in the world by gun collectors. In November 2021, a "Texas Paterson #5," so-called because it was popular with the Texas Rangers (the law enforcement group, not the baseball team), sold at auction for $431,250—or slightly less than a 2021 Jasson Dominguez baseball card. (Refer back to this book's Introduction if you've already forgotten who Jasson Dominguez is.)

A more exotic enterprise than gun-making also sprang up in Paterson, and lasted about as long. In February 1857, David Hower, who was a very poor shoemaker with a very large family, discovered there were pearls in the mussels he gathered for food in Notch Brook, a small stream that fed into the Passaic. Later that year, a carpenter named Jacob Quackenbush found a 91-grain pearl that he sold to Tiffany & Co. in nearby New York City for $1,500 ($54,300 in 2024 dollars.) The jewelry firm promptly sold it to the Empress Eugenie, wife of France's Napoleon III, for $2,000 (about $72,400.) Like Colt, however, Paterson's pearl rush was short-lived: The mussels were picked clean and the brook eventually dried up.

More successful than Colt and freshwater pearls were steel and railroad companies. Between 1852 and 1901, for example, the Cooke Locomotive Works churned out 2,600 railway engines. In 1919, the Wright Aeronautical Corp. moved its headquarters to Paterson, where it built the engine that powered Charles Lindbergh's *Spirit of St. Louis* across the Atlantic in 1927. In 1929, Wright merged with a company run by aviation pioneer Glen Curtiss. During World War II, the firm produced a whopping 142,00 aircraft engines.

In addition to train and airplane engines, Paterson produced a panoply of notable people. The Paterson-born poet William Carlos Williams wrote what might well be the longest ode to any American town when he published a five-volume epic entitled simply *Paterson* between 1946 and 1958. Williams, one of the most important American poets of the 20th century, was best known for short pieces. But in *Paterson*, he set out to portray every man as a city "beginning, seeking, achieving and concluding his life in ways which the various aspects of a city may embody—if imaginatively conceived:"

"Paterson lies in the valley under the Passaic Falls/ Its spent waters forming the outlines of his back. He / lies on his right side, head near the thunder of the waters filling his dreams!/ Eternally asleep, / his dreams walk about the city where he persists/ incognito. Butterflies settle on his stone ear./ Immortal, he neither moves nor rouses and is seldom/ seen, though he breathes and the subtleties of his machinations/ drawing their substance from the noise of his pouring river/ animate a thousand automatons."

You get the idea.

Other notable Patersonians, either born there or transplanted in their youth, include the poet Alan Ginsberg; boxer Rubin "Hurricane" Carter, falsely accused of a triple murder and immortalized in a Bob Dylan song; comedian Lou Costello; Garret A. Hobart, 24th vice president of the United States; Giuseppe Zangara, who tried to kill the newly elected president Franklin D. Roosevelt but fatally shot the mayor of Chicago by mistake instead, and Larry Doby, the Hall of Fame outfielder who was the first African American in the American League and the second black manager in the majors.

In fact, Paterson—and all of New Jersey—had a long and storied baseball history. The first game to be played under at least the rudiments of modern rules took place in October 1845 in Hoboken, just 15 miles south of Paterson. One of the teams in the first professional baseball league was located in Elizabeth, only 25 miles north of Paterson. And in 1896, the Paterson Silk Sox featured a bow-legged kid with hands the size of polar bear paws. His given name was Johannes Peter Wagner, but the Paterson papers dubbed him "Hannis." His nickname got changed to "Honus" on the way to the Hall of Fame as probably the greatest shortstop ever. Wagner ended up with a pretty famous baseball card too, which we'll get to later.

By 1946, the year Danny O'Connell III began his professional baseball career, Paterson had reached a population of 139,000, making it New Jersey's third-largest city. Most of its inhabitants were European immigrants or the descendants of European immigrants who had been lured by the promise of work in Paterson factories: English, Welsh, Scots, Germans, French, Swedes, Polish, Russians, Danes, Italians and Irish. One member of this last ethnic group was a Connecticut-born teenager who arrived sometime in the last few years of the 19th century. For the purposes of our story and to minimize confusion, we'll refer to him as the "original Danny O'Connell."

The first of the O'Connell clan—at least the one we're concerned with—reached American shores in 1859 at the age of 24. John O'Connell hailed from Irramore, a speck-sized village in County Kerry, near the southwest tip of Ireland. After a year or so working as a "day laborer" in Massachusetts, John married Mary Casey, another immigrant from County Kerry. The couple eventually settled on a farm in Litchfield County, Connecticut, tucked in the state's northwest corner.

As 19th century farm families were wont to do, John and Mary had eight children. The third of these was born in 1864. His birth name was David Daniel O'Connell, but somewhere along the line, according to various census and other public records, he became known as Daniel, and eventually Daniel Francis. It's unclear why, and it probably doesn't matter.

The original Danny O'Connell didn't take to farming, and apparently wasn't all that crazy about Litchfield County either. Sometime in his late teens, he left home and made his way 135 miles south to Paterson. What he did there is uncertain, except for the possibility he worked in a saloon and the fact that in 1897, he married 27-year-old Ellen "Ellie" Murphy. Ellie was a New Jersey native who worked as a "winder" in one of the Paterson silk mills and whose parents were Irish immigrants. Soon after, the couple moved back to Litchfield County, where they bought a house and Danny worked as a teamster. They also had four children, on a more-or-less regular schedule: Mary in 1900; Helen in 1902; John in 1903 and Daniel Jr. (whom we'll refer to as "Danny Jr.") in 1904.

By 1920, the O'Connells were back in Paterson, owners of a modest home on Carlisle Avenue in Stony Road, a neighborhood in the southwest corner of

Paterson. (It was actually formally designated on maps as "Stoney Road," but the locals left out the "e" and I'm going with the locals.) Like many industrial cities, Paterson had become apportioned into distinct neighborhoods whose inhabitants were almost always united by their socio-economic status, even if divided by their ethnicities. At the time the O'Connells arrived in Stony Road, it was far more Italian in its ethnic flavor than Irish. But it gradually became a colorful and generally peaceable mix of the two. And almost everyone was poor.

The original Danny had become an iron worker, and was good at it. "During his career," one of his obituaries reported, "(he) had supervised the construction of several large buildings and bridges in this vicinity." Family lore also has it that he was locally famous for being able to jump from a standing start into a waist-high (and presumably empty) beer barrel and out again. "All of the O'Connells were good athletes," his granddaughter Alice proudly recalled.

Unfortunately, there was little money to be made jumping in and out of beer barrels. And however skillful he was at working iron, paying the bills required more than just the original Danny's paycheck. At the age of 18, daughter Helen had married a printer, borne a son and moved down the street from her parents. But 20-year-old daughter Mary was still living at home and working as a silk mill weaver. Seventeen-year-old son John was a mechanical engineer at a railroad factory, on his way to a long career as a Paterson police officer and becoming well-known as one of the city's best bowlers. And 15-year-old Danny Jr. had left school after finishing 8th grade to work in a rubber plant.

Danny Jr. grew into a handsome brown-haired, blue-eyed young man. In his very early 20s, while working as a telephone company lineman, he met Myrtle Parliman, a Jersey-born girl who worked in one of the Paterson silk mills. Myrtle was the third of seven children of William and Stella Parliman. Her father was a night watchman at a chemical works plant. Danny Jr. and Myrtle married in 1926. He was 22, she was 18. The newlyweds moved into a $28-a-month house on Glover Avenue, a few blocks from Danny Jr.'s parents. And on January 21, 1929, Myrtle gave birth to Daniel Francis O'Connell III (whom we'll refer to as "Baseball Danny.") The event merited four lines in *The Morning Call*. The newspaper got the birthdate wrong.

From an economic standpoint, Baseball Danny picked a bad year to arrive.

Exactly 245 days after his birth, the U.S. stock market crashed. Although there were myriad and intertwined causes far more significant for what followed than the stock market collapse, it's historically convenient to cite "Black Thursday" as marking the advent of a crushing world-wide economic calamity that would last a decade.

It took a while for the Great Depression to reach Paterson, since relatively few Patersonians had any kind of a financial stake on Wall Street. But when it did, it came with a vengeance. Wages for silk workers fell 40 percent between 1929 and 1933, and the mills periodically closed altogether when business was slack. More than 140 New Jersey banks failed. By 1932, 38 percent of Paterson homeowners could not pay their property taxes.

At 106 Carlisle, the original Danny managed to hold on to his home. But sometime during the decade, he took in boarders: Danny Jr. and his family moved in. The original Danny apparently was not much of a sentimentalist, since he charged his son and family rent only slightly lower than what they had been paying on Glover Avenue. Two new mouths to feed arrived when Myrtle O'Connell gave birth to Bob in 1933 and Alice in 1935. Although Danny Jr. managed to move 10 doors down by 1942, it was a tough 10 years for everyone.

"I remember we had no hot water," Alice O'Connell said. "None. If I took a bath, then we would have to fill the tea kettle and heat it up so Bob or Danny could take one. And both places on Carlisle had plenty of cockroaches...looking back, I guess it was pretty horrible sometimes." There was also domestic friction from time to time: "My grandmother hated my grandfather," Alice said. "When she was angry at him, which was most of the time, she made him sleep in the garage."

But since most if not all of Stony Road's residents were in the same economic boat and many residences housed multiple generations, there was a familiar air of normalcy to the O'Connells' situation. And if things got too crowded or too tense, it was just three blocks to Pennington Park—and baseball. The park was tucked in a pocket bounded on three sides by a bend in the Passaic River and on the fourth by busy McBride Avenue, which served as Stony Road's commercial and retail hub. "It was perfect because it was within walking distance of home, but beyond shouting distance," recalled Chuck Pazzano, a childhood chum of Baseball Danny. "That gave you a good excuse when your mother asked why you didn't come running home when she screamed her head off for you."

Pazzano, who grew up to be a prolific writer, a co-founder of the Professional Bowlers Association and a charter member of the National Bowling Hall of Fame, said that of the Pennington Park regulars, Baseball Danny "wasn't the biggest, wasn't the fastest and in most cases wasn't the best in any one department. But he was always the best all-around player on the field, no matter what the sport. He was always the fastest thinker and always a step ahead of everyone else in anticipation and determination. His nickname was 'The Head.' Youngsters have a way of coming up with nicknames that make good sense."

Danny, Pezzano added, could be "a little crazy at times, a little irritating, but never proud or overbearing." He was quick to take the lead in whatever was going on, from marbles to drug-store-corner debates, but never dominant. And he got along with nearly everyone. Pazzano could recall seeing Danny in only one fight during their boyhoods, "and it wasn't much of a fight." Danny's brother Bob recalled that Danny was so well-liked in the neighborhood, "it got me out of a few situations" when he mentioned he was Danny's younger brother. Bob did not elaborate.

While Pennington Park was a solid three blocks from the O'Connell home on Carlisle Avenue, it may still have been within earshot of Myrtle O'Connell's voice. Baseball Danny's mom had a way of getting people's attention. "Myrtle was like 'what you see is what you get, in your face,'" Maureen O'Connell Hurley recalled of her paternal grandmother. "It was her way or the highway. We didn't realize until much later on that my grandfather (Danny Jr.) had a drinking problem, so I think she put up with a lot, and that may be why she always just seemed like such a tough cookie."

She also had a wicked sense of humor. "My mom and I went over to her house when I was seven or eight, and Myrtle asked me if I wanted a can of Coke," said John O'Connell, Baseball Danny's younger son, "which I thought was a great thing. So I said yeah and she asked me if I wanted a big can or a little can. And I of course said 'big can.' So she stuck her butt in my face and said 'here's a big can.' And I thought it was hilarious, but my mom was mortified."

Danny Jr., Myrtle's husband, was quieter, at least by comparison, although he too could be uncomfortably boisterous. "I didn't know my grandfather very well," said his namesake grandson, Danny O'Connell IV. "He didn't say much to me the times I saw him. But I never saw him without a beer in his hand." If Danny Jr. had a drinking problem, he also struggled to hold onto a steady job. At various times he was a telephone lineman, a road construction foreman, an aircraft factory laborer and a dye company worker, before retiring after a 15-year stint as the third-floor janitor at Paterson's Central High School.

But whatever their shortcomings, Myrtle and Danny Jr. were loving parents who encouraged their children's interests. And their son Danny's dominant interest from a very early age was baseball. "Before I went to grade school, I remember my father talking to other baseball fans around my home about the Doherty Silk Hose team of Paterson," he later recalled. "Those talks gave me the fever, and Dad made the fever boil when he took me by the hand and led me to the Polo Grounds to see the Giants play the Cubs."

Although a Giants fan, Danny's favorite player was Cubs star Stan Hack, probably the best third baseman in history who is nevertheless not in the Hall of Fame. "Hack came closest to an earthly manifestation of the ideal third baseman of the day," wrote author William Curran. "Tall, slender, handsome, confident—Hack was the idol of every sandlot urchin playing third base in a pair of torn knickers." Hack was an apt role model for Danny O'Connell, because they shared both self-confidence and winning personalities. "Smilin' Stan," an opposing player said, "has more friends than Leo Durocher has enemies."

When Danny Jr. couldn't take his son across the Hudson to see the Giants or Dodgers, the younger O'Connell occasionally found a spot on a Paterson Recreation Department bus full of kids, chaperoned by Paterson policemen, including his Uncle John. However he got to the Polo Grounds or Ebbets Field, he regarded it as paradise. "That was a dream," he said, "because all I wanted as a kid was to be in the big leagues."

Danny "The Head" O'Connell's intelligence wasn't confined to games at Pennington Park. In fact, he was a good enough grammar school student to skip fifth grade. That meant he entered St. Bonaventure Catholic High School, about six blocks from the O'Connell home, in September 1941 as a 12-year-old. He was all of 5'2" tall and weighed maybe 125 pounds with his shoes on. But he could play ball.

"An orchid to Danny O'Connell for his excellent playing against St. John's." said a student-written piece in the Paterson *News* during Danny's freshman year. "It was Danny's debut as a Bon's man." A week later, the paper noted "Danny O'Connell again repeated his excellent performance in baseball." And as his first prep season wound down, the *News'* St. Bon's correspondent reported "Danny O'Connell represented the superior skills to be displayed by our underclassmen in the forthcoming years."

By his senior year, Danny had crept up to 5'7" and 150 pounds. His athletic skills, meanwhile, had exploded. On the St. Bonaventure Indians baseball team, he not only made the Catholic All-Conference team as a pitcher, but also played shortstop, catcher and the outfield—and was team captain. In one game, he threw a one-hitter and drove in seven runs with two homers and a double. He won another game by tripling in the last inning and then stealing home. Against St. Bon's archrival, St. Mary's, he gave up hits to the first three batters he faced, loading the bases. He then retired 21 of the next 24 hitters, striking out 12 and winning 3-0.

And baseball wasn't even his best sport. "Any and all of St. Bon's students who have seen Danny dashing to and fro on the basketball court will tell you of his alertness, speed and all-around ability," it read in his 1945 high school yearbook, next to a photo of a cherubic and slightly floppy-eared O'Connell wearing a coat and tie and as serious an expression as he could muster. "A group of happy faces are always around Danny, testifying to his numerous attractions and enjoying the gems of his wit."

Among his "numerous attractions" was an ability to put a basketball through a basketball hoop. As captain of a St. Bon's team that went 17-4 in his senior year and won the city's Catholic Conference championship, Danny was far and away the team's top scorer: 18 of St. Bon's 34 total points in one game; 12 of 40 in another; and 18 of 21 in a third.

Moreover, he was clutch. In the championship game against St. Mary's, Danny scored more than a third of St. Bon's total, including a driving layup with 20 seconds left to win the game. According to his sister Alice, as he was carried off on the shoulders of admirers, one of his aunts slipped a dollar into his hand. If so, it was Danny O'Connell's first financial compensation for an athletic performance. In naming him to its seven-member All-Conference team, *The Morning Call* noted "the pride of the Indians is a snappy shot, and a good floorman."

And then it was over. By mid-June 1945, Danny O'Connell was a 16-year-old high school graduate with a scrapbook full of press clippings, dutifully assembled by his mother, and a fulltime job in a Paterson silk-dyeing plant, reluctantly arranged by his father. The O'Connells needed the money. Danny needed to play baseball.

So on nights and weekends the summer and fall after his graduation, Danny played ball with recreation-league and semi-pro teams and even the occasional pickup game at Pennington Park. Weekdays, he worked alongside his father at the dye plant, performing the same mind-numbing tasks with potentially dangerous chemicals, over and over, day after day.

As much as he hated the job, he also feared losing it. The war in Europe was over before he graduated. With the atom-bombing of Hiroshima and Nagasaki, the war in the Pacific was all but over by early August. Tens of thousands of New Jersey men would be coming home with the altogether reasonable expectation they would get back the jobs they had left. A 16-year-old runt of a kid would be at the bottom of any company's employee-preference list.

In the meantime, Danny's post-high school ballplaying had not gone unnoticed. Ben Marmo, a local coach and sometime sportswriter, was also a part-time scout for the Philadelphia Phillies. At Marmo's urging, the Phillies agreed in the spring of 1946 to give O'Connell a look. On April 1—April Fool's Day—Danny boarded a train for a Phillies tryout camp in Dover Delaware, 175 miles away. A week later, he was home. He had skills, Phillies officials told him, but he was too young and too small for professional baseball. Crushed, Danny went back to the dye plant.

A few weeks later, however, the Danny O'Connell roller coaster was back on track. Jack Brutchy, a semi-pro pitcher pal, told Danny about the Bloomingdale Troopers, a brand-new minor league team in a brand-new independent league in a town about 15 miles northwest of Paterson. "They were paying guys to play ball," O'Connell recalled in a 1963 interview. "I jumped at the opportunity. 'Imagine,' I thought, 'getting $70 a month to play ball.' That was pretty good money in those days."

His father, however wasn't so sure $70 a month ($1,128 in 2024 dollars) was enough. And since Baseball Danny was only 17, he needed parental approval to sign a contract. According to Mickey Weintraub, the then-24-year-old shortstop, manager and part-owner of the Troopers, Danny Jr., "although very anxious for [Baseball] Danny to get his chance, felt that the family was not in a position financially to give up the much greater earnings Danny could make on the outside."

So Weintraub went out on a limb. He guaranteed the O'Connells the club would raise the monthly $70 to $90 if Danny stuck with the team for 30 days. Further, he told them he was sure Danny would hit at least .300, and would positively get an offer from a major league organization by the end of the year. "Finally," Weintraub said, "Mr. O'Connell, who was just as much a fan as Danny, graciously consented to let him play, even though it was a financial sacrifice."

By the beginning of the Troopers' season on May 8, 1946, Daniel Francis O'Connell III was a professional baseball player.

CHAPTER 2 NOTES

It occurred in See Ron Chernow's *Alexander Hamilton*, pp. 371-385 for more detail on Paterson's early history as a manufacturing center. The Great Falls is now the centerpiece of a National Historical Park, which includes a statue of Hamilton. Hemmed in by narrow, traffic-choked streets, in the shadow of towering brick buildings and seemingly in a constant state of being repaired, I believe it to be just about the sorriest such park in America.

Historians generally regard A good overview of New Jersey history is *New Jersey: A History of the Garden State,* edited by Maxine N. Lurie and Richard Veit. Dermot Quin's *The Irish in New Jersey: Four Centuries of American Life* provides a solid and readable background about Irish immigration.

Other enterprises followed "Colt Gallops Away with Big Money at Auctions," *True West* magazine, Vol. 69, Issue 2 (Feb.-Mar. 2022), pp. 18-19.

A more exotic The "Empress Pearl," as it was dubbed, was given by the Empress to her dentist, an American who in turn gave it to his dental school at the University of Pennsylvania. From there it disappeared, although pearls claiming to be the original sometimes show up as either the "Empress Pearl" or the "Tiffany Pearl." It might be worth checking Grandma's jewelry box again.

"Paterson lies in" from William Carlos Williams' *Paterson*, p. 6 in the 1995 New Directions published version.

In fact, Paterson For more on the history of baseball in the Garden State, see *The Jersey Game*, by James M. DiClerico and Barry J. Pavelec.

The original Danny *The (Paterson NJ) Morning Call*, Nov. 7, 1940, p. 24; author's interview of Alice O'Connell, Aug. 5, 2022.

The junior Danny *The (Paterson NJ) Morning Call*, Feb. 1, 1929, p. 28.

It took a while Lurie, op cit., pp. 238-239.

"I remember we" Author's interview of Alice O'Connell, Aug. 5, 2022.

But since most *Bergen (NJ) County Record*, Oct. 4, 1969, p. 12.

Pazzano, who grew Ibid.

Danny, Pezzano added Ibid; author's interview of Bob O'Connell, Aug. 5, 2022.

While Pennington Park Author's interview of Maureen O'Connell Hurley, April 11, 2022.

She also had Author's interview of John O'Connell, July 30, 2022.

Danny Jr., Myrtle's Author's interview of Daniel O'Connell IV, Feb. 15, 2022.

But Whatever their *Pittsburgh Sun-Telegraph*, March 16, 1950, p. 33

Although a Giants Eric Hanauer, "Stan Hack," Society for American Baseball Research (SABR.org), April 25, 2022.

When Danny Jr. National Baseball Hall of Fame archives; *The Catholic Advance*, April 9, 1954, p. 12.

"An orchid to" *The (Paterson NJ) News*, April 28, 1942, p. 12; *The (Paterson NJ) News*, May 5, 1942, p. 12; *The (Paterson NJ) News,* May 19, 1942, p. 4.

Moreover, he was Author's interview of Alice O'Connell, Aug. 5, 2022; *The (Paterson NJ) Morning Call*, May 7, 1945, p. 14.

But a few weeks *The (Paterson NJ) Evening News*, March 6, 1963, p. 39.

Danny Jr., however, *The (Paterson NJ) Evening News*, April 15, 1950, p. 20.

So Weintraub went Ibid.

CHAPTER 3

"THIS COUNTRY IS GOING THROUGH A SOCIAL REVOLUTION"

DANNY'S WORLD

It was perhaps the most pivotal year in the history of baseball, and not just because Danny O'Connell made his professional debut. The National Pastime in 1946 wrestled with racism, labor unrest and even a threat from a foreign power.

In short, it almost perfectly reflected the post-war convulsions affecting the rest of the country. America began the year trying to navigate its way from the planet's most prominent wartime juggernaut to its most prosperous peacetime nation. It was not smooth sailing.

One problem was where to put all those soldiers, sailors and marines coming home. In 1945, there were 12.5 million Americans in military uniform, or nearly 9 percent of the nation's total population. In 1946, they were coming home at the rate of about one million per month. But during the war, new housing construction had ground to a halt as materials and labor were diverted to the war effort.

Coupled with soaring marriage and birth rates, the result was that by the end of 1946, an estimated 6.5 million families were living with friends, relatives or in housing that could only charitably be described as housing. In Fort Worth, that included chicken coops. In Chicago, an enterprising chap bought 2,000 surplus Army radio shelters for $150 each, connected them together in sets of three and sold them as housing for $1,400 (about $22,600 in 2024.) In Fargo North Dakota, housing officials "remodeled" surplus grain storage bins into rental apartments. And in New York City, which had a decided lack of grain storage bins, Mayor William O'Dwyer stated the Big Apple needed 785,500 new apartments to meet demand.

Almost all baseball players returning from the service were doubly affected, since they had to find housing in their hometowns as well as where they were based during the season. If they were traded or demoted to the minors during the season, the headache multiplied. Ten members of the Washington Senators were reduced to living in the team clubhouse for more than a week after spring training ended, and the Chicago White Sox offered season passes to anyone who provided housing leads to 20 players who were essentially homeless on Opening Day.

A dearth of housing wasn't the only post-war headache caused by the diversion of materials from consumer products to military supplies. Baseball card production, for example, skidded to a halt during the war because the cardboard and ink they were made of was needed for the mountains of paperwork required for running military operations. Card production didn't revive on a substantial scale until 1948.

The bubble gum the cards came with also disappeared during the conflict since supplies of the tree-born latex that gave the gum its elasticity was either behind enemy lines or needed for rubber production. Unlike the cards, bubble gum reappeared in limited quantities in 1946—and became a microcosmic example of America's surrealistic post-war economy.

Because it was scarce—like bread, meat, women's stockings and a host of other consumer products—bubble gum became both outrageously expensive and the object of frenzied behavior by those who sought it. In Kansas, the *Wichita Beacon* reported kids paying up to $2—200 times the pre-war price—for a single piece of gum. Five hundred youngsters thronged a Miami Beach newsstand for a chance to buy one of 150 pieces the vendor had procured. In Buffalo, 300 kids besieged a fire station after a specious rumor that the station was giving out free gum spread like, well, a wildfire.

Newspapers across the country tut-tutted about children mimicking their parents by engaging in black market profiteering. "Explaining to the small fry just what is wrong with profiteering on bubble gum is going to be some job," opined a wire service columnist. "One of them is likely to pop up with 'but Daddy bought Mama some nylons for $5,' or 'But Mama said she's sure the meat the butcher sells us is from under the counter.'"

Product shortages and pent-up consumer demand combined with the lifting of federal price controls to ignite a skyrocket of inflation. Food prices seemingly rose weekly. In January 1946, 63 cents ($9.63 in 2023) could get you a loaf of white bread, a box of breakfast cereal and a pound of pork chops. In December, the same items cost 82 cents ($12.53), a 30 percent increase. Between February 1946 and August 1948, annual inflation rates reached as high as 20 percent before things finally began settling down.

While prices on nearly everything went up, wages for almost everyone did not. During the war, organized labor had taken a no-strike pledge (which was occasionally reneged on) and agreed to work more hours for less money and fewer benefits. In exchange, labor expected things to at least return to their pre-war status once the conflict ceased. It didn't happen. The result was widespread labor unrest. By the end of the war, worker unhappiness manifested itself in more than 5,000 strikes across the nation, with more than 107 million working days lost. Union membership had more than doubled during the war, and the strikers ran the gamut from coal miners and casket makers to steel workers and stevedores.

And this is where baseball and the rest of 1946 America parted company. Players had no union, and were essentially at the mercy of the owners. They could be sold, traded, demoted to the minors or fired with 10 days' notice, 15 days' salary and a one-way railroad ticket home. Players were paid nothing for the weeks of spring training before the season began, and had to supply their own gloves and shoes. Worst of all, they couldn't take their talents to another team because a clause in every contract reserved their on-field performances to whatever team that had originally signed them.

This "reserve clause" had been adopted in 1880 in an effort to stymie the common practice of players jumping from club to club, sometimes in mid-season, whenever a more lucrative contract was dangled. But the clause was so one-sided it made virtual serfs of players, stripping them of the ability to move on even when their current contracts expired.

A player, in the bitterly sarcastic words of John Montgomery Ward, "goes where he is sent, takes what he is given and thanks the Lord for life." Ward said that in 1887. A star pitcher and infielder for the New York Giants, Ward was also the leader of the first players' union, which morphed into its own league, the Players League. Both union and league collapsed by 1890. In 1912, another union, The Baseball Players Fraternity was established but gone by the end of the decade. In 1914, the Federal League sprang into being, challenging the American and National leagues as the country's only major leagues. After two seasons, its franchises either went bankrupt or were bought out by AL and NL teams. Meanwhile, another players union came and fizzled.

In 1922, a unanimous decision by the U.S. Supreme Court cemented the unchallenged dominance of the American and National leagues. The court's logic in exempting baseball from the nation's anti-trust laws would have embarrassed a pre-law student. In essence, the court ruled that since any one game was played in only one state, and individual franchises existed in only one state, they were not subject to federal laws regarding interstate commerce. The facts that teams traveled between states to play games, and leagues encompassed clubs in multiple states, were deemed "incidental" by the court. Moreover, the court said, baseball was "a spontaneous human activity" and not really a business, like railroads or steel production. The reserve clause, which baseball's attorneys quietly admitted wasn't a binding legal obligation, remained in place.

In early 1946, three corporate lawyers whose clients included the New York Giants, penned a smugly matter-of-fact article for the *New York Law Review*. They acknowledged that the reserve clause meant "the club has an exclusive right to the services of the player during his baseball life," but did not opine on its legal validity. The article went on to point out that owners were legally powerless to prevent players from unionizing, but all such efforts had failed because "the players themselves have no desire to form such organizations." Finally, the attorney-authors asserted that the average player was in his 20s and making an average salary of $5,000 ($80,600 in 2024) for six-and-a-half months' work. "Thus it is that a ballplayer finds himself in an enviable position compared with the conditions of the average person of his age."

What the lawyers' patronizing article failed to take into account was that a baseball player's career was far shorter than that of "the average person of his age." In addition, many players had lost two, three, or in some cases four prime-earnings seasons to the war. When they returned, they expected more than just the status quo they had left. What the owners expected was for the players to behave and be grateful for the opportunities bestowed on them. "It is the express attitude of many owners," *Fortune* magazine noted, "that the average big-league player ought to be happy he's not back in Hoskins Corner driving a truck."

But the autocratic complacency of baseball's hierarchy was shaken by several events in 1946. One occurred before the season even started, in the form of a 39-year-old Mexican multi-millionaire who sported a charming smile, a $6,800 ($110,000 in 2024) diamond wristwatch and a pearl-handled pistol in the waistband of his immaculately tailored suits.

A fitness nut who favored orange juice over liquor, Jorge Pasquel was charming, generous, quick-tempered and touchy about his incipient baldness, He was also used to getting his own way. "Sure, you could say I'm a dictator," he told *Time* magazine. "Whatever I order is done."

Pasquel had turned a relatively modest shipping company he and his four brothers had inherited into a far-flung empire that included not only ships but real estate, cigar factories—and it was widely believed—large-scale smuggling. The Pasquel brothers also controlled the Liga Mexicana de Béisbol, a baseball league in which the brothers owned all or part of all eight teams and of which Jorge was the president.

During the war, the Pasquels enticed several top players from the Negro Leagues such as Williard Brown, Ray Dandridge and Monte Irvin to play in Mexico. Banned from the American big leagues, African Americans found that with Mexican fans, how they played was more important than what they looked like. "I am not faced with the racial problem (in Mexico)," said Willie Wells, whom Mexican fans dubbed "El Diablito" ["the little devil"] for his full-tilt hustle. Wells was a star infielder for the Negro Leagues who never played in the majors but was nonetheless elected to the Baseball Hall of Fame in 1997. "We stay in the best hotels, we eat in the best restaurants," he said. "We don't enjoy such privileges in the U.S....Here in Mexico, I am a man."

With the war's end, Jorge Pasquel turned his attention to the big leagues and players disenchanted with pre-war salaries and pre-war working conditions when they returned from military service. "We treat players right, not like slaves," Pasquel said. "U.S. players are bought and sold like so much cattle and have no control over the decision." Even heavyweight boxing champion Joe Louis, a huge baseball fan, was impressed by Pasquel. After knocking out challenger Billy Conn in June, Louis was asked what was next. "I dunno," he jokingly replied. "I may go down to the Mexican League. They tell me I hit pretty good."

As if to prove the truth of Pasquel's statement about the autocratic nature of pro baseball in America, Baseball Commissioner Albert "Happy" Chandler, the former Kentucky governor and U.S. senator who had succeeded Judge Kennesaw Mountain Landis as the game's titular boss, decreed on Opening Day that any player jumping to the Mexican League would be banned from pro ball in America for at least five years. (Pasquel promptly offered Chandler $50,006 to become commissioner of the Mexican League, $6 more than he was making as MLB commissioner.)

The first big leaguer to sign with Mexico was Danny Gardella, a New York Giants outfielder who had power at the plate but couldn't catch a ball if you handed it to him. Other notable Major League jumpers were star St. Louis Cardinals pitcher Max Lanier, Giants pitcher Sal Maglie and Dodgers catcher Mickey Owen. In all, 18 players moved south of the border. But Pasquel failed to land any of the game's superstars despite lavish offers that included a $75,000 ($1.1 million) cash signing bonus to the Cardinals' Stan Musial, who was making $13,500 with St. Louis at the time. Pasquel's offer to Ted Williams was so big, Williams reportedly replied "Are you going to give me four strikes too?"

None of the big names took the leap. Their reasons included Chandler's threat of a ban, suspicions about the worth of Pasquel's promises and even spouses adamantly opposed to the idea. "They promised Cadillacs if we'd go with them," recalled Yankees shortstop Phil Rizzuto. "… I had just gotten back from two years in the service and I was having a tough time adjusting to curve balls and getting base hits. I was thinking this might be the most money I'll ever make in baseball, but...[Rizzuto's wife] Cora said 'no way we are doing this.'"

As it turned out, almost all of the players who jumped soon found Mexico not to their taste. The difficulties they faced included difficulty collecting promised money, bad equipment, decrepit ballparks, hazardous travel conditions, mosquitos and gun-toting fans. As their complaints circulated back to the

United States, few players were tempted to join the early jumpers. The Pasquel raids stopped by the end of the '46 season.

Faced with legal action by banned players who wanted to come back, Commissioner Chandler rescinded his ban in 1949. The Mexican League sputtered along until 1955, when it joined Organized Baseball (the umbrella association that includes the major and minor leagues) as a Double-A league. Jorge Pasquel got out of the business in 1951 after being beaned by a beer bottle thrown by an irate fan during a game. He died in 1955 when the small plane he was traveling in to his secluded ranch crashed.

To outsiders, the Mexican League raids might have looked like a tempest in a teapot. But to MLB club owners, they were a sobering warning that the threat of outside competition was a real incentive to modernize their approach. "Scared owners granted concessions they would never have granted otherwise," Arthur Daley of *The New York Times* noted a few years later, "and the lot of athletes in the majors is much happier and more lucrative because of the Pasquels."

A second threat to the Baseball Establishment involved a 36-year-old ex-U.S. Navy lieutenant trying to win back his second-base job with the Seattle Rainiers of the Pacific Coast League.

Al Niemiec had a taste of the big leagues over a couple of seasons in the late 1930s. But from 1940 to 1942, he was merely a solid player for the PCL's Seattle club that won three consecutive pennants. In October 1942, he went into the Navy, emerging at war's end. In an act of patriotic benevolence, Organized Baseball had decided that all returning vets must be carried by their old clubs through at least Spring Training and the first two weeks of the season. Seattle met the requirement with Niemiec—and after 11 games, cut him loose with 15 days' pay and a first-class train ticket home to Connecticut.

Niemiec took the train and signed on with a Class B team in Providence, Rhode Island. He also took the Rainiers to federal court, claiming they had violated a provision of the G.I. Bill of Rights that Congress had unanimously approved in 1944. The provision required employers to give veterans their old jobs back for at least a year unless they could demonstrate "good cause" for not complying. Niemiec complained the team had cut him because they thought he was too old to finish a full season, without giving him a fair chance to show he could still play.

Seattle contended Niemiec had clearly lost a step on the base paths and in the field. The Rainiers' lawyers also offered the laughable assertion that baseball was exempt from the G.I. Bill's requirement because it was "a quasi-public institution not operated primarily for profit."

In late June, Judge Lloyd L. Black disagreed with the team. In ordering Seattle to pay Niemiec's full season's salary whether they played him or not, Lloyd said the Rainiers had not adequately demonstrated Niemiec's play was sufficiently deficient. Just in case his views on the case weren't clear, Lloyd delivered a two-hour oration during which he said baseball players had the same rights as plumbers, house painters or any other returning veterans.

"Since it has been argued correctly that baseball is the Great National American Game that it is," the judge said, "it certainly ought to bear its share in meeting obligations to servicemen...Youth must be served, but not at the expense of men who have worn the uniform, and contrary to law."

The decision sent shudders through baseball's bosses, who feared a tidal wave of similar cases. *The Sporting News* estimated 143 major league players and more than 1,000 minor leaguers might have the same legal beef as Niemiec. Commissioner Chandler hastily wired the Seattle club and urged them to appeal. Chandler said Organized Baseball would pay for legal expenses in all such cases.

But it never came to that. Niemiec accepted a payout of $2,905 ($44,400 in 2024), quit baseball and became a beer salesman and later a golf pro. Other clubs took a cue from Seattle's solution to the problem and simply paid off any players who raised the issue.

At the same time Niemiec was rattling baseball's chains in Seattle, a Boston attorney was stirring the pot throughout the big leagues. Robert F. Murphy was a 35-year-old Harvard-educated labor counselor for the National Labor Relations Board. He was also a huge baseball fan who thought professional baseball players in post-war America were getting a raw deal. He began talking informally to players on the two Boston clubs and visited some other teams during Spring Training. "I could talk for three days on some of the injustices done to ball players by the club owners," he said.

Murphy's talk soon turned into a lofty plan to strengthen players' bargaining position via an organization he dubbed the American Baseball Guild. Each major leaguer would pay 50 cents ($8.12 in 2024) per week in dues to fund operations. The Guild's opening negotiating points would include a minimum $7,500 ($120,900) annual salary for players, no maximum salary, mandatory arbitration on salary disputes, and bonus incentives and insurance in every contract. In addition, players would get half of the purchase price when sold to another team. And there was a vague demand that contracts be worded fairly for both sides, a roundabout challenge to the reserve clause.

With enthusiasm but no experience at labor organizing, Murphy took his pitch on the road, meeting with every team he could. Club owners reacted privately with alarm and publicly with bluster. The cranky cheapskate Clark Griffith, owner of the Washington Senators, contended "collective bargaining in baseball would be utterly impractical. There is no production line in the game. It's a matter of individual ability."

Baseball writers, who in the 1940s carried considerable weight in forming public opinion about the game, were divided over the prospect of player unionization. Some viewed Murphy's crusade as either a well-meaning but quixotic quest, or a thinly disguised ploy by Murphy to set himself up as a union boss. "It's going to take real salesmanship to the get the Guild going," wrote Dan Hall, sports editor of the *Tampa Bay Times*. Hall conceded that players probably needed at least $7,500 a year to meet spring training expenses and maintain in-season and off-season housing. "But try selling that idea to a $40-a-week clerk." Columnist John Wray of the *St. Louis Post-Dispatch* noted Murphy's operation had no formal support from organized labor in other fields. "If Organized Baseball can't lick a one-man agitation," Wray wrote, "it will show that its resourcefulness is lower than a baboon's IQ."

But widely syndicated conservative columnist Westbrook Pegler wrote that players might rightfully band together "against the cruel whims and rascality of the soulless corporations which operate the industry...Their standard form of contract is unfair, being a 20-year enlistment on the player's part from the date of his first agreement but subject to cancellation on 10 days' notice by the employers when an arm goes lame or the eyes grow dim, and always on the bosses' terms."

On June 4, Murphy said he had signed up 60 to 70 percent of the players on four National League teams and "over 90 percent" of the Pittsburgh Pirates. "We intend to get some of it done this season," he added. "We're not going to get tossed around." Murphy also announced he would test his influence first in Pittsburgh, with a players' vote on a strike if Pirates management declined to negotiate.

It was a choice fraught with promise and peril. Pittsburgh was a strong union town and several Pirate players had union connections through their families. Moreover, the plight of one of the Bucs players had engendered sympathy and solidarity. In 1945, 28-year-old rookie catcher Bill Salkeld had hit a solid .318 and led the team in home runs with 15. But the Pirates gave him only a $500 raise in 1946, to $6,000. Unable to find housing for his family in Pittsburgh, Salkeld first rented a hotel room, then sent them to live with in-laws in California. The hotel and train tickets ate up the raise and more, forcing him to borrow money from teammates.

At the same time, however, many Pirates players genuinely liked Bill Benswanger, the team's president. "I thought Murphy's ideas made sense," team captain Al Lopez recalled five years later, "but I also knew Bill Benswanger, our boss, was a thoroughly good guy." It didn't help Murphy's cause that the Pirates were also thought to already be one of the better-paid teams in the majors.

On June 7, Pirates players gathered in their clubhouse before a home game with the Giants to take a strike vote. They listened to a pep talk from a team official, but Murphy was banned from the clubhouse. They also heard from pitcher Truett "Rip" Sewell, who with a reported salary of $15,000 ($241,700) was reputed to be the highest-paid Pirate. Sewell flatly told his teammates they had all signed contracts to play, and he was going to pitch no matter what kind of team was behind him. (Anticipating a strike, the Pirates had a contingency plan to field a team that included 49-year-old manager Frankie Frisch and 72-year-old coach Honus Wagner.)

Then they voted 20-16 to strike, Unfortunately for Murphy, it had been decided it would take two-thirds approval to go forward. Pirates players took the field and took their frustrations out on the Giants, pounding out 15 hits in a 10-5 win. After the game, outfielder Johnny Barrett explained he voted against striking: "I have a wife and three children and I'm getting good money." An unnamed teammate who voted to strike angrily responded "The hell with the bunch of them. They lost their guts. They were all for a strike until the show-down came, and then they backed out."

The death blow to Murphy's crusade came a week later when the National Labor Relations Board rejected his charges that Pirates ownership had broken federal law by engaging in unfair labor practices. The board also declined to decide whether it even had jurisdiction over professional baseball.

The union was dead, killed as much by Murphy's starry-eyed inexperience at organizing as anything else. But not all the anti-union forces relaxed. "There is no witless Pollyanna among the magnates and officials who thinks the trouble has blown over for good and the majors no longer need concern themselves with the gripes of players," editorialized *The Sporting News*, the self-described "baseball Bible" that normally loathed changes in the game. "This country... is going through a social revolution. As America's national game, baseball is passing through that social upheaval, along with bread baking and wheat growing, coal mining and steel puddling, railroading and meat production. There is an insistence in many quarters that the baseball setup is antique. Whether it is or not should be ascertained."

Whether *The Sporting News* didn't know it or just didn't report it, the sustainability of baseball's setup was already being privately ascertained by the powers that were. Throughout July and into early August, a "Steering Committee" of four owners—Larry MacPhail of the Yankees, Tom Yawkey of the Red Sox, Phil Wrigley of the Cubs and Sam Breadon of the Cardinals—along with National League President Ford Frick and American League President Will Harridge, had been meeting secretly. Their goal was to formulate a plan to deal with the threats posed by Pasquel's Mexican League and the players' increasing restiveness.

The committee's de facto leader was MacPhail, a loud-talking, loud-dressing lawyer, department store owner and horse breeder. MacPhail was an adventurous fellow. Just after World War I, he was part of a scheme to snatch exiled German Kaiser Wilhelm II from his sanctuary in the Netherlands so he could be tried for war crimes. The caper failed, but for the rest of his life, MacPhail proudly displayed an ash tray he had stolen from the Kaiser's residence. In World War II, he volunteered as a private at the age of 50 and emerged as a colonel.

When he was sober, MacPhail was regarded as a baseball genius. Recognizing early on that working people could not easily attend day games during the week, he introduced the majors to night baseball in 1935 by installing lights while president of the Cincinnati Reds. He was among the first to discount ticket prices for women and children, broadening baseball's appeal. But when he was drunk, which was often, he could be downright nasty and more than a little nuts. "He never took personally what he said about someone else," quipped the ever-quotable Leo Durocher, who managed the Dodgers when MacPhail was the club's president and was fired and immediately rehired by MacPhail at least twice. "There is a thin line between genius and insanity, and in Larry's case it was sometimes so thin you could see him drifting back and forth."

MacPhail convinced the committee that the best way to preempt attempts by players to organize would be to invite some player representatives to meet with the owners and present their wish-list for better working conditions. "A healthier relationship between club and player will be effective in resisting attempts at unionization," he wrote, "or raids by outsiders."

To the owners' great relief, the players' priority was not abolishing the reserve clause, but establishing a pension plan. "The pension was 98 percent of the negotiations with the owners," said St. Louis Cardinals star shortstop Marty Marion, one of the player reps. "All the other stuff about minimum salaries and traveling expenses means comparatively little. What we want in baseball is some security for the future."

The players got their pension. Owners agreed to a plan, beginning in 1947, to fund a pension system in which each player, coach and manager would contribute $250 a year ($3,500 in 2024). Owners would match the amount. In addition, receipts from the broadcast rights for the World Series and revenues from the All-Star Game would go to the pension fund. Players with 10 years in the majors would be eligible for $100 a month ($1,400) at age 50, with lesser amounts for players who completed from five to nine seasons. The first pensions would be distributed in 1955, when it was estimated the fund would be large enough to cover the needs. Owners figured at the time that the pension system's solvency would be solely the players' worry. "Some of the club owners believe the players are (or will be) confronted with a tremendously baffling financial problem," *The Sporting News* reported.

The owners made other concessions as well. A minimum salary of $5,500 ($77,500 in 2024) was set. No player's pay could be cut more than 25 percent from season to season. Severance pay was increased from 10 days to 30. Players would get $25 ($350) per week for spring training expenses. No doubleheaders would be scheduled for the day after night games. Players cut loose because of injury would receive a full year's salary.

In return, the owners tried to add 14 games to the 154-game schedule to fund their part of the pension plan. But a loud chorus of protest from players, the press and baseball purists scuttled that idea. To recoup the money they had anticipated from the extra games, the owners cut the minimum seasonal salary they were granting by $500 ($7,050 in 2024.) They also added language to the standard 1947 contract meant to eliminate the players' ability to sue the club or to legally challenge the reserve clause.

As for the concessions made, the owners could certainly afford them: The collective net profit margin for all teams in 1946 was estimated at 20.9 percent, compared with a net loss of 1.3 percent in 1943. And the post-war baseball boom was just starting. Total major league baseball attendance leapt from 7.5 million in 1943 to 18.5 million in 1946 and more than 20 million in 1948 and 1949. The minor leagues' jump was equally impressive. The number of minor leagues had shrunk during the war from 44 to 12, and total attendance to less than 7 million. By 1947, there were a staggering 448 minor league clubs in 59 leagues, drawing 41.5 million fans.

"In the years immediately following World War II," the history writer David Halberstam noted, "professional baseball mesmerized the American people...Baseball, more than anything else, seemed to symbolize a return to normalcy and a return to life as it had been before Pearl Harbor."

If the players were disappointed with the scope of the concessions, they largely kept quiet about it. The more perceptive members of the press did not. John Lardner of *Newsweek* suggested the deal was akin to prison wardens providing their prisoners bigger cells. Red Smith of the *New York Herald-Tribune* rhetorically spit on both sides. Smith said the owners, shaken by the Mexican League and the threatened strike at Pittsburgh, "sought to forestall trouble by tossing the help a bone." The players, Smith added, were "unschooled, self-centered and reactionary...They are all capitalists or would-be capitalists, so they snoot at unions, refusing to see beyond their batting averages." Murphy, the young lawyer who had tried to unionize the players, resorted to metaphor to sum up the settlement. "The players have been offered an apple," he said, "but could have had an orchard."

MacPhail, meanwhile, was busy drafting a report to sum up the committee's findings. The document, which was meant to be for owners' and MLB officials' eyes only, was a scathing indictment of Organized Baseball's structure and practices. MacPhail wrote that the game's administration hadn't changed in 35 years while the rest of the country certainly had. The reserve clause was legally indefensible and would not "prevent a player from playing elsewhere or prevent outsiders from inducing a player to breach his contract." He also warned that Murphy's organizing efforts would have succeeded had he started by organizing minor league players. "… In that event, we would have probably awakened to a fait accompli."

The report shocked other owners and MLB officials enough that they destroyed it—or thought they had. In 1951, a tattered copy was found and turned over to a congressional committee looking into baseball's exemption from anti-trust laws. *The Sporting News* published sections of the MacPhail report. But left unpublished was the part in which MacPhail urged that one of baseball's longest-standing traditions be preserved: Black players should not be allowed in the big leagues.

Organized Baseball had banned African American players since 1880, not through any formal written rule but as—and you should excuse the expression—a "gentlemen's agreement" among club owners and league officials. For many, if not most, support of the ban was based on mindless, soulless racism.

But in his report, MacPhail put a different spin on it. His stated objections to integrating baseball were not so much based on being anti-black as in being pro-green, as in money. In his Steering Committee report and in a letter to a committee created by New York City Mayor Fiorello LaGuardia to investigate baseball's color line, MacPhail claimed African American players would undercut Major League Baseball's financial base.

In words that directly contradicted the 1922 U.S. Supreme Court ruling that said baseball was not really a business and therefore exempt from federal antitrust laws, MacPhail wrote that "professional baseball is a private enterprise which depends on profits for its existence, just like any other business." Those profits, he contended, would be threatened if Black ballplayers were permitted to play in the majors.

One effect would be that Black big leaguers would attract Black fans and thus make White fans uncomfortable enough to stop attending. "… A situation might be presented, if Negroes participate...in which the preponderance of Negro attendance in parks such as the Yankee Stadium, the Polo Grounds and [Chicago's] Comiskey Park could conceivably threaten the value of Major League franchises owned by those clubs."

In addition, MacPhail continued, many major league clubs made hundreds of thousands of dollars each year from renting their ballparks to Negro League franchises. If the best Black ballplayers moved to the majors, the Negro Leagues would collapse. "The Yankee organization [of which MacPhail was president] alone nets nearly $100,000 [$1.6 million in 2024] per year from rentals and concessions in connection with Negro League games."

In an effort to broaden his anti-integration arguments beyond the financially self-serving, MacPhail suggested few Black players were good enough for the majors, lacking the proper instruction and experience. White players gained theirs working their way up through the minor league system, which had also been closed to Black players. MacPhail also piously claimed it was not right for big-league clubs to interfere with the contractual relationships between Black players and Negro League clubs, even in cases where there was no current written contract. "In conclusion," he wrote to LaGuardia's committee, "I have no hesitation in saying that the Yankees have no intention of signing Negro players under control or reservation to Negro clubs."

MacPhail was well aware at the time of his writings that Brooklyn Dodgers chief Branch Rickey, MacPhail's one-time mentor and current arch-rival, had already signed Jackie Robinson in October 1945 to a minor league contract with Montreal, Brooklyn's top farm club, for the 1946 season. A splendid athlete and recently discharged Army officer, Robinson tore up the International League in 1946, leading the circuit with a .349 average and winning the Most Valuable Player Award. So MacPhail fired a rhetorical warning shot across Rickey's bow in the event Robinson was elevated to the majors in 1947. "The individual action of any one club may exert tremendous pressures upon the whole structure of Professional Baseball and could conceivably result in lessening the value of several Major League franchises," MacPhail wrote.

Branch Rickey, however, was not a man to be intimidated by lesser mortals, which in his mind included just about everyone. He was convinced he was doing the right thing in signing Robinson. In explaining his motives, Rickey often told a story about when he was the baseball coach at Ohio Wesleyan University. An African American player named Charles Thomas had been denied a hotel room on a team road trip to play the University of Notre Dame in Indiana. Rickey arranged for Thomas to get a cot in Rickey's room, on which Thomas sat and despairingly wept while roughly rubbing the backs of his hands and crying "black skin, black skin. If only I could make them white." Rickey recalled "I vowed that I would always do whatever I could to see that other Americans did not have to face the bitter humiliation that was heaped upon Charles Thomas."

But just like MacPhail, Rickey was also motivated by the color green. "Son," he told Dodgers traveling secretary Harold Parrott, "the greatest untapped resource of raw material in the history of our game is the black race. The Negro will make us winners for years to come. And for that I will happily bear being [called] a bleeding heart and a do-gooder and all that humanitarian rot."

So this was 17-year-old Danny O'Connell's baseball world in 1946. The pension plan that emerged from the year's labor struggles would figure prominently in Danny's quest to remain in the big leagues, as well as the financial future of his family. The increased competition engendered by the courageous struggle of Jackie Robinson to integrate the game (about 25 percent of major leaguers would be African American by 1960) would also make it that much more difficult for O'Connell to stay in the majors. But first he had to get there.

CHAPTER 3 NOTES

Coupled with soaring *Fort Worth Star-Telegram*, Apr. 8, 1946, p. 10; *Chicago Tribune*, June 16, 1946, p. 170; *Bismarck (ND) Tribune*, Feb. 25, 1946, p. 7; *New York Daily News*, March 16, 1946, p. 213.

Almost all baseball Robert Weintraub, *The Victory Season*, p. 100. This is an excellent recounting of the 1946 season.

Because it was *Wichita (Ks.) Beacon*, Sep. 27, 1946, p. 1; *Miami Herald*, Jan. 29, 1946, p. 17; *Buffalo News*, Oct. 11, 1946, p. 27.

Newspapers across the *Hope (Ark.) Star*, May 22, 1946, p. 4.

Product shortages and U.S. Bureau of Labor Statistics, *Monthly Labor Review*, April 2014; *Retail Prices of Food, 1946 and 1947*, May 31, 1948, p. 10.

In early 1946, Excerpted in *Baseball Digest*, Feb. 1946, p. 52.

What the lawyers' Weintraub, op. cit., pp. 271-272.

A fitness nut *Time Magazine*, March 11, 1946, p. 70.

With the war's Weintraub, op. cit., p. 96; *The Sporting News*, July 3, 1946, p. 2.

But none of Weintraub, op. cit., pp. 96-97.

But what to *The New York Times*, June 7, 1949, p. 36.

Seattle contended Niemiec Jeff Obermeyer, "Disposable Heroes: Returning World War II Veteran Al Niemiec Takes on Organized Baseball," *Society for American Baseball Research 2010 Summer Baseball Research Journal*.

"Since it has" *Eugene (Or.) Guard*, June 25, 1946, p. 6.

The decision sent *The Sporting News*, July 3, 1946, p. 8.

At the same Weintraub, op. cit., p. 180.

With enthusiasm but Weintraub, op. cit., p. 182.

Baseball writers, who *Tampa Bay (Fla.) Times*, June 2, 1946, p. 21; *The Sporting News*, June 19, 1946, p. 5.

But widely syndicated *Cincinnati Enquirer*, May 20, 1946, p. 2.

On the other, Weintraub, op. cit., p. 184.

On June 7, After the season Sewell was gifted a pricey wristwatch by Commissioner Chandler for helping to head off the Pirates' strike. A four-time All-Star, he was released by the Pirates after the 1949 season, played one season more in the minors, then retired. He remained an outspoken foe of players unionizing.

Then they voted *The Sporting News*, June 19, 1946, p. 4; *Pittsburgh Sun-Telegraph*, June 8, 1946, p. 2.

The union was *The Sporting News*, June 19, 1946, p. 12.

When he was Lee Lowenfish and Tony Lupien, *The Imperfect Diamond*, p. 148;

Ralph Berger, "Larry MacPhail," Society for American Baseball Research, SABR. org.

MacPhail convinced the *The Sporting News*, Oct. 24, 1951, p. 8.

To their great *Boston Globe*, Oct. 9, 1946, p. 9.

The players got *The Sporting News*, Dec. 11, 1946, p. 2.

The owners made The Spring Training money the players got for years afterward was referred to as "Murphy money," just about the only tribute paid to the organizing efforts of the Boston lawyer Robert Murphy.

A month later *The Sporting News* Oct. 31, 1951, p. 8.

In the years David Halberstam, *Summer of '49,* p. 14.

If the players *Boston Globe*, July 31, 1946, p. 20; Lowenfish, op. cit., p. 151.

In words that Quotes here and in following paragraphs are from the MacPhail Report, Baseball Hall of Fame archives and *New York Daily News*, Jan. 14, 2015, p. 56.

Branch Rickey, however, *The New York Times*, April 14, 2012, sports section P. 10.

But just like Weintraub, op. cit., p. 74

CHAPTER 4
"HE WAS JUST ALL BASEBALL"
BUSH LEAGUES, BUS RIDES & BRANCH RICKEY

Perhaps the nicest thing you could say about Danny O'Connell's first professional team was that its ineptitude was both pervasive and consistent. And sometimes entertaining.

To be fair, the Bloomingdale Troopers were starting from scratch in 1946. Maybe from somewhere farther back than scratch. So was the North Atlantic League, a Class D collection of small-town teams in New Jersey, New York and Pennsylvania. The Troopers' hometown of about 5,000 was 15 miles northeast of Danny's hometown of Paterson. Bloomingdale was best known for its rubber factory and as the site of a Revolutionary War mutiny by mostly drunk Continental Army troops. The mutiny was quickly quashed and the two ringleaders executed by order of George Washington. I mention this to show the bar wasn't set very high for the Troopers to make a name for themselves in the town.

Things didn't get off to an auspicious start. The team's first owner was the tax collector for the nearby city of Bayonne. He named the team "Troopers" to honor his son, a New Jersey state policeman killed in a car accident in 1944 while on patrol. The Troopers' first manager was a locally well-known semi-pro catcher who decided just a few weeks before the season began that managing would interfere too much with running his sporting goods store. So he quit. When he did, the tax collector sold the newborn franchise to three men who had played baseball together at the City College of New York and were looking to buy a minor league team.

The key member of the trio was Mickey Weintraub, a 24-year-old Brooklyn-born shortstop. Weintraub's major league aspirations were disrupted by the war and then terminated when he contracted malaria while building airfields for the Army in New Guinea. During a post-war tryout with the New York Giants, Weintraub's malaria flared up. He went temporarily blind on the practice field and had to be led off the field by the second baseman.

With his partners, Weintraub headed across the Hudson. They sank $10,000 ($161,600 in 2024) into DeLazier Field, Bloomingdale's 3,500-seat concrete ballpark, outfitting it with a new lighting system, concession stands and expanded restrooms. Then they began looking for players. Newspaper announcements were placed seeking "any aspiring ballplayers between the ages of 17 and 24 who are interested in a tryout." More than a hundred boys and men were interested. One of them, Weintraub recalled a few years later, was an "awkward and gawky and very young" Danny O'Connell.

"But after looking at him for only a couple of days, I felt he was a natural," Weintraub said. "(The) one thing that impressed me was his tremendous spirit and enthusiasm for the game. He was just all baseball, living and breathing it, and a boy like that, willing to learn, can't miss if he has any natural assets at all."

Once Weintraub had convinced Danny's dad (who had to sign the contract since Danny was under age) that O'Connell had a bright future in pro ball, the Troopers had their third baseman. Weintraub planned to play shortstop himself as well as manage. That left seven other positions to fill. None of them were filled with much in the way of baseball talent. Of the 63 players who donned Troopers uniforms in 1946, just two besides Danny would get a taste of the big leagues. One of them, Harold "Sour Mash Jack" Daniels, played 12 seasons in the minors and one in the majors, hitting .187 in 106 games for the 1952 Boston Braves. The other, Carl "Butch" Sawatski, played parts or all of 11 seasons in the big leagues, mostly as a backup catcher.

Like Danny, Sawatski was from Paterson. The two would often hitchhike the 15 miles home from Bloomingdale after night games, lugging their baseball gear—and sometimes poultry—at 1 or 2 in the morning. "We'd get a dollar or two from some of the fans for each homer we hit," O'Connell laughingly recalled a decade later, when he and Sawatski were reunited as teammates in the bigs. "My dad would start it off with $2 when I happened to get one. Sometimes they paid us off with live chickens and watermelons."

Hitchhiking home was only one of the "perks" of life at professional baseball's lowest level. The maximum salary allowed in the North Atlantic League was $90 ($1,450 in 2024) a month (which Danny had worked his way up to in June from the $70 he originally signed for). Players got $2 a day meal money while on road trips ($32), and the club took care of finding them a place to sleep, usually in the spare room of a private residence. The good news was that none of the league's seven other teams were in towns more than 130 miles from Bloomingdale. The not-so-good news? The Troopers' transportation consisted of a tired station wagon and whichever players' cars were working that week.

The team's owners had calculated they would have to draw 800 fans per game over the 128-game season to break even. But they hadn't calculated how bad the team would be. After losing their first two games 15-1 and 18-5, the Troopers somehow got worse in the third game, when they didn't get any hits at all. As the team stumbled between sixth and seventh place, fans stayed away in droves. Many of those who had pledged to buy season tickets changed their minds. Austerity measures were taken by the club: "The management of the Bloomingdale Troopers has asked that persons finding baseballs knocked out of bounds at DeLazier Field return them," a newspaper notice announced, "as the total has been quite high."

In fact, it took a 51-year-old fat guy who had become a worldwide legend precisely by knocking baseballs out of bounds to draw the biggest crowd of the season. Babe Ruth was passing through North Jersey on his way to a hunting and fishing trip when friends and local officials convinced him to take in a Troopers game. The Babe was just beginning to feel the effects of the rare cancer that would kill him two years later. But Ruth not only watched the game to the end, he graciously took the field afterward. With an old Yankees team-mate lobbing pitches to him, the Babe thrilled the crowd by lofting several balls over the stadium's right field wall and onto the roofs of houses across the street.

It was the highlight of the season, unless you counted the night the team's business manager was forced to play first base because of injuries and had his nose broken by a base runner. And there was "Danny O'Connell Night." In addition to the club and fans bestowing some small gifts of appreciation on Danny, the evening featured him hitting ground balls to the team's infielders while boys and girls on horseback galloped 90 feet to first base, where an umpire judged whether the horses beat the throws. Danny also got to help judge a bathing beauty contest.

"Danny has batted his way into the cleanup spot in the Troopers' lineup," one of O'Connell's hometown papers crowed, "… and he is already among the league leaders for the batting championship." Another paper noted, without any discernable hint of sarcasm, that after a very rough start, the Troopers had by late in the season "climbed from the depths of seventh place to a very secure position in sixth."

By the end of the season, Mickey Weintraub had sold his own contract to Portland in the Pacific Coast League, his two former partners had sold the Troopers to a local civic group, and Danny O'Connell had emerged as the team's one shining star. At the end of his first season, he led the team in games played, plate appearances, hits, runs, doubles, triples, runs-batted-in, batting average and needling umpires.

His performance paid off. A few days after the season ended, a three-paragraph article appeared in Paterson's *The Morning Call.* "Danny O'Connell, former St. Bonaventure's High athletic standout, has been sold by the Bloomingdale Troopers of the North Atlantic League to the Brooklyn Dodgers...and will report (next season) to the Class C Three Rivers club in the Canadian-American League."

O'Connell had been spotted by Clyde Sukeforth, a longtime Dodgers operative instrumental in signing Jackie Robinson the year before. (In a 1972 letter to Sukeforth, in fact, Robinson said that aside from Branch Rickey and Robinson's wife, no other person played a bigger part in the "Rickey-Robinson experiment" than Clyde Sukeforth.)

Sukeforth later told the Pirates' superstar Ralph Kiner that Troopers officials first asked for $500 for Danny's contract. When he readily agreed, they upped the price to $1,000 and then $1,500 (about $24,200 in 2024.) Danny got nothing—and didn't care. "I was just glad they asked me to sign," he told a reporter. "I was flattered. I just wanted the chance, and the Dodgers gave it to me."

A whole lot of Americans just wanted a chance to play baseball in 1946. As a *Time* magazine writer put it, "Never have so many been after so few jobs." Reporting from spring training in Florida, the unnamed scribe divided the prospective big leaguers into three groups: "1) a crop of rookies just blooming when draft boards nipped them; 2) big-name stars, back after a year or two in service and looking for their old spots; 3) the wartime stand-ins who refused to believe all the bad things said about them."

An estimated 1,200 hopefuls showed up at the Brooklyn Dodgers' camp in Vero Beach in 1946, most of them nursing a fantasy of just making one of the Dodgers' dozen minor league clubs. And that was *after* the Dodgers had already hosted 400 to 500 returning veterans at a pre-Spring Training camp for would-be ballplayers.

The prevailing feeling of most of the players, the *Time* writer noted, could be summed up in two words: "Job jitters. Nobody felt safe and everybody hustled. In the old days, if a player got his sweat shirt damp by working too hard, it usually took a leisurely hour in the clubhouse to change; now the men were back on the field in five minutes."

Even with the explosion of dozens of new minor league teams creating more opportunities ("every town with a filling station and a Piggly Wiggly thinks it needs a ballclub," groused one major league executive), competition was fierce. More than 4,000 minor league players had gone to war (143 did not come back), and at least that many untested players had grown old enough during the war years to challenge them for a job.

The St. Louis Browns, for example, held a six-week camp that saw 300 players vying for 50 jobs on the Browns' top two minor league clubs. One of them was Les Moss, a 21-year-old catcher who had spent two years in the Merchant Marines and whose career as a player, coach and manager would span 33 years. "There were many guys coming back from the service," Moss said, "and some of them had been over there three to five years. There were some pretty rough cookies. Every time you turned around, there was a fight going on." (Moss made the Browns' Triple-A club in Toledo, Ohio.)

"When I came back, I hoped to move up to Louisville, the Triple-A team" for the Boston Red Sox, recalled Al Kozar, who played for the Red Sox Double-A team in Scranton, Pa. before serving three years in the Army. "But they were filled up there, so I had to try to win my job back at Scranton. Our shortstop had to beat out 30 competitors for the job, and I had to beat out 17 at second base." (Kozar would play 830 games in the minors over eight seasons for a chance to play 285 games in the big leagues over three seasons.)

In early March 1947, Danny reported to a recently deactivated naval base in Pensacola, Florida. Along with 100-plus other players, O'Connell had been ordered by the Dodgers to take part in an innovative program the club was trying for the first time: "Speed-Up Camp."

It was, according to a club spokesman, "primarily an instruction camp where players with known weaknesses receive instruction in an effort to correct them. The camp is also designed by Mr. Rickey [Dodgers president and part-owner Branch Rickey] to help speed up the ascent of minor league players into the major leagues. For instance, if a boy has trouble hitting a curve ball, he'll practice overcoming that difficulty."

The month-long camp was overseen by a staff of 24 that included Dodger officials and imported instructors such as former St. Louis Cardinal star Pepper Martin and Hall of Fame member George Sisler. When it was over, O'Connell and most of the other participants moved to another part of the base where the Dodgers had established their regular Spring Training camp for 10 of the club's 12 minor league affiliates.

The players apparently kept their, uh, noses clean. When Rickey was told there had been only one reported case of venereal disease among the 400 or so minor league hopefuls, he triumphantly announced it to a large luncheon audience of Pensacola civic and business leaders. "They are clean-minded," he said without a trace of irony. "When one is around these boys on the field and in the dressing room, he gets to know character. I am proud of the boys."

Wesley Branch Rickey was a very moral man. Or at least moralistic. As a short-lived and mediocre major league catcher, he had refused to play games on Sundays. As an executive, he refused to attend them on the Sabbath. That didn't stop him, however, from making money by selling tickets and beer on Sundays to less observant baseball fans. As the caustic newspaperman Jimmy Breslin put it, Rickey "was a baseball man, and nowhere in his religious training did he take a vow of poverty."

His first name, by which no one ever called him, was taken from John Wesley, the founder of Methodism. He attended, taught and coached at a Methodist university. And he often spoke as a lay minister at Methodist services. Then again, Branch Rickey often spoke just about anywhere and just about anything. "Ask Branch what time it is," sniped Dodger manager Leo Durocher, "and he builds you a goddamned watch."

In addition to the sound of his own voice, Rickey loved money, and jealously guarded however much of it he could sweep into his grasp. He thus earned a widespread reputation as a tightwad. *New York Daily News* columnist Jimmy Powers dubbed him "El Cheapo" (a nickname Rickey despised.) One of Rickey's most time-tested ruses in negotiating with players was to have an assistant call him while he was in the midst of a contract talk. In a voice loud enough to be heard by both Rickey and the raise-seeking supplicant across Rickey's desk, the aide would pile on baloney about a brand new can't-miss prospect who had just been discovered and who just happened to play the same position the fellow in Rickey's office played. The not-so-subtle message was that no player in Rickey's world was irreplaceable. As the Hall of Fame outfielder Enos "Country" Slaughter put it, "Mr. Rickey likes ballplayers, and he likes money. What he don't like is the two of them getting together."

He was also a baseball innovator without peer: sliding practice pits, batting tees, networks of strings over home plate to help pitchers visualize the strike zone, protective batting helmets, classroom teaching of fundamentals. Rickey was also the first to hire a statistician to help formulate on-field strategy. His greatest innovation, if that's the correct term to use, was of course integrating major league baseball—and helping to spur the agonizingly slow and still-ongoing process of integrating the rest of America—by signing Jackie Robinson in late 1945.

But the Rickey "innovation" that would most immediately affect O'Connell was Rickey's mastery of the farm system. He did not invent the process of a major league team supplying players to minor league franchises in return for maintaining complete control of the players' future. He perfected it, however, while running the St. Louis Cardinals organization for 17 years and establishing it as the most successful club in the National League before he moved to the Dodgers in 1942. Rickey's philosophy when it came to signing players was quantity over quality. He instructed his scouts to nab any player with potential: "Don't be finicky," he told them. The best would climb the organizational ladder of minor league teams to the majors. The others would fall off or be sold to other clubs. By 1938, the Cardinals had so many players under contract that baseball Commissioner Kennesaw Mountain Landis (who privately referred to Rickey as "that sanctimonious son of a bitch") ordered St. Louis to release 91 players so they could sign with other organizations.

One result of Rickey's vacuum cleaner approach was that when an under-sized New Jersey kid named O'Connell showed up on the radar of a Dodger scout, it was no big deal to shell out $1,500 (about $24,200 in 2024) for the right to determine the path the kid's baseball career would take. But in addition to his approach to signing players, Rickey was also famous, or notorious, for believing there was only one proper way to play baseball—his way. His organizations had rigid standards for hitting, pitching, sliding, bunting, fielding, hustling, thinking and taking the game seriously.

"They really drummed in the fundamentals," Danny recalled of his time in the Dodger system. "They taught you to always be thinking, always hustling. You learned the game on all its levels, or you went home."

O'Connell's home for the 1947 season was roughly 450 miles north of Paterson—and 120 miles north of America. Trois Rivières ("Three Rivers") was an oddly named Canadian city about midway between Montreal and Quebec City. Founded in 1634, the town, despite its name, sat at the confluence of just two rivers, the Saint Maurice and the Saint Lawrence. Its name derived from the fact that two islands neatly trisected the Saint Maurice where it entered the Saint Lawrence, giving it the appearance of three rivers flowing into one.

Three Rivers was home to the Royals, who sprang into existence in 1946 as the Dodgers' farm club in the Class C Canadian-American League. They played a 140-game schedule against teams scattered around Quebec Province, New York and Massachusetts. After a fast start in 1947, the team faded, finishing sixth in the eight-team league. Danny's season was the reverse. He slumped early, perhaps the result of an 18-year-old Jersey kid being plunked down in a truly foreign environment. Or it may have been due to the growth spurt he underwent: From age 16 to age 18 he stretched up and filled out from 5' 7" and 150 pounds to 5'11" and 170 pounds.

Whatever the reason for the slow start, he had blossomed on the field by season's end. His .311 average was eighth in the league, and he led or was second on the team in hits, runs, doubles, triples, walks, batting average and on-base percentage. He made the league's All-Star team, and reporters who covered the Royals unanimously voted him the team's most valuable player, for which he received a gold wristwatch.

"The young Brooklyn athlete has before him a brilliant future if bad luck does not interfere," a local paper predicted (in French). "O'Connell is the leading hitter of the team. He is the best hitter of all the third basemen in the Canadian-American League... Dan defends his position with competence, precision and authority. There is no third baseman in the Canadian-American at present who beats O'Connell in the art of fielding bunts."

Danny would later recall the season with a mixture of cocky pride and relief it was over. "Playing ball in that league was a cinch," he said. "It was getting to the next town that was rough. The jump from Quebec City to Pittsfield, Massachusetts, was 500 miles. When we finished a series with Quebec, they would load both clubs—40 or so people—in one bus about noon and ride all night and part of the next day. They had seats in the aisle and nobody could move for 18 hours."

Bus rides in the minor leagues were indeed the stuff of nightmares. The vehicles themselves often barely qualified as vehicles. New players or those with insomnia were often "volunteered" by their teammates to sit just behind the driver. Their job was to keep the driver awake. And the bus rides were just part of the ordeal of minor league baseball. Players got from $1 to $3 per day ($16 to $48 in 2024) in meal money while on the road—and remember this was to feed young male athletes mostly in their late teens or early 20s. Some visitors' clubhouses had one shower for 25 players. A typical road-trip day would consist of playing a game, immediately boarding a beat-up bus, riding for hours to a grimy hotel, sleeping a few hours—two or three to a room—and playing another game that afternoon or evening.

But for 4,000 or so minor leaguers, including O'Connell, who were contending for a chance at 400 major league jobs occupied by men who wanted to keep them, the dream was worth the drudgery. "You'd stand on your head," said John R. "Red" Murff, "and let them pour hot lead in your butt if you could get to the big leagues." (Murff did get to the big leagues, as a 35-year-old relief pitcher who appeared in 26 games over two years with the Milwaukee Braves.)

After the season, O'Connell went home to Paterson. He lived with his parents, played baseball and basketball with various semi-pro and recreational teams, table shuffleboard at the nearby Lincoln Tavern and pinochle and poker in the basement of the local fire station. In October, the Dodgers informed him his next rung on the minor-league ladder would be 1,900 miles south of the last one.

Greenville, South Carolina, was notable for two things. It was one of the relatively few Southern cities to completely escape damage during the Civil War, and it was the center of the South's post-war textile industry. This explained why the city's team, the Spinners, was called the Spinners. In baseball circles, Greenville was best-known for being the home of "Shoeless Joe" Jackson, the semi-literate but baseball-brilliant player who was tossed out of professional baseball permanently for allegedly taking a bribe to throw the 1919 World Series as a member of the infamous Chicago "Black Sox." Unlike Danny's first two pro teams, the Spinners had a long history that harkened back to 1907. In fact, Joe Jackson began his spectacular if ultimately ill-fated career with the club. Greenville, the Dodgers' Single A farm club, was a member of the highly competitive South Atlantic—or "Sally"—League.

As in 1947, Danny got off to a slow start. An ankle injury during Spring Training ended his hopes of jumping to Brooklyn's AA team in Fort Worth, Texas. When the Spinners' season opened, O'Connell was on the bench, mostly because at 19 he was still relatively inexperienced and a whole four years younger than Fred Postolese, the incumbent third baseman.

Danny apparently filled some of his free time writing letters home to his folks, because his mom Myrtle snipped off the letterheads from stationery Danny used from the various hotels the team stayed in, and pasted them in scrapbooks. "Our team travels by bus to all the towns," he informed his parents in one letter in May 1948, before engaging in some uncharacteristic whining. "I have recently been having tough luck in my hitting," he complained. "The outfielders made three great catches on me in the Macon series."

Soon after, however, the "great catches" slowed and the hitting accelerated. By early June, Danny was playing regularly, and well. "O'Connell continues to show a lot of promise," noted local columnist Carter "Scoop" Latimer. "The third baseman with quick reactions fields capably, throws hard and accurately and is getting his share of base knocks. He has everything in his favor to go to the top in baseball." The legendary pitcher Carl Hubbell, scouting the Sally League for the New York Giants, pronounced O'Connell "the league's best National League prospect."

In addition to hitting and fielding, Danny also displayed two other skills that were highly prized in post-war baseball: holler and hustle. "Speaking of 'holler guys,'" *Charleston News and Courier* sports editor Doc Baker wrote after a game in July, "the Greenville Spinners really have a noisy pair in short-stop Rocky Bridges and third baseman Danny O'Connell. If Spinner pitcher Pete Mondorff was unaware of their presence behind him Thursday night...at least the fans knew that Bridges and O'Connell were around." A decade later, Spinners manager Greg Mulleavy recounted how he would sometimes call for a team workout the day after a night game. "Bridges and O'Connell would roll up some uniforms after the night game and go to sleep on the clubhouse floor to make sure they'd be there in time for the workout...I knew then they would make it to the major leagues."

The Spinners finished third during the regular season, then won the playoffs to take the league championship. O'Connell was named to both the mid-season and post-season All-Star teams. Although his average fell below .300 (.292), he was second or third on the team in games played, at-bats, doubles, triples, homers and total bases.

Danny's sterling performances in '47 and '48 presented the Dodgers with a pleasant but perplexing problem: what to do with him in '49. Ordinarily under Branch Rickey's rung-at-a-time system, Danny would next move to the Dodgers' farm team in the AA Texas League, the Fort Worth Cats. On a hunch, however, Brooklyn officials decided to give O'Connell a chance to make the AAA club in St. Paul, Minnesota.

The Saints' manager, Walter Alston, was initially unimpressed with Danny. But O'Connell made only one error in 17 spring training games with the Saints and led the team in RBIs. *St. Paul Pioneer-Press* columnist Joe Hennessey called O'Connell's play "the pleasant surprise of the spring," but also noted "he is determined to be a third baseman, and third basemen are as plentiful as oranges."

Even so, Danny broke camp with St. Paul as the team's starting third baseman. The Saints roared out of the gate, winning their first five games. But manager Alston still wasn't convinced, telling reporters he hoped the Dodgers would send him an infielder with more experience. "Don't get me wrong now," Alston said, "Dan O'Connell has been holding up well at third. But he's just a kid of 20 and may need some aid."

The next day, O'Connell doubled, walked, drove in two runs and scored two as the Saints won their sixth straight. In fact, St. Paul won its first 12 games and 18 of its first 20 before cooling off. O'Connell cooled off as well, and was briefly benched in mid-May. But while the Saints found themselves in a down-to-the-wire pennant race, Danny got hot and stayed hot. With his parents visiting St. Paul during a five-game series against Columbus in early June, for instance, O'Connell went 11 for 25 as the Saints swept the Red Birds.

"When we first assigned Danny to St. Paul, it was with the idea of getting him enough experience so he could take over regularly next year," exulted Dodger scout Wid Matthews. "But he fooled us. What a pair of hands that fellow has! And a terrific arm. You've never seen anyone with more hustle. He has it to burn. The day you see him loafing is the day I quit. Certainly he still has a lot of weaknesses...(but) it's the way he absorbs teaching that makes you so hopeful for his future."

O'Connell also developed new-found power at the plate, possibly as a result of having added 10 pounds before the season began. In a May 22 double-header against the Indianapolis Indians, St. Paul's chief rival, O'Connell hit a two-run homer in each game. Two weeks later against Toledo, he hit a grand-slam to win the game. In July, a two-run homer beat Louisville. By season's end, Danny had hit a team-leading 17 homers.

On the last day of the season, O'Connell went 4-8 with a two-run homer as the Saints won both games of a double-header. That earned them the American Association pennant by one-half game over Indianapolis. Each of the Saints players picked up an extra $500.46 (about $6,500 in 2024) for copping St. Paul's first flag in 11 years.

Danny hit .314 in 138 games and had 102 RBIs to go with his 17 homers. He was second in the voting for the league's rookie-of-the-year honors, and named to the second team on the post-season All-Star squad. The first-team third baseman was a fellow named Froilan "Nanny" Fernandez. A decade older than O'Connell, Fernandez had made it to the majors in 1942 with the Boston

Braves, only to lose the next three years to military service. After the war, he stuck with the Braves for two more years before being demoted to the minors in 1948. In 1949, he started the season with St. Paul as an outfielder, in large part because O'Connell had come out of nowhere to take over at third base. By mid-May, Fernandez had been traded to Indianapolis, where he wound up back at third, leading the league in RBIs and winning the league's Most Valuable Player Award.

Fernandez played with a chip on his shoulder. During the season, he was fined and suspended briefly for pushing an umpire. He also tangled with O'Connell during a game in St. Paul, and hard feelings between them lingered. The two would tangle again the following year, this time for a big-league job.

On September 22, after the St. Paul season ended, O'Connell and several other Saints were summoned by the Dodgers to join the club as Brooklyn battled St. Louis for the pennant in the waning days of the National League season. Danny was well aware he wouldn't get into a game. The Dodgers had the slick-fielding Billy Cox at third, backed up by veterans Spider Jorgensen and Eddie Miksis. But the idea was to give O'Connell a taste of the majors, as both a reward for his good season and an inducement to continue to play well. And maybe he was a good luck charm. After he joined the team, the Dodgers won four out of their last six games and took the pennant over the Cardinals by one game.

A week after joining the Dodgers, Danny climbed aboard the team bus in Boston and took a seat next to Jackie Robinson, who was on his way to winning the N.L.'s Most Valuable Player award. "Hello," said O'Connell. "Goodbye," said Robinson. "Didn't you see the item in the paper? You've just been sold to the Pirates." "You're kidding," Danny sputtered.

But Robinson wasn't kidding.

CHAPTER 4 NOTES

The key member *Jewish Chronicle of Pittsburgh*, Aug. 20, 2009 (online).

With his partners *Ridgewood (NJ) Herald-News*, April 4, 1946, p. 14.

"But after looking" *The (Paterson NJ) Evening News*, April 15, 1950, p. 20.

Like Danny, Sawatski *Milwaukee Sentinel*, March 4, 1957, p. 6.

"Danny has batted" *The (Paterson NJ) News*, Aug. 12, 1946, p. 49; *The (Paterson NJ) Morning Call*, Aug. 27, 1946, p. 16.

His performance paid *The (Paterson NJ) Morning Call*, Sept. 12, 1946, p. 4.

O'Connell had been Letter, Jackie Robinson to Clyde Sukeforth, July 21, 1972, National Baseball Hall of Fame Archives.

Sukeforth later told *Pittsburgh Press*, March 11, 1950, p. 6.

A whole lot *Time* magazine, March 20, 1946, p. 68. The "wartime stand-ins" the article referred to did indeed get hit with an avalanche of criticism for their relatively lackluster performances during the war. Much of it was deserved, and the overall quality of baseball at the major league level did indeed suffer—e.g., a one-armed outfielder, a 15-year-old pitcher. The 1944 All-Star Game rosters featured a total of only six future Hall of Famers while the 1946 game had double that number. The feckless level of wartime play did, however, lead to some great gallows humor. *New York Sun* writer Frank Graham described one game in the '45 World Series between the Chicago Cubs and Detroit Tigers as "the tall men against the fat men in a game of picnic baseball." A Chicago sportswriter, when asked which team he favored in the Series, replied "I don't think either one of them can win."

The St. Louis Browns Danny Peary (ed.) *We Played the Game*, p. 6

"When I came" Ibid., p. 5.

It was, according *Nashua (NH) Telegraph*, Feb. 27, 1947, p. 13.

The players apparently *Pensacola (Fla.) News Journal*, April 8, 1947, p. 3.

Wesley Branch Rickey Jimmy Breslin, *Branch Rickey*, p. 47.

In addition to Roger Kahn, *Rickey and Robinson*, p. 2.

But the Rickey G. Scott Thomas, *A Brand-New Ballgame*, p. 26; Kahn, op. cit., p. 9.

"They really drummed" *The (Paterson NJ) Evening News*, March 6, 1963, p. 39.

"The young Brooklyn" This was a translation of a Three Rivers article by Paterson's *The Morning Call,* Oct. 9, 1947, p. 26.

Danny would later *Pittsburgh Sun-Telegram*, March 16, 1950, p. 33.

Bus rides in Umpires in the lower minors had it even worse most of the time. They had no facilities to change in other than the ballparks' men's rooms, thus having to run a gauntlet of often-irate fans in their ump attire to get to their cars. Then they had to drive themselves to the next town. And there were a lot fewer big-league umpire jobs to hope for than player jobs.

But for 4,000 Gene Fehler, *When Baseball Was Still King,* p.12. After his playing days were over, Murff had a 31-year career as a scout, and is most remembered as the man who discovered and signed Hall of Fame pitcher Nolan Ryan to a New York Mets contract.

Greenville, South Carolina It's worth noting that Jackson hit .375 in the 1919 Series and had 12 hits, a number still unsurpassed for a single series. He was thus either innocent or a really inept cheater.

Danny apparently filled From a scrapbook scrap, courtesy of the O'Connell family.

Soon after, however *The Greenville (SC) News,* June 9, 1948, p. 11; *The Greenville (SC) News,* July 7, 1958, p. 8. Rocky Bridges had the unfortunate distinction of beginning his major league career in 1951 backing up Hall of Famers Pee Wee Reese and Jackie Robinson on the Dodgers. He thus didn't play much. But he nonetheless bounced around the big leagues for all or parts of 11 seasons, and even made the American League's 1958 All-Star squad while playing for the Washington Senators

Even so, Danny *Minneapolis Star Tribune,* April 28, 1949, p. 26.

A week after *The New York Times,* March 18, 1954, p. 35.

CHAPTER 5
"NOW I'M PLAYING FOR MONEY"
DANNY COMES UP SHORT(STOP)

The 1950 Pittsburgh Pirates were a team in transition, from not-so-good to truly awful. This was excellent news for Danny O'Connell. Simply put, it was easier for a player to move up in a moribund organization than a successful one. Danny had spent the last three years as part of the Brooklyn Dodgers system, and the Dodgers were very good. From 1947 through 1949, Brooklyn had won two pennants and finished third once.

The Pirates, on the other hand, finished seventh, fourth and sixth in those seasons. In fact, the Pirates hadn't played in a World Series since 1927. Their owners were a feckless bunch, their managers mediocre, their players quarrelsome and dissatisfied, and their top minor league team was probably better than the big-league club.

All in all, Danny's chances of making the majors at the age of 21 looked pretty good in late February 1950, as he stepped off the train in San Bernardino, California, for his first spring with the Pirates. And he knew it.

"I felt a warm glow all over," O'Connell told a Pittsburgh writer when asked how he felt about having been sold at the end of the 1949 season by the Dodgers to the Pirates for $50,000 ($652,000 in 2024 currency) and Jack Cassini, a minor league infielder. "It was surprising news, but welcome and I regard it as one of the best breaks I've had in baseball." A few days after arriving in camp, Danny candidly explained to another reporter why he thought so. "They [the Dodgers] simply have too many good ballplayers," he said, "and if I ever make good in the majors, it would be quite a job to make big money with that organization." Talking a few weeks later with his pal Joe Gooter, sports editor of the Paterson *News,* O'Connell sounded downright cocky. "From what I've seen, I've very confident," he said. "It hasn't been too hard to handle. I hope I stay lucky."

O'Connell was joining one of the oldest teams in the National League—
and also one of the least successful. The Pirates sprang from the Pittsburgh
Alleghanies, an American Association team that began in 1882. The club joined
the 11-year-old National League in 1887. Between 1901 and 1927, the Bucs
(short for "Buccaneers") won five pennants and two World Series. But in 1927,
the team was swept in the Series by the New York Yankees, the awe-inspiring
"Murderers' Row" team that featured Babe Ruth, Lou Gehrig and four other
Hall of Famers. The shellacking apparently shocked the Pirates into a semi-
permanent state of mediocrity. Over the following 22 seasons, the team won no
pennants and finished fourth or lower 16 times.

The Pirates were owned for nearly half a century by Barney Dreyfuss, a
German immigrant and distillery owner, and his heirs. But at the end of the
1946 season, the family sold the team to an eclectic quartet headed by Frank
E. McKinney, an Indianapolis banker and co-owner of the Pirates' Triple A
affiliate, the Indianapolis Indians. McKinney's partners included real estate
investor and prominent race horse breeder John Galbreath, Pittsburgh attorney
Thomas P. Johnson, and Hollywood luminary Bing Crosby. Although he was
the majority owner, McKinney's business interests kept him in Indiana most of
the time, which meant the Pittsburgh-located Galbreath served as the managing
partner. Crosby was the least involved of the owners. As such, his chief duty
was to show up once in a while for publicity photos.

In 1946, the new owners inherited a fractious bunch of ballplayers. Many
of them hated Pirates manager Frankie Frisch, a Hall of Fame player from the
'20s and '30s whose hard-nosed managing style was ill-suited for post-war
baseball. Having seen the horrors and deprivations of war up close, players
returning from military service were no longer impressed by the rants and rah-
rahs of baseball's old-timers.

The new owners fired Frisch, and replaced him with Billy Herman, another
Hall of Fame player. As player-manager, Herman got into all of 15 games, hit
.213 and managed the club to a last-place tie with the Phillies. Herman in turn
was replaced in 1948 by Billy Meyer, who most decidedly was not a Hall of
Fame player during his brief major league career, but was a successful minor
league manager. He was initially successful in the big leagues too, leading the

1948 Pirates to a surprising fourth place finish and earning him Manager of the Year honors in the National League. (Meyer and the Pirates came back to earth in 1949, finishing in sixth place with a 71-83 record.)

The 58-year-old Meyer was generally liked by players because they deemed him fair. But he suffered from a common managers' malady—stomach ulcers—and he could be downright nasty when his temper flared. During one particularly rough stretch, for example, he told his team "You clowns could go on [the television show] 'What's My Line?' in full uniform and stump the panel."

In addition to shuffling managers, the new owners poured more than $600,000 ($7.8 million in 2024) into refurbishing the Pirates' hallowed home park, Forbes Field, and several million more to buy men to play on it. Two things soon became clear: Galbreath, as managing partner, didn't know a player from a plumber; and he was a sucker for anyone wearing spikes if the Dodgers' Branch Rickey offered him for sale.

From the end of 1946 to the beginning of 1950, Rickey peddled Pittsburgh 17 players—including Danny O'Connell—for a total of more than $1 million ($13 million in 2024). At the same time, Rickey demonstrated one of his many other skills. "Branch Rickey," it was said, "could spot baseball talent from a moving train." So along with the cash from outright sales, the Dodgers plucked some flesh-and-blood gems from the Pirates, such as pitcher Preacher Roe and third baseman Billy Cox. Both Roe and Cox would help make the Dodgers the dominant team in the National League. But by 1950, only six of the 17 players the Pirates got from the Dodgers, including O'Connell, would still be with Pittsburgh.

Made painfully aware of his gullibility by the local press, Galbreath vowed in 1948 to stop dealing with Rickey. He reportedly bet the Dodgers' president a suit of clothes that the Pirates would never again pay more than $50,000 for a Brooklyn player. Then he promptly lost the bet by paying $50,001 for Monty Basgall, a minor league infielder. Basgall produced 110 hits over three seasons with the Pirates, or $456 per hit, before becoming a highly regarded longtime coach - for the Dodgers.

To be fair, it wasn't all because Galbreath was a baseball rube. Rickey was one hell of a marketer. During a meeting between Rickey and Pittsburgh owners in 1949 to sell yet another player, Bing Crosby got up and headed for the door. "Where are you going?" Rickey inquired. "I'm going out to hire a three-piece ensemble to play soft music while you put on this sales talk," Crosby replied.

Other teams' executives also fumed at Rickey's wheeling and dealing even while envying the Dodgers' success. "Rickey is the greatest salesman in baseball," sniped Jim Gallagher, vice president of the Chicago Cubs. "He never sold a player worth a quarter. But he has received millions for them." There was some truth in Gallagher's jab. Written into Rickey's contract with the Dodgers was a clause that allowed him to pocket 10 percent of the sales price for each player.

Rickey protested his innocence to the charges of bamboozling other teams in trades. He cited several solid players he had sold over the years. "I would recommend that Mr. Gallagher watch Danny O'Connell, the third baseman I've just sold to Pittsburgh from the St. Paul club," he retorted. "A fine prospect, that boy." But he also uncharacteristically expressed some understated contrition to a Pittsburgh reporter.

"I am sorry that a few of our deals with Pittsburgh did not turn out happily," Rickey said. "But I am glad they took O'Connell. He cannot miss."

In their first few years in charge, Pittsburgh's new owners had attempted to improve the team by acquiring once-productive players with the hope they still had a few good seasons in them. Billy Herman was one example. A far more expensive one was Hank Greenberg. The right-handed slugger had carved out a Hall of Fame career with the Detroit Tigers despite losing three full seasons to military service during World War II.

But after a salary dispute in which Greenberg threatened to retire rather than take a pay cut, Detroit sold his contract to Pittsburgh in 1947 for a whopping $75,000 ($1.1 million in 2023.) The Pirates not only agreed to pay Greenberg $90,000 ($1.3 million), they moved the left field fence 30 feet closer to home plate, from 360 to 330 feet, to give him an easier home run target. The truncated area was dubbed "Greenberg Gardens." Greenberg responded by hitting .249

with 25 homers, and then retiring after the '47 season because of back problems.

Their old-guys strategy having failed, the club owners changed course and undertook a youth movement. "We don't promise any pennant next season," manager Meyer said in January 1950. "But we do promise to give the Pittsburgh fans a young, hustling team that will be interesting at all times."

The promised youth movement should have augured well for Danny O'Connell, who was both young and a hustler. Moreover, his chief competitors at third base were neither young nor particularly good. One was the incumbent, Pete Castiglione, a 29-year-old who had played shortstop and the outfield as well as third in 1949, with average results. The other was none other than Nanny Fernandez, Danny's minor-league nemesis from the year before. Fernandez was coming off an excellent year at the Triple A level. But he was 31, and hadn't set the majors on fire in his earlier stint there.

During spring training, Meyer gave his younger players plenty of chances. "He looks good to me," Meyer said of O'Connell in late March. "I'm giving him every chance and certainly will carry him until at least the season opens— maybe a lot longer." While he showed flashes of promise, however—a couple of long home runs, some heads-up base-running and several dazzling fielding plays -- O'Connell was also inconsistent, had a long hitless streak and wound up with a .244 pre-season average.

On April 7, when the Pirates reached Chattanooga, Tennessee for an exhibition game, it was announced Danny would be assigned to the Indianapolis Indians in the American Association, the same league in which he had spent the 1949 season. O'Connell was disappointed, but not devastated. "I'll be back," he told friends and family. "I'll make them take me back."

Then he promptly pulled a leg muscle and missed the first week of the Indians' season. When he got back on the field, it was at an alien position. It turned out the Pirates were even worse off at shortstop than at third base and, unbeknownst to O'Connell, one of the reasons he had been sent to Indianapolis was to learn a position he hadn't played since high school.

With all due deference to third basemen everywhere, shortstop is a much tougher position to play. There's more ground to cover and more plays in which to be involved. Even on routine grounders, the shortstop must get rid of the ball quicker, since he's usually farther away when he gets the ball than the third baseman. Then there is the matter of taking part in more double play efforts and more stolen base attempts. If there's a consolation prize in playing short, it's that the position is so important defensively that an excellent-fielding shortstop can still make a living in the big leagues even if he's a crummy hitter.

None of this was lost on O'Connell. His best defensive attributes—quick reflexes, a strong throwing arm and a disregard for his front teeth on line drives screaming down the line from 90 feet away -- made him a natural third baseman. In fact, on a pre-season questionnaire, Danny had noted the reason he switched to third base in high school was "not good enough fielder for shortstop." But Pittsburgh officials decided they needed a shortstop to replace Stan Rojek, an anemic-hitting, average-fielding 31-year-old they had picked up from—who else?—Branch Rickey and the Dodgers. So O'Connell agreed to give it a try.

The results were almost immediate, and little short of amazing. In his first 19 games at the position for Indianapolis, O'Connell handled 78 chances with only one error. "Danny Boy is almost super elegant in his new position," rhapsodized Lester Koelling of the *Indianapolis News*. "Watching the Irishman in the short field, one would never suspect that O'Connell had always been a third baseman...Danny is making plays to either side that haven't been seen here in years. His powerful and accurate arm permits him to get off throws while off-balance on the dead run."

As scintillating as his fielding was, Danny's hitting was even more impressive. In his first game as an Indian, he homered, singled twice and scored three runs. A few games later, he singled, doubled and stole home with the winning run. Twice in one week, he hit walk-off bases-loaded singles. During an 11-game hitting streak in May, O'Connell went 22 for 45. He ended the month hitting .402. "Danny is the star of the club," said Gus Bell, an Indy teammate. "O'Connell has a wonderful arm, is a hustler and is hitting at a terrific clip."

When the Pirates sent O'Connell and several others to Indianapolis at the end of spring training, it was with the understanding they could be recalled to Pittsburgh with 24-hours' notice. After watching Danny slam three hits and make a sparkling backhand stab at shortstop in June, a friend of Indians (and Pirates) co-owner Frank McKinney asked if Danny was still on 24-hour recall. McKinney replied yes. "Well in that case," the friend quipped, "O'Connell just used up 16 hours."

By the end of June, O'Connell was leading the American Association in batting average, hits, total bases and walking on water. But Pirates officials insisted he still wasn't ready. "There are no plans to bring O'Connell to Pittsburgh at this time," General Manager Roy Hamey told reporters. "We believe O'Connell will be ready next year, but we want to keep him at Indianapolis this year, where he will get more experience."

The Pirates' brass received enthusiastic support for their stance from Indianapolis fans and newspapers. An editorial in the Clinton, Indiana *Daily Clintonian* suggested with tongue in cheek that it could be psychologically damaging to bring O'Connell up from a good Indy team to a bad Pittsburgh one: "A young fellow could get a defeatist complex playing with the Pirates and wind up with a beat-up psyche. The Pirates better suffer through the remainder of the season as quietly as possible and leave Indianapolis alone."

Danny's superhuman hitting eventually cooled down a bit. His average slipped all the way down to .366. Thirty of his 106 hits were for extra bases and he had played in every Indians game since missing the first week of the season. The Pirates, meanwhile, had achieved consistent awfulness. On June 21, the team was 15 games under .500 and in seventh place. A story surfaced about a players-only meeting in which the club owners were ripped as "idiots." The two players who had beat O'Connell out at third base, Pete Castiglione and Nanny Fernandez, were hitting .228 and .258 respectively, and Fernandez had made 11 errors in 60 games. Two other players had also been tried at third and found wanting. The Pittsburgh newspapers began a "We Want Danny" chant.

"This date is reckoned as the first day of summer," *Sun-Telegraph* columnist Charles "Chilly" Doyle wrote on June 21, after a game in which Fernandez made two errors in the same inning, leading to four unearned runs in a 7-3 loss to the Phillies. "But it might as well be the last for the Pirates if the club doesn't bring in Danny O'Connell or some other dependable infielder immediately. The time has come for an infield showdown."

A week later, under the headline "Bucs May Get O'Connell from Hoosiers," Doyle reported that club owners and Hamey had conferred about bringing Danny up "in a desperate attempt to prevent the permanent collapse of a major league entry that has cost the present owners several millions of dollars." By July 4, the Pirates had fallen into last place, and dug in.

If club officials weren't smart, however, they were stubborn. "O'Connell is going to make a great shortstop in time," said Indianapolis manager Al Lopez on July 1. "We're just breaking him into the position and he has several things to learn. One of his biggest weaknesses is going back on a pop fly. He is improving, though, and will be ready next year."

"Next year" came 10 days later. On July 11, McKinney, Johnson, Hamey and Meyer huddled in Chicago, where the All-Star Game was being played that day. They emerged to announce Danny O'Connell was being summoned to Pittsburgh, "in an effort," as one newspaper put it, "to aid the Bucs in getting out of last place." Naturally when it came to the Pirates, there was a wrinkle: After playing shortstop all season at Indianapolis, O'Connell would start his major league career at third base. To make room, the team sent Nanny Fernandez to Indianapolis. He would never play in the big leagues again.

In explaining the position shift, manager Meyer said, "Stan Rojek is doing such a great job lately at shortstop, I don't want to disturb him. O'Connell will take over at third and if we need help at short later on, he can move over." At the time, Rojek was hitting .219 with no home runs and was playing a so-so shortstop, which shows how "doing such great work" was for the 1950 Pirates a relative phrase.

For his part, O'Connell professed not to care if he played third, short or the harpsichord. "I had heard rumors I might come up earlier," he said, "but when I didn't get the word by July 4, I gave up hope. But it sure is nice to be in the majors."

Forbes Field, the Pirates' home ballpark, opened in 1909. A 10-minute trolley ride from downtown, it was named after an adjacent street, which in turn was named after the British brigadier general who in 1758 founded the settlement that became Pittsburgh. The park was a scenic and comfortable three-story structure, with ivy-covered red-brick outfield walls and innovations such as elevators and circular walkways to the upper decks rather than stairs. It seated slightly more than 34,000. Somewhat improbably given the Pirates'

generally woeful performances, it was often nearly full of spectators.

"The ex-Smoky City has the darndest bunch of baseball bugs in the country," the International News Service (INS) noted in January 1950. "They flock to the park, win or lose, and in recent years it's been mostly the latter."

The Bucs' attendance figures backed up the wire service's assertion. Despite losing 69 games more than it won from 1947 through 1950, the club drew an average of 1.35 million fans per season. In the National League, only the mighty Dodgers drew more, with a team that won the pennant or contended for it each of those years. Pittsburgh was a blue-collar, lunch-bucket town that loved baseball on just about every level.

But if there was a single key factor for fans flocking to Forbes, it was in the form of a 6'2" 195-lb. ruggedly handsome left fielder from New Mexico. Ralph Kiner broke in with the Pirates in 1946 at the age of 23, and promptly led the National League in home runs. He did it again in 1947. And 1948. And 1949. And so on, through 1953. Over that seven-year period, Kiner averaged 42 homeruns a year. The left field enclosure at Forbes Field that had been dubbed "Greenberg Gardens" was re-named "Kiner's Korner."

Young, strong and charismatic, Kiner was the dreamboat of hundreds of Pittsburgh bobbysoxers. He dated Hollywood beauties such as Elizabeth Taylor and Janet Leigh, endorsed every product in sight, had a regular (and probably ghost-written) column in one of the local newspapers and even hosted radio and television shows. Most of all, he hit majestic homers. "His home runs were fan-friendly," Cincinnati Reds pitcher Joe Nuxhall ruefully joked, "because you watched them for a l-o-n-g time."

Kiner liked the limelight, and the money that came with it. But he graciously welcomed Danny in his "Kiner's Liners" column in the *Pittsburgh Press*. "Clyde Sukeforth, the Dodgers coach, told me at the All-Star Game (in which Kiner hit a 9th-inning home run to tie the game that the National League won in 14 innings) that the Pirates were getting a prize in Danny O'Connell," Kiner wrote (or had written for him). "As if we didn't know it!" Kiner and O'Connell would become good pals and remain so even when they were no longer teammates, particularly due to their mutual love of wagering a dollar or two on horse racing.

For their part, Pittsburgh's papers and fans enthusiastically welcomed

O'Connell. All three of the city's major dailies ran photos of Danny chatting with manager Meyer in the dugout or discussing batting grips with Kiner or being mobbed by dozens of autograph-seeking kids even before his first official appearance on a big-league field.

That came on July 14, in a night game at Forbes Field against the Giants. The weather was seasonally rainy (for Pittsburgh in the summer) but unseasonably cool, with temperatures hovering in the mid-50s at game time. Although the Giants weren't quite as hopeless as the Pirates, they were in the midst of a six-game losing streak, hanging around sixth place, and no sort of a box-office draw.

Even so, an impressively large crowd of 29,323 showed up. As usual, many were there to see Kiner, who had hit seven long balls in his last 10 games and was tied for the major league lead in homers. But they were also drawn by the first appearance of an admittedly very nervous O'Connell. Management and media had built up the Indianapolis wunderkind as a sort of mini-Moses who would help lead the Bucs out of the cellar to the Promised Land—or at least seventh place.

Neither Kiner nor O'Connell disappointed. Kiner slammed a 450-foot drive over the left-centerfield wall, and threw in a double and a triple. Batting sixth, Danny came to bat with two out in the bottom of the first inning and a runner on third. He hit the first pitch he saw as a big leaguer sharply into left for his first hit and first run-batted-in. The Pirates scored three runs in the first inning, a highly unusual occurrence. (Unfortunately, the Pirates' pitching staff had given up seven runs in the top of the inning, which was a much more usual occurrence.)

In the fourth inning, Danny singled again on the first pitch, this time off Sal Maglie, one of the best pitchers in the league. He came around to score the first run of his career. The next inning, he was robbed of extra bases on a one-handed leaping catch at the fence by Giants right fielder Don Mueller, and in his last at-bat of the day popped out to second. True to form, the Pirates lost. No matter—Pittsburgh sports writers were sure a star had risen over the Steel City.

"O'Connell looked the part of a big leaguer," wrote Les Biederman of the *Press*, "and the fans wondered why he had been held at Indianapolis so long."

"O'Connell won the hearts of the banner throng the minute he stepped to the plate in the first inning and banged a liner like a rifle shot into left field," the *Sun-Telegraph's* "Chilly" Doyle claimed, adding that a play Danny made at third base to start a double play "would have been a credit to [Pirates Hall of Famer] Pie Traynor at his best." And Jack Hernon of the *Post-Gazette* positively gushed: "Danny O'Connell looks like the answer to the third-base situation...O'Connell can set up stakes in Pittsburgh for a long while off his debut."

Two games later, O'Connell hit his first home run. Then a belated case of the jitters set in. Over the next three games he went 0-12, striking out five times, and contributing to what had to be one of the most entertaining plays of the Pirates' season.

On July 19, in the 11th inning of a game against Philadelphia, the Phillies' Bill Nicholson hit a towering pop fly about six feet in front of home plate. Pirate catcher Clyde McCullough called loudly that he had it. But Danny, charging in from third, didn't hear him. O'Connell slammed into his teammate. The ball landed in fair territory, then rolled toward the stands behind the plate. Before anyone could retrieve it, Nicholson was chugging into third base. Since neither O'Connell nor McCullough had touched the ball, it was ruled a triple—perhaps the shortest in baseball history. The next Phillies hitter smacked a home run to win the game.

The flub, which manager Meyer shrugged off as a hustle play gone wrong, might have jarred Danny free of his anxiety, at least temporarily. He rebounded with a 5-for-9 performance in the next two games, adding his first major league double and stolen base to his first-week-in-the-big-leagues collection. He also earned praise for his defense (notwithstanding the six-foot triple.)

"Danny plays that spot as if it were made for him," said Frankie Gustine, a much-loved Pirates coach who in his own playing days had been a three-time All-Star at third base. "And what a hustler he is!"

Of course this being the 1950 Pittsburgh Pirates, O'Connell began his second week in the majors at a different position. On July19, Frank McKinney sold his share of the team to co-owners Galbreath and Johnson. On his first day as the new majority owner, Galbreath spent $50,000 (about $652,000 in 2024) to buy third baseman Bob Dillinger from the poverty-stricken Philadelphia Athletics.

At the time of the deal, the bespectacled Dillinger was leading the American League in triples and stolen bases and hitting .310. A five-year big leaguer, Dillinger was a lifetime .300 hitter with blazing speed, but he had virtually no power and as a fielder was rated between indifferent and horrible. Moreover, his lackadaisical attitude was the chief reason no other American League team wanted him. "He doesn't try and he doesn't hustle," Yankees General Manager George Weiss summed up.

With Dillinger's arrival, the dithering Pirates decided to bench O'Connell. "I realize there will be plenty of fans who would like to have me send hustling Danny O'Connell into the shortstop role at once," explained manager Meyer, "but after weighing this question for a long time, I'm convinced that I should wait a few days before he is moved to the bigger position."

Meyer waited two days before inserting Danny at shortstop and into the fifth slot in the batting order. Except for a few games at third while Dillinger was nursing a sore leg, O'Connell remained at short the rest of the season. He also played like what he was—a promising rookie who took a while to adjust to the roller-coaster of success and failure that was the majors.

In late July and early August, the Pirates embarked on a 10-game road trip to Philadelphia, Brooklyn and New York. Against the Phillies—and in front of his parents, who had journeyed the 100 miles from Paterson to see their boy play—Danny sparkled. In the four-game set, he had six hits in 16 at-bats, including two homers, two doubles and his first triple. But in the six games against the Dodgers and Giants, he fizzled. There was a costly error in one game and another collision with Pirates catcher McCullough while both chased after a pop foul. At the plate, Danny went a feeble 1-for-21. His season's average dropped to .219.

O'Connell's poor showing in New York might well have been due to the pressure of playing in the equivalent of his backyard. Three busloads of Patersonians had come to the Polo Grounds for his first game in the ballpark he frequented as a kid. *The Morning Call* invaded his folks' house on Carlisle Avenue and ran a full-page article that featured hokey photos of Danny in his tee-shirt at the kitchen table, eating some of Myrtle's baked chicken while his dad poured him another glass of milk. "You ask me what one factor contributed to my making the major leagues," the article quoted O'Connell, "and I have to tell you it is my mother's cooking."

Danny admitted he was feeling "a little more pressure than usual." But Billy Meyer hastened to promise the home folks that the Pirates' mercurial management had decided to stick with O'Connell for the duration. "He'll stay up," Meyer told Joe Gooter of Paterson's *The News*. "There's no question about that. O'Connell will be our first-string shortstop. He is assured of that position for the season, even if we have to move him to third now and then because of injuries." Meyer added that "there's pressure on a rookie all the time, but O'Connell isn't the type to scare easily...He's a good boy, is coming along and will be okay."

And even while slumping, Danny impressed people with his high baseball IQ. While playing third base in a game against the Giants, he faked a throw to second base, whirled and tagged out a startled Giants runner who had wandered a few steps off third. The next game, the Giants' Monte Irvin drove a ball against the right field wall but stopped at second when O'Connell faked catching a throw at third even though the ball was still in the outfield. "That kid," Giants manager Leo Durocher said, "might win more games with his brains than his bat."

Whether it was Meyer's pep talk in the press, a few days of Myrtle's home cooking or just getting out of New York, O'Connell snapped out of his slump. Over the last two dozen games in August, Danny hit .333 with three home runs and six doubles. Playing every game, he made only four errors. In September, he hit safely in 23 of the season's last 29 games, missing what was at the time considered a key benchmark of success in baseball -- a .300 batting average -- by going 0-8 in the last day's doubleheader and finishing at a still-creditable .292.

Despite playing just a bit more than half a season with the Pirates, O'Connell was third on the team in home runs, second in stolen bases, sixth in total bases and second in sacrifices. Of all National League shortstops who played as many games at the position as Danny (65), only Marty Marion of St.

Louis had a higher fielding percentage, and no one made fewer errors.

O'Connell's total 79-game performance earned him third place in the Rookie of the Year balloting by sportswriters. Both of those he trailed—Boston outfielder Sam Jethroe and Philadelphia pitcher Bob Miller—benefited from a full year in the majors. He was named to *The Sporting News'* all-rookie team. Danny's showing also earned him praise from someone as close to God as there was in Pittsburgh baseball circles. O'Connell, noted the iconic Honus Wagner, had "the skills to be a great, great player. I don't like to gauge a player definitely on short notice, but O'Connell's improving in everything." The peerless former Pirate added that he particularly admired O'Connell's "ability to think one play ahead all the time."

Even with Danny's fine season and another stellar year from Ralph Kiner, the Pirates stumbled to a 57-96-1 record, the club's worst since 1917. "I'm looking forward to a fresh start," team skipper Meyer said in September. "This thing, this year, has been a nightmare." In a Page One story in the *Post-Gazette*, Meyer singled out the collective and individual failings of various players while declining to assign any of the blame to himself. But he did praise the play of four of the younger Bucs: pitchers Vern Law and Bill McDonald, outfielder Gus Bell, and O'Connell. "Danny O'Connell is going to be a great player in time because he has the ability, instinct and will to win. Just watch that lad."

O'Connell echoed his manager's confidence—in himself. "I'm glad I'm up here," he said during the season. "I feel that this half-season in the majors will teach me a lot when I start out next year. I was disappointed when I was sent down at the start of the season because I was sure I could make the grade in the big time. But now that I'm back, I intend to stay."

Danny's off-season proved to be almost as momentous as the season itself. A few days after his last 1950 game with the Pirates, O'Connell joined a barnstorming team of big leaguers that included the Dodgers' Carl Furillo, the Braves' Vern Bickford, the Phillies' Del Ennis and Pirates teammate Danny Murtaugh. For most of October, the team toured southern and mid-Atlantic states, playing local amateur and college teams. The barnstormers evenly divided the gate receipts, less expenses and the promoter's cut. "The boys are satisfied," columnist Joe Gooter wrote. "They figure it's better than driving a truck."

For the still-21-year-old O'Connell, the highlight was hanging around with established big leaguers in a relaxed atmosphere. The lowlight was almost certainly in Norfolk Virginia, where thieves stole Danny's topcoat and traveling bag from the promoter's car. O'Connell lost all the spare clothes he had and was forced to buy a new wardrobe on the road. But he took it in stride. "No doubt," he deadpanned, "there is one well-dressed man somewhere in Norfolk."

When the barnstorming tour ended, Danny returned to his parents' home in Paterson. He played basketball with a team put together by New York Yankee outfielder Gene Woodling, who lived in nearby Fair Lawn. He also took a Christmas season job with the U.S. Post Office as a mail carrier to earn a little extra money. His total baseball income for 1950 was probably less than $5,000 (about $65,200 in 2024.)

But while the Pirates owners were inept, they weren't cheap. Based on his year, O'Connell expected to do much better financially in 1951, and said as much. At a Pittsburgh country club banquet as the season was wrapping up, Danny and Kiner were the guests of honor. An audience member praised O'Connell's season and asked him how he liked playing in Pittsburgh after his years with the Brooklyn Dodgers organization. "I like it great," Danny quipped. "I've played for Branch Rickey. Now I'm playing for money."

It was funny—and wrong. On November 3, the Pirates announced that Branch Rickey was the club's new general manager. Rickey had lost a fight with Dodgers majority owner Walter O'Malley over control of the Brooklyn club. He thereupon took a $1 million buyout consolation prize ($13 million in 2023) and moved to Pittsburgh. There he vowed to use his genius to revive the franchise.

That, however, wasn't even the most unsettling off-season news for Danny O'Connell. Two weeks before Rickey was announced as his new boss for 1951, O'Connell heard from an even higher authority: Uncle Sam. Danny had registered for the draft in 1947 and heard nothing since. But in mid-October, with the four-month-old Korean War heating up, his draft board informed him he had been classified 1A. Assuming he passed his physical, he could expect to be wearing a different kind of uniform in the coming year.

"I had high hopes for 1951," Danny wrote sportswriter Les Biederman a few days before Christmas," but I guess I'll have to wait a couple of years. I hope I'll be able to play enough baseball in the Army to stay in shape."

Though his playing plans for 1951 had been derailed, however, O'Connell would nonetheless realize in the coming year a dream shared by millions of American boys before and since. Sometime in the coming spring, his likeness would appear on a baseball card.

CHAPTER 5 NOTES

"I felt a" *Pittsburgh Press*, Jan. 24, 1950, p. 22; *Pittsburgh Press*, March 2, 1950, p. 18; *The (Paterson NJ) News*, March 21, 1950, p. 58. Cassini, the player thrown in as part of the deal, played 12 seasons in the minors, led different leagues six times in stolen bases, managed in the minors for many years, but never got a big-league at-bat.

On the Pirates Steve Ziantis, *100 Things Pirates Fans Should Know and Do Before They Die*, p. 136.

The 58-year-old, Ibid.

Made painfully aware Andrew O'Toole, *Branch Rickey in Pittsburgh*, pp. 11-14.

To be fair, *The (Paterson NJ) News*, Nov. 11, 1949, p. 24.

Other teams' executives *The Sporting News*, Nov. 4, 1949, p. 5.

Rickey protested his *The (Paterson NJ) News*, Nov. 11, 1949, p. 24.

"I am sorry" *Pittsburgh Press*, Oct. 27, 1949, p. 43.

Their "Old Guys" *Newport (RI) Daily News*, January 11, 1950, p. 14.

During Spring Training *The (Paterson NJ) News*, March 21, 1950, p. 58.

None of this National Baseball Hall of Fame archives.

The results were *Indianapolis News,* May 12, 1950, p. 36.

As scintillating as *Pittsburgh Sun-Telegraph*, June 1, 1950, p. 28.

By the end *Pittsburgh Post-Gazette*, June 28, 1950, p.16.

The Pirates brass *Clinton (Ind.) Daily Clintonian*, July 6, 1950, p. 7.

"This date is" *Pittsburgh Sun-Telegraph*, June 21, 1950, p. 22.

A week later, *Pittsburgh Sun-Telegraph*, June 28, 1950, p. 22.

If club officials *Pittsburgh Post-Gazette*, July 1, 1950, p. 10.

"Next year" came *Pittsburgh Press*, July 11, 1950, p. 25.

In explaining the *Pittsburgh Press*, July 14, 1950, p. 26.

For his part Ibid.

"The ex-Smoky" *Tyrone (PA) Daily Herald*, Jan. 26, 1950, p. 5.

Young, strong and Ziantis, op. cit., pp. 65-66.

Kiner liked the *Pittsburgh Press*, July 16, 1950, p. 33.

"O'Connell looked the" *Pittsburgh Press*, July 15, 1950, p. 6; *Pittsburgh Sun-Telegraph*, July 15, 1950, p. 9; *Pittsburgh Post-Gazette*, July 15, 1950, p. 10.

Two games later Danny's first homer was duly noted by *The New York Times* on Page 27 of its July 17, 1950 edition. Three columns over on the same page, *The*

Times allotted three paragraphs to reporting that Uruguay had upset Brazil 2-1 to win the 1950 World Cup in soccer. Just shows how the times have changed.

Danny plays that" *Pittsburgh Sun-Telegraph*, July 17, 1950, p. 14.

At the time *The Sporting News*, Aug. 2, 1950, p. 9.

With Dillinger's arrival *Pittsburgh Sun-Telegraph*, July 21, 1950, p. 12. Dillinger hit .288 in 58 games for Pittsburgh the rest of the season, was deemed a slacker and sold to the Chicago White Sox.

O'Connell's poor showing *The (Paterson NJ) Morning Call*, Aug. 2, 1950, p. 10.

Danny admitted he *The (Paterson NJ) News*, Aug. 2, 1950, p. 2.

And even while *New York Daily News*, Aug. 5, 1950, p. 164.

Whether it was For much of baseball history, players who hit .300 (three hits in every 10 at-bats) were considered in the upper tier of their craft. The development of other statistical measures in the recent years has diminished batting average as a yardstick by which to gauge a player's worth.

O'Connell's total *Tyrone (Pa.) Daily Herald*, Oct. 3, 1950, p. 16.

Even with Danny's *Pittsburgh Post-Gazette*, Sep. 2, 1950, p. 1.

O'Connell echoed his *The (Paterson NJ) News*, Aug. 2, 1950, p. 62.

Danny's off-season *The (Paterson NJ) News*, Oct. 17, 1950, p. 24.

For the still *Bloomsburg (Pa.) Morning Press,* Oct. 12, 1950, p. 13; *Pittsburgh Press*, Dec. 24, 1950, p. 21.

But while the *The (Paterson NJ) Morning Call*, Sept. 5, 1950, p. 20.

"I had high" *Pittsburgh Press*, Dec. 24, 1950, p. 21.

CHAPTER 6

"ACTRESSES, BASEBALL PLAYERS AND OTHER DREADFUL PEOPLE"

ALSO CIGARETTES, BUBBLE GUM AND STILL MORE DREADFUL THINGS

T he company that produced the first major league baseball card featuring Danny O'Connell was presided over by a man who:

1) Once tried to make a living by catching green sea turtles in the Gulf of Mexico but gave up the idea after his boat foundered and all the turtles escaped.

2) Got fired from the Los Angeles Police Department after being caught with his squad car full of young women.

3) Was married, divorced and bankrupt by the time he was 21, a multi-millionaire by the time he was 41, and rich enough, according to a 1947 *Saturday Evening Post* profile, "to maintain four ex-wives on alimony totaling almost as much as President Truman's salary."

But more about him in a minute or two. First there is the matter of Danny O'Connell's debut big-league card, which measures 2 1/16 by 3 1/8 inches. On the front is an image of Danny from the chest up, with the word "Pirates" emblazoned on his uniform jersey and a confident smile on his face. The image is actually a black and white photograph that artists colorized with paint. On the back of the card, O'Connell's height is listed (5'11) as well as his weight (168 lbs.) and his 1950 season statistics. The card also mentions he was a third baseman who had mainly played shortstop in 1950. And it points out that he had "entered the service"—a polite way of saying he had been drafted—which meant his first major league baseball card would be issued for a season in which he would not participate.

Danny's card was No. 93 in a set of 324 issued by Bowman Gum, Inc., a then-24-year-old Philadelphia-based company. For those keeping score at home, No. 92 in the set is Vern "Junior" Stephens, an eight-time All-Star infielder who had once signed a five-year contract with the Mexican League, only to be "rescued" by his brother and father and driven back across the border after only one day in Mexico. Number 94 is Clyde McCullough, the Pittsburgh catcher with whom Danny had twice collided during the 1950 season while the two were chasing pop flies. O'Connell, Stephens and McCullough were each paid $100 (about $1,200 in 2024) for allowing their likenesses to be used by Bowman exclusively for baseball cards sold with gum.

There were other players in the 1951 Bowman set who, like O'Connell, were appearing on their first cards. Number 253, for example, featured a 19-year-old blonde rookie from Commerce, Oklahoma, who had recently been converted from shortstop to outfielder. His name is Mickey Mantle, and his 1951 Bowman rookie card sold at auction in 2022 for $3.2 million. Fifty-two cards farther on is the rookie card of a 20-year-old African American outfielder from Westfield, Alabama, named Mays. Willie Mays. A '51 Willie Mays Bowman card in mint shape in 2023 was a comparative bargain at $800,000. And a mint-condition Danny O'Connell is an even more reasonable $400 as of this writing, or about $36 in 1951 currency.

At the time, these future cardboard treasures could be had for a penny apiece (about 12 cents in 2024) or six cards for a nickel (60 cents). Either way, they came in a waxed paper wrapper and included a hard slab of synthetic rubber and resins, hydrogenated vegetable oil, "a fruity characteristic" and food coloring. "When thoroughly chewed," *Life* magazine observed, "it becomes a nasty-looking pink mess with the elasticity of a fairly old piece of rubber." (*Author's Note:* I don't recall it being even that good.)

The "good-natured, jovial bon vivant" purveyor of these cards and gum was Jacob Warren Bowman, a larger-than-life personality - or at 6'3" and 220 lbs., he sure seemed like it. *Time* magazine called him "one of Philadelphia's lustiest characters...whose business adventures have been many and remarkable." That was putting it mildly.

Bowman—his many friends called him Warren - was born in 1895 on a Pennsylvania farm and raised on a New Mexico cattle ranch. At the age of 18, he ventured west to Los Angeles, where he opened a used car business. Trouble was, he didn't have any cars. Undaunted, Bowman persuaded friends and acquaintances to park their cars on his lot. If someone made an offer on one of the vehicles, he then talked the owner into selling, with Bowman pocketing a commission. World War I ended the car business, and Bowman became a Los Angeles police officer. While patrolling one evening, he pulled over a fellow who just happened to be the assistant police chief. The chief couldn't help but notice Bowman's squad car contained several young women whose presence Bowman could not readily explain. Thus ended his law enforcement career.

His subsequent jobs included running a one-car limousine service and driving a produce truck. When he heard that the Mexican town of Tampico could use a steam-cleaning laundry for the area's grimy oil workers, he and a friend headed south, only to find some locals had beat them to it. So, Bowman and his pal journeyed into the tropical forests of southeastern Mexico, where they felled mahogany trees with the intention of floating them downriver to waiting sawmills. This proved unwise. The heavier-than-water mahogany logs sank. After that came the aforementioned sea turtle-hunting debacle, running a café in Veracruz and trying in vain to develop a caffeine-laden coffee-flavored hard candy.

Back in the States and down to his last $25, Bowman was on a boat from Cleveland to Detroit, where a friend had offered him a job selling used cars. On the boat Bowman struck up a conversation with a traveling gum salesman, who boasted he was making $60 a week (about $1,065 in 2024). That was enough to get J. Warren Bowman into the gum business. He began as a salesman, offering retailers prizes such as steak knives and "genuine Indian blankets" for placing large orders. After a false start or two, one of which involved buying 180 pinball-like machines and rigging them to pay off in pieces of gum, he borrowed enough money in 1927 to open Gum, Inc., later changed to Bowman Gum. In 1929, the year Danny O'Connell was born, Bowman's company began producing Blony bubble gum. (More about how bubble gum was invented later in this chapter.)

The year before the start of the Great Depression was not a particularly auspicious time for launching a business based on a non-essential item. But a penny-priced product whose target customers didn't have to worry about paying rent or making car payments with their money was about as good as it got. By 1937, Bowman had cornered 60 percent of the American bubble gum market—and bubble gum was a very popular product. Bowman's gross sales amounted to $800,000 a month ($17.5 million in 2024.) The Bowman gum's appeal, other than its obvious ability to annoy parents and teachers, was its weight: At almost a half-ounce, Blony pieces were bigger than the competition's gum. "Three big bites for the penny" turned out to be one eye-catching slogan for kids.

It was not all smooth sailing for the former turtle hunter during the '30s. A protracted and bitter legal battle ensued when Bowman tried to squeeze out of a contract with the New York pharmacist who had supplied the gum's base (the part that makes gum chewy) since the company started. Bowman had found a cheaper and better base in Chicago, and began buying it. The New York pharmacist sued, and Bowman's board of directors was so panicked about the suit, he was even pushed out as president for a while. But he was restored to power after he persuaded the judge hearing the lawsuit to try samples of the gum made with the two different bases. The judge ruled in favor of Bowman and the Chicago base after finding the New York stuff stuck to his dentures.

Like its Depression-era rivals, Bowman's company used various trading cards to accompany its gum and enhance its appeal. But while Bowman and other issuers of trading cards in the first half of the 20th century viewed the cards mainly as tools to sell gum or candy, their 19th century counterparts produced cards to peddle a far more controversial and impactful product.

Deciding what constitutes America's first baseball card is a bone of contention among serious collectors, who by the way are every bit as contentious as devotees of baseball statistics. Members of both groups can be seriously nerdy about stuff like this. The author included.

A big part of the problem is defining just what a baseball card is. Some historians contend that the Adam and Eve of cards is of unknown origin and was printed sometime between 1810 and 1830. It features a boy pitching a ball to another boy holding what could be a bat while a third boy stands near what could be construed as first base. The caption reads "Boys delight with ball to play."

The eminent baseball historian John Thorn disagrees. Thorn maintains the first card was actually a ticket, on heavy card stock with a silver-mirrored finish, to a Feb. 9, 1844 game in Hoboken New Jersey (just 17 miles south of Danny O'Connell's hometown of Paterson.) As Thorn explains it, the $1 ticket (about $42 in 2024), which is illustrated with what is clearly some kind of baseball game, was meant to be kept as a souvenir of the event. "This ticket is the first depiction of men playing baseball in America," he contends, "and it may also be, depending upon one's taxonomic convictions, the first baseball card."

In a 2015 exhibit, the Library of Congress claimed the first cards were team photos of the Brooklyn Atlantics from the 1860s. One of these was sold at auction the same year for $179,000 (the equivalent of $237,000 just eight years later) by the great-grand niece of one of the team's outfielders.

Others believe the first true baseball cards were those of the 1866 Unions, a team from Lansingburgh, New York, a community near Albany. The Unions, also known as the Troy Haymakers, posed for solo photos sold by the photographer via mail order as well as handed out by the players as *cartes de visite,* or "visiting cards." The argument here is that these cards were the first to feature individual players and sold to the general public. Plus, the Unions were charter members of America's first professional baseball league, the National Association of Professional Baseball Players, even though they went broke and disappeared after just one season.

As for me, I'll take the cards issued by Peck & Snyder. Andrew Peck was a New York City orphan who served in the Union Army during the Civil War. At war's end, Peck eased into a career making and selling sporting goods. Teaming with a fellow named W. Irwin Snyder, Peck opened a store on Nassau Street in Lower Manhattan. There they made and sold bats and baseballs. The two also came up with innovations such as rubber-soled, canvas-topped shoes—the forerunners of today's tennis shoe—and inline roller skates.

In 1869, Peck & Snyder put out 3 ¼ x 4 ½- inch cards bearing photographs of teams such as the Cincinnati Red Stockings (generally regarded as America's first truly professional baseball team and who compiled a 57-0 record in 1869), and the Mutual Green Stockings (a New York City club notorious for throwing games after betting on the other team.) On the back of the cards, which were handed out on street corners, was an advertisement for the sporting goods company. Thus we have the combination of a baseball-related image *and* the grand American tradition of trying to sell something. Variations of this combo became the basis for most baseball cards until well into the 20th century.

In the first few decades after the Civil War, the product cards were most often used to push cigarettes. And although it may come as something of a surprise, cigarettes in the mid-19th century needed all the help they could get. It was true that Europeans began chewing tobacco or lighting it on fire and inhaling the smoke about 10 minutes after arriving in the New World and observing the practice by Native Americans. But most smoking was done via pipes or cigars. Cigarettes were a pain to roll, didn't last very long and were generally considered tobacco conveyances for the lower classes.

The exigencies of the Civil War, however, made them much more popular. "The fixins"—rolling paper and tobacco in pouches—were more portable for soldiers on the march and less breakable than pipes or cigars. Post-war innovations by tobacco companies, such as pre-rolled cigarettes in packs (first rolled by hand and then by machines) increased their popularity even more. Based on federal tax revenue reports, it was estimated that domestic cigarette smoking quintupled between 1870 and 1885. Even so, cigarettes lagged well behind other tobacco products. While manufacturers churned out an estimated 1.3 billion cigarettes in 1885, an average of 22.1 per American, they made 3.6 billion cigars, or 59.2 each for everyone in the country.

Enter advertising. Developments in photography during and after the Civil War resulted in the rise of a cottage industry built around "cabinet cards." Originally, most of these cards, usually 4 ½ by 6 ½ inches in size, were photo images of personal events, such as weddings. By the early 1880s, however, studios were churning out thousands of copies of photos featuring celebrities who ranged from opera divas and stage actresses to notable military figures and famous writers. "The business of making and selling portraits of well-known people has increased with wonderful rapidity during the last five or six years," *The New York Times* reported in February 1883. *The Times* said the price of the cards ranged from 5 cents to $5 ($1.55 to $155 in 2024), depending on the celebrity's popularity at the moment.

Trade cards, such as the Peck & Snyder baseball cards previously mentioned, were offshoots of the celebrity cards. But they took on extra value as advertising vehicles as a result of the 1876 Centennial Exposition in Philadelphia. What amounted to America's first World's Fair was an immensely popular event. Almost 10 million people attended during its six-month run—equivalent to 20 percent of the nation's entire population. Many attendees were so dazzled by the Expo's wonders—from the telephone and typewriter to Heinz ketchup and a tropical fruit called the banana—that they collected scores of trade cards featuring the inventions and innovations and pasted them in scrapbooks to share with the folks back home. Card collecting became a popular pastime.

Which brings us back to cigarettes. In the early 1880s, several of the nation's plethora of tobacco companies hit upon the idea of inserting picture cards in their cigarette packs. This served to help advertise their brands *and* stiffen the soft packages to help protect the smoke sticks. At first, the most popular subjects were amply curved women, some of them well-known actresses and singers and some of them just amply curved. After all, the companies' target consumer was the adult male. Following the time-honored business practice of "monkey see, monkey do," virtually every tobacco company of any appreciable size joined the picture card stampede. By 1887, a single New York plant was producing 75,000 cards per day and operating on a round-the-clock schedule.

Cigarette makers improved on the gimmick by marketing individual cards as parts of sets. This helped create brand loyalty as customers tried to complete their collections of a particular set. It also turned them into advertisers for the brand when they showed off their cards. In the wake of adverse publicity and protests from the clergy and other groups against "smut peddling," the companies expanded their cards' subjects from flirty females to wildlife, flags of nations, famous sailing ships, Wild West figures—and baseball players.

Major tobacco companies such as Allen & Ginter, Duke, and Lone Jack all issued baseball card sets. But Goodwin and Co., a New York City firm, took it to another level. Starting with a modest 12-card set of the hometown New York Giants, the company over several years distributed more than 2,000 cards of more than 500 players on more than 40 major and minor league teams. This "super-set" became known as the "Old Judge" cards, after one of Goodwin's cigarette brands.

Even though flags, ships, athletes and cowboys were more acceptable subjects than saucy young ladies showing too much ankle, cigarette cards were still frowned upon by quite a few people. When a young woman in Boston was asked by a reporter if she would like to have her picture on a card, she recoiled in indignation: "What a horrid suggestion! Only actresses, baseball players and other dreadful people have such things taken."

If young Boston ladies were repelled by the cards, however, they opened up an immense new market for cigarette makers: boys. Putting locally and nationally known baseball players on cards—along with pirates, trains, Indian chiefs and gunslingers—made the cards more attractive to sons, grandsons and nephews than to dads, grandads and uncles. Boys begged their elders to buy a particular brand so they could collect cards from favorite sets. Companies encouraged the practice by offering card binders and albums in return for x number of tickets or coupons from empty packages. And if begging didn't work, boys eliminated the older middleman and began smoking themselves.

"The cigarette would lie down and die tomorrow if it were not for the small boy," a wholesaler told a *Chicago Tribune* reporter in June 1889. "There is a law [in Illinois] against selling them to boys under 16," a newsstand owner told the same reporter, "but I never saw the boy yet, even if he couldn't reach up to the counter, who wasn't willing to swear he was 16."

A few months later, another vendor told a *Tribune* reporter that because his youthful customers "like to make collections of the pictures...I have to keep all the different kinds [of cigarettes] I can get...If the kids would switch to cigars it wouldn't be so bad. But the younger generation growing up is a cigarette generation...If there was a law prohibiting the giving away of pictures [cards] it would be more effective than an age law."

The vendor's comment about how the boys would be better off smoking cigars reflected a widespread belief that tobacco use in forms other than cigarettes was somehow more benign. Writing in the *New York Medical Journal* in 1888, a Dr. C.W. Lyman noted that while tobacco use in any form was injurious to human health, "cigarettes are responsible for a greater source of mischief... because smokers—and they are often boys or very young men—are apt to use them continuously or at frequent intervals...Thus the nerves are under the constant influence of the drug [nicotine]...one of the most powerful of the 'nerve poisons' known."

Since 19th century tobacco companies had the collective moral compass of a rabid congressman (not at all dissimilar from their 21st century counterparts), the fact that young boys were smoking almost certainly did not bother them in the least. What did bother them was the fact that manufacturing and distributing baseball and other cards with their tobacco products was costing them a fortune. One executive estimated that 35 percent to 40 percent of his company's expenses were due to the cost of the various sets of cards they produced.

When the city of Charleston, South Carolina, banned cigarette cards in 1887, tobacco magnate J.B. "Buck" Duke applauded the move and said he wished it was nationwide "as it would save us $180,000 per year ($5.9 million in 2024), or nearly $2,000,000 ($66.2 million) in the next ten years. Competition has forced us to adopt this method of advertising." Another company president called the cards "an advertising madhouse" and expressed the fervent wish to get out of the "damned picture [card] business."

In April 1889, the five biggest tobacco companies met in New York and came up with a solution to their card problem that perfectly captured the monopolistic spirit of the Gilded Age in which they functioned: They merged into a trust, with Buck Duke, who was head of the largest company, as president. They called it the American Tobacco Company.

"The central object of the trust is to reduce the cost of advertising to a minimum," the *Philadelphia Press* noted, "and as the pictorial end has been the most expensive, it is sure to be dropped altogether. For years, the small boy has been begging, 'Won't yer give me the picture?' He has collected a valuable collection of Indians painted in their most villainous dye, or sturdy athletes, baseball players...All these delights are to be relegated to ancient history by the big trust."

Editorial moralists rejoiced. "It would be well if we could entirely abolish the paper-covered passports to the hereafter and send people back to the more wholesome cigar and pipe," huffed the *Detroit Free Press*. "If, however, we must have cigarettes, it is a comfort to know there is a movement among the manufacturers to abolish the pestilential cigarette picture. The universal enclosure of these pictures has developed an entirely new class of cranks, young and old."

The formation of the tobacco trust ended neither baseball cards nor the proliferation of cigarettes. In fact, the trust flourished in its production of the latter. In its first full year, the American Tobacco Company manufactured nine of every 10 cigarettes in the country. By 1910, it had absorbed more than 250 competitive firms and was churning out 10 billion cigarettes a year, enough to supply every American man, woman and child 108 each.

A typical pack cost a dime ($3.30 in 2024) and contained 10 smokes. Depending on the brand, it also contained a baseball card. The cards were part of a collection eventually known as the T206 set, after its designation in a seminal 1951 card set catalog. After a 20-year lull, the trust returned to inserting cards in 16 of its brands of cigarettes and loose tobacco to boost sales. Released over a three-year period, the T206 set consisted of 524 color cards, most of which were 1 7/16 by 2 5/8 inches. More than a hundred of them bore the likenesses of minor league players, and some major leaguers appeared on more than one card.

One of the T206 cards became the centerpiece of a legend that spread beyond the galaxy of baseball card collectors and even the baseball universe itself, and I would be remiss to not at least perfunctorily mention it here. The card in question bore the visage of a pleasantly homely 35-year-old man with a prominent schnozz and a stolid expression. The fellow's name was Johannes Peter Wagner, but everyone called him Hans or Honus or "The Flying Dutchman."

By whatever appellation, he was a baseball god, one of the Hall of Fame's five charter members. Despite his freakishly long arms, giant hands and almost cartoonishly bowed legs, Wagner was lightning-fast on the bases, a vacuum cleaner on defense and a hitting machine at the plate. His Hall of Fame plaque unabashedly declares him "the greatest shortstop in baseball history."

But his greatest distinction when it comes to baseball cards is that he didn't want to be on one—at least not one in the American Tobacco Company's T206 set. The company thought differently. It offered to pay a good pal of Wagner's, *Pittsburgh Gazette* sportswriter John Gruber, $10 ($331) to get Wagner's permission to put him on a card. Meanwhile, it printed from 50 to 200 Wagner cards—no one knows for sure how many—and waited for Wagner's okay. But Wagner kindly and cryptically refused. He even sent his friend Gruber a check for $10 so he wouldn't lose out on the deal.

The tobacco company thereupon did not print any more Wagner cards, making them exceedingly scarce. Their scarcity alone makes the existing Wagner T206s exceedingly prized by card collectors, and therefore exceedingly expensive. But its rarity is only a slice of the legend. Another piece is just why Wagner refused. For decades it's been argued that he was opposed to tobacco and didn't want to be viewed as encouraging kids to smoke. That argument is partially refuted by the fact that Wagner's likeness adorned cigar boxes, and that at least one baseball card from the late 1940s, when Wagner was a coach, shows him with a wad of chewing tobacco in his cheek that could choke a medium-sized blue whale. Still, it may be that he just didn't want kids to smoke even if it was okay for him to indulge as an adult.

A more contemporaneous argument, put forth in 1912 in *The Sporting News*, was that his refusal "demonstrated that the mania for money which has seized many professional ballplayers has not contaminated him [Wagner] in the least." This theory also appears to be baloney, since Wagner had a demonstrated fondness for money and routinely suggested throughout his long career that he was going to retire, only to reconsider when offered a raise. He also endorsed products from time to time, such as Coca-Cola, which according to a 1912 ad was "the only beverage he ever drank that has vim, vigor and go to it…".

In addition to the mystery surrounding the reason for his refusal, the Wagner T206's history has been chock-full of other colorful tidbits. Various versions of the card have been stolen, trimmed or counterfeited. They have been owned by famous actors, star hockey players and convicted criminals. In 2010, a group of nuns in Baltimore who had been bequeathed a Wagner T206 sold it for $262,000 (about $377,600 in 2024) to support various charities.

And the prices the cards fetch keep going up. In July 2022, a Wagner card graded a lowly 2 on the 1-to-10 grading scale baseball card appraisers use, sold for $7.25 million. "There is nothing on the earth like a T206 card," said Ken Goldin, the founder and chairman of the auction house that oversaw the private sale. "There's a reason no Wagner T206 card has ever sold for less than it was purchased for—the card is art, it's history, it's folklore."

It was also part of the tobacco trust's swansong when it came to baseball cards. In 1911, the United States Supreme Court declared the American Tobacco Company in violation of federal anti-trust laws and ordered its dismemberment into several different companies. The world of baseball cards soon became something of a barren landscape. It was as if the cards were searching for a new and reliable product to which they could tie their future and secure their place in the nation's cultural history.

Various candy companies gave it a try. The American Caramel Co.

sporadically included individual wrapped cards in its boxes from 1908 to 1927. One 1911 card even featured Honus Wagner. But it sorely lacks the cachet of the T206, and one in "excellent" condition can be had for a mere $50,000. Cracker Jack, that American confectionary mainstay, put out sets of 144 and 176 cards respectively in 1914 and 1915—one card to a box—but decided it was too expensive a promotion and gave it up.

A Chicago printer named Felix Mendelsohn also gave it the old Peck & Snyder try. In 1916, Mendelsohn produced a 200-card set, the backs of which bore ads for more than a dozen different businesses that included men's clothing stores, breweries, bakeries, a Chicago theater and even *The Sporting News*. Among the players on the fronts were the Olympic superstar Jim Thorpe, on his only major league baseball card, and a young moon-faced left-handed pitcher for the Boston Red Sox named Babe Ruth.

Then in the fall of 1928, the perfect companion to baseball cards was birthed by a 23-year-old cost accountant who was bored.

Walter Diemer worked for the Fleer Corporation, a Philadelphia candy company. One afternoon, he was asked to man the telephone in the company's lab while the technicians stepped out for a few minutes. The company had been searching in vain for a method of making its own base for its gum products rather than buying it. Diemer was no chemist, but he liked to fool around in the lab in his spare time.

So when no one called while he was in the lab, he began fiddling around with an old formula for making gum base. Somehow, he endowed it with more elasticity than regular gum which allowed it to stretch thinner without breaking. "It was an accident," Diemer recalled decades later. "I was doing something else and ended up with something with bubbles."

It took a few months, but Diemer eventually came up with a substance worthy of testing on the world outside the lab. He made up a five-pound batch, added pink food coloring because it was the only color he could find, enveloped 100 pieces of it in taffy wrappers and, on the day after Christmas 1928, took them to a local grocery store. They sold out in two hours.

Fleer began marketing the concoction as "Dubble Bubble." Diemer, who would eventually become the firm's executive vice president and live until the ripe old age of 94, conducted bubble-blowing classes for the company's salesmen—and the undersides of restaurant tables, school desks and movie theater seats have never been the same.

The gum became wildly popular, and almost immediately the subject of wild speculation: It contained poison and/or dangerous acids, it was said, and led to measles, loss of teeth and permanent jaw damage. "It would not surprise us in the least to hear it rumored that bubble gum was responsible for the late world war," an indignant Fleer company spokesman said. "No mysterious or harmful ingredients are necessary for the making of a good bubble gum like Dubble Bubble."

Fleer doubled down on its denials by paying for newspaper ads around the country. The ads were "signed" by local wholesalers who advised "that the rumor that Fleer's DUBBLE BUBBLE Gum is injurious is ABSOLUTELY FALSE." To buttress the point, the ad contained a newspaper excerpt reporting that the chief of the City of Cleveland's Bureau of Food Inspection had given the gum a clean bill of health.

The assurance of a Cleveland food inspector evidently carried more weight than you might think, because by the end of the 1930s, Fleer was making $4.5 million a year (more than $100 million in 2024) from the gum. But neither Diemer or the company had bothered to patent Dubble Bubble. A dozen or so imitations soon sprang up, including one by J. Warren Bowman's company.

Some of the firms, including Bowman's, packaged their gum with cards. The subjects of Bowman's cards in the early 1930s included pirates, Wild West characters, Hollywood stars and "Heroes of Law Enforcement." The company generally steered clear of baseball cards because they involved getting players under contract for using their likenesses and were thus more expensive and time-consuming.

But while Bowman steered clear of cards with baseball as the subject until the end of the decade, other companies didn't. The most successful of these was a Boston company founded by a Canadian, Enos. G. Goudey. The 240-card set Goudey put out in 1933 is considered one of the most significant in baseball card history for several reasons, not the least of which is that the company actually issued only 239 cards. Missing was No. 106, of Napoleon "Larry" Lajoie, who retired in 1916 and was elected to the Hall of Fame in 1937. The company contended it was a mistake. Hordes of angry parents loudly complained it was a deliberate ruse to keep kids buying gum and cards in an impossible quest to complete the set. Some threatened legal action. Without admitting chicanery of any kind, Goudey did issue a Lajoie card the following year.

It also sold a bunch of gum. Eventually, Goudey decided it could sell gum just as successfully without the cards as with them, and got out of the card game altogether. But Warren Bowman's company did not. Always the innovator, Warren Bowman in 1937 came up with the first set of bubble gum trading cards to spark an international furor. Inspired by a radio broadcast he heard about Japanese atrocities in Japan's undeclared war with China, Bowman teamed up with George Moll, a highly creative and deeply religious Philadelphia advertising man, to produce a set called "Horrors of War." The set's 288 cards depicted—in sanguinary detail—events from the Japan-China conflict, the Spanish Civil War and the Italian incursion into Ethiopia. At the bottom of the back of each card was the message the pacifistic Moll wanted to impart: "To Know the Horrors of War is to Want Peace."

Kids snapped up more than 100 million of what was popularly known among the bubble-blowing set as "war cards" between 1937 and 1939, at a penny for one card and one piece of gum. The cards' popularity almost certainly wasn't due to a widespread juvenile wish for world peace. It almost certainly was because many of the full-color lithographic images depicted gory scenes such as a woman photographer being run over by a tank. The pictures were accompanied by graphic descriptions such as "mangled bodies lying in great pools of blood!" and "pieces of arms and legs flying through the air!"

Adults were generally less enamored with the "Horrors of War" set. "A few years back I used to collect bubble gum cards with baseball players' pictures," a Chicago parent complained, "but what warlike element is now being allowed to implant itself in the minds of our children?" The Japanese government was incensed enough to lodge a formal complaint with the U.S. State Department and ban all Bowman products from Japanese shores. And when an elevator at the Bowman factory in Philadelphia snapped a cable in mid-1938 and plunged five floors, badly injuring two workers, it was immediately thought to be the work of Japanese saboteurs.

It wasn't. Nonetheless, between 1939 and 1941 Bowman turned to the less controversial subject of baseball for its cards. The "Play Ball" sets proved to be quite popular. And then America's entry into the war halted card production altogether for the next six years.

With the end of the war and the post-war popularity surge of the Grand Old Game, Bowman stuck mainly to baseball when card production resumed in 1948. The '48 set wasn't much. Although Bowman claimed to have 106 major leaguers under contract, there were only 48 black and white cards, probably because the company lacked photos of many of the players under contract.

Despite such a small set, Bowman's copy writers were apparently hard pressed to think up something to say about each player on the back, even when a fair amount of the space was already taken up by an ad for Blony Bubble Gum. Pitcher Bill McCahan (No. 31), for example, was "another hometown boy made good." Snuffy Stirnweiss (No. 35, and I'm not making these names up) was "another hometown boy makes good." Perhaps desperate for just a little variety, Buddy Kerr (No. 20) was "a boy who's made good in his home town."

The cards got better. For 1949, the company claimed to have signed 272 Major League and Pacific Coast League players to exclusive contracts, and produced a set of 240 cards that were partially colorized photos. When the rival Leaf company issued cards with some of Bowman's under-contract players on them, Bowman successfully sued, forcing Leaf into agreeing to stop making baseball cards for two years. In 1950, the set's size climbed to 252 and featured full-color paintings. The '50 set included the first card of trail-blazer Jackie Robinson, and the cards' backs provided information generally more useful than that the players had home towns and had "made good."

In 1951, Bowman once more strayed from the National Pastime to international affairs. Post-war America was as obsessed with the threat of communism -- both real and imagined—as it was about baseball. In 1947, the House Un-American Activities Committee (HUAC) began a hunt for communists within and without the federal government. Joseph R. McCarthy, a duplicitous and alcoholic U.S. senator from Wisconsin, claimed to have a list of 200 "known communists" who worked in the State Department. "Tail-Gunner Joe" (so-nicknamed because he claimed to have been a combat-seasoned bomber tail-gunner although he was actually never in a battle) seemingly made headlines every other day with new accusations and revelations. Most of them were base-less, but they kept the subject at the forefront of Americans' consciousness. The communist countries of China and the Soviet Union, both of which had been wartime allies of the United States, became America's arch-foes. Neither country even played baseball.

So, in addition to its 1951 baseball set featuring Danny O'Connell's first card (okay, and those of Mantle and Mays), Bowman issued a 48-card set that decried the evils of communism. "Our main concern is selling bubble gum," a company spokesman explained. "Although we are not too interested in sending 'messages,' we decided that children would be interested in an anti-communist series and we think it is good for them." The full-color cards included a picture of Chinese leader Mao Tse-Tung captioned "Warmaker," and a card showing a "Chinese engineer" having his hands chopped off. "That is one of the more bloodthirsty cards," the spokesman admitted, "but we wanted to give a realistic, well-rounded picture of communism."

Like the war cards of the 1930s, the anti-commie cards sold well. By 1951, Warren Bowman was the "King of Bubble Gum." His company was producing a quarter of the world's bubble gum and grossing $1 million ($11.4 million) a month. His main product had survived an investigation by the U.S. Food and Drug Administration after an avalanche of rumors and allegations (mostly spread by parents) about the harmful effects of bubble gum. After diligent test-ing that involved feeding it to monkeys, dogs and cows, the FDA concluded bubble gum was no more damaging than most things kids put in their mouths.

Bowman also had come up with a package of regular gum that had eight sticks rather than the usual five. The eight sticks were smaller and amounted to no more actual gum by volume than the regular five, but Bowman successfully marketed it as gum for people who liked to move their jaws less.

As he sat in his refrigerator-cold sound-proofed fifth-floor private office, however, and stared out an entire wall of windows looking down at the Germantown section of Philadelphia, or studied the murals of Mexican deserts painted on his office's other walls, Warren Bowman was restless. He owned a mansion in Philadelphia, a beachfront estate near Tampa, and fleets of speed-boats and automobiles. He was busy developing a luxury housing development in Florida, complete with a posh hotel. In his spare time, he was going through a divorce with his fifth wife, who was 27 years his junior.

Bowman was sagacious enough to know his gum company's dominance in both bubble gum and baseball cards wouldn't last forever. He knew the 1949 legal battle with Leaf over the rights to put ballplayers' images on cardboard wouldn't be the last such fight. Already a Brooklyn gum company was tentatively testing the market, and Bowman Gum was taking legal steps to squash the interloper. Whatever his motivation, in May 1951, Bowman sold his interests in the company he had founded almost a quarter of a century before to an outfit called Haelan Laboratories, and "retired" to Florida.

His retirement included dabbling in real estate, paper bag manufacturing, food processing, throwing lavish parties and lots of fishing. His death at the age of 67 merited an obituary in *The New York Times*. "Mr. Bowman's chance meeting with a chewing-gum salesman...started him on one of the most spectacular business careers of his time," *The Times* wrote.

As for the titular hero of this tome, Danny O'Connell's next baseball card would be produced by a company that in its first try at making cards nearly poisoned its customers. But first Danny had a war to fight.

CHAPTER 6 NOTES

The company that *The Saturday Evening Post*, Nov. 1, 1947, p. 20. O'Connell's Bowman card actually wasn't his first appearance on a card. In 1950, the Sawyer Biscuit Company, a Chicago-based cookie and cracker manufacturer, produced a set of cards featuring players from the Triple-A Indianapolis Indians. Danny was among them.

At the time, *Life* magazine, May 9, 1938, p. 6.

The "good -natured" *Tampa Bay Times*, Feb. 10, 1962, p. 11; *Time* magazine, Sept. 13, 1937, p. 60.

The eminent baseball John Thorn, *Baseball in the Garden of Eden*, p. 95.

Others believe the Michael Clair, "What Was the First Baseball Card Ever Made?" *MLB.com*, Feb. 28, 2022.

As for me Dave Jamieson, *Mint Condition*, pp. 13-14. This is a splendid overview of baseball card history whose only flaw is that it was written way back in 2010. An updated edition is sorely needed by the world in general and baseball fans in particular.

The exigencies of *The Grenada (Miss.) Sentinel*, Sept. 18, 1886, p. 7.

Enter advertising. *The New York Times*, Feb. 25, 1883, p. 6.

Trade cards, such Steve Wiegand, *1876: Year of the Gun*, p. 136.

Which brings us Jamieson, op. cit., p. 26.

Cigarette makers improved Jamieson, op. cit., p. 19.

Even though flags *New Orleans Times-Picayune*, July29, 1888, p. 12.

"The cigarette would" *Chicago Tribune*, June 23, 1889, p. 29.

A few months *Chicago Tribune*, Nov. 12, 1889, p. 7.

The vendor's comment *The Sunday Leader* (Wilkes Barre Pa.), Dec. 2, 1888, p. 7.

When the city Jamieson, op. cit., pp. 26-27.

"The central object" *Philadelphia Press,* reprinted in the *New Orleans Times-Picayune*, June 11, 1890, p. 2.

Editorial moralists rejoiced *Detroit Free Press*, June 10, 1890, p. 4.

The formation of Patrick Porter, "Origins of the American Tobacco Company." *Business History Review*, Duke University, 1969, p. 59.

A more contemporaneous *The Sporting News*, Oct. 24, 1912, p. 2; *The Sporting News*, April 11, 1912, p. 8.

So when no *Philadelphia Inquirer*, Jan. 11, 1998, p. 46.

The gum became *Union (Mo.) Republican Tribune*, March 28, 1930, p.6.

Fleer doubled down *The Springfield (Ohio) Daily News*, March 25, 1930, p. 9.

Adults were generally *Chicago Tribune*, July 31, 1938, p. 10.

So in addition *Sydney (Aus.) Morning Herald*, May 18, 1951, p. 2.

His retirement included *The New York Times*, Feb. 10, 1962, p. 23.

CHAPTER 7

"THEY'RE SOLDIERS FIRST AND BASEBALL PLAYERS SECOND"

THEY ALSO SERVE WHO ONLY PLAY SHORTSTOP

Danny O'Connell played a lot of baseball on the day Kenneth Shadrick died. O'Connell's Indianapolis Indians had squared off against the Louisville Colonels in a 4th of July twi-night double-header before a largest-of-the-season home crowd of 14,466. Danny went 3 for 8, padding his league-leading hits total to 106 and pushing his batting average a bit higher, to .361. The Indians won both games, which put them in a virtual first-place tie with the Minneapolis Millers in the race for the 1950 American Association pennant. But because of a long rain delay, it took until just after midnight to finish the second game.

Fourteen time zones and 6,700 miles west of Owen J. Bush Stadium, Kenny Shadrick was also outdoors under rainy skies. Only he was in a Korean graveyard, fighting for his life. Shadrick was a month shy of his 19th birthday. The son of a West Virginia coal miner and the third of 10 children, Kenny had grown up in the nearly invisible town of Skin Fork, 400 miles southeast of Indianapolis and close to nowhere.

He was a quiet, skinny kid who liked to ride his bicycle and read Wild West and science fiction books and magazines. He also liked football, and when he reached high school, he tried out for the team despite weighing just 130 pounds. Pineville High was too poor to provide uniforms or equipment. But Kenny's dad Theodore managed to scrape together $5 ($65 in 2024) for what Kenny needed to play. And then one day someone stole his football gear, and Kenny promptly quit school.

At the age of 17, with his parents' permission, Shadrick joined the Army.

According to his brother Roy, "he just wanted to see the world." What he saw was Fort Knox, Kentucky, where he completed basic training; the Fort Lewis army base near Seattle, Washington, and then Kyushu, Japan, where he was assigned to a bazooka squad that was part of the 34th Infantry Regiment of the 24th Infantry Division. He initially liked Japan. But as the months went by, he liked it less and less. "Mom," he wrote in a June 24th letter, "this place is getting me down."

On July 5, 1950, just 10 days after tens of thousands of North Korean soldiers had poured into South Korea and eight days after President Harry Truman announced the United States would militarily support South Korea, Private Shadrick found himself in a cemetery on the outskirts of the tiny village of Sojong-ni. Hiding behind burial mounds, Kenny's squad spotted two North Korean tanks and began firing at them. About 4 p.m.—or about two hours after the Indians' doubleheader in Indianapolis concluded -- Shadrick stood up to see how effective the bazooka rounds had been. A machine gun on one of the tanks opened fire. Shadrick was hit in the right arm and chest.

According to a combat photographer who was with Shadrick's squad, "he moaned 'oh my arm,' and I noticed the bone between the elbow and shoulder was shattered. As he fell forward a lieutenant rushed to his aid. I said it was too late because I had seen the hole in his chest...in 30 seconds, Shadrick was dead."

Kenny's parents were having breakfast the next day when a friend rushed into their four-room home to tell them what he had just heard on the radio: Their son had become the first American ground soldier killed in the new war in Korea. Reporters flocked to Skin Fork, although it turned out later that the first U.S. combat infantry fatality had actually occurred a few hours earlier.

"What was Kenny fighting for?" a *Time* magazine reporter asked his father. "Against some kind of government," Theodore Shadrick replied. "Where was Korea? He didn't know -- out there somewhere, where his boy was killed."

"I don't think they should have sent 18- and 19-year-old boys in there to fight," his weeping mother Lucille said. "I guess there will be lots more."

Lucille Shadrick was right—there were "lots more." By the time an armistice was agreed upon three years after her son Kenny's death, more than 36,000 Americans were killed or missing in action and another 100,000-plus wounded.

But in the second half of 1950, no one was sure how long or how widespread what President Harry Truman labeled a "police action" would last. And as baseball executives gathered in St. Petersburg, Florida, in December 1950 for the annual winter meeting, they had no clue as to how much impact the war would have on their industry.

Baseball had played through during World War II. Answering a written query from then-Commissioner Kennesaw Mountain Landis as to whether the game should shut down, President Franklin D. Roosevelt replied, "I honestly feel it would be best for the country to keep baseball going." In what became known as the "Green Light Letter," Roosevelt said the war would require Americans "to work longer hours and harder than ever before. And that means that they ought to have a chance for recreation and for taking their minds off their work more than ever before." Five thousand major and minor-league players providing entertainment for 20 million Americans, Roosevelt said, was "in my judgment thoroughly worthwhile." So the game went on, even if teams had to scrape near the bottom of the talent barrel, as in 15-year-old Joe Nuxhall pitching for the Cincinnati Reds or one-armed Pete Gray chasing flies in the St. Louis Browns' outfield.

When the Korean War broke out, Landis' successor, Happy Chandler, eschewed writing a letter and went directly to the White House to meet with Roosevelt's successor. President Truman assured Chandler that every effort would be made to keep the National Pastime playing. That did not mean, however, that baseball would escape the effects of the conflict in Korea unscathed.

The military draft created before the start of World War II had expired in 1947. As a result, the number of Americans in uniform plunged from more than 11 million in 1945 to about 1.4 million in 1948. More concerning, only 671,000 of those were deemed combat-ready ground troops, and that number turned out to be optimistic. Alarmed by the confrontational international actions of the Soviet Union, Truman had successfully pushed for the draft's "temporary" reinstatement in 1948. After the North Korean invasion of South Korea in mid-1950, Congress extended compulsory military service for men between the ages of 18-1/2 and 35, while exempting those who had served in World War II. That left a smaller pool of potential draftees. But it included most major league ballplayers.

"There is no getting away from it, the grim prospect of World War III already is laying a heavy hand on what otherwise would be a very promising outlook for baseball's 1951 season," wrote John Drebinger of *The New York Times* from the winter meetings. Drebinger noted that clubs were nearly paralyzed with indecision when it came to making trades because of the uncertainty created by the draft. "… No one will let go of an old player because no one is certain that by next summer that old hand will be a key man on the club. No one wants to risk trading for a youngster because by tomorrow he may be on his way to a military base."

In the end, about a hundred major leaguers swapped their baseball uniforms for military ones. Few did it willingly, and even fewer saw any kind of combat. "Army life was tough," joked New York Yankees pitcher Ed "Whitey" Ford, who like Danny O'Connell was drafted after his rookie season in 1950. "Would you believe it? They actually wanted me to pitch three times a week."

There were notable exceptions among the ranks of reluctant player-warriors. Jerry Coleman, the Yankees' second baseman, flew 63 combat missions as a U.S. Marine pilot of an F4V Corsair bomber. The 1949 American League Rookie of the Year winner and 1950 World Series most valuable player, Coleman was all the more heroic because he also flew 57 missions during World War II, making him the only major league player to see action in both wars.

On one mission in Korea, his plane flipped upside down because of a stalled engine, and he was nearly strangled by the chin strap on his helmet. "It wasn't much fun," recalled Coleman, who for nearly 50 years was the radio voice of the San Diego Padres and was so beloved they erected a statue of him outside the Padres' ballpark. "But I have no regrets."

One of Coleman's brothers-in-arms was a baseball god. Ted Williams had been deemed too good a pilot to risk in combat during World War II. Instead, his superb flying skills were used to teach new pilots. But in Korea, Williams flew 39 combat missions in F9F Panther fighters. On one low-level flight, Williams' jet was hit by anti-aircraft fire and set ablaze. His wingman, future astronaut and U.S. Senator John Glenn, motioned from his own jet for Williams to gain altitude rapidly to put out the flames. But there was nothing Glenn could do to fix Williams' other major problem, which was his destroyed landing gear. Fearing his 6'4" frame would get stuck if he attempted to eject, Williams landed the plane on its belly, pancaking down the runway for several thousand feet.

Williams scrambled out of the jet as soon as it skidded to a halt and ran for his life from the once-again blazing aircraft. Among the anxiously waiting crowd on the runway was Coleman. "Hey Ted," he yelled, "That's a lot faster than you ever ran around the bases."

"How would you know?" Williams shot back. "You never get on base." Or so the story goes.

For the most part, however, ballplayers were inclined to choose playing ball over combat. "Naturally, I'm not too interested in the Army," Willie Mays, the National League's 1951 Rookie of the Year award winner, told a reporter. "But if I have to go, I'll make the best of it...Maybe I'll learn some baseball in the Army." Mays had applied for a hardship deferment on the grounds he was the sole financial support of his mother and four siblings. The application was denied and Mays was inducted in June 1952.

Another renowned rookie in 1951 was classified physically unfit. Mickey Mantle had injured an ankle in his teens and developed osteomyelitis, an inflammation of the bone. "I'll play baseball for the Army or fight for it, whatever they want me to do," Mantle said after failing a second physical exam. "But if I don't go into the Army, I want to play baseball."

The classification of Mantle and other professional athletes as physically unfit drew snorts of derision. Representative Carl Vinson, a Georgia Democrat who was chairman of the House Armed Services Committee, said it was troubling "when we see a great baseball player, a great football player or some prize fighter is 4F and able to draw $10,000 a year [about $121,000 in 2024], (and) do all the hard work of a star athlete, but nonetheless can't carry a rifle, throw a grenade or do kitchen police (KP) work because he isn't able."

Baseball's self-styled "paper of record," *The Sporting News*, leapt to the players' defense. "Neither the player nor the game is to blame—it was merely the policies of the Selective Service...equal treatment is all the ballplayer has ever asked, with no special favors for the game." If more players were called into military service, the paper editorialized, "baseball will carry on to the best of its ability, proud of whatever sacrifices it may be called upon to make in behalf of the common good."

Despite such stalwart support, the charges of favored treatment for players continued, particularly in the case of Mantle. Stung by the criticism, Mantle agreed to take a third physical in 1952. He failed again, this time because of a knee injury he suffered while chasing a flyball in the 1951 World Series. For all you trivia fans, the guy who hit the ball was a New York Giants rookie, name of Mays.

Danny O'Connell had dutifully registered with the Selective Service in January 1947, just six days after his 18th birthday, and just before the draft was temporarily suspended. His registration card listed his parents' address on Carlisle Avenue as his domicile and his occupation as "unemployed at present (plays professional ball in summer.)" It also described him as being 5'11" tall and weighing 165 lbs., with brown hair, hazel eyes, "ruddy" complexion and bearing a 1-inch scar on an unspecified knee as the result of an unspecified accident.

In mid-October, 1950, his local Selective Service board informed him he had been classified 1A, and on Feb. 7, 1951, he was notified to report for induction. Then things got confusing. A day or two after being told to report, Danny was notified that due to a backlog of inductees, America could fight the war without him until late March or early April at the earliest.

So the Pirates decided he should report for Spring Training in California. "It was reasoned that even a month's work at San Bernardino would benefit the youngster, who is one of the best shortstop prospects to come to the Pirates in years," the *Pittsburgh Press* reported.

Then Uncle Sam changed his mind. O'Connell was ordered to report on Feb. 14—Valentine's Day. After one more short delay, he was finally inducted on Feb. 21, along with 47 others from the Paterson area, and bused 82 miles south to Fort Dix New Jersey. "I hope I can at least keep in shape," Danny told an AP reporter at Fort Dix. "I'd like to go back to the Pirates when I get out."

His apprehension concerning staying in shape for baseball was very quickly put to rest. Even before he completed basic training at Fort Dix, Danny wrote to Pirates teammate Pete Castiglione "the athletic heads already have me tagged for baseball action."

More formally, O'Connell had been tagged to join Company H of the 3rd Infantry Regiment at Fort Myer, Virginia. In what was almost certainly not a coincidence, Danny arrived at the base on April 3, the same day as two other major league players: Pitcher Johnny Antonelli of the Boston Braves and catcher Sam Calderone of the New York Giants. With what might have been a straight face, Captain O.S. Stone, the company commander, announced "They're soldiers first and baseball players second as far as we're concerned. Of course, if they want to play ball in their spare time, I'm all for it."

Stone's statement was unmitigated baloney. Everyone on the base and possibly even the North Korean high command knew they were there to play baseball for the Fort Myer Colonials. By the time the team played its first game in late April, every player on the roster but one had played professional baseball at the Double-A level or higher. (The lone exception was a second baseman, Joe Montebaro, who had been a star high school player in Asbury Park, New Jersey.)

Just being assigned to the 3rd Infantry at Fort Myer was considered a prize posting whether you played baseball or not. The base was adjacent to Arlington National Cemetery, on land the federal government had confiscated from the wife of Confederate Gen. Robert E. Lee when the Civil War began. Because of its proximity to Washington, D.C., Fort Myer was home to the Army's ceremonial units, such as the Army Band.

The regiment was known as "the President's Honor Guard." It provided military escort to foreign dignitaries visiting Washington and added to the pomp and circumstance surrounding various events in and around the Capitol. "We meet all the big shots who arrive and leave," O'Connell wrote to a Pittsburgh sportswriter near the end of Danny's two-year-hitch. "And in this past year we've met Queen Elizabeth (when she was still just a princess), Queen Juliana of The Netherlands, Prime Minister Churchill and President Truman quite often." Fort Myer was also the home base for the Army's chief of staff, so naturally it needed a good baseball team.

Danny was astute enough to not mess up a good thing by bragging about it. After all, he'd made close to $5,000 in 1950 playing for the Pirates and was only getting $82.50 a month (about $997 in 2024) to play for the Army. "Danny says he arises at 5:45 each morning," *The Sporting News* reported in July, "and is doing a lot of women's work in the Army such as scrubbing floors, sweeping and washing dishes."

O'Connell and *The Sporting News* tactfully failed to mention he was also playing a lot of baseball for Fort Myer. A teammate was not so reticent. "We played in big-league parks, ate the best food, and wound up our Army careers on a baseball tour of Japan," utility player Sam Scarpone recalled in 1955. Unsurprisingly, the three big leaguers were the heart of the Fort Myer team. Sam Calderone was a 25-year-old native of Beverly, New Jersey, a suburban town near Philadelphia. Like O'Connell, Calderone came up in the Dodgers' system and sparkled in three minor league seasons. But the Dodgers had a future Hall of Fame catcher, Roy Campenella, and in 1950 Brooklyn allowed Calderone to be picked up by the rival Giants. As a backup catcher, Calderone hit .299 in 34 games before being drafted. A burly 5'10" and 185 pounds, he would return to the majors in 1953 and play sparingly for the Giants and Milwaukee Braves before finishing his career in the high minor leagues.

Unlike the unheralded Calderone, Johnny Antonelli was enmeshed in a vast net of unwanted notoriety. The son of an Italian immigrant, the 21-year-old left-hander was a three-sport high school star in Rochester New York when the Boston Braves signed him for a then-absurdly large $75,000 bonus in 1948 ($978,000 in 2024.) That was far more than the total salary any of the Braves veterans made for three years' play, and they resented it. Antonelli pitched only four innings for the Braves in their 1948 pennant-winning season, and the other players voted him no part of their World Series purse while giving the team's batboys $381 each (about $4,970.) Antonelli was rarely used by Boston in '49 and '50, and after returning from the Army to the Braves in 1953, he had a so-so season. In 1954, he would be traded to the Giants, where he would become a star.

The Fort Myer Colonials' 1951 season got off to an inauspicious start. They lost their first game to Kent State University, with Danny going one for five, Calderone not playing at all and Antonelli inexplicably playing right field.

But it was a short losing streak. The team played other military posts' clubs in the Mid-Atlantic Interservice League as well as college, semi-pro and amateur teams. It would be more accurate, however, to say Fort Myer toyed with the opposition rather than played them. The Colonials finished the year with a 72-11 record overall, and won 27 of 28 league contests.

Antonelli was almost unhittable. Shutting out a Fort Eustis, Virginia team, he gave up only four hits and struck out 18. Against a Fort Meade, Maryland team that featured Cleveland outfielder Jim Lemon and soon-to-be big league pitcher Jim Brosnan, Antonelli gave up only two hits and struck out 17. He finished the season with a surreal 26-0 record. Calderone hit a ridiculous .395 with eight home runs and O'Connell hit .380 with 13 homers. Danny also took over as the team's manager when the regular manager had to attend to annoying Army duties.

In the league tournament at the end of the season, Antonelli gave up a total of two runs in four games as Fort Myer swept to the title. In one 5-0 win, O'Connell tripled in the first two runs and scored the third, while Calderone drove in the other two with a home run. In a 3-2 victory, Danny had three hits and stole second and third before scoring the winning run on a grounder.

O'Connell even got to play a game with the Pirates, albeit one that didn't count. On July 9, Pittsburgh played an exhibition game against a team of ex-Pirates and a few ringers such as pitching legend Bob Feller. The game was a benefit for Julius "Moose" Solters, a popular Pittsburgh tavern owner and former big-league outfielder who had gradually lost his sight after being hit in the head by a thrown ball a decade before. Through the intercession of a U.S. senator from Idaho who was a Pirates fan, Danny was granted a three-day pass so he could play in the game. His sixth-inning single put the game's only run on third, the Pirates won 1-0, and Solters was given $15,000 (about $181,300 in 2024.)

When the baseball season ended, O'Connell's military duties were mostly menial and mundane. But he apparently did not miss mess call too often. "Reports from Fort Myer, where he has been stationed, have it that Danny has put on considerable weight," O'Connell's old pal Joe Gooter wrote in his Paterson *News* column. "Of course he can slice surplus poundage when he does come back to baseball, but the report merely accentuates the handicaps which the Patersonian will be facing when he doffs khakis and dons his old uniform."

In Pittsburgh, meanwhile, even a fat Danny O'Connell might have been a most welcome sight.

Anyone who doubted Branch Rickey was a baseball genius needed only to ask him, because no one had a higher opinion of Branch Rickey than Branch Rickey.

He had built highly successful franchises in St. Louis and Brooklyn, and he saw no reason he couldn't do the same in Pittsburgh when he took over as the Pirates' general manager and vice president in late 1950. But Rickey was wise enough to know it wouldn't happen overnight, and clever enough to make sure everyone understood that while he would be the chief engineer behind any future success, he was inheriting a bad team.

"The Pirates finished eighth [in 1950] strictly on merit," he told reporters at the beginning of spring training. "But today, March 1, 1951, the Pittsburgh club is NOT looking forward to finishing in seventh place, nor sixth, fifth, fourth or anywhere else. We are shooting for first place."

When the writers stopped laughing, Rickey added, "now you boys know it won't be this year, but these boys [the players] are going to be impressed with the thought of setting their sights on only one spot, first place. We'll get there. When we will reach that objective is the problem we start working on today."

Rickey's approach to building a pennant contender in Pittsburgh was to comb the country for young prospects and lure them to the Pirates by paying them hefty bonuses. While known as a cheapskate when it came to negotiating salaries of players already with the team, Rickey didn't mind at all using the Pirates owners' money to land new prospects. To that end, he spent nearly $500,000 ($6 million in 2024) to sign potential stars. A few would justify the money by putting together solid major league careers. But most of Rickey's "bonus babies" quickly faded into obscurity.

Moreover, the Pirates' strategy of signing hordes of young players while the Korean War was ongoing and the military draft in full swing meant many of the young players couldn't play—at least not for the Pirates. A January 1951 survey of the organization by the *Pittsburgh Sun-Telegraph* found that 26 players under contract to the club were in the military already (including Danny O'Connell); another 29 were classified 1A and six were on active reserve.

Rickey professed to be unconcerned. "I'm confident that unless we have an all-out war, I will be able to show some progress in a couple of years. If there is an atomic war, it will be over in 10 days," he said, apparently without a whiff of facetiousness. "If we win, baseball will go on to still greater heights. If we lose, well, we must not think in those terms." Still, he hedged his bets by signing several players for 1951 whose glory days were well behind them but were at least too old to be drafted.

Pirates manager Billy Meyer was a bit more guarded in his assessment of the team's '51 hopes, pointing out that with the exception of Ralph Kiner and Wally Westlake in the outfield, who was going to play where remained a mystery. Meyer said 22 different infielders were tried during the 1950 season, "and it was not until Danny O'Connell joined us in mid-season at shortstop that we got anything like steadiness at that important post." (By the end of the '51 season, Kiner had been tried at first base and Westlake at third.)

O'Connell's replacement at shortstop was George Strickland, who had hit .111 in 27 at-bats as a rookie in 1950. In 1951, he nearly doubled his average, to .216, in 138 games. He also made 37 errors, the second-most of any National Leaguer at any position. Except for Kiner, who once again led the league in homers and pitcher Murry Dickson, who somehow won 20 games, the '51 Pirates ranged from lackluster to crummy. But the team could legitimately claim some progress: The Pirates finished seventh in 1951 as opposed to eighth and last in 1950, even though the team won seven fewer games. It turned out that the Chicago Cubs were even more hapless.

Rickey contended he wasn't surprised or overly disappointed. "I'm afraid that Pittsburgh will have to bear with at least one more season before we can offer them a respectable, winning ballclub," he said. "... We don't have a good ballclub and there's no use trying to believe that we do." He listed several of the team's weaknesses, but pointed out the infield was by far the most worrisome concern. "It's the worst I have ever seen...unless we do something about that infield it will be the year 2000 before we move out of the cellar."

Always the innovator, Rickey came up with the idea to hold a post-season instructional camp in Florida for the flock of young players he had signed. For four weeks in October 1951, the 70-year-old Rickey oversaw a military-style operation in which 61 potential Pirates were drilled in baseball fundamentals on the field and in classrooms, where Rickey delivered lectures on topics such as "How to Think Like a Winner."

"We accomplished so much in such a short time with the [players] that the results are overwhelming," he gushed to *The Sporting News* after the camp ended. "The biggest single purpose of the school was to find the difference between a ball and a strike for everybody, and I'm certain we achieved our goal." A few months later, as the Pirates prepared for the beginning of the 1952 season, Rickey brashly predicted the team would finish no lower than fourth place—in 1953, in large part because "that great young shortstop Danny O'Connell will be back to open the 1953 season."

Rickey prudently avoided making any predictions about how the '52 team would do, which turned out to be a wise move indeed. "We got off to a slow start," Pirates catcher Joe Garagiola joked in recalling the '52 season. "We lost 10 out of the first 14, and then hit a slump." Garagiola was exaggerating: The Pirates actually lost 12 of their first 14. By mid-season, the Bucs were 21-59, 34 games out of first place and 11 games behind the next-worst club, the Boston Braves. "We don't have too much to brag about on our team," a Braves player confided to a Pittsburgh sportswriter, "… but this Pittsburgh outfit takes the cake, with or without icing, for being the weakest I've ever seen."

The Pirates' ineptitude tried the patience of even Pittsburgh fans, who were among the most patient and faithful in the country. Attendance dropped to its lowest level since the end of World War II. As the club's finances sank, due in no small part to Rickey's profligate spending on bonuses to untried players, the team was forced to cut all the corners it could. To save money, Rickey sometimes allowed only 21 of the team's 25 players to travel on road trips.

If there was a bright spot, it was Dick Groat, a 21-year-old Pittsburgh-area native who had been an All-American basketball player at Duke University and signed a $75,000 contract-and-bonus package ($889,400 in 2024) to play for the Pirates right out of college. Groat was a shortstop—the position the Pirates had pushed Danny O'Connell into playing. In 95 games, Groat hit a creditable

.284 and was at least competent on defense.

But Groat was about it. Since the Pirates were legally obligated to finish the season, they did, thus cementing a place in the sub-basement of Major League Baseball's All-Time Worst Teams. "We should have finished lower than eighth," catcher Garagiola remembered, "but there were only eight teams in the league." The Pirates were last in the league in batting average, last in doubles, triples, home runs and runs scored. Their pitchers gave up the most runs and their defense made the most errors. Their longest winning streak all season was two, and they were eliminated from the pennant race on August 6, a full seven weeks before the season ended.

Two games before the season ended, Pittsburgh manager Billy Meyer called it quits, citing ill health that being around the Pirates was not helping. "This is the longest year I've ever put in throughout my baseball career," Meyer said in announcing his resignation. Most of the players were sorry to see him go. "He's the greatest fellow I ever played for," said Ralph Kiner. "He deserves to go out with a better ball club than this." But waiting around another season to go out with a better ball club was no sure thing.

"There's nothing on the immediate future horizon...to indicate the Pittsburgh club will make the first division in 1953," sighed Al Abrams, sports editor of the *Pittsburgh Post-Gazette*. "Not even the expected return of three valued rookies from Uncle Sam's service, pitcher Bill McDonald, shortstop Danny O'Connell and first baseman Al Grunwald next year, will bring about this miracle."

Like the Pirates, the Fort Myer Colonials fared worse in 1952 than they did the previous year. In 1951, the team won 87 percent of its games. In 1952, only 81 percent. The prior season's trio of major leaguers—O'Connell, Antonelli and Calderone—were joined by St, Louis Cardinals pitcher Tom Poholsky and a bit later by pitcher Bob Purkey, a top minor league prospect from the Pirates organization and future five-time All-Star.

Playing an assortment of college, semi-pro and military teams, the

Colonials got off to an 11-1 start and never really slowed down. On their way to a 59-14 record, Fort Myer lost two games in a row only once all season, and that was to a Fort Eustis, Virginia team that featured Pirates pitcher Vern Law and the New York Giants' Willie Mays. O'Connell hit .410 with 12 home runs, Antonelli struck out 1.5 batters per inning pitched, and Calderone averaged more than one RBI per game.

They were at their best in tournaments. In a 32-team double elimination tourney in July to decide the semi-pro championship of Virginia, the Colonials buzzed through undefeated, even getting revenge against the Mays-led Fort Eustis Wheelers team by beating them twice. Calderone was the tournament's MVP; O'Connell the "outstanding defensive player" award winner, and Poholsky the best pitcher. Mays had to settle for the "most sportsmanlike" trophy.

Next came a best-of-five series against the West Virginia semi-pro champion. Fort Myer won three straight, which gave the Colonials a berth in the 18th annual National Amateur Baseball Tournament in Wichita, Kansas.

The tournament was the brainchild of Raymond "Hap" Dumont, a Wichita promoter who longed to bring a major (if not major league) baseball event to America's heartland. No military team had won the tournament since 1945. But the presence of so many professional ballplayers on service clubs because of the draft meant a lot of military installations around the country had pretty good baseball teams. That in turn resulted in 12 of the tournament's 18 competing teams in 1952 hailing from various Army, Navy or Marine bases. (The non-military teams included squads from a Wichita airplane builder, an Oklahoma oil company, a labor union from Alaska, an Arizona cotton cooperative and the North Miami Police Department.)

Before heading to Kansas, Danny wrangled a short leave in early August and went home to Paterson, where he managed to touch off a bit of a family feud. His younger sister Alice, who had recently been described by one of the town's newspapers as "a dark-haired 17-year-old Irish beauty," was the star pitcher and best hitter on a girls' softball team that had won the city championship in 1951 and would win it again in 1952, 1953 and 1955.

Alice's team was set to play a for-fun game against the girls' fathers. Danny finagled an invite to pitch for the pops' team. Despite giving up 12 hits, Danny hung on to lead the dads to a 7-5 win. He even laced a double off his sister.

Seventy years after the fact, Alice O'Connell was still steamed about it. "Danny was a ringer and had no business in the game. He was a professional too, and that was just unfair," she told me at an O'Connell family gathering at a Hawthorne, New Jersey restaurant owned by the family of Alice's sister-in-law. No one argued the point because A) Alice picked up the tab for lunch, and B) Long experience had taught everyone it was not a good idea to argue with Alice.

It would probably be small consolation to Alice O'Connell, but *The Sporting News* in 1952 had the same misgivings about her older brother playing against amateurs. The paper ran down the list of big-league and top minor league players in Wichita and commented that "the presence of all these professionals competing for a 'semi-pro' or 'non-pro' title raises the question whether the tournament has lost its identity as a sandlot event...What chance has a team made up strictly of semi-pros to compete for the title on even terms?"

The answer to *The Sporting News'* rhetorical question turned out to be "not much." Over a cold and soggy two weeks, Fort Myer combined talent, luck and atrocious umpiring to win all seven of its games and claim the championship.

In the first game, Antonelli threw a three-hit shutout against a San Diego Marine base, striking out 15. O'Connell drove in the first run and scored the second in the 2-0 victory. In the second game, the Colonials could muster only two hits against a Navy team, but won 5-2 anyway when errors, walks and a single by Danny led to them scoring three runs in the eighth inning without hitting the ball out of the infield.

The atrocious umpiring occurred in the Colonial's penultimate game. "It was the most exciting game of the tournament by far," the *Wichita Eagle* exclaimed, "in fact, one of the best ever played in any tournament." Facing an Army team from Fort Ord California, O'Connell came to bat in the first inning with a runner on first and hit a long drive to right field that appeared to most of the crowd of 5,000-plus to carom off a flagpole that was clearly in foul territory and bounce into the right field stands. But the home plate ump saw it differently and immediately signaled it a home run.

As Danny trotted around the bases, the furious Fort Ord team charged home plate *en masse* and surrounded the umpire. Badly shaken, the ump abruptly changed his mind and called it a foul ball. This brought the Fort Myer bench charging onto the field, and the rattled arbiter reversed his reversal. O'Connell was credited with a homer, and the Colonials held on to win 6-5 in 12 innings.

They won another nail-biter the next day, 5-4, to cop the title. Antonelli, Poholsky and Calderone were named to the all-tournament team. O'Connell was not only named the best shortstop, he was voted the tourney's Most Valuable Player award after hitting .320 "and covering shortstop like an Army blanket." *Wichita Eagle* sports editor Pete Lightner noted that O'Connell "turned out to be almost an entire infield by himself. Without him, the Colonials would not have won."

The prize for winning the tournament was an 18-day "good will" trip to Japan, with a four-day stopover in Hawaii. Playing before crowds as large as 90,000 in the baseball-crazy country, the Colonials won a best-of-seven series against the top Japanese amateur team in five games, then went 1-1-1 in three games against an all-star team from Japan's professional clubs.

"I even got overseas pay for the trip," Danny joked on the team's return, "and I got a bonus of a hundred bucks (about $1,200 in 2024) for the trip too... Besides playing our games, they took us on sight-seeing trips and we had a good time."

In December, with only two months to go until his discharge, O'Connell wrote a letter to *Pittsburgh Sun-Telegraph* writer Chilly Doyle. "I followed the Pirates very closely last season," he wrote. "I think we will do better next year." He also made it clear he wasn't bothered by the stories that the team was grooming the bonus baby Dick Groat to play shortstop "because I would like to go to third base. I like it better than shortstop."

Among O'Connell's last official Army duties was to march in the inaugural parade of President-elect Dwight Eisenhower in January 1953. He had wisely saved furlough time so he could spend the last weeks of his Army service out of uniform and in Paterson, where he began getting into shape at the local YMCA. Although he had played with the Fort Myer basketball team after returning from the Japan trip, O'Connell, at 185 pounds, was still five pounds heavier than he had been in his rookie season. One Feb. 20, he was formally discharged. Two days later, he headed for Cuba.

CHAPTER 7 NOTES

He was a quiet *The News* (Frederick, Md.), July 7, 1950, p. 7.

At the age *Time* magazine, July 17, 1950, p. 12.

According to a *Greeley (Co.) Tribune*, July 7, 1950, p. 5.

"What was Kenny" *Time* magazine, July 17, 1950, p. 12, *Knoxville (Tn) Journal*, July 9, 1950, p. 4.

Baseball had played Baseball Hall of Fame archives.

"There is no" *The New York Times*, Dec. 7, 1950, p. 59.

In the end, *USA Today*, July 21, 2013.

On one mission Ibid.

Williams scrambled out Richard Sisk, "Jerry Coleman & Ted Williams, Korea Battle Buddies," *Military.com*, Jan. 13, 2014.

For the most *Decatur (Ga.) Daily*, Jan. 17, 1952, p. 9.

Another much-heralded *The New York Times*, April 14, 1951, p. 24.

The classification of *The Sporting News*, Feb. 7, 1951, p. 10.

Baseball's self-styled Ibid.

So the Pirates *Pittsburgh Press*, Feb. 11, 1951, p. 37.

Then Uncle Sam *The Herald-News* (Passaic NJ), Feb. 22, 1951, p. 30; *Pittsburgh Sun-Telegraph*, March 5, 1951, p. 16.

More formally, O'Connell *Pittsburgh Press*, April 3, 1951, p. 40.

The regiment was *Pittsburgh Press*, Jan. 11, 1953, p. 43.

Danny was astute *The Sporting News*, July 18, 1951, p. 10; *The Sporting News*, Jan. 19, 1955, p. 10.

With the baseball *The News* (Paterson NJ), Nov. 17, 1951, p. 12.

"The Pirates finished" *Pittsburgh Post-Gazette*, March 2, 1951, p. 18.

Moreover, the Pirates' *Pittsburgh Sun-Telegraph*, Jan. 4, 1951, p. 26.

Rickey professed to be *The Sporting News*, Dec. 27, 1950, p. 2.

Pirates manager Billy *The Herald-News* (Passaic NJ), Jan. 25, 1951, p. 36.

Rickey contended he *Pittsburgh Post-Gazette*, Sep. 21, 1951, p. 22.

"We accomplished so *The Sporting News*, Nov. 14, 1951, p. 11; *Pittsburgh Sun-Telegraph*, March 23, 1952, p. 31.

Rickey prudently avoided Andrew O'Toole, *Branch Rickey in Pittsburgh*, p. 66; *Pittsburgh Press*, Sept. 27, 1952, p. 23.

"There's nothing on" *Pittsburgh Post-Gazette*, Aug. 7, 1952, p. 14.

Before heading to *The News* (Paterson NJ), June 4, 1952, p. 42.

Seventy years after Author's interview with Alice O'Connell, Aug. 5, 2022.

It would probably *The Sporting News*, Sept. 3, 1952, p. 10.

The atrocious umpiring *Wichita Eagle*, Aug. 31, 1952, p. 1

They won another *Pittsburgh Post-Gazette*, Sept. 4, 1952, p. 20; *Wichita Eagle*, Sept. 3, 1952, p. 12.

"I even got" *Pittsburgh Post-Gazette*, March 5, 1953, p. 19.

In December, with *Pittsburgh Sun-Telegraph*, Dec. 14, 1952, p. 34.

By mid-season *Pittsburgh Post-Gazette*, July 3, 1952, p. 14.

Among O'Connell's last *The News* (Paterson, NJ), Feb. 2, 1953, p. 52.

CHAPTER 8

"HE'S OUR BEST BALLPLAYER"

DANNY'S YEAR

February 23, 1953 was a Monday. It was also a federal holiday, since George Washington's 221st birthday the day before had fallen on a Sunday. So Dwight David Eisenhower, who had been inaugurated Washington's 33rd successor as America's president barely a month before and was thus a federal employee, took the day off.

The 62-year-old World War II hero attended a service at the Christ Episcopal Church in Alexandria, Virginia, then played a round of golf at the Burning Tree Club, a private males-only course in Bethesda, Maryland. (He sent an aide to lay a wreath at Washington's tomb.) Eisenhower liked golf far more than baseball or being president. He had already laid out a rudimentary driving range on the south lawn of the White House, sometimes hitting a hundred balls in a session. Previous presidents had used the area mostly to stage the annual Presidential Easter Egg Hunt, although William Howard Taft had allowed Pauline, his pet Holstein cow, to roam around the lawn from time to time.

Elsewhere in America, farmers were loudly complaining about falling prices for their products while grocery shoppers were just as vociferously moaning about spending a "record high" average of $14.20 a week ($167 in 2024) to feed a family of four. Newspaper editorialists opined the problem was that the "middlemen" between farmer and consumer were taking too big a slice of the pie, noting farmers only got 48 cents of every food dollar, down from 50 cents the year before. "It would be healthier if the farmer's two cents could be returned to him," the Greenville, South Carolina *News* noted, "without an increase in food prices."

The February 23 edition of *Life* magazine featured a cover photo of "America's Prettiest School Teacher." Twenty-one-year-old Nell Owen of Dallas, Texas, had been so-named by the *Our Miss Brooks* radio show, purportedly to dispel the stereotype - perpetuated in no small part by the radio show itself—that female school teachers were generally homely spinsters who wanted most of all to meet a nice man and become a housewife. Mrs. Owen, described as having "proved herself durable as well as fetching," won a trip to Hollywood, where she and her husband met various movie stars.

Many Americans with the day off might have perused one of the current best-selling books. These included the latest John Steinbeck novel, *East of Eden*; the immensely popular self-help book *The Power of Positive Thinking*, by Protestant clergyman Norman Vincent Peal, or *The Silent World*, which offered an intriguing look under the sea and was written by a former French naval officer, Capt. J.Y. Cousteau.

For those with less literary predilections, there was television. A month earlier, a staggering 73.9 percent of all American TV sets were tuned to Episode 16 of the second season of *I Love Lucy*, in which the title character, Lucy Ricardo, gave birth to a son. The show, which had been taped a few months before, aired 12 hours after the show's star, Lucille Ball, gave birth to a son in real life. The episode proved far more popular than Eisenhower's televised inauguration the next day.

Television sets had proliferated like so many randy bunnies. In 1950, there were three million TV set owners in America; by 1960, 55 million. On Feb. 23, 1953, a Sylvania, Philco or Emerson set could be had for as little as $200 ($2,350 in 2024.) Of course that was for the model with the 17-inch screen. The giant 25-inch screen model was considerably more costly.

Somewhere in Korea, meanwhile, a 24-year-old infantry sergeant from Detroit was five months and four days from dying. On July 27, Sgt. Harold R. Cross Jr., who had spent nearly a decade in the Merchant Marine, U.S. Navy and U.S. Army, would become nationally known as the last American ground trooper to be killed before an armistice between the warring factions in the three-year-old Korean conflict went into effect. Cross, who was killed by an artillery round while crouching in a bunker with his squad, would join an estimated 36,573 other Americans who died in a struggle that essentially ended in a stalemate and became known as the country's "forgotten war."

And sometime late in the afternoon of February 23, Danny O'Connell got off a plane in Havana Cuba and reported for work with the Pittsburgh Pirates.

Just what O'Connell's job was going to be was uncertain. Danny had joined the Pirates as a third baseman, the position he much preferred. But the club had decided he was needed more at shortstop, which is where he played in his 1950 rookie season and then for two years in the Army. "O'Connell is by far the one athlete the Bucs are counting on most heavily," *The Sporting News* learnedly reported in January, "because the infield is the weakest link and the shortstop berth has already been reserved for his unusual talents."

Apparently no one at "baseball's Bible" had bothered to ask Fred Haney, the Pirates' new manager. "I've got four or five players I can use in the infield," Haney said early in spring training. "But from what I've seen so far, my best third baseman is O'Connell, my best shortstop is O'Connell and my best second baseman is O'Connell. But if I use Danny at third or short, I have nobody who can do as good a job at second base...I can put him anywhere, and he could do better than anyone else. He's our best ballplayer."

Haney's comments were not only high praise for O'Connell, but a clear indication that the Pirates' new skipper understood from the beginning that he was not taking over the '27 Yankees. "I am fully aware that managing the Pirates is not going to be a bed of roses," he wrote in a pre-spring training article that was part of an Associated Press series penned by managers of all 16 big league clubs. "However, if I am permitted one cliché, I will say that the Pirates will be an interesting team to watch."

Unlike the easy-going Billy Meyer, whom he had replaced as manager, the 57-year-old Haney was a hard-nosed, old-school baseball man. Born in New Mexico and raised in Los Angeles, Haney had been a three-sport star in high school. At 5 feet 6 inches and 170 pounds, he acquired the nickname "Pudge." But he was deceptively fast and led several of the minor leagues in which he played in stolen bases. He broke into the majors in 1922 on a Detroit Tigers team managed by Ty Cobb, the Hall of Fame player who, legend has it, used to sharpen his shoe cleats on the dugout steps in full view of opposing teams and was the poster boy for the take-no-prisoners approach to the game. The irascible Cobb immediately took Haney under his wing. But in baseball, scrappiness does not fully compensate for limited talent, and Haney's seven-year major league career as an infielder was unremarkable.

After his playing days were over, Haney became a minor league manager, and then managed the lowly St. Louis Browns in the American League for three forgettable seasons. After a few years as a broadcaster for the Los Angeles Angels and Hollywood Stars in the Pacific Coast League, he took over as the Stars' manager in 1949, leading them to two pennants in four years. Even so, Haney was not the first choice of Branch Rickey, the Pirates' general manager. The notoriously cheap Rickey had hoped to sign a manager who could also play, thus saving an extra salary. But Haney's resumé was sound, and Rickey realized the Pirates needed a firmer hand than they had under Meyer.

"There will be no lying around the field as long as I'm in charge," Haney barked on the first day of spring training. He told the Pirates they had 10 days to get in game shape. "You don't have to show me a thing during that period except hustle. And I warn you, if you can't show me that, I won't be interested in anything else."

Haney's warning was not aimed anywhere near O'Connell. One particularly hot and muggy afternoon, he told Danny to take a break from infield drills. A bit later, the manager looked up to see O'Connell running wind sprints in the outfield. "I had to stop him," Haney recalled. "He was working harder than if he had been in the regular workout. I had to order him into the clubhouse and out of uniform for the day."

That the Pirates were in Cuba in the first place was the result of Branch Rickey's lust for a bargain and Fulgencio Batista's desire to scrape off some of the slime he had draped on his island country's international reputation. Batista, an astoundingly corrupt and appallingly brutal dictator, had been Cuba's de facto boss since leading a coup in 1933, except for the eight years he spent in self-exile in the United States after failing to sufficiently fix the 1944 presidential race in his country.

In 1952, he rectified his mistake by staging another coup and installing himself as president. Working with American organized crime bosses, "El Hombre" ("The Man") harvested tens of millions of dollars from Cuba's thriving gambling and prostitution industries. Working with large U.S. companies only slightly less larcenous than the Mob, he also received a share of their profits in return for allowing them to dominate Cuba's economy. Batista's secret police forces kept order by routinely imprisoning, torturing and/or murdering political dissidents and other trouble makers.

But Batista wanted to add to the island's prestige and allure by getting the country's name into news stories that did not include the words "brothels" or "death squads." So the general had his brother-in-law, who just happened to be Cuba's sports commissioner, make an offer to Rickey. In return for a Pirates agreement to spend spring training in Cuba for three seasons, the Cuban government would pay all the team's expenses. In return, the government would keep the box office receipts from all the Pirates' exhibition games, which were sure to draw giant crowds of baseball-crazy Cubans. Rickey happily agreed. He covered the venality of the deal by telling reporters that springtime in California, where the Pirates had trained the last few years, was too rainy.

The team was housed in a five-story apartment building about seven miles north of Havana, with hastily constructed practice facilities across the street and exhibition games played in a nearby sports stadium. "The boys will love this place," Haney predicted after scouting the environs two weeks before training camp opened. "They'll be only a few feet from the beach."

While the proximity to the beach allowed the Pirates to be, in the words of one writer, "the best-tanned team that ever opened a major league season," the seven-week camp was by and large a disaster. "In all my travels to baseball training camps, I have never seen a more disgruntled group of players," wrote Al Abrams, sports editor of the *Pittsburgh Sun-Telegraph*. "They are openly hostile about the living accommodations, the food they have to eat and innumerable other minor details."

One player told Abrams "the toilet facilities are the most horrible I've ever seen. We can't shower or bathe because there's no water. The other morning I had to go across the street to borrow water just to flush the commode." First-floor apartments flooded every time it rained, bed linens were changed only after two weeks of complaining, and the food was considered just above the inedible level. Abrams described trying a steak "that was tougher than [catcher] Joe Garagiola's glove."

Living conditions proved to be only one of the problems. Because all the other big-league clubs were training in Florida, Arizona or California, the Pirates' total major league competition in the spring consisted of two games against the Philadelphia Athletics. The rest of the schedule was against a Class C team from Florida and a team of locals, "The Cuban All Stars." Only the Florida team never made it because of transportation troubles and the Cuban team only showed up when it felt like it, which it didn't on more than a dozen occasions. So the Bucs played a lot of intra-squad games.

Unsurprisingly, the Cuban populace wasn't interested in watching an eighth-place U.S. team play against itself. Deepening Cuban disinterest was the fact that the only Pirate most of them had heard of wasn't there. Slugger Ralph Kiner, incensed by Rickey's offer of a 25 percent pay cut to his $90,000 (a bit over $1 million in 2024) salary, was holding out. Despite tying for the league home run lead in 1952, Kiner had a generally crappy year. Plus Rickey disliked stars in general and he particularly disliked Kiner, a prima donna who basked in his own celebrity. During the '52 season, Rickey had written a 15-page letter to Pirates co-owner John Galbreath that laid out in tedious detail all of Kiner's sins. These ranged from insisting on flying on some road trips (at Kiner's own expense) rather than taking the train with his teammates because the slugger suffered from hay fever, to sharing an apartment during the season with a fellow Rickey claimed was "well known for his promiscuous domestic infidelity." During contract negotiations in the off-season, Rickey famously told Kiner, "We finished last with you, and we can certainly finish last without you."

Kiner finally showed up in mid-March after accepting a 15 percent cut. By then, it was too late to make many Cubans care. The "crowd" at one game was comprised of 16 people, and that included two stadium cops and the Pirates' bus driver. Attendance was so bad, the Cuban government quit charging admission - and also quit turning on the stadium's lights to cut down the electric bill. Games thus had to be played under the steamy afternoon sun. "This is no way," a player summed up, "to treat even a last-place ballclub."

In spite of disgruntled teammates, non-flushing toilets and catcher's-mitt steaks, O'Connell took to second base like a congressman to a free lunch. At shortstop, Haney installed Dick Cole, a 27-year-old light-hitting, slick-fielding fellow who had played for Haney's PCL pennant winners, and predicted that by mid-season, O'Connell and Cole would be among the best double-play combinations in the league.

Even the umpires were impressed with Danny's play. "I never saw O'Connell before, but he certainly impressed me," said Frank Secory, one of four National League umps assigned to Cuba on a one-at-a-time rotation. "He made plays around second base that would do justice to any second sacker and is as smooth as silk...I got a good close look at Danny, and he's strictly a major leaguer. I like the way he handles the bat too. I never saw a player so young who can hit behind a runner like O'Connell."

In early April, the Pirates at last left Cuba and headed for the season opener at Brooklyn by way of New Orleans (where they played an exhibition with their Double A farm team) and Pittsburgh. The baseball world let out a collective yawn. "The Pittsburgh Pirates are so without hope that they face the National League pennant race without fear," a wire service opined. "It is clear, after seven weeks of training, that the Pirates are doomed to another eighth-place finish."

Nevada oddsmakers agreed. The Yankees and Dodgers were tabbed as the favorites to meet in the World Series, as they had in 1952. The Pirates' chance of making it was set at 300 to 1, "probably the longest price ever placed against a big-league club." The next-lowest teams' chances were set at 30 to 1.

Even folks who had no business piling on, piled on. When Frank "Trader" Lane, the loquacious general manager of the Chicago White Sox, was asked how he could pick Pittsburgh to finish last and yet also list them as the most improved team, he replied "Easy. They have one ballplayer this year in Danny O'Connell. Last year, they had none." The White Sox, by the way, had not been to the World Series themselves since 1919, and they threw that one in the "Black Sox" scandal that grievously wounded the National Pastime.

Not everyone was as downbeat about the Bucs. "O'Connell has definitely made a vast difference in the Pittsburgh infield with his steady all-around play," Danny's hometown *Morning Call* proclaimed. "In fact, Danny is the leader of a group of young upstarts who are scoffing at what the experts have predicted as the season starts." Manager Haney was equally defiant. "I firmly believe that after watching the team through spring training, we are not going to finish last again," he said. "I want the ballclub to have the same confidence in themselves as I have in their ability."

And then the season started.

For O'Connell, it was a season of "almost" - of high praise and higher expectations; of shining individual moments in a dreary sea of collective failure, and most of all of bright promise of things to come.

Pittsburgh opened in Brooklyn against the defending National League champion Dodgers, before 12,433 spectators enthusiastic enough to brave mid-40s temperatures and a cutting wind that made it feel much colder. The Pirates jumped to a quick 4-0 lead, and then reverted to form. Homers by Roy Campanella and Duke Snider, both of whom Branch Rickey had brought to Brooklyn back when he was running the Dodgers and was still a genius, gave the Dodgers an 8-5 win.

Kiner made it interesting in the ninth when he blasted a shot to deep left-center with two runners on. But the wind knocked it down enough for Snider to catch up with it. At the plate, O'Connell doubled, walked and scored a run in four at-bats. In the field, he made an acrobatic stop of an errant throw from catcher Joe Garagiola and then dove back across second base to tag out a would-be Dodger base-stealer.

The Pirates lost the next day too, 4-2, on a bases-loaded double by Dodger shortstop Pee Wee Reese that wiped out a 2-1 Pirate lead. Then they headed home, for what turned out to be a highly entertaining home opener against the Philadelphia Phillies. The weather at Forbes Field was somehow even more miserable than it had been in Brooklyn: gloomy, drizzly and a bracing 34 degrees at game time. The Pirates scored a run in the first on two hits and two Phillies errors, and the Phils scored two in the fourth on a homer by Willie "Puddinhead" Jones. Then things got weird.

In the bottom of the fourth, the Pirates sent 12 men to the plate, seven of whom scored to make it 8-2, Pittsburgh. Danny singled and walked. Undaunted, the Phils, who were a pretty good team and would finish third in '53, sent 15 men to the plate in the top of the fifth and scored nine runs to take an 11-8 lead.

Undaunted by the Phillies' undauntedness, the Pirates responded briskly in the bottom of the inning. Two walks, two singles and an error brought O'Connell up with two out, two runners on base and the score now knotted at 11 apiece. Danny smashed the second pitch he saw over the left-field wall. The Pirates held on to win their first game of the season, and sent home happy those of the 16,220 in attendance who hadn't suffered frostbite.

For Pittsburgh fans, it was easily one of the season's high points. By the end of April, the Pirates were 5-9, and by the end of May, 13-28, good for last place and 14.5 games behind the front-running Dodgers, although just 1.5 games back of the seventh-place Chicago Cubs. Rickey, meanwhile, continued to run the club as if he were relying on a Ouija board and a monkey's paw to tell him what to do.

Much to the amusement of players on other clubs, Pirates hitters were ordered to wear fiberglass batting helmets that had long peaks but no protective pieces over the ear and were uncomfortably tight. "They fit like a glove," Garagiola cracked. "I wish they fit like a cap." Less funny was the fact the club had ordered only 15 new uniforms for the season, meaning almost half the team sported threadbare jerseys and windbreakers that in some cases were three years old. (Danny was one of the lucky ones who got a new uni.)

On June 4, Rickey rid himself of his biggest personnel headache by unloading Kiner, along with the wise-cracking catcher Joe Garagiola, pitcher Howie Pollet and first baseman George "Catfish" Metkovich to the Chicago Cubs. In return, the Pirates received six players named "who?" None of the players the Bucs got from the Cubs was hitting above .230 at the time of the trade, and none of them hit more than .210 after. But what Rickey really wanted was cash, and he got it. The Cubs sweetened the deal by throwing in an additional $100,000 ($1.2 million in 2024.) Moreover, the six ex-Cubs' contractual salaries were collectively $67,000 ($788,000) less than those of the departing Pirates. Apparently giddy with the deal, The Pirates climbed into 6th place after beating the Cubs 6-1 the day of the trade. The giddiness was fleeting. Three days later, they were back in the league basement.

While trading mediocre players for even more mediocre players, Rickey also continued "rebuilding" the Pirates by installing three rosy-cheeked rookies who were actually better at sports other than baseball. Eddie and Johnny

O'Brien were 22-year-old identical twins from South Amboy New Jersey. (Eddie was 12 minutes older.) Although only 5'8" tall, the O'Briens had been outstanding college basketball players. Their Seattle University team actually defeated the legendary Harlem Globetrotters back when the 'Trotters played contested games rather than exhibitions. The O'Briens were also pretty good college baseball players. That, coupled with the almost irresistible novelty of fielding identical twins, led eight major league teams to compete for their services. The Pirates won out, in part because of lobbying by mega-star and Pittsburgh minority owner Bing Crosby and in part by the $40,000 bonuses ($470,800 in 2024) Rickey dangled before them.

For a much less comprehensible reason, he also paid $25,000 ($294,000) to Vic Janowicz, an Ohio State halfback and winner of the 1950 Heisman Trophy as the best college football player of the year. Rickey was convinced he could make a big-league catcher out of him.

None of the three "bonus babies" amounted to much as baseball players. The O'Briens combined for a .243 average and two homers before involuntarily departing the team toward the end of the season for the Army. Janowicz, who eventually left baseball for a brief career in the National Football League, hit .252 in 42 games. (At a dinner after the season, O'Connell joked that "this year, we may pay a bonus for a baseball player." Rickey was not amused.) Worse, because of a major league rule that Rickey had vigorously pushed for back when he opposed big bonuses for untried players, any player who received more than $4,000 (about $47,000 in 2024) had to stay with the big-league club for two seasons and couldn't be sent down to the minors. Thus the equivalent of 12 percent of the Pirates' 25-man roster was fixed no matter how lousy they were.

What all this had to do with O'Connell was Rickey's insistence that the O'Briens be penciled in as the Pirates' regular shortstop and second baseman. That meant Danny moved back to familiar territory in mid-June. "I came up to the Pirates as a third baseman and was sent to Indianapolis to learn to play shortstop," O'Connell told a luncheon crowd in early July. "When I came back from the Army, I found myself at second, and now I'm back where I belong, at third base."

And while "Rickey's Wrecks" floundered, O'Connell shone. In an early-season series against the Giants, Danny hit a 400-foot triple to win one game and helped win another by kicking the ball out of the catcher's hand as O'Connell arrived at home plate just after a throw from the outfield. Against Milwaukee, he hit two home runs in one game against future Hall of Famer Warren Spahn, and two days later took a fast ball in the ribs from Braves pitcher Lew Burdette with the bases loaded in the 10th inning to win the game. In a July 4 double-header against the Dodgers before an Ebbets Field crowd of 30,029 that included his proud parents, O'Connell went six for nine with a double, a walk and three runs scored.

To be sure, there were valleys among the peaks. A six-for-41 slump in early June dropped his batting average from .302 to a season-low .264. In a game against St. Louis in May, O'Connell made errors on two consecutive plays, giving the Cardinals both their runs in a 2-1 loss. Adding to the misery: Danny went zip for four at the plate, striking out once and grounding out thrice, once with the bases loaded and once with two runners on. And occasionally he outsmarted himself.

In a game against the Cardinals, St. Louis had a runner on first with Cards' pitcher Wilmer "Vinegar Bend" Mizell at the plate and a 2-0 count. O'Connell figured Cardinals manager Eddie Stanky would signal Mizell to take the next pitch and try to coax a walk. So on the pitch, Danny broke from his second-base position to sneak behind the St. Louis runner at first and draw a pickoff throw from the catcher. Only Stanky didn't put on the take sign and Mizell hit the ball directly at the spot O'Connell had just vacated and into centerfield.

"I guess I pulled a rock," a chagrinned O'Connell told Pirates manager Haney after the inning was over. "Sure you did," Haney replied, "and if you don't do it again, I'll fine you. You had an idea that just didn't work out. You can't play this game mechanically. You've got to have plans and the confidence to try them." Cardinals manager Stanky concurred. "That kid's a good ballplayer," he said. "He didn't make a mistake. It was good thinking. It just backfired."

Stanky's praise was echoed by a veritable pantheon of baseball men. "Danny O'Connell is a real pro," said the Dodgers' Jackie Robinson. "He could play anywhere." Cincinnati Reds manager Rogers Hornsby, quite probably the best-hitting second baseman ever and a world-class cantankerous old fart, positively gushed (at least for Hornsby): "That kid is a throwback to the Old Timers...O'Connell fights all the time...O'Connell fields better than [Braves third baseman] Ed Mathews and hits better than [Dodgers third baseman] Billy Cox." Former Pirates third baseman and Hall of Fame member Pie Traynor said "O'Connell is one of those rare athletes who can play anywhere in the infield...He's the best man I've seen in years at getting the ball away fast." Chicago Cubs super scout Ray Blades called Danny "one of the standouts of the National League...He isn't what one would call spectacular, but he's a steady, reliable player. Danny is so smooth you hardly notice him. That's the real test of a real player."

Danny naturally agreed. In a highly flattering piece in *Sport* magazine, veteran baseball writer Milt Richman noted, "if there is anything that character-izes O'Connell, it is confidence. He brims over with it, just as he does with Irish wit and song. He thinks he's good and he has no reluctance to tell anybody what he thinks."

"Why shouldn't I feel that way?" Danny responded. "... I don't have a glaring weakness that a guy is going to get me out on...The way I figure it, anybody can field. To be a big-leaguer, you got to hit."

And why shouldn't he have felt that way? He was 24 and healthy, miss-ing only five games over the season, all the result of an injured thigh muscle incurred while dashing from first to third on an infield single. He was well-liked by his teammates. Pitcher Bob Friend, who roomed with O'Connell on road trips, used terms like "jokester" and "good old Irishman" to describe him. His humor and enthusiasm were welcome in a Pirates clubhouse that endured far more losses than enjoyed wins. During a trip to St. Louis, for example, O'Connell took the O'Brien twins and rookie outfielders Carlos Bernier and Jose Montemayor to the city's world-famous zoo. "Danny is a good guy," Eddie O'Brien said. "He makes everybody, even us rookies, feel like part of the team." Of course friendship only went so far: Les Biederman of the *Pittsburgh Press* noted that "O'Connell is the sharpest card player on the Pirates, so none of the boys will play with him."

With the departure of Kiner, Danny also became the most in-demand Pirate as a product endorser. He signed with an agent, Frank Scott, who landed O'Connell appearances in radio, TV and print ads for a dairy, a grocery store chain and a men's clothing store. He was also a sought-after lunch and dinner speaker. At a Pirates boosters' club lunch in July, "O'Connell started out by saying that he isn't much of a public speaker because he's not long out of the Army and in the Army a man doesn't get much chance to talk," the *Sun-Telegraph* reported, "and then dispelled that by rolling his audience in the aisles with his witty remarks." Noting, for example, the wildly enthusiastic crowds in Milwaukee, where the Braves were in their first season, O'Connell said "Why, they even cheer the umpires! Of course they'll learn more about the right way to act at the ballpark as the season goes on."

Even the press loved him. At the end of the season, *The Sporting News* polled 100 writers and editors who covered the majors to rank players on each team in 44 categories that included character traits as well as on-field talent. The categories ranged from "most feared hitter in the clutch" to "best dancer" and "most conceited." On the Pirates, Danny was ranked first in nine categories:

- Most feared hitter in the clutch
- Most relaxed on the field
- Has done most for team
- Least temperamental
- Happiest
- Most friendly to fans
- Best student of game
- Wittiest
- Best conversationalist

In the National League, only St. Louis superstar Stan Musial ranked first in more categories for his team. But baseball is a lot like life, or vice versa. Both are full of "almost," of accomplishments that fall just a bit short of success, of achievements that are one small step below well-established levels of excellence. For Danny O'Connell, the 1953 season was one of tantalizing, not quite fully satisfying, *almost*.

He was *almost* an All-Star. In baseball, being chosen for an All-Star team is tantamount to an actor being nominated for an Academy Award, a journalist being a finalist for a Pulitzer Prize or a Louisiana politician not being indicted. Whatever the rest of a career brings, the words "former All-Star" will happily accompany the player through his obituary and beyond. "Danny O'Connell doesn't know how close he came to being selected to the National League All-Star team in the very first season he had a chance to compete," the *Pittsburgh Press* reported on July 12, the day before the season's traditional All-Star break.

In '53, fans elected each league's eight starting position players. The manager of the team that won the pennant the year before chose the pitchers and reserve players. In this case the manager was Charlie Dressen of the Dodgers. "I like that kid," Dressen said of O'Connell, "like him a lot. He can fit in anywhere and would have come in handy for us since he swings the bat pretty good. But I simply didn't have room for him."

As Dressen explained it, Danny's spot was needed so the team could carry an extra catcher who could handle pitches from knuckleballer Hoyt Wilhelm of the Giants. (Knuckleballs are notoriously unpredictable. The catcher/comedian Bob Uecker once advised that the best way to handle a knuckleball was "wait until it stops rolling and pick it up.") "So," Dressen said, "I took [catcher] Del Rice from the Cardinals and regretted leaving O'Connell off. But if anything happens between now and [the game], I'll make a pitch for Danny."

But nothing happened to make room for Danny. As it turned out, Dressen inexplicably carried five catchers. Of the quintet, only the fans' choice, Roy Campanella of Brooklyn, played. Wilhelm did not pitch at all in the National League's 5-1 win. "There'll be other years and other All-Star games for O'Connell," the *Press'* Les Biederman philosophized, "but it would have been quite a feather in Danny's fiberglass cap he wears if he made the grade this year. Danny can play anywhere in the infield and can hit with authority...He can do everything, and do it well."

The next *almost* for O'Connell was not as prestigious as an All-Star berth, but was more memorable for its longevity—and its extraordinary conclusion. It began on a Monday in Brooklyn with an eighth-inning groundball single to centerfield that drove in a run and gave the Pirates a 2-0 lead they would quite naturally squander. It ended on a Saturday in Upper Manhattan with a nifty tumbling catch by an outfielder normally far better at hitting the ball than catching it.

In between, O'Connell would collect at least one hit in the next 25 games the Pirates played, and two or more in half of them. In all, he would go 41-for-118 (a .347 average) and set the team's all-time record for consecutive games in a single season with at least one base hit.

"It was a big deal back then because we didn't have a lot going on with that 1953 team," Danny's roomie, Bob Friend, recalled a half-century later. "When he reached 10 games, everyone started to get interested...it was amazing how he handled the bat...Danny was a guy who knew the strike zone. He couldn't hit for a lot of power, but he could hit to all fields. He was a guy who knew how to play the game."

There was actually very little drama during most of the streak. In only one game did O'Connell go into his last at-bat needing a hit. But it might not have been all that pleasant having a clubhouse locker next to his. On his 1950 rookie self-profile, O'Connell had written that while he was not particularly superstitious, he made it a point not to change his sweat shirt until he went hitless in a game. On September 16, in a game against the Braves in Milwaukee that turned out to be the Pirates' 100th loss of the season, Danny tied the Pirates' record of 25 set by Charlie Grimm in 1923 and matched by Freddie Lindstrom in 1933. Grimm just happened to be the Braves' manager in 1953, and the two posed together for photographs. "I dunno," the "not superstitious" O'Connell grinned, "Maybe I shouldn't have my picture taken. Probably jinx me."

It almost did in the next game, the first game of a double-header against the Giants at the Polo Grounds. Danny came up in the 6th inning with a runner on first, having grounded out and walked in his first two plate appearances. The Pirates already trailed 4-0 and the outcome of the game was essentially meaningless to both teams. (It was so meaningless to Giants fans that only 2,744 attended, the smallest Polo Grounds crowd of the year.) But O'Connell did what baseball tradition at the time dictated: He laid down a sacrifice bunt rather than hit away in an effort to extend the streak. His selflessness was rewarded. In the eighth, with two runners on, he lined a single into right field, plating the Pirates' only run of the game and setting the team's new single-season record for most consecutive games with at least one hit.

In the second game, he grounded weakly to the pitcher in his first at-bat; flied deep to left in his second; grounded to second in his third; and struck out in his fourth. Now, in the ninth, he was scheduled to be the fourth Pirate to hit. The first two batters were retired on a pop-fly to first and a strikeout. The third hitter was Brandy Davis, a rookie hitting .192. Davis was appearing in only his 12th game - and playing in this game only because the reliable regular left fielder Gene Hermanski was 33, in the last week of his 10-year career and needed a rest after playing in the first game.

But Pirates manager Fred Haney, in an effort to better O'Connell's chance at a final at-bat, pinch-hit Toby Atwell for Davis. Atwell was a seldom-used catcher only marginally more experienced than Davis, and merely a slightly better hitter. He promptly hit a hard ground ball right back at Giants pitcher Marv Grissom—who just as promptly heightened the drama by having it bounce off his glove. Atwell was safe at first, and O'Connell was up.

Grissom quickly worked the count to 0-2, and O'Connell changed bats. On the third pitch, Danny looped a soft line drive just beyond and between first and second base. Giants right fielder Don Mueller raced in, stuck out his glove, snared the ball just below his knees and tucked into a somersault. He also held on, "and that," the *Pittsburgh Press* sighed, "was that."

Mueller's nickname was "Mandrake," after the comic-strip magician, because of his bat-handling talents. But he was no great shakes as an outfielder and the play he made on O'Connell's liner was, according to New York observers, "the best catch of his six-year major league career." For O'Connell, it was a deflating end to the streak, made all the more painful because the following day—of all days—was "Danny O'Connell Day."

Danny's day had been in the works almost as soon as the season started when it became clear to his hometown that O'Connell was in the majors to stay. A committee of Paterson's civic and business leaders negotiated with the Giants, who were happy to host a day for a rival player mostly because one-third of all the tickets eventually sold for the game were bought by Paterson folks. The committee also solicited gifts and organized a bus caravan that carried 1,500 Patersonians from the front of Wurzberg's sporting goods store on Market Street to the Polo Grounds on September 20.

"They are for him all the way," wrote Bob Whiting of *The Morning Call*, "because every sports fan likes an athlete who fights his way to the top against big odds, and Danny has been doing that from the start."

The ceremony, emceed by Giants radio announcer Russ Hodges, was broadcast over WPIX, one of five television stations emanating from New York City. Danny was showered with gifts: a set of golf clubs, a clock radio (from his teammates), a record player, a gift certificate from a men's clothing store, a year's supply of shoes and a year's supply of barbecue relish from Paterson's very own Welworth Pickle Co. Best of all (unless you really like barbecue relish) was a brand-new Buick Riviera convertible. Even the weather cooperated when it ignored a forecast of cloudy with a chance of rain and bestowed a mild and mostly sunny afternoon.

"It's hard for me to find exactly the right words," a choked-up O'Connell said while his beaming family looked on. "It's a wonderful feeling. I'd like to thank the people of Paterson and Stony Road, and the [organizing] committee for their hard work. Above all, I'd like to thank my mom and dad for their encouragement and guidance, which put me where I am today. This is a wonderful day for me."

Then he went none for four. "I figured that with my whole gang here today they'd have something to yell about," he moaned to a teammate after the game. "I let them down by getting horse-collared...They ought to take the gifts back."

They didn't. But the gods of baseball took something else away, and replaced it with another *almost*. Danny had entered the game hitting exactly .300. Until relatively recently in baseball history, when it was shoved aside in favor of more sophisticated statistical measures, hitting .300 had always been considered a key benchmark of excellence. Someone purportedly asked Cap Anson, professional baseball's first superstar, how he'd like his tombstone to be inscribed. "I guess one line will be enough," he replied: 'Here lies a man who batted .300.'" Anson can rest easy—his lifetime mark was .334. Another pretty good hitter, Ted Williams (lifetime mark .344), pointed out that hitting a baseball consistently was so tough that "baseball is the only field of endeavor where a man can succeed three times out of ten and be considered a good performer."

O'Connell, however, would end the '53 season hitting .294. Just four more hits added to his 173 would have done it. Danny went to the plate 684 times during the year. Turn just 0.8 percent of the 511 times he did not get credit for a hit, when his at-bats amounted to outs, walks, reached-base-on-errors, sacrifices, hit-by-pitches, and he would have reached the platform of excellence conferred by hitting .300 in a full big-league season.

In the last seven games of the season, all of which were against the Giants and Dodgers, Danny went two for 23. "I just couldn't buy a hit that last week," O'Connell sadly told Arthur Daley of *The New York Times*. "It got so brutal that I couldn't even get a hit when Alvin Dark [normally the Giants shortstop, whom manager Leo Durocher allowed to pitch a bit at season's end] pitched for the Giants against us. [Dark walked O'Connell.] I smacked two balls solidly the last day, but Wes Westrum [the Giants' slow-moving catcher]—of all people, he was playing third base—went into the hole to rob me of one hit and Don Mueller, who is no DiMaggio [and who earlier had ended Danny's consecutive-games hitting streak] robbed me of another. I guess I wasn't supposed to reach .300 last year."

Even with that disappointment, however, it was a very good year. The "Grandstand Managers," the Pirates' official booster club, voted O'Connell the team's most outstanding player. He led the club in games played, plate appearances, hits, doubles, triples, batting average and total bases, was second in walks and on-base percentage and third in slugging average. Despite not reaching the magic .300 mark, his .294 was 29 points higher than the league average and good for 19th in the National League. (Nine of the 18 hitters in front of him wound up in the Hall of Fame.) He tied for 12th in hits, and finished 16th in voting for the NL's Most Valuable Player award.

After the season ended, Danny lingered for a week in Pittsburgh to have some unspecified surgery described in the papers only as "minor." Then he went home to Paterson for an off-season that was uneventful. *Almost.*

At home, Danny went to work gaining back a few of the 12 pounds he had lost during the season and shaving a stroke or two from his golf handicap at the North Jersey Country Club. There were burgers to eat at the City Line Luncheonette, cards and beer at Gamptece's Bar & Grill and pickup basketball games at the Paterson YMCA. There was a two-week fishing trip with Sam De Gise and J.J. Mangeny, a couple of pals who had spearheaded the effort behind "Danny O'Connell Day" at the Polo Grounds. He even worked as a delivery driver for United Parcels during the Christmas rush for exercise and an extra bit of spending money. "Boy, going up those stairs from 8 in the morning until 10 at night keeps you in shape all right," he told a reporter for *The Sporting News*.

And there was the occasional girl. Danny's sister Alice recalled him bringing home a young lady from Pittsburgh to meet the O'Connells. "I don't know how much he really liked her," Alice said. "She spent most of the time checking herself out in the reflection from the china cabinet [glass] in the living room. She brought her sister, and the sister had Bob [Danny's younger brother] in a bear hug, trying to get him to dance with her."

In early November, Danny bought the O'Connell family a new house in the slightly more upscale community of Totowa, maybe a 20-minute walk from their Stony Road house and on the other side of the Passaic River. Alice said he borrowed $4,000 ($47,800 in 2024) from an aunt to help with the down payment. If so, Danny put down another $2,000 ($23,900) himself and assumed a $10,500 ($123,500) mortgage on what his newspaper buddy Joe Gooter called "a modest house...a one-family wooden frame home."

And in his spare time, O'Connell pondered where he might be playing in 1954. Danny knew he was the most valuable commodity the Pirates had—and the Pirates needed money. If he were sold or traded, he told a reporter in late November, he hoped it would be to Milwaukee because the Braves had the pitching to beat the Dodgers and win the pennant, or to the Giants, because they were just across the Hudson River and were in essence his hometown team.

In Pittsburgh, meanwhile, Branch Rickey was privately studying his options while publicly trying to soften up Pirates fans to the very real possibility they would be losing their favorite player. Club treasurer Jim Herron had estimated in August the Pirates would lose maybe $250,000 ($2.9 million in 2024) for the 1953 season, and Herron turned out to be an optimist: The final figure was closer to $350,000 ($4.1 million.) Pittsburgh finished the season drawing fewer fans than any other National League team except Cincinnati, and 1954's attendance prospects were no rosier.

"I don't want to trade O'Connell," Rickey claimed. "He is the type of player we need on this club. Not that one man will make a difference on the Pirates," he added as an aside, possibly to remind fans the team had finished last with and without Ralph Kiner and could do the same with or without O'Connell. Shifting gears again, Rickey said "O'Connell is the one boy we can figure on as an important part of the club when it gets into contention. But then again," he rhetorically swerved, "if we see a chance to get two or three players who will help when we get started in Pittsburgh, I would trade anyone."

What Rickey left unsaid was that any deal involving Danny would also involve a pile of money for the cash-strapped Pirates. Manager Fred Haney was more direct. "If O'Connell goes," he said at baseball's winter meetings in New York City in early December, "it will probably be a matter of financing. If we find we need more money to operate in 1954, then it wouldn't surprise me to see O'Connell sold. He's the best asset we have."

O'Connell spent Christmas Eve making celebrity appearances at five local movie theaters staging free shows for orphans and underprivileged kids. The day after Christmas, Danny was playing pinochle with friends at a local social club when a shirtless Frank "Ace" Molinaro rushed in with news. Nine years older than O'Connell, Molinaro was Danny's sandlot baseball coach. The Molinaros had been members of St. Bonaventure's parish since the late 19th century and "Ace" (the nickname sprang from a contest in which he had made 196 of 200 free throws) was a star basketball player at St. Bons and went on to teach and coach at the school for half a century. Molinaro's news—which he obtained from a radio report while lounging around the house in his underwear—was that O'Connell had been dealt to the Milwaukee Braves. "I might not have believed him," Danny said later, "if Ace had stopped to put on his shirt, but when I saw that he was so excited he ran over half-dressed, I knew it had to be true."

In return for O'Connell, the Pirates received veteran third baseman Sid Gordon, outfielder Sam Jethroe and pitchers Max Surkont, Curt Raydon, Fred Waters and Larry Lassalle—and a reported $100,000 (about $1.2 million in 2024.) It was the first six-for-one trade in major league history.

Danny was delighted. "They can't call it off, can they?" he joked to a reporter. "They'd better not. This is a wonderful Christmas present. It's the best break I've gotten in my baseball career. I'm with a team that has a good chance for the pennant."

The Braves were happy. "Getting O'Connell was a great deal for us," said Milwaukee manager Charlie Grimm. "He is a winning-type player: adds speed, gives us extra infield insurance and swings a potent bat. He's my second baseman…." Milwaukee fans were generally happy. Someone penned a celebratory ditty to mark the occasion, to the tune, naturally, of "Danny Boy:"

"Oh Danny Boy, the Braves, the Braves have beckoned you;

From Pirates' den to Braveland's Pennant heights.

When summer comes, and base hits must be falling;

It's you it's you will hit and we'll get by.

You'll come to bat with bases loaded Danny;

Bring in those runs to make us shout with glee.

And we will bend an elbow to you Danny;

Oh Danny Boy, Oh Danny Boy, we love you so."

Rickey was defensive and defiant. "I was looking to the future in this deal," he said. "I know the fans will not be pleased at O'Connell going to Milwaukee, but I have never lost out on a long-range transaction such as this one…O'Connell is a fine player. Not a great one in my estimation, but a good one." Rickey also insisted that pitchers Raydon and Lassalle were key to the trade, the players he really wanted. But Pirates fans weren't buying it.

The day after the trade, *Pittsburgh Sun-Telegraph* writer Chilly Doyle conducted an informal on-the-street poll, and concluded 90 percent of Pirates fans were generally livid. When Doyle suggested to one fan that six-for-one was a sound business ratio, the fellow replied "Listen wise guy, we can finish last with a guy like Danny and still look like a ballclub most of the time. Stick around and watch the 1954 jerks …".

As it turned out for Pittsburgh, Gordon, who produced a solid overall major league career, had a good year in 1954 with the Pirates, was traded in 1955 to the Giants and played sparingly that season before retiring; Jethroe got into two games in '54, then finished his career in the minors; Surkont won 16 games for the Pirates over two seasons before being traded to the Cardinals; Raydon spent four years in the minors before making it to Pittsburgh in 1958 for a single season; Waters appeared in 25 games over two years as a relief pitcher with the Pirates before being released, and LaSalle never made it to the majors. The Pirates finished last in both 1954 and 1955. Rickey and Haney were fired after the 1955 season. Haney, however, would surface again in O'Connell's life, and not in a good way.

The day after the trade was announced, Danny played with a St. Bonaventure alumni team in a basketball game against the current St. Bons team. The alums lost, with Danny being held to only six points. Paterson's *Evening News* carried a report on the game the next day, along with a photo spread of O'Connell celebrating his trade with friends and family, and a congratulatory column by Joe Gooter. "Danny is single," Gooter pointed out, "and goes on dates occasionally. There is a girl in Pittsburgh he prefers to the others. But he has revealed no definite plans yet."

Gooter was right about O'Connell preferring one girl, but he was wrong about her location. Actually, she was in a photo two columns over, smiling up at Danny as he held a bat in his hands. The caption described her as "a friend, Vera Sharkey."

CHAPTER 8 NOTES

Elsewhere in America *Greenville (SC) News*, Feb. 23, 1953, p. 4.

The Feb. 23 edition *Life* magazine, Vol. 34, No. 8, Feb. 23, 1953, p. 106.

Somewhere in Korea *Detroit Free Press*, Aug. 2, 1953, p. 1.

Just what O'Connell's *The Sporting News*, Jan. 21, 1953, p. 8.

"There will be" *Pittsburgh Sun-Telegraph*, Feb. 24, 1953, p. 18.

Haney's warning was *Sport* magazine, Vol. 16, No. 2 (Feb. 1954), p. 67.

In 1952, he Batista was overthrown in late December 1958 by communist insurgents. He fled the country and spent the rest of his life in the kind of exile only $300 million in plundered loot can bring, dying in 1973 in Spain. The communists were led by a would-be pitcher, Fidel Castro, whose baseball skills have been vastly inflated over the years. The fact is Castro wasn't even good enough to make his college team.

The team was housed *The Sporting News*, Feb. 11, 1953, p. 13.

While the proximity *The Sporting News*, April 1, 1953, p. 23; *Pittsburgh Sun-Telegraph*, March 18, 1953, p. 18.

Unsurprisingly, the Cuban *Pittsburgh Sun-Telegraph*, March 18, 1953, p. 18; Andrew O'Toole, *Branch Rickey in Pittsburgh*, p. 93. The Pirates' stay cost Cuba $53,000 (almost $600,000 in 2023.) The venture proved so distasteful to both parties that they agreed to forget about the two years left on the agreement. Pittsburgh trained in Fort Pierce, Florida in 1954.

Even the umpires *Pittsburgh Press*, March 18, 1953, p. 31.

In early April *The (Huntingdon, PA.) Daily News*, April 8, 1953, p. 4.

Nevada oddsmakers *Pittsburgh Press*, April 11, 1953, p. 6.

Even folks who *The Sporting News*, April 15, 1953, p. 14.

Not everyone was *The (Paterson NJ) Morning Call*, April 15, 1953, p. 12; O'Toole, op. cit., p. 101.

Much to the *Pittsburgh Post-Dispatch*, April 17, 1953, p. 22.

None of the three *The (Paterson NJ) News*, Nov. 23, 1953, p. 37.

What all this *Pittsburgh Sun-Telegraph*, July 1, 1953, p. 16.

In a game against Mizell would go on to become a three-term congressman from North Carolina. The "Vinegar Bend" nickname stems from the Alabama town where he began his baseball career. Just thought you should know.

"I guess I" *Sport* magazine, Vol. 16, No. 2 (Feb. 1954), p. 64; *Pittsburgh Post-Gazette*, May 6, 1953, p. 23.

Stanky's praise was *Pittsburgh Press*, July 8, 1953, p. 25; *The (Paterson NJ) News*, Aug. 12, 1953, p. 30; *Pittsburgh Sun-Telegraph*, May 10, 1953, p. 10; *The*

Sporting News, July 29, 1953, p. 6.

Danny naturally agreed *Sport* magazine, Vol. 16, No. 2 (Feb. 1954), p. 64.

And why shouldn't *Pittsburgh Press*, May 23, 1953; *Pittsburgh Press,* Sept. 19, 1953.

With the departure *Pittsburgh Sun-Telegraph*, July 1, 1953, p. 16.

He was almost *Pittsburgh Press*, July 12, 1953, p. 42.

In '53, fans Ibid.

As Dressen explained Ibid.

But nothing happened Ibid.

"It was a big" *Pittsburgh Post-Gazette*, May 20, 2003, p. 19.

There was actually *Pittsburgh Post-Gazette*, Sept. 17, 1953, p. 22.

Grissom quickly worked *Pittsburgh Press*, Sept. 20, 1953, p. 63.

For Mueller, whose *The Sporting News*, Sept. 30, 1953, p. 31.

Danny's day had For those who like a certain symmetry to life, Wurzberg's was the sponsor of the girls' softball teams that Danny's sister Alice led to three straight Paterson city championships in the early '50s.

"They are for" *The (Paterson NJ) Morning Call*, Sept. 18, 1953, p. 12.

"It's hard for" *The (Paterson NJ) News*, Sept. 21, 1953, p. 24.

Then he went *Sport* magazine, Vol. 16, No. 2 (Feb. 1954), p. 65.

In the last *The New York Times*, March 17, 1954, p. 35.

At home, Danny *The Sporting News*, Jan. 20, 1954, p. 4.

And there was Author interview of Alice O'Connell, Aug. 5, 2022.

In early November Ibid.

And in his *Newark (NJ) Star-Ledger*, Nov. 28, 1953, p. 8.

"I don't want" *The Sporting News*, Nov. 25, 1953, p. 12.

What Rickey left *Pittsburgh Press*, Dec. 7, 1953, p. 24.

O'Connell spent Christmas Eve *The (Paterson NJ) Morning Call*, Dec. 28, 1953, p. 22.

Danny was delighted *Pittsburgh Press*, Dec. 27, 1953, p. 25.

The Braves were *The Sporting News*, Jan. 6, 1954, p. 4.

Rickey was defensive Ibid.

The day after *Pittsburgh Sun-Telegraph*, Dec. 28, 1953, p. 10.

The day after *The (Paterson NJ) Evening News*, Dec. 28, 1953, p. 36.

CHAPTER 9

"IT WAS A LITTLE LIKE ROMEO AND JULIET"

VERA, JACK AND THE BRAVES' NEW WORLD

Precisely when and where Danny first met Vera is lost in the mists of time and North Jersey. We can narrow it down to sometime in the fall of 1953, after Danny's satisfying season with the Pirates had concluded and he went home to Paterson. Family lore has it that Ace Molinaro, Danny's sandlot coach and mentor/pal, was responsible. Molinaro somehow knew Madeline "Maddie" Sharkey, Vera's older sister. "Initially he [Ace] had been interested in fixing up my father with my Aunt Maddie," said Maureen O'Connell Hurley, "and my Aunt Maddie said 'no, no, I'm too old for him, but he should meet my younger sister.' And that's how the whole thing came to pass."

If it wasn't love at first sight, it was close, despite a somewhat bumpy start. According to Danny's younger brother Bob, the first date ended with Danny taking part in a bar fight. Other family members contend O'Connell was merely a spectator to the fracas. Either way, it's a good bet the evening was a novel experience for the 26-year-old Miss Sharkey.

"My mother and father, it was a little like Romeo and Juliet," said Danny O'Connell IV, the couple's oldest son. "When they were dating, he would take her home and my mom's family would be upstairs saying the rosary. My dad would go home to his house and they'd be playing pinochle and poker. My mom and dad had very different backgrounds."

Born in 1928, Veronica Cecilia Sharkey was one of six children, one of whom died in childhood. Her father, Dominic Thomas Sharkey, had arrived in America in 1912, at the age of 19, from an Irish village called Frenchpark, in County Roscommon. Dominic had a sixth-grade education, $44 (about $1,425 in 2024) in his pocket and a brother waiting for him in New Jersey.

By the time Dominic was 23, he was working as a farmhand in Montclair, New Jersey. By the time he was 24, he was in the U.S. Army as World War I dragged through its last year. And by the time he was 25, he was married. Delia Murray had arrived in America from Ireland's County Mayo a year after Dominic. Like her husband, the diminutive Delia was 19 when she stepped off the boat and had a sibling living in Jersey. Unlike Dominic, she had only $10 ($317) to her name. Delia found work as a cook for the family of a wealthy leather company executive.

Dominic and Delia married in 1919, prospered, and multiplied. The 1930 census reported Dominic working as a fireman and owning a house in Upper Montclair that he estimated was worth $12,000 (about $225,800 in 2024), which was a few thousand more than his neighbors reckoned their own houses were worth. For most of his working life, Dominic was the chief mechanical systems engineer for a county mental hospital.

And while Danny O'Connell was tearing up the playing fields of Stony Road, Vera Sharkey was trying a little of this, a little of that in the tonier environs of Upper Montclair—and doing pretty well at most of them. At Bloomfield Elementary, she belonged to the Junior Red Cross and performed in school piano recitals. At Montclair High, she was second soprano in the school choir and on the student council. "Little girl...big ideas," it read under her senior picture in the high school yearbook. "… She hopes to become a nurse." Instead, she enrolled after graduation in the Berkely Secretarial School. "It was the classic 1940s, 1950s thing for young women post-high school," her daughter Maureen said.

According to John O'Connell, their younger son, Danny and Vera became "engaged to be engaged" near the end of 1953 or at the beginning of 1954, before Danny reported to spring training. When the news came of Danny's acquisition by Milwaukee the day after Christmas, Vera was on hand at the O'Connell home for the celebration. "Danny believes he found the girl of his dreams," a Milwaukee paper chattered, "but won't announce the happy day. All he'll reveal is that his intended lives in Montclair, N.J., and does secretarial work. 'I think we'll announce our engagement during the summer,' the personable athlete says with a twinkle in his eye. Whoever becomes Mrs. O'Connell, she'll have to be a good cook. Danny loves steaks and roast beef."

In addition to cooking various cuts of dead cattle, she would also have to be able to put up with an often-overbearing mother-in-law. "My Grandmother Sharkey was just this lovely quiet religious woman," elder daughter Maureen recalled, "and Myrtle O'Connell was anything but that." An example of how domineering Myrtle could be: When Danny and Vera were contemplating names for their first-born. "My mom liked Kelly Ann and Grandma (O'Connell) hated it, and said things like 'what if she's fat and they call her Kelly Big Belly?' So they settled on Maureen Ann."

And Danny's future wife would need to become accustomed to being married to a man who was in love with a game she didn't know much about and which would consume a big piece of each year. Danny, meanwhile, who had called his trade to the Braves "the best Christmas present ever," would soon confront the truthfulness of an old truism: Be careful what you wish for.

As he stepped off the plane in his new baseball hometown, he had to have felt the pressure. More than the aching cold of a mid-January Milwaukee morning and the bite of a wind born over ice-choked Lake Michigan, Danny O'Connell must have felt the probing stabs of self-doubt. They had to be testing the walls of self-confidence he had built for himself over the past eight years of steady success as a ballplayer.

He smiled his cocky smile for the gaggle of reporters, photographers and club officials waiting at the bottom of the stairs and was whisked off to Milwaukee's year-old County Stadium. There he was fitted with his new uniform, with No. 4 on the back. He also signed a $13,000 contract ($153,700 in 2024) for the upcoming season, considerably more than the $8,500 ($99,000) he earned in 1953 and about five times more than the average American adult male would make in 1954.

"I am very happy with the contract offer," he told the gathered sportswriters, "and I know I am going to like playing here. The fans are wonderful and it will be great to play with a team like [Braves manager] Charlie Grimm has." Asked if he thought he would hit better with the Braves than the Pirates, Danny joked, "Yeah, I think so. I won't have to hit against those Braves pitchers and I'll get some cracks against the Pirates too. I might even get to .400, but I'll settle for .303." *Sentinel* writer Red Thisted added his own chipper assessment: "O'Connell likes Milwaukee, and Milwaukee is certainly going to like O'Connell."

Thisted and a chorus of his press box peers had been singing Danny's praises since O'Connell's trade from Pittsburgh had been announced. "Around the league they're suggesting that if Danny is as good as he was in 1953," *The Sporting News* said, "he will be the catalytic agent which sets off the already-torrid Milwaukee club and spurs it to a pennant."

But among the cheery predictions there were quieter queries. "The big question mark is how good will O'Connell be," an NEA wire service writer mused. "He's squarely on the spot—he has to make good. The question is: Will that cause him to press and try so hard that he may lose his easy confidence of the past?" Closer to home, columnist Bob Whiting of Paterson's *Morning Call* noted "the pressure will be on him from the start...At Pittsburgh he was easily the best man on the squad (in the infield)...He may still be at Milwaukee, but he'll have to prove it."

In addition to the expectations O'Connell would be the boost the Braves needed to push to the pennant, there was renewed speculation as to just how much Danny had cost Milwaukee. When the deal was announced, the conventional guess was O'Connell's price tag had been a heretofore unheard-of six players *and* $100,000 ($1.2 million in 2024) in cash.

But in late January, Barney Kalemenko of the *New York Journal-American* reported the Braves had forked over $200,000 ($2.4 million) to Pittsburgh for O'Connell. If so, that amount, even adjusting for inflation, would have been considerably more than the New York Yankees had paid the Boston Red Sox in 1920 for outfielder-pitcher Babe Ruth. Kalemenko's source was a New York Giants official who said the Giants had been willing "to go well over $100,000 as well as give up two or three good players" for O'Connell, only to be told it was too late and not enough. The report gained credibility when Gabe Paul, Cincinnati's general manager, confirmed the Reds had vainly offered Pittsburgh $150,000 and six players for Danny.

And then there was second base. Although he had started 1953 at second,

O'Connell played only 47 games there before switching to third base, which he preferred and where most baseball mavens thought he belonged. While signing his contract, Danny acknowledged, "I'll have to brush up on my double-play technique if second base is the place Grimm is going to use me, but it should not be difficult to make the switch from third."

Bravado aside, it's doubtful as sagacious a player as O'Connell could actually believe that. Playing second base requires a different skill set from playing third (the author said, as if he knew first-hand what he was talking about.) Third base requires a strong throwing arm; second base doesn't. It does require quick hands, which Danny had. What he didn't have and would need to acquire was mastery of the pivot—the ability to dance across the bag to catch a toss from another infielder and then throw to first for a double play—all the while avoiding a grown man running directly at you and doing his best to prevent you from accomplishing your task.

"If a second baseman doesn't pivot right," said Jackie Robinson, who like O'Connell had to learn the intricacies of playing second while in the big leagues, "he won't pivot often. He'll be belted, bruised, spiked and stepped-on, and he won't make double plays." O'Connell's ability to pivot adroitly was an open question as the 1954 season approached. "O'Connell is one of the future greats," said Billy Meyer, Danny's manager with the Pirates in 1950, "but I believe of the three infield positions, Danny is least effective at second. He's so much better at short or third." Bob Carpenter, president of the Philadelphia Phillies, said "there is no assurance that O'Connell can play second base. He's no cat at that spot...They [the Braves] are going to have their headaches."

O'Connell was certainly giving a headache to a Brave in Elkader, Iowa, a small town about 200 miles due west of Milwaukee. The Brave in question was Jack Dittmer. The 26-year-old son of an Elkader auto dealer, Dittmer in 1953 had been Milwaukee's starting second baseman. He intended to keep the job in 1954. "I don't concede O'Connell one thing," Dittmer said in early February. "He is a good ballplayer, but not what the writers are trying to make him out to be...By no means do I feel he is a cinch to play second over me, if I'm given the chance to beat him out in spring training."

Jack and Danny were polar opposites in almost everything. Dittmer was a corn-fed Midwesterner; O'Connell was a corned-beef-and-cabbage Jersey kid.

Dittmer was a left-handed hitter; Danny hit from the right side. Dittmer was a college graduate who had starred in three sports at the University of Iowa; O'Connell's "college" had consisted of four-and-a-half years in the minors. Dittmer got a $6,000 bonus (about $72,500 in 2024) to sign with the Braves at the age of 22; O'Connell got zilch to sign with the Dodgers at 17. Dittmer was excused from military duty due to asthma and hay fever; O'Connell served exactly two years in the Army (mostly playing baseball.) Dittmer was so laid-back some scouts erroneously believed he was lazy; O'Connell was so energetic you sometimes wanted to swat him on the nose with a rolled-up newspaper. Dittmer was strictly a second baseman; O'Connell did everything on the field but pitch, catch and sell popcorn.

Dittmer joined the Braves in 1952 in mid-season after a year and a half in the minors. He hit poorly but fielded well enough to win the job at second in 1953, the Braves' first season in Milwaukee. He hit .263 with eight homers and 63 RBIs, but also led National League second basemen in errors and had a fielding percentage that ranked fifth among the league's eight starters at second. He was nonetheless quite popular with fans and teammates because of his easy-going personality, good sense of humor—and an endearing and well-publicized incident in which he wrote a scorekeeper to ask that an error charged to his close pal, Milwaukee shortstop Johnny Logan, be charged to him instead. (The scorekeeper was not sufficiently moved to make the change.)

O'Connell was therefore fighting a headwind with both fans and Braves players when he arrived in Milwaukee. The aforementioned Logan, for example, whose wife had been a maid of honor at Dittmer's wedding, tried to be diplomatic. "Remember, I played alongside Jack Dittmer for two seasons," he said. "He's a great second baseman in my opinion. I think we were a smooth combination...Danny is a big-league infielder. So is Dittmer. All I can say is that may the better man win the second base job." For his part, Dittmer made no effort to be diplomatic. "I'm a better ballplayer—maybe I should say I'm a better second baseman—than O'Connell," he said. "If O'Connell is going to replace me at second, he'll do it only after a tough fight."

For his part, Danny avoided stirring up a storm while acknowledging he understood the situation. At a dinner in Pittsburgh, O'Connell said he wouldn't be taking his golf clubs to spring training. "I figured on going to [Florida] this year with the Pirates and taking my clubs along," he said. "I had my job sewed up. Now I have something to fight for with the Braves."

If Milwaukee sports writers were hoping for a prolonged, personal and unprofessional O'Connell-Dittmer spat when spring training opened in Bradenton, Florida, they were dismayed to find that the competition didn't seem to affect camaraderie between the two teammates. "They greeted each other warmly and carried on a few minutes of genial conversation," Lou Chapman of the *Sentinel* reported. "... After the workout, Jack even asked Danny if he could give him a lift" to the hotel.

Manager Charlie Grimm, however, was not at all reticent to keep the Braves' second base situation uncertain. "My biggest problem in spring training will be to pick a second baseman," Grimm said in early February. "Danny O'Connell will have a real fight on his hands to win the second base job from Jack Dittmer...Jack is my kind of player. He loves to win. He proved himself beyond all doubt in his first full season last year."

Whether Grimm was trying to boost Dittmer's spirits, warn O'Connell not to be complacent, pretend the money and players the front office had parted with for Danny didn't enter into his on-field decision-making, or really didn't know who would start, is uncertain. But "Jolly Cholly" Grimm was a more substantive baseball man than his nickname might indicate.

Charles John Grimm is one of the most deserving members of the Baseball Hall of Fame who *isn't* in the Hall of Fame. Born in St. Louis in 1898, Grimm quit school after sixth grade and became, by turns, a painter in a brewery, a ballpark peanut vendor and, at the age of 17, a major league first baseman. In a 19-year playing career Grimm produced more than 2,200 hits and was one of the better fielding first basemen of his time. As a big-league manager, he won two pennants with the Chicago Cubs and was instrumental in winning a third. He is in fact one of handful of Americans to have played at least 2,000 major league games and managed in at least 2,000 more.

He was also renowned for being a first-class entertainer: a banjo-strumming, joke-cracking fellow who livened up dull games by sliding into third base—while coaching—or lying down in the batter's box before the opposing pitcher had the chance to knock him down.

"That is Grimm's secret" as a manager, noted writer Tom Meany in his 1954 book *Milwaukee's Miracle Braves*: "complete cooperation from his players. He keeps them relaxed and happy. There is no Gestapo system. He does not second-guess on failures and mistakes."

But Grimm wasn't above playing his players. The day before spring training began, he penciled in O'Connell as his starting second baseman, batting fifth. The next day Dittmer played with the starters in the first intrasquad game. The pattern continued throughout the spring. Danny would play a game; Jack would play the next day. Neither made it easy for Grimm to choose. Through March 25, three weeks before the season began, O'Connell was hitting .354 in 17 games, with a homer, two doubles and two errors in 66 chances. Dittmer was hitting .357 with four doubles, a triple and zero errors in 46 chances.

O'Connell had the advantage of versatility. As various Braves were injured, Danny was there to sub. In one game, he played second, third and short. "It's great to have fellows like O'Connell around, "Grimm said. "He fits in anywhere you ask him to play. He also has the aggressive winning spirit I like in ballplayers. Whatever we paid for him was worth it."

Dittmer's hopes rose as the Braves broke camp and headed toward Milwaukee while playing a series of exhibition games in various Southern cities against the Boston Red Sox. While Danny slumped badly, Jack continued to hit at a torrid pace and field flawlessly. But Dittmer was competing not only against O'Connell, but the deal that had brought him to Milwaukee. "The Luck of the Irish—and a six-figure price tag—are serving Danny O'Connell pretty well this spring," wrote Chris Edmonds of the Associated Press. "Although Jack Dittmer...is out-hitting and out-fielding him, O'Connell seems a cinch to be in the starting lineup for the National League opener."

But Opening Day starting lineups are fragile things. That of the 1954 Braves was settled only after events that involved a player immortalized by a single at-bat; a future Hall of Famer who didn't like playing Danny O'Connell's favorite position at third; and a promising rookie who had spent 1953 in the minors, playing O'Connell's current position at second.

The first of these was the slugging outfielder Bobby Thomson, who on Oct.

3, 1951, launched "The Shot Heard 'Round the World:" a line-drive three-run ninth-inning homer that gave the New York Giants a 5-4 pennant-clinching playoff victory over the arch-rival Brooklyn Dodgers. The 30-year-old Thomson, whose nickname was "the Flying Scot" because he was fast on his feet and had been born in Glasgow Scotland, was a formidable hitter. From 1949 to 1953 he averaged 27 home runs and 102 RBIs per season and made three All-Star teams. But the Giants had a highly promising slugging outfielder returning from the Army—Willie Mays—and they needed pitching.

So on February 1, Thomson was traded to Milwaukee for four players and $50,000 ($584,000 in 2024). The key Brave going to New York was southpaw pitcher Johnny Antonelli, Danny O'Connell's buddy from the Army. In New York, he flourished, winning 21 games in 1954 as a member of the World Series-winning Giants, making the All-Star team and leading the league in shutouts, earned run average and winning percentage. Antonelli went on to complete a respectable 12-year major league career before retiring in 1961 to operate a tire dealership in Rochester New York. He and O'Connell would be teammates and pals on the Giants, and fans often confused the two darkly handsome men for each other when seeking autographs.

For his part, Thomson seemed the solution to the Braves' vacancy in left field, just as O'Connell had been ballyhooed as Milwaukee's second base savior. On March 13, however, in an exhibition game against the Yankees, Thomson slid awkwardly into second base. His right ankle snapped in three places. His season's start was postponed until well into July.

Enter Eddie Mathews, the Braves' slugging third baseman whose 512 career home runs would punch his ticket to Cooperstown. A temperamental 22-year-old, Mathews liked slugging: In his first two years in the majors, he smacked a total of 72 homers. But he wasn't crazy about third base: Over that two-year span, he made 49 errors, many of them on throws that threatened the well-being of those seated behind first base. For this he was sometimes booed, and he did not care for it. Even before Thomson was hurt, Mathews announced he'd rather play left field.

"It would be ideal for us," he told reporters. "Suppose Jack Dittmer goes good at second base and Danny O'Connell at third. Then my shift to left would be a natural." O'Connell, Mathews said, "is a good hitter as well as a fine defensive player." Dittmer, he continued, was "a good second baseman, one of the best in the National League at making the double play."

Manager Grimm wasn't buying it. "There has been some talk that O'Connell would play third base and Eddie Mathews would shift to the outfield," he said. "That's not true. Mathews is our third baseman." Besides, Grimm added, the Braves had a kid who in 1953 had played with Milwaukee's Triple A club in Jacksonville, Florida. "He is a second baseman but I've been told he can play the outfield too."

A lot of people thought the kid could. One of them was Branch Rickey, Danny's old boss at Pittsburgh. Watching a Braves-Pirates spring game with a Pittsburgh reporter, Rickey pointed to the kid, who was deceptively slender and looked so relaxed he might have been sleeping standing up. The kid was one of the best prospects around, Rickey said, then confided that the Braves had offered to trade him straight up for O'Connell. But Rickey turned the deal down because it did not involve any cash, which the Pirates desperately needed.

So 20-year-old Henry Aaron remained a Brave and would spend most of the 1954 season in left field, at least until he broke his ankle in early September. Mathews would stay at third base, and Danny O'Connell and Jack Dittmer would bite their fingernails all the way to Milwaukee.

The 1954 Milwaukee City Directory listed one barrel maker; 14 book stores; 77 bowling alleys; seven breweries; 29 sausage makers; 88 beer distributors—and at South 44th Street on the West Side, on the site of an old landfill—The Milwaukee Braves Baseball Club.

The Braves had moved to Milwaukee from Boston the year before. The reason was simple. From 1950 to 1952, the club had lost a total of more than $1 million (about $11.9 million in 2024.) And even though team owner Lou Perini had dropped out of school after eighth grade to haul water buckets at his father's construction sites, he was no fool. Boston wasn't big enough for two major league teams, and its heart belonged to the Red Sox.

Milwaukee, on the other hand, promised to love any team that would have it. Although it was America's 13th-largest city in 1953, it was known mostly for its heavily German-influenced culture, its bratwurst, its beer, its cheese and for being less than a hundred miles from the "real" city of Chicago. Of course there was more to Milwaukee than that. Beginning as a trading post in 1785, Milwaukee (the name came from an Algonquin word meaning "pleasant land") was a magnet for tens of thousands of German immigrants, followed by thousands of Polish newcomers. It was home to Allen-Bradley, a company that made electronics parts; A.O. Smith, which made steel frames for everything from Cadillacs to baby carriages; and Allis-Chalmers, a farm machinery manufacturer.

And Milwaukeeans prided themselves on producing oodles of *Gemütlichkeit*—loosely, "good fellowship"—and that was enough for Lou Perini. Louis Robert Perini was one of 14 children born to Italian immigrants. At 5'8" and 175 lbs., Perini was built a bit like one of the bulldozers his vast construction company owned. His threadbare neckties, calloused hands and leather-tanned face belied his status as one of the country's wealthiest builders of bridges, highways and dams. He was by his own admission not a baseball man. But by most accounts he was a pleasant, patient and a very astute businessman. And he knew business was highly unlikely to get better anytime soon for his Braves in Boston.

Milwaukee, however, offered real potential. At the top of its attractions was a brand new 36,000-seat stadium, built on a former garbage dump and having the distinction of being America's first publicly financed ballpark, paid for through a $5 million ($58.5 million) city-county bond issuance. The unimaginatively named County Stadium had ostensibly been built for the Milwaukee Brewers, the city's Triple A team that was the top farm club for the Braves. But everyone knew it was bait for the big leagues. In fact, local officials let it be known they were willing to lease the park to a big-league team for a paltry $1,000 a year.

Perini wanted to move, but not until the 1954 season. And he wanted to keep his desire quiet so at least a few Bostonians would show up for what would be the Braves' 1953 lame-duck season. But in 1952, Bill Veeck, owner of the hapless St. Louis Browns, let it be known he wanted to move the Browns to Milwaukee. Because the Braves controlled the city's minor league team, they controlled the major leagues' territorial rights to Milwaukee. That meant to move, Veeck needed Perini's assent as well as those of other major league team owners.

Perini wavered. Milwaukee's movers and shakers, from newspaper editorialists to brewery owner Fred Miller, began to put the squeeze on, demanding that either Perini move the Braves to town, or let Veeck move the Browns. Other major league owners much preferred it to be the Braves. They generally liked Perini, and generally loathed the outspoken and iconoclastic Veeck.

The club owner's dislike for Veeck was for a variety of reasons. These ranged from his integration of the American League in 1947 by signing Larry Doby (of Paterson, New Jersey) when Veeck owned the Cleveland Indians, to publicity stunts they deemed undignified, such as when Veeck sent 3'7" Eddie Gaedel to the plate in 1951 as a pinch-hitter. (Gaedel walked, was pinch-run for and promptly banned by American League President Will Harridge from ever appearing again.) Veeck also refused to wear a necktie, in large part just because he was expected to wear one. He was that kind of guy. There was also pressure on big league owners from some members of Congress, who broadly hinted that baseball's exemption from federal anti-trust laws might be jeopardized if the game didn't loosen up its geographic strictures and give the rest of America a chance to see big-league ball.

With just a few weeks before the start of the 1953 season, Perini decided to move. The Braves thus became the first major league team to switch cities in half a century. The move was so abrupt, tens of thousands of tickets and programs already printed for the "1953 Boston Braves" had to be destroyed even as their Milwaukee counterparts were being printed. More than a few of the National Pastime's pundits sneeringly suggested there was no need to print too many new tickets, as it was doubtful big-league baseball would go over in "Bushville."

"A big-league park doesn't make a big-league town," sniffed *Washington Post* columnist Shirley Povich, adding that Milwaukee was "the last outpost of the 10-cent bottle of beer," [as if there was something wrong with that,] and sniping that "Milwaukee fans are not noted for being fast with a buck...A bit more than half a century ago, Milwaukee was in the majors for a spell, but the city has been bush ever since."

Povich and his like-minded ilk, however, were forced to eat their words and wash them down with 10-cent beers. The Braves were a smash hit in their new home. In its last year in Boston, the team drew 281,278 spectators. In 1953, it hosted 1,826,397 fans, a new National League record. Moving his team to Milwaukee, Perini crowed late in the season, "is one of the greatest contributions to modern baseball."

If Milwaukee fans didn't invent the pre-game tailgate party, they perfected it. They arrived hours before the game to fill the parking lots with smoke from grilling brats and the heady aroma of Miller High Life, "the champagne of bottled beers." The libation wasn't confined to the parking lots. The Braves generously allowed spectators to bring beer into the stadium, even if it meant losing some concession sales. Third baseman Eddie Mathews joked that fans bought a minimum of three extra tickets—"one for the wife, one for the kid, and one for the cooler."

Seventy years later, one of the 1.8 million-plus people who poured into County Stadium in '53 still savored the experience of a major league game in 1950s America. "My dad took me to a double-header the day after July 4," recalled Bob Buege, a lifelong Milwaukee resident and author of several books on the Braves. "It was like magic; I had never seen anything like it before. I remember everyone was wearing suits and fedoras, and it seemed like most of the men were smoking cigars—don't see that anymore. The field was so green, it almost hurt your eyes. I remember the smells of the food, and the steady noise. I thought it was a palace."

A quarter of the 1953 attendees came from outside the Milwaukee metro region. One fellow drove 500 miles from Ely Minnesota, in a 1934 Plymouth, to see a game. When Perini learned of it, he gave the guy use of his personal box for two weeks. The Braves owner was even more munificent with Milwaukee government. Instead of the $1,000 in rent he legally owed for use of County Stadium, he paid $250,000.

Braves players were elevated to demi-god status. "The people of Milwaukee just couldn't do enough for you if you were a Brave," Hank Aaron recounted in his autobiography. "We'd go into a store to buy a suit and they wouldn't let us pay for it. They gave us free cigars, candy, eggs, jewelry, dry cleaning, haircuts." Star pitcher Warren Spahn was given a tractor; hometown outfielder

Andy Pafko a Cadillac, and outfielder Billy Bruton a down payment for a house.

On the eve of the 1954 season, with Milwaukee fans' high hopes of the team improving on its surprising 1953 second-place showing, there was no reason to think the "Bushville" love-fest wouldn't continue for any and all of the deserving Braves' players. Now Danny O'Connell had to become one of them.

The first step in achieving that goal came a few days before the season started. A crowd estimated at 30,000 turned out in Milwaukee for a 25-block ticker-tape parade to greet the Braves as they arrived from spring training. "While a chilly breeze whipped in off Lake Michigan," *The Sporting News* reported, "a lot of teenaged girls in blouses lined the curbs and cheered wildly as their heroes—Eddie Mathews, Joe Adcock and Danny O'Connell, the club's bachelors—rode by." Even the non-teenaged girls had cheers for the new Brave. "This smiling Irishman is destined to become a favorite of the baseball fans of Milwaukee and Wisconsin during the 1954 pennant race," one reporter breezily predicted.

Step two came on Opening Day in Cincinnati against the "Redlegs." (As a sign of the times, the team had formally changed its nickname from "Reds" to avoid any taint from the "communist menace," and didn't change it back until 1959.) Danny was in the starting lineup. Precisely why he started over the incumbent Dittmer was left unexplained, although it probably had a great deal to do with the Braves' front office being loath to give any indication it might have made a six-player, $200,000 mistake.

In any event, O'Connell shone even if the Braves didn't. Batting second, Danny singled twice, drove in three runs, scored once and handled five fielding chances flawlessly. Milwaukee's 9-8 loss was made more painful by leftfielder Andy Pafko's beaning by Redlegs pitcher Joe Nuxhall after Pafko had doubled three times. Pafko missed the next six games with a concussion, and escaped more serious injury only because he was one of five Braves who wore protective rubber-lined plastic caps. (The others were first baseman Joe Adcock, catcher Del Crandall, shortstop Johnny Logan...and O'Connell.)

Step three came in the home opener against St. Louis, before a noisy crowd of nearly 40,000 that included Danny's dad and uncle, who had flown six hours from Paterson in a small private plane owned and piloted by a prominent Paterson businessman. In his first four plate appearances, Danny singled, walked and laid down a sacrifice bunt. But he saved the best for the 11th inning. With centerfielder Bill Bruton on first, O'Connell singled sharply to right. Cardinals right fielder Rip Repulski briefly bobbled the ball, and Bruton, probably the fastest player in the league, scored all the way from first. The cherry on top for Danny was taking part in four double plays, one of them in the ninth and one in the 10th.

Driving in the winning run on Opening Day at home was almost certainly enough to win over the hearts and minds of Milwaukeeans, but O'Connell was just getting started. "Danny O'Connell pulled a trick the Globetrotters could use," the *Milwaukee Sentinel* marveled after the next game. "In the fourth inning on Johnny Temple's grounder, with Jim Greengrass on first, Danny picked up the ball and flipped it backhanded to Johnny Logan" for the force-out. "It was a dazzling maneuver."

O'Connell finished the season's first week with hits in all five games for a .364 average. That was good for a $250 ($2,900 in 2024) gift certificate from Blatz Brewing as the "Brave of the Week." The certificate was "redeemable at any retail store in Milwaukee," and not just for beer. He had at least one hit in 15 of the first 17 games, ending the month at .345. When Bruton came down with a nasty virus and Mathews moved—temporarily—to fill the outfield vacancy, Danny filled in at third. Over those first 17 games, he handled 110 chances with zero errors.

His off-the-field charms were also beguiling teammates and reporters as well as ordinary citizens: "Danny has a flair for dry comedy and saves clippings of old jokes which he resurrects at the most propitious times"..."The new Braves infielder has a rich tenor voice that would be the pride of all Killarney"..."Braves teammates of Danny O'Connell are sure they're hearing singer Eddie Fisher when they close their eyes and listen to Danny render 'O Mein Papa.'"

He had also already established himself as the best hearts, fan tan and gin rummy player on the team (poker was not allowed in the Braves clubhouse), and teammates paid him the ultimate compliment for a pro athlete—they ragged on him. "O'Connell is the kind of guy who may look knock-kneed out there on the field to an opposing player," George "Catfish" Metkovich, Danny's roommate on the team, told a reporter. "His uniform doesn't fit and he doesn't appear too bright a guy. But you realize Danny's real worth when he's on your team...He's smart and dangerous every time he takes a cut at the plate." (This from a guy whose nickname was bestowed upon him by the peerless Casey Stengel because Metkovich once injured himself stepping on a catfish.)

O'Connell parlayed his entertainment skills into endorsements that paid cash and also made gratis appearances around town that enhanced his popularity. He was one of 11 Braves whose likenesses and autographs were imprinted on tee-shirts sold by the W.T. Grant variety store chain. He appeared in ads for Sherkow Formal Wear sporting a classy dinner jacket. Over the course of a single week, he was at Gimbel's Department Store to sign copies of a book about the Braves, at the grand opening of a batting range owned by Eddie Mathews, and at Carroll University for an athletic awards banquet. And he appeared as a regular panelist with other Braves players on WTMJ's new quiz show, *Play Ball.*

Except for the fact the Braves got off to a slow start, Danny's new professional life in Milwaukee was going swimmingly. And then things began to go sideways. On May 1, Mathews returned to third base and O'Connell went back to the still-unfamiliar environs of second. Perhaps coincidentally—perhaps not—he also quit hitting. Over the first 15 games of the month, Danny went an anemic 12 for 61, a .197 average.

Part of the cause was self-generated pressure. Playing in Pittsburgh for the first time since being traded by the Pirates, O'Connell went 0-12 over three games and made three errors. "Danny's just in one of those slumps," manager Grimm shrugged after the third game, "and a few days' rest should do the trick. The kid may have been pressing a bit too hard being back in Pittsburgh, but he's too good a ballplayer for me to worry about."

But not too good for the gentlemen of the press. In the *Journal,* the slumping O'Connell was now "the Braves' $200,000 second baseman." In the *Sentinel,* he was "the Dead-End Kid," or "the expensive acquisition from the Pirates." Associated Press scribe Chris Edmonds wrote that "the tavern talk around town is that the Braves got the short end of the winter dealings...One of the saddest lads in the Braves' clubhouse the past fortnight has been Danny O'Connell, the $200,000 boy from Pittsburgh...The Irish Thrush who's been having trouble at the plate has been singing nothing but the blues."

After Pittsburgh, Danny flew to New York ahead of the rest of the team so he could make a surprise appearance at his high school reunion in Paterson. "His classmates were thrilled," *The Morning Call* reported. "Referring to his present hitting slump, Danny felt sure that seeing his former classmates again would be an ample morale-builder." It wasn't. Despite the presence of Vera and his folks at two games against the Giants, O'Connell went 0-8. "I was up there tighter than a drum," he moaned afterward. "Next time we go East, I'm going to tell the folks to stay home."

Grimm, who three days earlier had professed not to be concerned about O'Connell, was worried enough when the Braves moved on to Philadelphia to announce a major shakeup. Henceforth, he decreed, O'Connell would sit against right-handed pitchers and Dittmer would start in those games. So Danny sat—for all of one game. Dittmer went none for five, dropping his season's average to an almost-invisible .150, and O'Connell returned to the lineup.

For the rest of May, Danny hit .293, More important, the Braves won nine of the month's last 11 games to start June in first place, 1.5 games ahead of the Giants, Dodgers and Phillies. But Milwaukee's lead was short-lived and the glow of the season's first weeks dimmed considerably for both the team and O'Connell.

For most of the rest of the season, Danny was remarkably consistent. At the end of May, he was hitting .275; at the end of June, .278; on July 31, .276; on Aug. 30, .279 and at the end of the season, .279. That was a batting average considered in 1954 between respectable and could-be-better, although in 2022 it would have been good for 10th-highest in the National League. In a statistical measure deemed more important in 2024, O'Connell's WAR (Wins Above Replacement) was 3.1, or fourth on the team among non-pitchers. (Loosely defined, WAR estimates the number of wins a player adds to the team above what a replacement player would add. I'm pretty sure it's derived through various algebraic formulas and waving chicken bones over the *Sports Illustrated* swimsuit issue.)

Only Johnny Logan appeared in more games for Milwaukee than O'Connell. Danny led the team in doubles and sacrifices and was third in hits. He was third in the league in fielding percentage for second basemen, and also in "total fielding runs above average," a complex stat that measures how many runs a player saved his team defensively above the league average. Among third basemen in that category, he was first. And he was versatile: 102 games at second base, 36 at third, eight at first and one at shortstop.

As for the Braves, they were tantalizingly and frustratingly good but not great. Milwaukee won 10 in a row three times and lost as many as five in a row only twice. But the team was only average when it came to close games, losing 12 of 20 extra-inning contests and 26 of 50 one-run games. They finished a respectable 89-65, good for third place, eight games behind the Giants and three behind the Dodgers.

While disappointed in the results, Milwaukee fans lost none of their enthusiasm. Thanks in part to the addition of 7,000 seats at County Stadium, by the end of August the Braves broke the National League attendance mark they had set the year before, and ended up drawing an impressive 2.1 million in a metropolitan region of 836,000.

Despite playing reasonably well with a good major league team in front of large crowds for the first time in his career, however, 1954 was not all beer and skittles for O'Connell. June 22, for example, had its distractions. The Paterson *Evening News* carried a photo that day of Danny and Vera, along with the news the couple had formally announced their engagement the night before at a private dinner with their families. Later that day, about 1,200 Republicans from Danny's home county of Passaic descended on the Polo Grounds for a game between the Braves and Giants and to fete both Danny and a local congressman running for his sixth term. O'Connell received a gift certificate and an engraved wallet. The now-officially engaged Vera got "a huge corsage," and Danny's folks got their picture in the paper with the congressman.

On the field, however, Danny did not rise to the occasion, going two for

11 in three games in New York. In fact, he was consistently bad in front of the home folks who crossed the Hudson to see him play in '54. In 11 games, he hit a paltry .184 at the Polo Grounds.

Much more distressing than hometown distractions was the $200,000/ six-player price tag still hanging from Danny's neck. In late June, *Sentinel* writer Red Thisted labeled Mathews, catcher Del Crandall and O'Connell as the Braves' "major disappointments." At the time, Mathews was hitting .240, Crandall .210—and O'Connell .278. By the end of July, the local newspapers were speculating that Milwaukee would get rid of the popular Dittmer "because Danny O'Connell beat him out for second and the Braves paid too much for O'Connell to let him go."

At the end of July, manager Grimm offered a lengthy defense of Danny after a spate of shots from the press and a scattering of boos from the stands. "Remember," Grimm said, "he's had to familiarize himself with a brand-new position and he's had to make adjustments from playing with a last-place club to a first-division team...and bear in mind that the pressure has been on him from the standpoint of the fans. The boy we had at second last year, Jack Dittmer, is a fine player himself. What's more, Jack was very well-liked by the Milwaukee fans, and it's rough to replace someone else in their affections."

Grimm also made a startling admission: He had been too hasty at the start of the season, he said, in refusing to put Eddie Mathews in left field after Bobby Thomson was injured and letting O'Connell play third. "There's no question in my mind that O'Connell is the best third baseman in the league."

A few weeks after Grimm's apologia, he fanned the flames of the team's second base controversy. When Mathews split a finger at the end of August, Grimm moved O'Connell to third and inserted Dittmer at second. Jack promptly went on a tear with his bat, going 19 for 40 (.475) with five home runs and 11 RBIs. When Mathews came back, O'Connell went to the bench."Jack Dittmer has been sensational—both afield and at bat since I put him in there," Grimm told an Iowa newspaper. "He's been so good that I've had to keep O'Connell on the bench most of the time."

Dittmer was gratified to the point of smugness. "Frankly, I expected to be on the bench when the Braves bought Danny O'Connell," Dittmer contended. "A ball club doesn't put out so much for a player and not figure to use him regularly. But I never lost confidence. I knew I had the stuff and that someday I could prove it." Then he promptly stopped proving it. In the season's last 19 games, Dittmer hit .233 with no home runs, to finish the season at a mediocre .245. O'Connell, meanwhile, played in only 13 of the last 19, mainly as a pinch hitter and defensive substitute. That included eight games at first base, which he played using his fielder's glove and not a first baseman's mitt.

He lost his temper at least once. In a rain-soaked game against the Dodgers, O'Connell was ejected by umpire Frank Secory "for uncomplimentary remarks about his [Secory's] eyesight." In the same game, he squawked long and loud when umpires refused to stop the game because of the rain, only to call it the next inning after Brooklyn had taken the lead and the game had progressed enough to officially become a Dodger victory. For complaining, O'Connell was fined $25 ($290 in 2024) by the league.

But he generally kept his sense of humor despite his diminished role. In a meaningless game at the end of the year against Cincinnati, the umpires gathered near first to discuss a possible interference call against a Redlegs runner. Danny, who was playing first base, wandered over to the huddle. When one of the umps asked what he thought he was doing, O'Connell replied "I just want to hear what you're saying in a spot like this. I may want to be an umpire someday."

"That was good enough for a laugh," the *Sentinel* reported, "but not good enough to keep Danny in the conversation."

With the season over, O'Connell began the 1950s ballplayer's post-season ritual of trying to make money at other occupations. For Danny, this was particularly necessary because he moved out of the house he had bought his folks and into a rented place in Fair Lawn, about eight miles away. He and Vera had also set a January 22 1955 date for their wedding.

The Braves' third-place share of World Series receipts came to $1,227.67 apiece (or $14,346 in 2024 dollars.) There was a few hundred bucks from a barnstorming tour through the Northeast and Canada cut short by bad weather.

The lost barnstorming money was made up when a cadre of civic organizations hired O'Connell and other major leaguers to give speeches to youth groups around the country on the theme that playing sports would make kids upright citizens.

But his main offseason job was provided by Milwaukee brewer Fred Miller. It consisted of traveling to various Eastern cities and showing a film called "The Milwaukee Story" and talking up the town. "This is a good job," O'Connell told a Pittsburgh reporter. "I am out mostly in the evenings and played a lot of golf until it got too cold."

Danny being Danny, he directly answered a question about the 1955 season, even at the risk of leading Milwaukee fans into thinking he didn't want to return. "I might be traded," he said. "I've already read where [pitcher] Chet Nichols and myself are going to St. Louis for [second baseman] Red Schoendienst...There's been talk that maybe the Phillies will get me. I wouldn't mind either place. You have to take those things when they happen in baseball."

In Elkader Iowa, meanwhile, Jack Dittmer was selling cars at his dad's dealership and stewing about his second-string status. "I won't be satisfied to come back to the Braves as just a spare infielder," he said. "All I ask is to be given an equal chance to make the team for next season. If given that...then I will have no kick coming, but I wouldn't like to put in another year like last season."

Neither, said O'Connell, would he. "I meet people who say I only had a fair season with the Braves," he wrote to the *Milwaukee Journal*. "Well, I know I can do much better. And I'll prove it next year."

CHAPTER 9 NOTES

Precisely when and Much of the material for this section was gleaned through in-person, e-mail and telephone interviews of Danny and Vera's children: Maureen O'Connell Hurley, Daniel F. O'Connell IV, Nancy O'Connell Mellin and John O'Connell, as well as Danny's sister and brother, Alice O'Connell and John O'Connell.

According to John *Milwaukee Sentinel*, March 3, 1954, p. 5.

"I am very" *Milwaukee Sentinel*, Jan. 17, 1954, p. 39; *Wisconsin (Madison) State Journal*, Jan. 17, 1954, p. 42.

Thisted and a *The Sporting News*, Jan. 20, 1954, p. 3.

But among the *Mount Olive (NJ) Chronicle*, March 13, 1954; *The (Paterson NJ) Morning Call*, Jan. 18, 1954, p. 16.

And then there *Milwaukee Sentinel*, Jan. 17, 1954, p. 39.

"If a second baseman" Roger Khan and Al Helford (eds.) *The (1954) Mutual Baseball Almanac*, p. 22; *The Sporting News,* March 24, 1954, p. 25; *The Sporting News*, Jan. 20, 1954.

O'Connell was certainly *The Sporting News,* Feb. 10, 1954, p. 31.

O'Connell was therefore *Milwaukee Journal*, Jan. 4, 1954, p. 26; *Milwaukee Journal*, Feb. 27, 1954, p. 10.

If Milwaukee sports *Milwaukee Sentinel*, Feb. 27, 1954, p. 15.

Manager Charlie Grimm *Milwaukee Journal*, Feb. 10, 1954, p. 47.

"That is Grimm's" Tom Meany, *Milwaukee's Miracle Braves*, p. 45.

O'Connell had the *Pittsburgh Post-Gazette*, March 24, 1954, p. 16.

"The Luck of" *The (Appleton, Wisc.) Post-Crescent*, April 6, 1954, p. 23.

So on Feb. Antonelli would go 21-7 for the World-Series-winning Giants in 1954, leading the league in winning percentage, shutouts and earned run average.

"It would be" *Milwaukee Sentinel*, Jan. 17, 1954, p. 16; *Milwaukee Journal*, Jan. 18, 1954, p. 27.

Manager Grimm wasn't *Janesville (Wisc.) Daily Gazette*, Feb. 9, 1954, p. 10.

Milwaukee however, offered The bonds were paid off in 1964, two years after Perini sold the club and 18 months before the Braves skipped town for Atlanta.

The club owners' The Browns were allowed by other owners to move to Baltimore for the 1954 season, but only on the condition that Veeck sell the team. He resurfaced eventually, buying the Chicago White Sox later in the decade and enjoying a last laugh of sorts when the White Sox won the 1959 A.L. pennant.

"A big-league park" John Klima, *Bushville Wins!*, p. 12.

Povich and his *The Sporting News*, Sept. 8, 1953, p. 8

Seventy years later, Author telephone interview of Bob Buege, March 12, 2022.

A quarter of Lou Perini letter to Wm. J. Brandt, Aug. 2, 1953, Baseball Hall of Fame Archives.

Braves players were Henry Aaron, *I Had a Hammer*, p. 126.

The first step *The Sporting News*, April 21, 1954, p. 8; *Waukesha (Wisc.) Daily Freeman*, March 18, 1954, p. 12.

Driving in the *Milwaukee Sentinel*, April 18, 1954, p. 43.

His off-the-field *Milwaukee Sentinel*, March 21, 1954, p. 48; *Milwaukee Sentinel,* March 28, 1954, p. 25.

He had also *Milwaukee Sentinel,* March 21, 1954, p. 48.

Part of the cause *Milwaukee Sentinel*, May 17, 1954, p. 20.

But not too *Milwaukee Journal*, May 18, 1954, p. 39; *Milwaukee Sentinel*, March 18, 1954, p. 20*; Eau Claire (Wisc.) Daily Telegraph,* May 18, 1954, p. 4; *Janesville (Wisc.) Daily Gazette*, March 19, 1954, p. 11.

After Pittsburgh, Danny *The (Paterson NJ) Morning Call*, May 17, 1954, p. 15; *Milwaukee Sentinel*, May 21, 1954, p. 42.

Grimm, who three *The (Wisconsin Rapids, Wisc.) Daily Tribune*, May 19, 1954, p. 8.

Despite playing reasonably *The (Paterson NJ) Evening News*, June 23, 1954, p. 41.

Much more distressing *Milwaukee Sentinel*, June 28, 1954, p. 44; *Green Bay(Wisc.) Press-Gazette*, July 30, 1954, p. 18.

At the end *Milwaukee Journal*, Aug. 1, 1954, p. 32.

Grimm also made Ibid.

A few weeks after *Des Moines Register*, Sept. 17, 1954, p. 17.

Dittmer was gratified *Milwaukee Sentinel*, Sept. 8, 1954, p. 18.

He lost his *Milwaukee Sentinel*, Sept. 11, 1954, p. 14.

But he generally *Milwaukee Sentinel*, Sept. 24, 1954, p. 27.

But his main *Pittsburgh Post-Gazette*, Dec. 3, 1954, p. 23.

Danny being Danny Ibid.

In Elkader Iowa, *Milwaukee Journal*, Dec. 5, 1954, p. 71.

Neither, said O'Connell, Ibid

CHAPTER 10

"O'CONNELL'S A NATURAL POP-OFF"

TALKING TOO MUCH AND HITTING TOO LITTLE

It was an interesting year for Danny O'Connell baseball cards. It was a generally awful year for Danny O'Connell. The single best event of 1955 for Danny, in fact, came just 22 days into the year.

It occurred on a snowy Saturday at St. Cassian Roman Catholic Church in Montclair New Jersey. Sometime before noon, Veronica Cecilia Sharkey and Daniel Francis O'Connell III were wed. "The bride was attired in a blush satin gown with an Alencon lace bodice," reported one of the several newspapers that covered the event. "Her French tulle veil fell from a coronet headpiece and she carried a bouquet of mixed winter blossoms." Danny wore a tuxedo he had modeled in a newspaper ad for a Milwaukee formal wear store.

Among Vera's bridesmaids were Danny's sister Alice as well as Vera's own sisters. Danny's best man was John Monopoli, a childhood pal from the old Stony Road neighborhood, and one of his ushers was Vera's brother, Cliff Sharkey. At the reception, which was hosted by the Montclair Women's Club, the band played "Take Me Out to the Ball Game." The song was easily one of Danny's top 10 baseball-related moments of the year.

The newlyweds spent their honeymoon on a wedding cruise to Bermuda, followed by a few days at Grossinger's, the most famous of the "kosher" resorts in the heart of the "Borscht Belt" of hotels in the Catskill Mountains of New York. These catered primarily to a Jewish clientele often banned from other resorts. Grossinger's was famous as a breeding ground for future great comedians and its generous mealtime portions, both of which Danny enjoyed immensely. According to the couple's eldest child, Maureen O'Connell Hurley, "my dad didn't like the beach. He hated getting sand all over him." So Danny probably enjoyed Grossinger's more than Bermuda.

Whichever he preferred, O'Connell could afford to splurge a bit. Despite under-performing in the eyes of Braves officials in 1954, the team gave Danny a $2,000 raise ($22,500 in 2024) over the $13,000 ($146,000) he collected in 1954. That was a comfortable 15.4 percent salary hike. By comparison, the average American family's income was $4,400 in 1955, up just 6 percent from the year before.

But money had never been much of a motivating factor for O'Connell when it came to baseball. He truly loved playing the game, and even more so when he played it well. In the upcoming season, he was determined to improve his pretty-good performance of the year before. "I'm afraid my hitting was somewhat of a disappointment last year," he said. "But I've done a lot of practice swinging with a heavy bat over the winter, and I'm sure it'll be a different story this year. Don't be surprised if I hit over .300."

When not getting married or swinging a heavy bat over the winter, Danny also did a lot of talking, to service clubs, youth baseball groups and just about any lunch or dinner crowd that invited him. And one night about two weeks before he was wed, he talked too much.

Speaking to a business group in Waterbury Connecticut, about 30 miles southwest of Hartford, O'Connell was asked about the perception the Braves were a bit too laid-back in their play. "I think our lack of fire might be due to our easy-going manager, Charlie Grimm," Danny responded with typical guileless candor. "Charlie is a wonderful guy, but sometimes I think he didn't get us mad enough to win the pennant."

O'Connell compounded his verbal faux pas by criticizing Braves pitchers for not knocking down opposing batters enough after Milwaukee hitters were plunked. "Our batters were thrown at plenty by rivals last season and except for Lew Burdette, our pitchers didn't reciprocate," Danny said. "They just wouldn't throw dusters. We took plenty and didn't dish it out in return. If we had dished it out, I think we could have won instead of finishing third."

Milwaukee pitchers, at least publicly, ignored O'Connell's observations about their collective timidity after his comments somehow found their way into *The Sporting News*. But Grimm responded with measured anger. "That's O'Connell's version," he told one newspaper. "It's his privilege if he wants to pop off, and his popping off won't make me change my system of managing. I think I'm aggressive in my own way."

To another reporter, Grimm said it "was the first time in all my years of managing that a player of mine has popped off publicly. But I'm not upset," he insisted. "... The sad part of it all is that it may not do O'Connell any good with the fans if he doesn't go well in the field. It certainly won't bother me. I don't hold a grudge."

Wisconsin sportswriters' reactions varied. *Wisconsin State Journal* columnist Henry McCormick huffed that "O'Connell's implied criticism of Grimm is in bad taste for a fellow who fell so far below expectations during the season he is discussing." *Milwaukee Sentinel* sports editor Lloyd Larson, on the other hand, opined that Danny was probably misquoted, since O'Connell had never bad-mouthed Grimm within anyone's hearing during the '54 season. Closer to home, *Hackensack Record* columnist Al Del Greco pointed out the obvious: "O'Connell's a natural pop-off—not a mean one either. But he can get himself in a mess of trouble."

As for Danny, he ruefully tried to downplay the incident while sending a letter of apology to Grimm. "That quote of mine out of Waterbury the other day was just one of those things," he said. "... I didn't mean anything by it, but there's apparently a difference when you just say something and it comes out in cold black and white."

Danny O'Connell's "cold black and white" print pop-off problems were infinitesimal compared to America's centuries-old Black and White racial issues that continued to fester in the mid-1950s. Nine decades had passed since a horrific fratricidal war and a trio of constitutional amendments had begun the process of expiation from the nation's "Original Sin" of slavery. More than two million African-Americans had served in World War II and the Korean War, fighting totalitarian foreign governments rooted in genocide, xenophobia and religious intolerance.

And yet in Wichita, Kansas, an eight-year-old girl had to walk or ride a bus more than two miles to attend a public school when there was another public school just seven blocks from her home. In Montgomery, Alabama, a 42-year-old seamstress was arrested for refusing to give up the public bus seat she had paid for, simply to convenience another passenger deemed more worthy in the eyes of local law. And near the tiny town of Drew, Mississippi, a 14-year-old boy was murdered for allegedly getting fresh with the woman clerk of a country store.

The commonality of Linda Carol Brown, Rosa Parks and Emmett Till was their race. They were American citizens who in the parlance of the time were "Negroes," "coloreds," or any of a host of derogatory epithets. Even African-Americans who were generally admired for some talent or other were invariably described in the media to make it clear they were other than white: "the dusky slugger" Willie Mays; "the ebony crooner" Nat King Cole, "the colored novelist" James Baldwin.

More than three centuries after enslaved Africans arrived in Virginia from Africa, America was still a country beset by racism. But America's greatness as a nation has never rested on its nobility or distinction at any given point in its history, but in its striving to be better than it was. So it was that on May 17, 1954, the United States Supreme Court unanimously decreed it was illogical, immoral and most importantly unconstitutional to force Linda Carol Brown to attend a school far from her home simply because of her skin color.

The court's decision overturned an 1896 Supreme Court ruling that asserted racial segregation of public facilities was permissible if facilities of equal quality were made available to each race—a situation that in the real world very rarely, if ever, occurred. In its 1954 decision, the court ruled that even the provision of "separate but equal" institutions was intrinsically harmful. "To separate (black children) from others of similar age and qualifications solely because of their race generates a feeling of inferiority as to their status in the community that may affect their hearts and minds in a way unlikely to ever be undone," wrote Chief Justice Earl Warren...."We conclude that in the field of education the doctrine of 'separate but equal' has no place."

Precisely 468 days after the court's ruling, while Danny O'Connell and the Braves were losing a doubleheader to the Pirates in Pittsburgh, two white men savagely beat a 14-year-old Black boy near a rural Mississippi town because he had reportedly said "bye baby" to a white woman clerk after buying two cents' worth of bubble gum. When Emmett Till refused to acknowledge he was inferior to the men after the beating, one of them shot him in the head. They then tied a 72-pound mill fan around his neck with barbed wire and dumped his body in a river.

The killers were acquitted after a farcical trial. They even bragged about their crime in a national magazine that shamefully paid them for their interviews. But the brutality of the killing and the blatant miscarriage of justice galvanized the nation's nascent civil rights movement.

Ninety-five days after Till's murder, Rosa Parks was on her way home from a long day at the Montgomery department store where she worked. The bus she was on was full, so when several white people boarded, Parks and three other African Americans were ordered by the driver to give up their seats and stand toward the back of the bus. But Parks was tired from work, and tired of being pushed around. She refused, and was subsequently arrested and fined $14 ($164 in 2024.) "I thought of Emmett Till," she recalled later, "and I just couldn't go back."

Parks' arrest sparked a boycott of the transit system by Montgomery's African-American community, which made up a sizeable portion of the bus company's clientele. It took more than a year, but coupled with a U.S. Supreme Court decision that declared racial segregation on public transit unconstitutional, the boycott worked. The bus company dropped its race-based seating charts in 1957. The boycott also served to bring a young and charismatic Atlanta clergyman, Martin Luther King Jr., to the forefront of the Civil Rights Movement that would grip the country in the following decade.

Baseball, meanwhile, justifiably congratulated itself on being the first major American cultural institution to integrate its workforce (and has somewhat tediously continued to pat itself on the back in the succeeding decades since.) But the initial integration between the foul lines did not magically translate to "Kumbaya" in the clubhouse.

"The feeling among many people is that after Jackie Robinson and Larry Doby integrated baseball, it was easy for the Black ballplayers who followed," said Jim "Mudcat" Grant, a solid big-league pitcher for 14 seasons, from 1958 to 1971. "That's bullshit. Major League baseball, from the beginning, was slow to react to the problems of Black players and that never changed."

Henry Aaron recalled the indignities of being referred to in the papers as "Stepan Fetchit" by Braves manager Charlie Grimm, or hearing a white teammate jokingly asking "what's black and catches flies? The Braves' outfield." He remembered the humiliation of being told to go to the back of the Dairy Queen across the street from Milwaukee's spring training facility in Bradenton, Florida, if he wanted an ice cream cone, or sharing an apartment with other Black and Latin American players above the garage of a local school teacher while their white teammates rented apartments or stayed at the team hotel.

"I soon realized I could never be just another major-league player," Aaron wrote in his autobiography. "I was a Black player, and that meant I would be separate most of the time from most of the players on the team."

There were small victories. Before spring training opened in '55, for example, several Black players were invited to play in the National Baseball Players Golf Tournament in Miami, at a course normally open to African Americans "only on Mondays, when business is off," a New Jersey paper noted. "... We're waiting for reaction from Miami." Fortunately, none came.

Still, it took 12 years after Jackie Robinson debuted with the Brooklyn Dodgers in 1947 for the last major league team to field an African American. That was the Boston Red Sox, owned by Tom Yawkey, perhaps the most unabashedly racist owner of a big-league club. Even the mighty Yankees— fearful, in the words of George Weiss, their general manager, that wealthy box seat patrons might refuse "to sit with niggers"—did not sign a Black player until 1955.

"When I finally get a nigger," Yankees manager Casey Stengel remarked, "I get the only one who can't run." Stengel's reference was to catcher-outfielder Elston Howard, whom Stengel referred to as "Eightball." Howard's 20-year career in the Negro and Major Leagues featured 12 All-Star appearances and a Most Valuable Player award—and proved that Stengel, who sometimes enjoyed pretending to be an idiot, wasn't always pretending.

O'Connell's second spring training with the Braves was markedly different

Danny's first taste of celebrity:
getting his photo in the
local paper as a 14-year-old
sophomore on the varsity
baseball team.
*–The (Paterson NJ.)
Morning Call.*

DAN O'CONNELL
. . . starred for Bons

Danny's high school
yearbook picture.
*–Courtesy St. Bonaventure's
Catholic Church, Paterson,
New Jersey.*

petition under Coach Bob Dia-
mond's administration.
O'Connell Shines
At Pennington Park, St. Bon's
downed the Academy team, 2-0.
The winning team scored 1 in

DANIEL F. O'CONNELL

Year Book Sports Editor
Dramatics 4
Basketball 2, 3, 4
Baseball 1, 2, 3, 4

Any and all of Bon's students who have
seen Danny dashing to and fro on the basketball court will tell you of his alertness,
speed, and all-round ability. A group of
happy faces are always around Danny testifying to his numerous attractions and enjoying the gems of his wit.

Veronica Sharkey
VERA
Little girl . . . big ideas . . .
she adores driving (under
B. A.'s supervision) . . .
hopes to become a nurse.

Veronica Sharkey's senior
Montclair High School yearbook
picture. No one seems to know
who "B.A." referred to in the
caption.
–*Montclair High School
1945 yearbook.*

A shirtless Danny looks on at
practice, 1946.
–*The (Paterson NJ) Evening News.*

St. Bonaventure's 1946 championship basketball squad. That's Danny–St. Bon's star
player–with the ball in the front row.
–*Courtesy St. Bonaventure's Catholic Church, Paterson, New Jersey.*

A 19-year-old Danny sporting his Greenville (S.C.)
Spinners uniform in his third season in pro baseball.
His perpetual 5 o'clock shadow, which as an adult
showed up about 5 a.m., has not yet appeared.
–*Courtesy of the O'Connell family.*

Danny as a rookie big leaguer with
the Pittsburgh Pirates in 1950.
–*Courtesy National Baseball Hall
of Fame and Museum.*

Danny shows off his trophy from being named to the 1950 Sporting News All-Rookie Team to his mom Myrtle.
–The (Paterson NJ) Evening News.

While brother Bob holds Danny's army uniform, sister Alice holds up his Pirates jersey the day after Danny's two-year military hitch ended in February, 1953.
–The (Paterson NJ) Evening News.

O'Connell takes the throw at third base as the Dodgers' Jackie Robinson steals the bag in a game in Brooklyn in May 1953. The ump is Lon Warneke.
–Courtesy Associated Press.

1869 Cincinnati Red Stockings Card issued by New York Sporting Goods retailers Peck & Snyder. It's widely credited as the first true baseball card, since the back is an ad for the retailers, so it was used as a sales device for another product or business besides just the card.

An 1887 tobacco card of James Francis "Pud" Galvin, baseball's first 300-game winner. This card is one of more than 2,000 issued over several years by Goodwin & Co., a New York firm. The cards are referred to in the hobby as "The Old Judge Set," after one of the cigarette brands they came in.
–Courtesy National Baseball Hall of Fame and Museum.

A studio-posed 1887 "Old Judge" cigarette card of Washington second baseman Jack Farrell.
–Courtesy National Baseball Hall of Fame and Museum.

Danny's first appearance on a major
league baseball card as part of the
1951 Bowman set.
–Author's collection.

A serious O'Connell on his
first Topps card in 1953.
–Author's collection.

Danny on a 1955 card
distributed by Johnston's
Cookies of Milwaukee.
–Author's collection.

O'Connell on TV – or at least a 1955 Bowman
card. Between the dials it reads "color TV," just in
case card buyers weren't sure what it was.
—*Author's collection.*

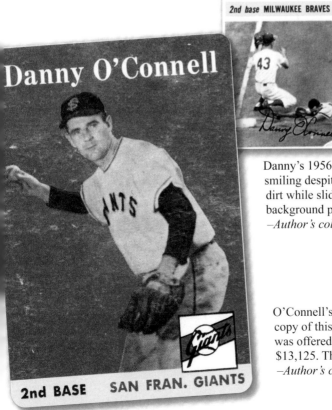

Danny's 1956 Topps card. He's
smiling despite apparently eating
dirt while sliding into third in the
background photo.
—*Author's collection.*

O'Connell's 1958 Topps card. A
copy of this card in mint condition
was offered on eBay in 2022 for
$13,125. This one was $4.
—*Author's collection.*

Danny on a 1958 Hires Root Beer card, part of a 66-card set. One card came with each six-pack, and if you pulled off the detachable tab the cards came with and sent it and two bottle caps in, you got to be a member of something or other. —*Author's collection.*

DANNY O'CONNELL
INFIELD—SAN FRANCISCO GIANTS

DANNY O'CONNELL
SAN FRANCISCO GIANTS   INFIELD

The 1960 Topps O'Connell card that was the bane of the author's existence at the age of eight. I had probably 42 Danny O'Connells and zero Willie Mayses. —*Author's collection.*

Danny's last baseball card, a 1962 Topps. —*Author's collection.*

DANNY O'CONNELL
WASH. SENATORS 3B

Vera and Danny, flanked by their
parents, pose for a wedding day
picture on Jan. 22, 1955.
–*Courtesy of the O'Connell family.*

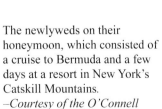

The newlyweds on their
honeymoon, which consisted of
a cruise to Bermuda and a few
days at a resort in New York's
Catskill Mountains.
–*Courtesy of the O'Connell
family.*

Danny's one-page 1956 contract with the Braves. Almost all players' contracts were exactly the same – except for the amount of salary typed in.
–Courtesy of the O'Connell family.

O'Connell scraping
his bat handle to get a
better-feeling grip in
1956.
–*Courtesy National
Baseball Hall of Fame
and Museum.*

Danny and Bobby Thomson yuk it up before a 1954 game. Roommates and golfing
buddies, their friendship would survive despite O'Connell inexplicably revealing
a secret that would tarnish Thomson's legendary "Shot Heard 'Round the World"
homer in 1951. –*Courtesy Getty Images.*

Danny as a San Francisco Giant during spring training in 1958.
–Courtesy National Baseball Hall of Fame and Museum.

St. Louis Cardinals' runner Don Blasingame barrels into Danny at second base in trying to break up a double play in a June 1958 game.
–Courtesy Getty Images.

Danny signs an autograph for former child movie star and future diplomat Shirley Temple Black while Giants teammate Darryl Spencer looks on before the start of the 1958 season. Black would be appointed U.S. ambassador to Ghana in 1972 and later hold other federal diplomatic posts. Spencer would play baseball in Japan.
–*Courtesy of the O'Connell family.*

Danny in an ad for a Washington D.C. formal wear company in 1961 – *Courtesy of the O'Connell family.*

O'Connell's last year as a player was in 1962 with the Washington Senators. The Nats' often-bumbling play might explain that puzzled look on his face.
–*Courtesy National Baseball Hall of Fame and Museum.*

The O'Connells in early 1963, not long after Danny was named manager of the York White Roses. That's Danny IV on Danny III's lap, flanked by daughters Nancy, right and Maureen, left, next to Vera. – *Courtesy of the O'Connell family.*

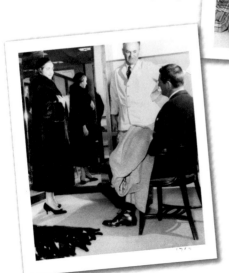

Vera tries on a fur coat at a Newark furrier. She wasn't really getting a coat. It was a publicity still that was part of the O'Connells trying to land advertising gigs in Northern New Jersey.
–*Courtesy of the O'Connell family.*

Danny's plaque as a member of the Irish American Baseball Hall of Fame, which up until the Covid pandemic hit in March 2020 was housed in Foley's NY Pub & Restaurant on 33rd Street in Manhattan. The Hall has been looking for a new home ever since. –*Author's photo.*

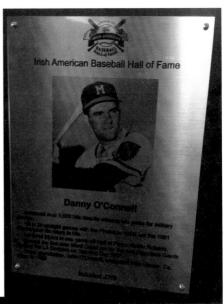

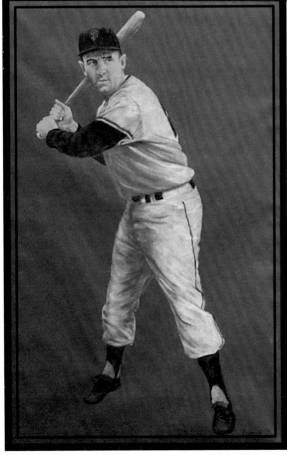

Portrait of Danny in a Giants uniform, probably presented to him as a gift for playing in a 1968 Old Timers game against the Dodgers in San Francisco. –*Courtesy of the O'Connell family.*

Paul Jones, owner of the world's largest private collection of baseball cards, stands in his man-cave of memorabilia in Idaho Falls, Idaho. Most of Jones' four million-plus cards are housed in boxes and file cabinets of his parents' garage. —*Author's photo.*

Foul Ball
PAUL JONES

Known throughout the baseball world as "Foul Ball Paul," Jones has been a guest bat boy at scores of minor league parks as well as for the big clubs in spring training. Here he does his thing for the now-defunct Tucson (Az.) Toros. —*Courtesy Paul, Lorraine and Barry Jones.*

Danny and Vera share a headstone in the "Irish Section" of the Immaculate Conception Cemetery in Montclair, New Jersey. That's an American Legion medallion near Danny's side. —*Author's photo.*

from his first. For one thing, his bride of less than two months came along. Almost as soon as their honeymoon ended, Vera and Danny headed south. Danny was one of the 20 invitees to the big leaguers' golf tournament in Miami (he shot an 85 and was knocked out in the first round), and one of a dozen Braves who reported to Bradenton before spring training officially began. Their eagerness resulted in a $50 fine ($566 in 2024) from Commissioner Ford Frick for violating a major league decree that spring training start on exactly the same day for all clubs. Braves officials, appreciative of the players' enthusiasm, paid the fines.

One of the other early arrivals was Bobby Thomson, the slugging out-fielder who achieved mythic status with his 1951 pennant-winning homer for the Giants in their playoff with the Dodgers. Despite vastly different personalities—Danny was outgoing and enjoyed poking fun at himself as well as others while Thomson was reserved and prone to withdraw into bouts of self-doubt—the two had several things in common. Both had been traded to the Braves before the 1954 season with the expectation they would plug the team's biggest holes and lead Milwaukee to a pennant. Both fell short, and both were often reminded of it by fans, sportswriters and the club's executives.

Beginning with the '55 season, the two were roommates when the team was on the road. They often played golf together in the off-season, sometimes with their wives. "We play about the same," O'Connell said when asked whether he or Thomson was the better golfer. He was less diplomatic when asked how Vera and Thomson's wife Elaine fared. "They're all right," Danny said. "They can hit the ball okay when they stop talking."

Vera O'Connell and Elaine Thomson, whom everyone called "Winkie," became fast friends. "Wink and I are looking forward to meeting the O'Connells in Florida to settle some old golf bets," Thomson wrote in a *Milwaukee Journal* column sponsored by a dry-cleaning company. "Danny is an unusually light-hearted kid who makes the biggest hit with the youngsters around the ballpark in Bradenton." When the Braves broke camp and headed north at the end of spring training, Vera stayed with Winkie at the Thomson's Milwaukee apart-ment while she and three other new Braves wives were "anxiously looking for housing," the *Sentinel* reported. "If you can help them, call WEst 3-8650, the ball club's office."

Finally, Thomson and O'Connell were tied together by a dark secret Danny knew about Bobby, a secret that when he carelessly let it slip almost a decade later, would tarnish Thomson's status in baseball history.

Another spring training change for O'Connell was on the back of his uniform. He switched his number from 4 to 27. "Single numbers are for sluggers," he explained. "Fellows who hit like me wear double numbers." He then hit a long home run with two out in the ninth inning of the Braves' last exhibition game to tie the score against Cleveland. Henry Aaron, who the day before had switched numbers from 5 to 44 based on the opposite theory that sluggers wore double digits, hit a two-run homer to win the game in the 10th.

But one thing that didn't change from the previous spring was the uncertainty surrounding who was going to be the Braves' starting second baseman: O'Connell or Jack Dittmer. At the end of '54, before O'Connell had offhandedly questioned Charlie Grimm's managerial skills, Grimm said his '55 lineup would feature O'Connell hitting second and playing it, "with Danny promising a better year."

A few days after Danny "popped off," however, Grimm began hedging his bets. "O'Connell improved steadily in his play around second and I believe he can add 20 points to his batting average," the manager told *The Sporting News*. "But I know what Dittmer can do, and if he can run Danny off the job, well, that's all right with me."

Danny started well. "O'Connell appears to have given up his 57 varieties of batting stances and stands up there and meets the ball where it is pitched," the *Sentinel* observed in early March. The story was accompanied by a large photo of Danny and Dittmer smiling, ostensibly sincerely, at each other. "... He [O'Connell] also has gained somewhat in sheer exuberance of spirit." He was so exuberant, in fact, that his teammates began calling him "Sgt. Bilko" by the end of the season, after the fast-talking, wise-cracking character portrayed by comedian Phil Silvers on a popular television show.

But while taking batting practice in mid-March, O'Connell collapsed in pain after fouling off a pitch. For almost all of the rest of spring training, he nursed a badly sprained back, the treatment for which involved sleeping on a board on the floor and refraining from all baseball activity.

"That's too bad, he has my sympathy, really," Dittmer said, ostensibly sincerely. "But with Danny out, it gives me the chance to play every day instead of alternating with him. I'm satisfied that I'll be the regular second baseman on the club...I saw from the start of spring training that I was to get a thorough chance to beat out O'Connell." At the time, Dittmer was hitting .225, and ended the spring on a zero-for-11 streak. His confidence was unswayed. "There's going to be one starter at second base this season," he declared. "His name is Dittmer...I think I've done a much better job this spring than last."

Danny did get a tepid vote of confidence from the Braves' general manager. "I'll admit I was disappointed in O'Connell [in '54]," said John Quinn. "But after all, he had limited experience at second base and the shift in position hurt his batting. He'll come through for us yet."

Grimm, meanwhile, seemed to change his mind more often than he did his underwear. A few days after O'Connell's injury, the manager announced that when Danny returned, he would hit second in the lineup and Henry Aaron would hit sixth. A week later, Grimm said "We have a mighty fine second baseman in Jack Dittmer, but I would feel a lot better if we had both of them on hand." Just before the regular season began, Grimm said the pair would platoon, with Dittmer starting against opposing right-handed pitchers and O'Connell against lefties: "Dittmer will see a lot of action this season. He deserves it." Grimm even played Aaron at second during the spring, pointing out that was Henry's position in the minor leagues.

O'Connell recovered in time to play in the Braves' last few exhibition games. But he was on the bench when Milwaukee opened the 1955 season with a 4-2 win over Cincinnati. Dittmer, hitting seventh in the lineup, went zip for three. Following Grimm's platooning strategy, O'Connell started the second game, against St. Louis, and hit a three-run homer in a losing cause. In Game 3, again playing Cincinnati, Dittmer started, went none for three and was pinch-hit for by Danny, who finished the game one for two. Then Dittmer in Games 4 and 5 and O'Connell in the next six. By the end of April, Danny was hitting.279, Dittmer .133, and Grimm's second base platoon scheme was over, at least for the time being. The Braves ended the month in second place with a creditable 9-6 record. But the first-place Dodgers won 14 of their first 16 games, and already had a 4.5-game lead. It was going to be a long and frustrating season in Milwaukee.

In a season that would be pock-marked with low spots, two highlights for Danny O'Connell in 1955 came in the form of small pieces of cardboard, one issued by a venerable and beloved Milwaukee baking company and the other by a litigation-weary gum-making subsidiary of a Philadelphia corrugated box company.

"Danny never collected baseball cards that I can remember," his sister Alice told me at a family lunch in 2022, "but he really loved seeing himself on them when he made it to the majors. I think it was like proof to himself that he really was a big leaguer like all those other fellows on the cards."

After his first appearance on a 1951 Bowman Gum card after his 1950 rookie year, Danny was absent from the 1952 cardboard galleries because of being in the army. He was back in 1953, wearing a bemused expression in a portrait painted from a photograph on card No. 107 of a 274-card set produced by the Brooklyn-based Topps Company, more about which we'll discuss in a few pages.

In 1954, there was a bumper crop of Danny O'Connell cards, at least in quantity if not quality. One was issued by Spic and Span, a chain of Milwaukee-area dry-cleaning stores. The 4" x 6" black and white cards were actually perfectly mailable post cards of Braves players. Danny's featured him posed as if leaping into the air and throwing to first to complete a double play. A second card, from Bowman, was a rather sad affair, with subdued colors, a bewildered-looking Danny and as arcane a trivia question on the back as has ever graced a baseball card: "Which player hit into zero double plays in 154 games during the 1935 season?" Look it up. (Just kidding: It was Augie Galan, who as most of you probably know had a 16-year career as an outfielder, played in three World Series, was a three-time All-Star, led the National League in stolen bases twice and hit exactly 100 home runs in his career. All of which could comprise another arcane baseball trivia question: "What was the goofiest thing ever asked on the back of a Danny O'Connell baseball card?")

The last of Danny's 1954 cards, and also one of his 1955 cardboard badges of validation, came from the Johnston Cookie Company, a Milwaukee institution that was established in 1848 by a Scottish immigrant. Johnston, situated in a multi-story red brick building that included a bank vault where they kept the silver dollars workers were paid with until the 1940s, was perhaps the most pleasant-smelling company in the Midwest. It made several products, including crackers and ice cream toppings, but it was cookies—macaroons, vanilla wafers, chocolate marshmallow—that made it famous far beyond Milwaukee. Making it even more beloved was the company's practice of bundling its broken cookies into two-pound bags and selling them once a week for 35 cents (about $4 in 2024). Kids would bus, bike or pull a wagon to the company at the intersection of 41st and National on Saturday mornings for a bag that - assuming they didn't share with their siblings - might last them well into Sunday afternoon.

From 1953 through 1955, Johnston also offered Braves baseball cards in six-card sheets. These could be obtained by mailing in a nickel and a box end, label or wrapper from a Johnston product. There was also a wall hanger available in which to display the 36-card set that even included cards of team executives.

Danny's 1955 Johnston card is a large (2 7/8" x 4") handsome color photo depicting him crouched over a grounder and in a determined position to throw the ball. The back-of-card blurb aptly describes him as "a very steady and brainy player (who) is known as a 'ball player's player.'" It adds that "his hobbies are golf and cards."

O'Connell's other 1955 card, again by the Bowman company, was dichotomously distinctive. The card portrays Danny with a bat over his shoulder, framed as if on the screen of a wood-boxed color TV (which we know is a color TV because it says so between the dials on the front of the set). The cards' design was a harbinger of how vital television would become to the economic well-being of baseball. The card's back also featured an innovative idea. In place of the usual banal summary of a player's off-season activities or a platitude along the lines of how he loved dogs and small children, there was a brief autobiographical blurb purportedly written by the player.

Danny's was a 91–word mini-essay entitled "My Biggest Thrill in

Baseball." It read: *"My biggest thrill in baseball was playing in my first major league game. I remember when I was a child I would go to Ebbets Field and the Polo Grounds with my father. I used to watch the games and think it would be impossible for me to ever play on one of those fields. But I finally made it with the Pittsburgh Pirates in 1950, and when I think that only about 400 boys in the country are major leaguers every year, I feel lucky to be one of them."*

A less successful innovation of the '55 Bowman set was the inclusion of 30 cards bearing the likenesses of major league umpires. This doubtless thrilled absolutely not a single kid in America unless one of the umps was a relative, and maybe not even then.

But Bowman's attempt at breathing new life into its cards in 1955 was actually the company's last gasp. Warren Bowman, the entrepreneurial genius/ nut job who founded his namesake company in 1928, had sold it in mid-1951 to an outfit called Haelan Laboratories and gone on to build Florida hotels, buy expensive fishing boats and marry and divorce various women. In 1955, Haelan was acquired by Connelly Containers, Inc., a Philadelphia company that made cardboard boxes and had little to no interest in making cardboard likenesses of baseball players.

Connelly's lack of interest was firmly rooted in the fact that since taking over from Warren Bowman, Haelan Labs had been locked in constant and expensive legal combat with a company that got into the bubble gum business a decade after Warren Bowman and into the baseball card business the year he sold out.

Topps, which was to become the most iconic name in the history of the baseball card industry, sprang fittingly enough from a tobacco company, since baseball cards themselves were essentially descendants of the noxious plant. In 1890, Russian immigrant Morris Shorin founded the American Leaf Tobacco Company in Boston. The firm, which Shorin and his four sons moved to Brooklyn not long after 1900, imported tobacco mostly from Turkey and wholesaled it to U.S. cigar and cigarette makers.

The company had its ups and downs. World War I dramatically reduced its access to Turkish tobacco and the Great Depression was no financial picnic either. The Shorins decided the company should diversify into a product that could take advantage of its existing and impressive distribution system.

Produce was considered and discarded as too fragile a commodity. Chewing gum, however, was not only durable but increasingly popular.

So in 1938, the Topps Chewing Gum Company was formed. The name was chosen to suggest the gum was so much better than the competition it needed two Ps. The six-story brick factory on Brooklyn's 36th Street near the waterfront was enveloped in a sugary aroma and the floors were covered with the white marble dust used to keep the gum from sticking to the wrapper.

Topps' first offering was a fruit-flavored cube that sold for a penny and promoted to retailers as a "change-maker," an impulse product that could sit on the counter near the cash register and lure customers into taking a piece or two in lieu of a few pennies' change. During World War II, Topps did well, in part because despite rationing, it managed to secure enough sugar to make its product sweeter than its rivals. It also came up with a catchy slogan: "Don't talk chum, chew Topps gum." It was a play off the anti-espionage maxim "Loose lips sink ships."

After the war, Topps introduced Bazooka Bubble Gum, which included a mini-comic strip wrapped around the gum. The strip featured the adventures of Bazooka Joe, an eyepatch-wearing kid modeled loosely after a company executive. Bazooka sold okay, but the post-war gum market was fiercely competitive. The Shorins decided they needed a further inducement to separate America's youth from their pennies and nickels.

So they did two things. One was to start marketing gum with trading cards that featured celebrities such as TV and movie cowboy star Hopalong Cassidy or "bring 'em back alive" animal collector Frank Buck. Celebrities' popularity, however, waxed and waned, and kids' tastes could be fickle. The second thing the Shorins did solved that problem. They hired an avid baseball fan and salesman force-of-nature named Sy Berger.

Seymour Perry Berger is the George Washington of the modern baseball card. The son of a furrier, Berger was born in New York City's Lower East Side in 1923 and raised in the Bronx. While he rather indiscriminately rooted for both the Yankees and Giants, Sy's favorite player was Boston Braves outfielder Wally Berger. The namesake slugger was no relation, but he once snuck Sy into the Polo Grounds and let him sit in the visitors' dugout before a game, for which Sy was forever grateful.

After graduation from Bucknell University and Army service in Europe, Berger landed a job in Topps' publicity department thanks to an intercession from a college chum who happened to be a son of one of the Shorin brothers. Berger's first day at Topps coincided with the release of the firm's Bazooka Bubble Gum, and his last day came a half century later. In between, he revolutionized the baseball card industry, although he rather modestly insisted before his death in 2014 that "I was basically in the children's entertainment business."

Berger's brainchild struggled through a painful birth. In 1951, he convinced Topps officials to replace its celebrity cards with those featuring ballplayers, putting the company in direct competition with Bowman. The first year's offerings were pitiable. For one thing, the set's 104 cards were about the size of postage stamps. For another, the backs were dominated by single words such as "strike" or "flyout," and were supposed to be part of a game that it is safe to say not more than 30 or 40 kids in America ever even tried to play. And then there was the piece of taffy that came with two cards for a penny.

Because Bowman claimed it was the only company that could legally offer gum with baseball cards, Topps decided to use taffy. Trouble was the taffy absorbed the varnish used on the cards. "You wouldn't dare put that taffy near your mouth," Berger recalled with a rueful grin years later. "That '51 series was really a disaster."

In 1952, however, Topps rebounded in spectacular fashion. The company's 407-card set is widely considered by collectors the best post-World War II batch of cards, if not the best set ever. Designed by Berger and the eccentric commercial artist Woody Gelman, the cards were bigger than before: 2-5/8" by 3-3/4". The pictures were black and white photos painstakingly colorized to match the player's real-life skin tones. There were bold team logos and facsimile autographs on the front and a wealth of statistics and personal data on the backs, from lifetime homer totals to hair color. In addition, there were laudatory paragraphs about each player.

"I used to write all the copy for the cards myself, in my living room on weekends," Berger said in a 1972 interview. "Jesus, it was murder. You don't know the agony of trying to think up something nice to say about some guy who hit .176 and made 25 errors. What can you say: 'This guy stinks?'"

Topps also dropped the taffy and replaced it with bubble gum, since it figured it was going to be fighting with Bowman in court over other issues anyway. The biggest issue centered on which company had the rights to issue cards for which players. Bowman paid players $100 to appear on its cards (about $1,100 in 2024), while Topps paid $75 ($884), or $125 (about $1,500) for an "exclusive" deal.

But a lot of players didn't worry too much about the legal niceties of "exclusive" deals, and signed contracts with both companies. "You could walk up to one of these players and offer him $50 to commit suicide," one gum company lawyer told *Sports Illustrated*. "He wouldn't read the contract or ask what it required him to do. He'd just grab the pen and sign and then pick up his glove and run out for fielding practice."

Bowman sued, contending Topps had infringed on its existing rights with players. Topps countered that Bowman's contracts with the players guaranteed only that the players wouldn't sue the gum company for using their likenesses. Further, Topps argued, the players had the right to sell their names and faces to a multiplicity of buyers. It took three years of legal wrangling. Bowman won the battle in the courtroom, but lost the war in the marketplace. The company's legal costs exceeded $300,000 ($3.5 million in 2024). At the same time, its revenues from card sales plummeted, mainly because most of their sets were markedly inferior to Topps'.

In 1956, the fight was settled by Topps paying Bowman's parent company, Connelly Containers, $200,000 ($2.3 million.) In return, Connelly handed over all of its card and gum assets, including whatever contracts it had with players, and agreed to stay out of the business for a minimum of five years. It never came back.

Topps would essentially monopolize the industry into the 1980s. Sy Berger's self-deprecating sense of humor, abundant affability - and apparently equally abundant expense account to wine and dine players and baseball officials and executives - charmed everyone. Topps signed nearly every major leaguer and potential major leaguer to five-year contracts, for $5. If the player lasted a month on a big-league roster, he got another $125 (about $1,500 in 2024.) By 1961, Topps had 6,500 current and former major leaguers under contract, including 446 of the 450 players who started the 1961 season.

Topps also produced an annual catalog from which players could pick items ranging from aquariums to shotguns in lieu of cash payments. Berger was so adept at his job, he encouraged players and their wives to call him at home to inquire about catalog products. (The Hall of Fame has a letter from Willie Mays to Berger, complaining about a broken toaster.)

"We get this stuff wholesale from RCA, General Electric," Berger said when talking about the catalog in the early 1970s. "It's got everything in it but replacement pitching arms. They [the players] can save their payoffs from year to year to get even bigger 'prizes.'"

In the O'Connell household, the dining room featured a giant phonograph courtesy of the Topps catalog. "I think we were the first ones on the street to have one of the big 'hi-fi' record players," Danny's older daughter Maureen recalled, "and we knew it was because Dad had his picture on the baseball cards. I remember that vividly because friends would come over and we would get to play albums on it...and I was the only one allowed to put the needle on the record because my little brother and sister would wreck it."

The Topps Company made tens of millions of dollars throughout the 1950s while players received small-cash payments or catalog trinkets, at least until they became organized enough in the mid-1960s to demand and receive a much more lucrative piece of the baseball card pie. Meanwhile, the O'Connells could listen to all the Eddie Fisher records they wanted. And Willie Mays presumably got a replacement toaster.

Danny O'Connell's 1955 offensive production was, in a word, offensive. It got off to a decent enough start. After hitting .279 in April and wresting the second base job from Jack Dittmer, Danny followed with a .284 average in May, playing in every game. Over one six-game stretch in the middle of the month, he hit .458 "and his fielding won standing ovations from the Braves fans."

One play, in the 11th inning of a game against the Dodgers, was "worth the price of admission alone," according to a *Sentinel* reporter. "… Danny made a miraculous diving stop on Duke Snider's sizzling grounder and a throw to match while flat on his back." The *Journal* noted that even Dodgers president

Walter O'Malley "gave O'Connell a standing ovation for that defensive gem."
Milwaukee won the game in the bottom of the inning on a Del Crandall homer.

O'Connell drew as much praise for his brainy play as for his bat and glove.
"Does the box score report anything about Danny O'Connell's intangible contributions in making a win possible?" the *Sentinel's* Lou Chapman rhetorically
inquired. "Not even the faintest hint of a suggestion. The box score can't begin
to record the smart moves Danny makes on the field."

In a game against St. Louis, for example, the Cards had runners on first
and third with two out in the bottom of the 10th inning when the batter singled
into right field. The winning run apparently scored from third. But O'Connell
noticed the runner on first had never touched second as dictated by the rules.
Danny yelled for the ball, stepped on second and the "winning" run didn't
count. In a game against the Phillies, Philadelphia had a runner on first when
the batter rifled a shot into right field. Danny, however, dove to the ground and
pretended he had stopped the ball. The runner on first slid into second instead of
continuing to third. Two pitches later, O'Connell snuck behind him and tagged
him out after taking a pickoff throw from the catcher.

"He's always thinking and making smart moves," said teammate Eddie
Mathews. "He's one guy who can be aggressive out there and still be well-
liked. Danny has a lot of friends [on other teams] despite his firebrand type of
play." Manager Grimm chimed in. "Danny is a real money man. I don't care if
he only hits .260. He proves his worth out in the field."

And then came June. Over the first half of the month, O'Connell went 9 for
59, a microscopic .153 batting average—or 107 points below the .260 Grimm
had deemed acceptable in mid-May. Analyses of the slump ranged from back
problems that lingered from his spring training injury, to constantly reverting to
his career-long habit of changing his batting stance. He fidgeted so much at the
plate, in fact, that it became a running joke among teammates that if O'Connell
was standing still while at bat, someone better check his pulse.

The saving grace that kept him in the lineup was his fielding. In a story
opining how Milwaukee's overall defense in '55 was worse than the season
before, the *Sentinel's* Lou Chapman wrote, "only Danny O'Connell has appre-
ciably elevated his station defensively. He is first among second basemen in the
league."

Sometimes—make that very rarely—Danny's bat saved his glove. In a game against the Giants in mid-June, O'Connell botched a routine double-play ball in the eighth inning to allow the tying run to score, then won the game in the 10th with a walk-off single. "Say, that's a good title for a book," he joked after the game. "'From Bum to Hero in Two Easy Lessons'—I mean 'Innings.'"

But for the most part, O'Connell's 1955 plate appearances were a good time for Braves fans to visit the rest rooms or the hot dog stands. Teammates, opponents and even the more astute sportswriters noted the naturally upbeat O'Connell was unnaturally quiet. In early July, with Danny hitting .233 and the even more hapless Dittmer hitting .130, manager Grimm installed Henry Aaron at second base. Over a 15-game stretch Danny sat on the bench while Aaron, who was hitting .318 before the position change, hit .250 during his stint at second. He fielded respectably at the position, but was clearly not as accomplished with the glove as O'Connell.

Only a second-year big leaguer, Aaron dutifully played where he was told—but he didn't like it. "There are too many things to worry about at second base," he said. "I suppose I could learn to like it, but I'd like to have a whole season to get it down pat."

So Grimm shrugged and reinserted Danny in the lineup. "This could be just one of those years where everything goes wrong for him, which has happened to other good players," the manager philosophized, referring to O'Connell. "I haven't given up on him. He may come back with a rush before the season is out."

What Danny came back with might be termed a "rushlet" rather than a rush. Once back as a regular, he embarked on a nine-game hitting streak, with 11 hits in 33 at-bats, and a continuation of heroics in the field. Then he reverted to pathetic at the plate. For a while, it looked like he might go 0-for-August. His first hit of the month came in the 15th game, followed by eight more in the next five games. In a memorable game against the Giants, he hit a home run in the first inning off his old Army pal Johnny Antonelli, and another in the 11th to win the game.

But it was a faint light in a dark year. O'Connell finished the year hitting .225—the lowest mark of any regular player in the league. His two homers in the game against the Giants represented one-third of his total for the season, He did lead the Braves in being hit by pitches, with five.

If there was consolation to be found for Danny, it was afield. His .980 fielding average set a club record for second basemen, and trailed only Red Schoendienst of St. Louis in the league. In 114 games at second, seven at third and one at shortstop, he made only 10 errors, most of them throwing miscues.

The Braves, meanwhile, could take consolation at the bank. The team again drew over two million, double that of the second-best fan-drawing team, the Dodgers. Milwaukee also hosted the All-Star game, with five Braves—Aaron, Mathews, Johnny Logan, Del Crandall and pitcher Gene Conley—appearing. And for finishing second in the standings to Brooklyn, Braves players garnered $1,694.05 (about $19,800 in 2024) from the World Series receipts.

But from the average fan's perspective, it was a disappointing season. The Dodgers jumped off to a 23-4 record on their way to the franchise's first World Series victory. Milwaukee spent not one day in first place, never got closer than seven games behind after July 7 and finished a distant 13.5 games out of first.

The season's poster boy was a 28-year-old unemployed house painter from Pennsylvania. On June 23, Bill Sherwood ascended a "flagpole" platform 75 feet above the ground over a shopping area on Milwaukee's Teutonia Avenue and vowed not to come down until the Braves won seven games in a row. He stayed there 89 days, during which time Milwaukee won six in a row thrice, but failed to win a seventh. Sherwood came down on September 19, when there were only six games left in the season. Like the Braves' front-office, Sherwood could console himself by looking at his bank book. His fan fanaticism had actually been fueled by the fact he was paid $1,335 ($15,500 in 2024) plus a bonus for his stunt by a group of local businessmen to promote the area.

And while Sherwood bore none of the blame for the Braves falling short, O'Connell and Bobby Thomson, who missed a third of the season with various injuries, were vigorously scapegoated. "It was a question whether Thomson or O'Connell was the biggest disappointment," wrote Bob Wolf of the *Journal*. "Thompson at no time looked like the slugger who cost so much two winters ago, but injuries had a lot to do with his failure...O'Connell's flop can't be explained that easily. It is difficult to understand how a player can be a .294 hitter with the Pittsburgh Pirates one year and a .230 hitter with the Braves two years later."

Braves officials were more disappointed in Thomson than O'Connell since Danny's defense was sound, he played through his aches and pains, and they were paying Thomson double what O'Connell was earning. So both general manager John Quinn and manager Charlie Grimm offered what sounded more like stays of execution than endorsements when discussing Danny's 1956 prospects with *The Sporting News*. "As for second base, if we can't get somebody in a trade, we'll have to go with O'Connell," Grimm said. "I know he's a much better player than he showed last season." Quinn added "I know he had a terrible year [at the plate], but I know he can't be as bad as last season."

Quinn also said one of the reasons the Braves hired recently fired Pittsburgh manager Fred Haney as a coach for the '56 season was to tutor O'Connell, who had played for Haney with the Pirates. Milwaukee newspapers applauded Haney's hiring. "As for second base," *Journal* sports editor R.G. Lynch wrote, "Danny O'Connell can play all of it the Braves will ever need. All he needs is 20 or 30 more points on his batting average, and the new coach Fred Haney is just the man to put him there...He knows what O'Connell can do and Danny will listen to him."

Privately, every sportswriter with an IQ higher than a doorknob's knew Haney had really been hired as the Braves' manager-in-waiting in case Grimm failed to spur the Braves quickly out of the gate in '56. Despite all the public scolding of O'Connell for criticizing "Jolly Cholly" for not being tougher before the season, more than a few players and club officials privately agreed with Danny's assessment by mid-season. "In an off-guard moment, some of the players will admit that Charlie is a little too easy-going," the *Sentinel* had reported in June, "and that he should crack the whip more." With no little irony, Grimm's only defender willing to be quoted by name was Danny O'Connell. "He's doing everything possible to shake us out of it," Danny said, "… But we've got to do it ourselves."

At home after the season, O'Connell worked out at the Paterson YMCA with other big leaguers who lived in the area, kept up a busy public speaking schedule and doted on Vera, who was well along in the couple's first pregnancy. His pal at the Paterson *News*, Joe Gooter, wrote that O'Connell "regards 1956 as the most important year of his life...because this is the one where he gets the chance to prove himself after the most disappointing season of his career."

But if he was feeling the pressure of making a comeback, Danny wore it well. At an elementary school PTA-sponsored "sports night" in December, Danny agreed to field questions from the kids:

Q: Could you tell us how to play second base?

A: *"I wish somebody would tell me how."*

Q: Is it an easy position?

A: *"Yes. All you have to do is get in front of the ball. When it bounces off your chest, you still have time to throw out the runner."*

Q: How many homers did you hit last season?

A: *"Six. I hit two in one game against the Giants. It seems to me that was the only good day I had last year."*

Q: Could you give us advice on how to become big leaguers?

A: *"Work hard at it and don't become discouraged. I know they told me when I started to play [professionally] to avoid smoking, drinking, late hours and going out with girls. The first three were easy."*

Q. Were you ever in arguments?

A. *"Only a few times. But I was always right."*

Danny should have quit while he was ahead in the verbal sparring with the kids. But he couldn't help adding a bit of bragging about the Braves: "We had a good team last year. Actually, there isn't much room for improvement." To which a diminutive member of the audience from the middle rows snapped: "Except if you finish first!"

CHAPTER 10 NOTES

It occurred on *The (Paterson NJ) News*, Jan. 24, 1955, p. 10.

The newlyweds spent Author's interview of Maureen O'Connell Hurley, April 10, 2022.

Whichever he preferred *The (Paterson NJ) News*, March 21, 1955, p. 34; *U.S. Bureau of the Census Report No. P60-24*, April 1957.

But money had *Chippewa (Wisc.) Herald-Telegram*, March 2, 1955, p. 13.

Speaking to a *The Sporting News*, Jan. 19, 1955, p. 24.

Milwaukee pitchers publicly *Chicago Tribune*, Jan. 18, 1955, p. 42.

To another reporter *Wisconsin Rapids (Wisc.) Daily Tribune*, Jan. 20, 1955.

Wisconsin sportswriters' reactions (Madison) *Wisconsin State Journal*, Jan. 18, 1955, p. 20; *The (Hackensack NJ) Record*, Jan. 19, 1955, p. 38.

As for Danny *The (Passaic NJ) Herald-News*, Jan. 21, 1955, p. 38.

The killers were Stephen J. Whitfield, *A Death in the Delta*, p. 60.

"The feeling among" Danny Peary (ed.) *We Played the Game*, p. 440.

"I soon realized," Hank Aaron, *I Had a Hammer*, p. 129.

There were small *Hackensack (NJ) Record*, Feb. 8, 1955, p. 20.

Still, it took David Quentin Vogt, *American Baseball, Vol. III*, p. 129.

"When I finally" Ibid.

Beginning with the *New York Daily News*, Nov. 8, 1954, p. 47.

Vera O'Connell *Milwaukee Journal*, Jan. 4, 1955, p. 23; *Milwaukee Sentinel*, April 30, 1955, p. 27.

Another spring training *Chicago Tribune*, April 11, 1955, p. 54.

But one thing *Green Bay (Wisc.) Press-Gazette,* Nov. 17, 1954, p. 38.

A few days *The Sporting News*, Jan. 19, 1955, p. 10.

Danny started well. *Milwaukee Sentinel*, March 3, 1955, p. 19.

"That's too bad" *Milwaukee Journal*, March 29, 1955, p. 49; *The La Crosse (Wisc.) Tribune*, March 25, 1955, p. 6.

Danny did get *The Racine (Wisc.) Journal-Times,* April 4, 1955, p. 17.

"Danny never collected" Author interview of Alice O'Connell, Aug. 5, 2022.

After graduation from *Jewish Daily Forward*, Dec. 16, 2014.

Because Bowman claimed *The New York Times*, Dec. 14, 2014, p. 17.

In 1952, however, The set doesn't include a Danny O'Connell card because he was in the Army. Once again, O'Connell just missed being included in a big chapter in baseball history.

"I used to write" Brendan Boyd and Fred C. Harris, *The Great American Baseball Card Flipping, Trading and Bubble Gum Book,* p. 20. This is one of the finest books ever written. Period.

But a lot *Sports Illustrated*, Aug. 16, 1954, p. 38.

"We get this" Boyd and Harris, op. cit., p. 23.

In the O'Connell Author's interview of Maureen O'Connell Hurley, April 11, 2022.

Danny O'Connell's *Neenah (Wisc.) News-Record*, May 24, 1955, p. 5.

One play, in *Milwaukee Sentinel*, May 14, 1955, p. 17; *Milwaukee Journal*, May 13, 1955, p. 40.

O'Connell drew as *Milwaukee Sentinel*, May 15, 1955, p. 23.

"He's always thinking" Ibid.

The saving grace *Milwaukee Sentinel*, June 19, 1955, p. 24.

Sometimes—make that *Milwaukee Sentinel*, June 18, 1955, p. 16.

Only a second-year *Milwaukee Sentinel*, Aug. 8, 1955, p. 14.

So Grimm shrugged *Milwaukee Sentinel*, July 24, 1955, p. 18.

And while Sherwood *Milwaukee Journal*, Sept. 25, 1955, p. 45.

Braves officials were *The Sporting News*, Dec. 14, 1955, p. 21; *The Sporting News*, Nov. 23, 1955, p. 12.

Quinn also said *Milwaukee Journal*, Dec. 4, 1955, p. 69.

Privately, every sportswriter *Milwaukee Sentinel*, June 5, 1955, p. 20.

At home after *The (Paterson NJ) News*, Dec. 3, 1955, p. 10.

But if he was Ibid.

Danny should have Ibid.

CHAPTER 11
"THIS IS THE BEST BALL TEAM IN AMERICA"
ALMOST

The fabulously talented infielder Ernie Banks appeared in 2,528 games over 19 years for the Chicago Cubs. Not one of those games was part of a World Series. Neither were any of the 2,055 games played by the .340-lifetime-batting-average icon George Sisler. Nor any of the thousands of games played by at least three dozen other members of baseball's Hall of Fame. Or by an estimated 90 percent of the 20,300-plus men who, as of this writing, have played major league baseball.

The point is that it was, and still is, very difficult to participate as a player in what to baseball fans is the most venerated of America's annual events. "The best possible thing in baseball is winning the World Series," said Tommy Lasorda, who managed in four World Series but never played in one. "The second-best is losing the World Series."

In the 1950s, playing in the Fall Classic meant something far more economically important than the accolades or the champions' rings (which became a tradition in the 1920s): It meant money in meaningful amounts. Ed Roebuck, for example, was a rookie pitcher for the Dodgers when they finally defeated the Yankees in 1955 after losing to them in '47. '49, '52 and '53. He thus felt none of the Dodger veterans' elation at having the loser monkeys off their backs. "I was making $6,000 or $6,500 (about $70,000 to $76,000 in 2024)," Roebuck said, "and we got World Series shares of $9,700 ($115,000). That's what it meant to me. Even the losers' share was more than my salary. [Just] getting to the World Series was it."

As players' salaries grew - and then soared - over the decades, the prospect of a post-season payday lost much of its luster. In 1955, the average salary for big-league players was about $14,000 ($163,220 in 2024). That meant the Dodgers' winning 1955 Series shares were equivalent to a hefty 70 percent of what the average player made for an entire season. In 2022, the average big-league salary was $4.4 million. The Series-winning Houston Astros' share was $516,347—or less than 12 percent of the average salary. "When we played," summed up Dodgers pitcher Don Drysdale, who played in five World Series during his career, "World Series checks meant something. Now all they do is screw up your taxes."

Although teams in the '50s got a slice of the World Series gate receipt pie for finishing second, third and fourth, the difference in the slices' size was significant. For finishing second in 1955, for example, Danny O'Connell and his Braves teammates got $1,694.05 each, or about one-sixth what the Dodgers got for winning the Series. Moreover, the $1,694.05 represented a "full share" of money from the Series. The players on each qualifying club voted on how to divvy up the loot—and not all shares were equal.

"Players never talked about each other's salaries," recalled Jim Landis, who had an 11-year career as an outfielder, mostly for the Chicago White Sox. "Most players didn't have salary gripes. The only time it got comical is when we cut up our World Series shares at the end of the year. People would complain that guys who only played half a year were getting too much. There would be a big debate."

Absent a big bonus from a World Series appearance, most players looked for ways to make some off-season dough. Landis spent his winters making bath tubs in a California factory. The Braves' Warren Spahn had an Oklahoma cattle ranch, while fellow Milwaukee pitcher Gene Conley played professional basketball. Pitcher Jim Brosnan worked in a Chicago advertising agency while gingerly stepping into a writing career by penning a few articles for the nascent magazine *Sports Illustrated.* In 1949, Jackie Robinson, fresh off winning the N.L.'s MVP award, sold television sets in a New York appliance store. (Robinson himself was the proud owner of a 16-inch set.)

As for O'Connell, he spent the winter of '55 delivering parcels during the holidays, giving speeches to service clubs, youth groups and business associations, and making celebrity appearances at automobile dealerships and grand openings of furniture stores. (He also proved to be politically adept, gracing various events for both Democratic and Republican officeholders and candidates.)

When he spoke to youth groups, he advised them not to follow the path he had taken if they wanted to play baseball for a living. "Don't be in too much of a hurry to sign a contract in organized ball," he would say. "Get a college education by all means...College ball is on a par now with top minor league play. If you do well [in college baseball] you can get yourself a good bonus and eliminate two or three years of minor league ball. Furthermore, if you don't make good, you can fall back on your education, They can't take that away from you."

The O'Connells, although still making much more than the average American family in the 1950s, could use any extra money Danny's verbal and package delivery skills could bring in. Two days before his 27th birthday, O'Connell signed his contract with the Braves for 1956. Reflecting his lousy '55 season, the $13,000 ($149,300 in 2024) salary it called for was $2,000 less than the year before, a 13.3 percent cut. Moreover, he and Vera had been compelled to find a larger and more expensive apartment in the Paterson area to make room for an addition to the family.

"Danny O'Connell, former St. Bons athlete and now a second baseman for the Milwaukee Braves, has a new rooter in the family," the Paterson *News* announced in mid-January. "His wife, the former Vera Sharkey of Montclair, gave birth to a seven-pound, five oz. Irish Coleen who answers to the moniker of Maureen Ann Friday evening [January 13] at St. Vincent's Hospital, Montclair. Both mother and daughter are doing fine and will be on hand for the opening day of the baseball season."

"I was glad to see the item in your column about the baby," Danny deadpanned while making the rounds of local media outlets to hand out cigars and accept congratulations. "It was the first I knew about it." A couple of weeks after Maureen's birth, Danny and Vera went bowling. Asked who was minding the baby, Danny said "Oh, we don't have baby sitters...We have benchwarmers. If my mother can't make it, then my mother-in-law pinch hits."

But beneath the public frivolity, Danny and Vera had to be feeling the pressures that all new parents feel—and then some. Less than six weeks after Maureen's arrival, the O'Connells were packing for spring training in Florida, then re-packing for Milwaukee. In 1955, it had taken several weeks for Vera to find a furnished apartment in a city she knew nothing about. On the plus side in 1956, she knew more about Milwaukee. On the stress side, she was moving with an infant.

Vera was also leaving behind a wide and deep roster of reliable and supportive friends and relatives. Even the priest who officiated at the O'Connells' wedding was a cousin of Vera's from Jersey City. There were her parents, a brother and sisters. Her mother-in-law could be a headache-and-a-half, but she was also a doting grandma.

"Mom had very strong family support at home [in New Jersey]," said daughter Maureen. "There was always a strong tie to the Sharkey family, and they were always there when she needed them...I think there were a lot of lonely times for Mom when they were living in so many different places. I remember that she would occasionally get together with the other players' wives, but that was really an exception. She never liked the spotlight."

Still, Vera was sometimes impressed by the baseball world. Once, according to the O'Connells' younger son John, she and Danny went to see the Manhattan apartment belonging to Ralph Kiner, Danny's old Pirate teammate. At the time, Kiner was married to the glamourous professional tennis player Nancy Chaffee. "Mom was impressed not only by the fact that Nancy Chaffee was giving her tennis tips," John said, "but also that her [Chaffee's] living room was big enough to swing a racket in and not hit any walls or furniture."

In later years, Vera would sometimes tell her kids stories about other players' wives, particularly those she was close to, like Bobby Thomson's wife Winkie, Johnny Logan's wife Dorothy or Henry Aaron's wife Barbara. While she liked Barbara Aaron, however, Vera did not care for Henry. "She didn't like that Aaron wrote in his [2007] autobiography that he rejected his 1956 contract by telling the Braves it was so low they must have sent him Danny O'Connell's contract by mistake," John said. "She was mad at that, and also that Aaron divorced his first wife [in 1971], because Mom really liked her. My mom's story was that Aaron would go on the road and forget to leave any money, so my mom went out and bought her groceries."

Much as she might have disliked it, Vera also voluntarily ventured into the public spotlight from time to time. She appeared at least twice with other Braves' wives on the local television quiz show *Play Ball*. She also posed with other players' wives in newspaper ads that depicted them pulling their dresses all the way up to six inches below their knees to display their "Perfect Plus" hosiery. With logic discernable only to advertising writers, the photos were accompanied by prose such as "pretty wives of famous men anywhere are generally first to discover a good thing." In this case, the "good thing" cost $1.19 ($13.70 in 2024). That was roughly five times what a pound of ground beef was going for then in Milwaukee grocery stores.

Although not a fervent fan, Vera also attended home games when she could find a sitter for baby Maureen. In one game, she was sitting next to Betty Gillespie, the wife of Braves radio play-by-play announcer Earl Gillespie, when Danny came up in a crucial late-inning situation. "I noticed Vera had her eyes closed and was muttering under her breath," Betty Gillespie laughingly recalled to a local sportswriter, "so I gently nudged her. 'Was I praying too loud?' Vera asked. 'Apparently not,' I told her. 'Danny just singled.'"

Danny O'Connell's 1956 baseball card (Topps No. 272) features a closeup of him wearing either a grin or a grimace—it's hard to tell which—while in the background he's sliding face-first into third base. The back of the card contains the usual stats, plus three cartoons that inform the viewer that Danny can play multiple positions in the infield; hit over .280 in both 1950 and 1953, and drove in the winning run in three different games against the Giants in 1955.

It says nothing about his morale during the previous season, nor anything about the pressure he was feeling from being a rookie dad whose baseball career was at a crossroad. But—unsurprisingly—Danny had plenty to say.

"What really gets me down is not playing every day," he told a Paterson reporter in early January while talking about his '55 experience. "The uncertainty of a job is tough to take when you're used to playing regularly. When you don't feel sure of being on the field every game, you can't help wondering about it, because you realize that two bad days at the plate and you'll be riding the bench."

A month later, Danny wrote a letter to the *Milwaukee Sentinel's* Lou Chapman, and "with characteristic frankness, the Braves' second baseman refused to alibi about, as he puts it, 'the worst year a guy could have.'" O'Connell told Chapman "I could make all kinds of excuses, but that's all they would be—excuses." Danny said that while his back had bothered him all season, neither it nor concern about Vera's pregnancy was why he hit so poorly. "When you're up there hitting, there's no one to help you. You have to do it yourself, and you're not thinking of anything or anybody when you're up there."

For the third straight year, Milwaukee manager Charlie Grimm irked O'Connell, infuriated Jack Dittmer and confused Braves fans when he talked about who would start at second base in the coming season. At the end of the '55 season, Grimm responded to reports that Dittmer would be traded by announcing O'Connell would start in '56. "Although he didn't do much with the bat [in '55]," Grimm said, "I'm sure he can fill the bill. Besides, he's good insurance if something should happen to Eddie Mathews at third." Of Dittmer, Grimm said "He's one of those ballplayers who maybe could do a little better somewhere else. Maybe he's not a bench player. Maybe it's my fault he didn't do better, but he had enough chances."

But in January, after Milwaukee failed to unload Dittmer, Grimm began to waffle. "Jack will get every chance to make it this spring," he said. "... If O'Connell comes through with the kind of performance he's capable of, then we'll be pretty well set at second. But I'm not counting out Dittmer yet."

Dittmer, meanwhile, angrily threatened to quit. "They want to cut my salary and I won't stand for it," he said. "... I've always figured on going into the automobile business with my father." He sulked in Iowa until just before spring training began on March 1, then showed up in Florida and reluctantly signed his contract.

With the dour Dittmer seemingly out of the picture, there was talk the Braves might try outfielder/shortstop Jim Pendleton at second. But Pendleton, who had a fondness for liquor and big sacks of White Castle hamburgers, and carried a chip on his shoulder from what he considered misuse of his marginal talents, drank, ate and pouted his way onto the bench.

And Danny, who reported to camp three pounds under his playing weight and 13 pounds lighter than the previous spring, was considerably cheered up by the presence of Fred Haney, his manager at Pittsburgh who had been hired as a Braves coach in the off-season. One of Haney's much-publicized tasks was to see what he could do to restore O'Connell's performance at the plate. "It did look at times last season that his dauber was down," Haney said in what sounded like English, "and that no matter what he tried, the result would be the same. He got discouraged...Certainly he doesn't belong down there with the .235 hitters." Haney moved O'Connell closer to the plate, closed his stance a bit and got him to wait on the ball more and take a more compact swing.

Haney also wanted O'Connell to have more of a take-charge presence on the field. "I tried it one day," Danny recalled years later, "and trotted up to big Gene Conley when he was pitching. Gene [who was 6'8", weighed 225 pounds and played basketball for the Boston Celtics when the baseball season ended] told me 'Get back there and learn to play second base before you try and tell me how to pitch.' So mostly after that, I stayed around second."

Whether it was Haney's advice or just renewed confidence, O'Connell had a great spring on and off the field. On it, he went 7 for 14 in the first three exhibition games and finished the spring hitting .339. "O'Connell has improved at least 40 percent since last year," declared shortstop Johnny Logan. "He's a different man this season and I think it's all because of his old Pittsburgh manager, Fred Haney. Fred's given Danny a real shot in the arm."

Off the field, O'Connell sang clubhouse duets of "Dungaree Doll" and "Everyone Has a Home But Me," with assistant trainer Joe Taylor; marched and twirled bats with catchers Del Rice and Del Crandall when a team of national champion baton twirlers visited training camp, and organized—and with Logan won—a team shuffleboard tournament. "The old Danny is back," the *Sentinel's* Lou Chapman noted. "He is getting his hits...but more important, Danny is the same carefree wisecracking Irishman of old. Gone is the sullen dispirited player of 1955...". Also back was the number 4 on his back. Having switched uniform numbers from 4 to 27 in 1955, O'Connell switched back to the single digit for the upcoming season. "It must've been the number that caused the slump," he explained with a wink.

In the final exhibition game, against Cleveland, Danny went 3 for 3, and Grimm not only announced Danny was indisputably his second baseman for 1956, but would hit leadoff instead of seventh in the lineup. O'Connell's job, in fact, seemed more secure than the manager's. "Grimm's hold on his job is slipping fast," one columnist wrote on a theme prevalent among pre-season prognostications. "This year Charley must get off to a good start or he'll be devoured by the Milwaukee wolves. The feeling about the Braves is they don't hustle enough...The Braves have the stuff to tow in the flag, but they won't because they are strictly 9 to 5 guys. There is no doubt that the fanatical Milwaukee patrons have spoiled their heroes. They just aren't hungry ball players."

It was a pennant race for the ages. When it ended, just two games separated the top three teams in the standings, which hadn't happened in the National League since 1927. And as with most human endeavors worthy of historical notice, it was chock-full of what-ifs and if-onlys.

The trio of contending teams had distinct personalities. Having already bowed to the anti-communist fervor of the era a few years previous by changing the club's 84-year-old name from "Reds" to "Redlegs," Cincinnati dropped the word "Reds" from its home jerseys in 1956. But however politically obeisant they were in off-the-field matters, the Redlegs were beasts at the plate. Cincy not only led the league in runs scored, it tied a single-season major league record for most home runs by a team, with 221. Five players had 28 or more homers: catcher Ed Bailey, first baseman Ted Kluszewski and outfielders Wally Post, Gus Bell and Frank Robinson.

Robinson was a fiercely competitive 20-year-old athlete from Oakland, California, whose 38 home runs in '56 set a major league record for rookies. Unwilling to yield a single square inch of the plate to pitchers, Robinson also led the league by being hit by pitched balls 20 times. To put that in perspective, that was as many or more than half of the teams in the league. On his way to the Hall of Fame - in part by being the only player to win MVP awards in both major leagues - Robinson would become the first African American big-league manager in 1975. In 1956, he was also an ingredient in one of the season's intriguing what-ifs.

During spring training, Redlegs manager Birdie Tebbetts was raving about his rookie outfielder when he revealed that in 1953, Pittsburgh general manager

Branch Rickey "was talking to [Cincinnati general manager] Gabe Paul, trying to make a deal for Danny O'Connell. When Rickey said he must have a kid named Robinson [then a 17-year-old playing in a Class C league], I pricked up my ears. I knew if Rickey wanted him, he must be good. Gabe turned him down, and now I'm glad."

In addition to bashing the ball, the Redlegs were a solid team on defense. Their weakness was pitching. They were fifth in team earned run average, fifth in WHIP (Walks and Hits per Innings Pitched) and last in shutouts. Their top three starters did not go deep in games, and combined for just 44, or 37.4 percent, of the team's victories.

The defending champion Dodgers were solid in every facet of the game. They committed the fewest errors of any NL team and were second only to Cincinnati in runs scored and homers. They had the league's best pitcher in Don Newcombe, who won not only the 1956 Most Valuable Player Award, but also the newly created Cy Young Award for the majors' most accomplished hurler. They also had a deep bullpen and the confidence that came with having won four of the last seven National League pennants. The Dodgers' biggest perceived weakness was age: Their starting lineup averaged more than 3.5 years older than Cincinnati's or Milwaukee's, and in baseball most players age in dog-years, not people-years.

The Braves' major strength was starting pitching. Warren Spahn (20 wins), Lew Burdette (19) and Bob Buhl (18) collected 62 percent of the club's wins. Buhl proved to be a Dodger-killer, winning eight games against Brooklyn in '56. Milwaukee's staff earned run average was better than that of the runner-up Dodgers by nearly half a run per game. It was first in shutouts and complete games, and second in WHIP. The Braves' defense was also good. But the team's hitting prowess lagged behind both its chief rivals. Worse, its batting slumps seemed to be contagious. "Usually two or three fellas slump," said 11-year veteran catcher Del Rice after a 10-game streak in June in which the team collectively hit .192. "But I've never seen an entire team collapse at the same time the way we have."

The Braves produced 1,350 base hits in 1956. The first of these came in the fourth inning of Milwaukee's inaugural game when Danny O'Connell singled sharply into center field off the Chicago Cubs' Bob Rush. Danny promptly took off for second and was gunned down when Braves shortstop Johnny Logan failed to swing on a hit-and-run play called by manager Charlie Grimm. There were scattered boos among the crowd of nearly 40,000 Milwaukee fans who had braved rain, snow flurries, 25-mph winds and a citywide bus strike to attend.

The Braves won anyway in a game that featured Grimm's 38th Opening Day in a big-league uniform as a player or manager and a five-hit shutout by Burdette. But the bad weather—and the boos—were portents of things to come. Milwaukee won four of its first six games, but had five others postponed because of inclement weather. By the end of May, every other team in the league had played at least five more games than the Braves. Making up the postponements would result in the club playing 21 double-headers in '56 and eat into the already small bag of days off during the season. In August, for example, Milwaukee played 36 games in 31 days.

Despite their soggy start, the Braves finished May in first place, but only one game up on St. Louis, two on Cincinnati and Pittsburgh and three on Brooklyn. O'Connell led off in all but one of the team's first 29 games, with decidedly mixed results. In mid-May, Danny was hitting a robust .290. Moreover, he'd been on base at least once in 14 of the first 16 games. "A pleasant surprise has been the pleasing performance of Danny O'Connell both at bat and in the field," the *Sentinel* noted. "Danny...is rolling along at close to a .300 pace and looks smooth defensively."

Of course not everyone loved him. In early May, a magazine polled major league players and managers as to whom they thought were the most overrated and underrated players at each position. Danny was named the most overrated second baseman in the National League, mostly due to his awful 1955. But at least he was in good company: Other "overrated" players included future Hall of Famers Mickey Mantle and Richie Ashburn; 11-time All-Star Del Crandall and four-time All-Star Ted Kluszewski, and pitcher Don Newcombe, the 1956 National League MVP.

In his defense, the *Milwaukee Journal* wrote: "O'Connell admirers, and he still has many, regard him as one of the real pros on the club. They like his constant jittery fielding movements to throw the opposition off balance. They like the way he works on the [opposing] pitchers too, waiting for a good pitch."

"They"—who included his teammates as well as fans—also liked the little things he did that weren't easily measurable statistically but helped win games. In a tie game against the Cubs, for example, the Braves had the bases loaded in the eighth inning with O'Connell occupying second. The batter grounded to third; the third baseman threw home for the force out and the Cubs' catcher threw to first in a vain effort to complete a double play. But O'Connell never stopped running, racing around third as soon as he saw the catcher's throw to first and sliding home to beat the startled first baseman's return throw. Against the Dodgers, Danny began the game with none for four. But in his last at-bat, he walked, went to second on a sacrifice, stole third and scored what proved to be the winning run when Dodgers catcher Roy Campanella's throw in an effort to nab O'Connell sailed into left field.

They were the kind of plays that kept Danny O'Connell in the big leagues. Unfortunately, the hitting drought he fell into the last half of May was the kind of thing that kept him constantly clawing to stay there. Over the month's last 14 games, Danny went 10 for 51 and finished May hitting .257. He wasn't the only Brave slumping. "I've lifted my head so much to watch popups," moaned manager Grimm, "I've added a few more wrinkles to my neck."

But O'Connell not only failed to get on base, he began having mental lapses, such as missing signs and failing to get down sacrifice bunts. In a game against the Giants, he even tried to tag up at first and move to second on a medium-deep fly ball to center field. Willie Mays' throw beat O'Connell to the bag by about three days. On June 1, Grimm benched him in favor of Jack Dittmer. The Braves promptly lost seven of their next nine games, Dittmer managed four hits in 33 at-bats and Danny was reinserted into the starting lineup. He responded by going on a nine-for-21 tear culminating with a performance that would be chronicled on the backs of most of his baseball cards for the rest of his career.

Leading off the home half of the first inning in a mid-June Wednesday night game against the Philadelphia Phillies before a crowd of 22,011, Danny tripled to right field off future Hall of Famer Robin Roberts. In the third inning, he again tripled to right. The next inning, perhaps just for a bit of variety, he tripled again, but this time to center. Undoubtedly tired from all that running, he only walked in the eighth. Nonetheless, he became only the 16th major leaguer to triple thrice in a game. He raised his average from .276 to .290. The Braves won 8-6.

But they were in fifth place now, two games behind Cincinnati and Pittsburgh and 1.5 behind St. Louis and Brooklyn. That was far too crowded at the top of the National League standings to suit Braves owner Lou Perini and general manager John Quinn. Three days after Danny's three-triple feat, and following a 3-2 loss to the Dodgers, manager Charlie Grimm was fired.

The Braves brass tried to make it look voluntary, and a reluctant Grimm agreed to go along with the charade. "I've decided to let somebody else take a crack at the job," he told reporters at a Milwaukee hotel after meeting with Perini and Quinn. But in his autobiography, Grimm contended, "Actually, I had been fired. Deep down, I was convinced I'd done a good job. I think they wanted a whip-cracker, but I was too old to change."

The post-mortem reviews of Grimm's departure were mixed. In his 1973 memoir, former Braves executive Donald Davidson said Grimm "gave players a free rein, feeling that they were professionals who would not take advantage of him. Unfortunately, it didn't work out that way." In other words, "Jolly Cholly" was too easy on his players, which was exactly what Danny O'Connell had been roasted for saying in public 18 months before Grimm's firing. At the time of the dismissal, an anonymous Brave said, "Charlie was playing scared baseball all the time. He acted like a man under a sword that was going to fall any minute."

To almost no one's surprise, Grimm was replaced by Fred Haney, the Braves coach who had been O'Connell's manager with the Pirates. Haney wasted no time in making clear there would be a new way of doing things. "You don't play baseball," he said at his introductory press conference, "you work baseball...Baseball is all business." Haney was short, deeply tanned, a dapper dresser and almost comically cantankerous. This last trait was greatly exacerbated during the '56 season by a mouthful of aching teeth, six of which had to be yanked at the beginning of September.

While the players' nickname for him behind his back was "the Little Napoleon," they were publicly reticent to assess his prospects. Except

O'Connell. Noting that Haney had never been successful at the big-league level, Danny said, "I want to see what he can do with a winning club like the Braves. Remember, at Pittsburgh we had a last-place team." While his comments were both honest and neutral, O'Connell's candor had to have raised the hackles of the prickly Haney.

Of course since it was already mid-June and the season was well under way, Danny's mouth had naturally already raised hackles. Two weeks before Grimm's firing, while O'Connell was riding the bench, the Braves lost three straight to the Pirates. Pittsburgh had surprised most of Western Civilization by taking over first place, but Danny wasn't impressed by his old club. "They won't finish higher than sixth," he said. "Right now they're getting all the breaks, but just wait. They'll settle down to their level."

The Pirates were understandably irritated. Referring to the high price the Braves had paid to get O'Connell from Pittsburgh after the '53 season, and the fact Danny's chief role at the time was to pitch batting practice, Pirates pitcher Ron Kline snorted, "Milwaukee is the only team in the majors with a $175,000 batting practice pitcher." At the time, O'Connell was admittedly stung. He would get his revenge in two weeks.

The Braves, meanwhile, reacted to their new leadership by reeling off 11 straight wins: two against the Dodgers, four each over the Giants and Pirates and one against the Phillies. And O'Connell reacted with arguably the most impressive offensive stretch of his career. During the winning streak, Danny had 12 hits, seven of them for extra bases. He also walked seven times, scored seven runs and drove in 12. A ninth-inning homer won a 2-1 game against New York, followed the next day by a three-run homer in the eighth that broke a 2-2 tie. Against Pittsburgh, he went seven for 15 in a four-game set, with two doubles, a triple and six RBIs. Two of the hits came off Kline. "That oughta shut him up," Danny grinned after the game.

At the beginning of the streak, Milwaukee was in fifth place, 3.5 games behind Pittsburgh, three behind Brooklyn, 2.5 behind Cincinnati and one behind St. Louis. At the end, the Braves were in first, two games ahead of Cincy and 3.5 over Brooklyn. But as with all good things, Milwaukee's winning ways—and Danny's—sputtered to an end. The Braves lost eight of the 14 games between the end of the winning streak and the break in the schedule for the All-Star Game, falling 1.5 games behind the Redlegs and only a half-game ahead of the Dodgers.

O'Connell fared even worse. Between June 25 and July 8, Danny hit a miserable .170. Haney dropped him to eighth in the batting order and even benched him for a game for Dittmer. "Danny O'Connell is finding the going getting tougher and tougher," the *Sentinel* sniped, "...The Braves better start looking for a second baseman." Danny candidly agreed with the paper's assessment of his hitting woes, if not its call for a new second baseman. "They'll be champagne in my room tonight if I get a hit today," he half-joked before going two for three with a walk, a double, an RBI and a run scored. The next day he went two for four. leading off the game with a triple.

But what kept O'Connell in the lineup was his glove. In a single game against Chicago, he robbed three Cubs of hits by backhanding a line drive, going deep behind second to snare a grounder and throw out the hitter, and diving to his left to cut off another grounder. "Danny O'Connell didn't do anything spectacular Wednesday night," the *Journal* noted after another game, "but the ubiquitous Irishman is second only to the old master, Red Schoendienst, among the league's second baseman. Red has fielded .991, Danny .988...that's a handsome fielding percentage for a man who goes after everything."

Besides, Danny wasn't the only Brave with hitting anemia. After losing 7-1 to the Cubs on July 5, Haney ripped into the team in a clubhouse meeting and ordered O'Connell, Mathews, Bruton, Thomson and Aaron to take extra batting practice. When a reporter pointed out Aaron had hit safely in 10 of the last 11 games and was hitting .309, Haney snapped "Yeah, but do you mean to tell me that Henry's hitting up to his capabilities? He should do better than a hit a game."

Whether it was Haney's tirade, the extra batting practice or just the three-day break afforded the team by the All-Star Game (except for Milwaukee participants Spahn, Mathews, Aaron and Crandall), Milwaukee rebounded over the last half of July. The Braves won 16 of 21, including seven straight, to finish the month two games ahead of Cincinnati and four up on Brooklyn.

O'Connell hit just .240 over that span, but he continued to get on base via the walk. By the end of July, Danny had walked 50 times. In 1955, the Braves' leadoff man, Billy Bruton, walked just 53 times the entire year. His on-base percentage (OBP) was .353, while the team's average OBP was .270. "August 1 is almost here," the *Journal* reported," and the Irish Thrush is still leading off. Manager Fred Haney calls his second baseman one of the best lead-off hitters in the National League."

In the first game of a double-header against Pittsburgh on July 15, O'Connell walked to lead off the game and scored on a Mathews home run; walked again in the fifth and seventh innings, and a fourth time in the eighth with the bases loaded to "drive" in the winning run. But in the second game, Haney was much less pleased with his leadoff man. In the bottom of the third, Danny hit a weak grounder to Bucs first baseman Dale Long, who let it roll up his arm. O'Connell, assuming he was an easy out, turned toward the dugout while the Pirates pitcher recovered the ball and strolled to the bag for the out.

"That'll cost you $50 ($575 in 2024)," Haney roared when Danny sheepishly reached the dugout. "You didn't even run 60 feet." O'Connell couldn't resist a chirp. "Sure I did," he retorted. "I ran at least 65 feet." Even Haney could not suppress a grin. "Okay," he replied, "I'll make it $25—a dollar a foot you didn't run." Haney later added "that won't happen again for 10 years—at least not to O'Connell."

Haney apparently didn't hold a grudge regarding Danny's inexplicable and uncharacteristic lack of hustle. Later in the season, the manager found himself defending the club against the oft-repeated criticism the Braves were too lackadaisical. "I'll admit they don't always look like they're going all out," he said, "but that doesn't mean they aren't. Some ballplayers are like that. They don't spout fire and sparks like some I played with and managed. Danny O'Connell is just the opposite. He's one of the fiercest competitors in the league. Maybe we could use more like him."

If the Braves players didn't seem overly excited about the pennant race, their owner did. In Toronto for an exhibition game against the Triple-A International League All-Stars, Milwaukee owner Lou Perini introduced his players at a banquet: "This is the best ball team in America. If I were as certain of a good seat [at the World Series] as I am of winning the pennant, I would be a happy man."

Perini's happiness took a hit as August began, with Milwaukee dropping three of four to the Dodgers in Brooklyn. Danny opened the month 1 for 19, and

Haney benched him for a few games, along with left fielder Bobby Thomson and shortstop Johnny Logan. "I felt they were getting a little heavy-legged," Haney explained, "and they haven't been hitting like they should. So with eight games coming up in five days, I thought I'd give them some rest. Then they would be ready when we get home."

In O'Connell's case, the rest cure worked. From August 7 to August 19, Milwaukee played 15 games in 13 days, and Danny hit safely in all of them. In addition to hitting .350 over the two weeks, he walked seven times, scored 11 runs and drove in seven. He played in 33 of the month's 36 games, leading off in 32 of them and hitting a respectable .270 overall. But the Braves could not shake the Reds or Dodgers. They began August 2.5 games ahead of Cincinnati; they ended it 2.5 games ahead of Brooklyn.

And for the first time since their arrival in Milwaukee in 1953, the team began to hear boos at home with unsettling regularity. For the fourth year in a row, Milwaukee's home attendance would lead the league. But even while continuing to show up at the ballpark, the fans had become more sophisticated, or just more restless. "It was said of the Braves' rooters that they cheered every time one of their boys got so much as a loud foul," Bob Wolf wrote in *The Sporting News.* "… Gradually the hysteria wore off, as it was bound to, and Milwaukee today is a grown-up big-league city...They even boo one of their heroes now if they feel he deserves such treatment."

As a four-game series began with Cincinnati on September 3, Danny O'Connell brashly predicted that if Milwaukee could win three of four, it would knock the Redlegs out of the pennant race. Instead, O'Connell went one for 13 and it was the Redlegs who won three of four. The Braves' lead shrank from 3.5 games to 1.5 over Cincinnati and two over Brooklyn.

Actually, Danny was right about the Redlegs even while wrong about the series results. Cincinnati wouldn't get closer to the league lead than the 1.5 games behind it reached on September 5. The Dodgers, however, were another story.

Leading by a game on September 11, the Braves trekked into Brooklyn for a two-game showdown. Milwaukee sent their Dodger-killer, Bob Buhl, to the mound. A burly former boxer who had quit the ring after nearly killing an opponent, Buhl had already beaten the Dodgers an astonishing seven times during the season. His mound opponent was a 39-year-old has-been who had once enjoyed being among the most-hated men in the borough of Brooklyn, and whom the Dodgers had signed in mid-May after he had flubbed a comeback try with the Cleveland Indians.

Salvatore Anthony Maglie broke into the big leagues in 1945 with the New York Giants; jumped to the Mexican League in 1946, and returned to the Giants in 1950 to become a key component of New York's pennant-winning teams in 1951 and 1954. As such, he was loathed by Dodger fans. Brooklyn players disliked him because of his fondness for throwing the ball at them should they deign to dig in against him at the plate. The newspapers and newspaper-reading public called Maglie "the Barber" because of his unshaven countenance and his predilection for "shaving" opposing hitters with the baseball. The Dodgers themselves called him by the much less politically correct nickname "the Dago." As longtime Dodger pitcher Carl Erskine put it, "When I saw Maglie standing in *our* clubhouse wearing *our* uniform, I knew nothing in the world would ever surprise me again."

Suffering from severe back problems and advancing years, Maglie was released by the Giants in 1955, and then picked up and let go by Cleveland in May '56. With a need for additional pitching, Brooklyn took a chance on him. It paid off spectacularly. The Barber won 13 games for the Dodgers, including a no-hitter in late September against the Phillies. So great was his contribution that he finished second to teammate Don Newcombe in the vote for the league's Most Valuable Player Award.

On the 11th, Maglie's sweeping curve and deceptive fastball limited the Braves to two runs on eight hits. He struck out six and walked none. He even delivered a bases-loaded single that drove in the decisive runs. (O'Connell went one for three with a sacrifice.) Dodger-killer Buhl lasted only into the fourth inning, walking seven. The Dodgers won 4-2. For the first time since June 3, the Milwaukee Braves were not alone in first place.

The next day, after a roller coaster 8-7 win over Brooklyn that O'Connell nearly gave away with his glove, they snatched back first place. With one out and the bases loaded and the Braves leading 7-5 in the seventh inning, Dodger hitter Sandy Amoros rolled a routine double-play grounder to Danny, who muffed it. Two runs scored, tying the game. "If there was a hole in the ground, I'd have climbed into it," he said after the game. "I kept thinking that I would be responsible for each of our guys losing $10,000 [in World Series shares.]"

But redemption came quickly. After the Braves scored in the eighth to retake the lead, the Dodgers had a runner on first and two out in the ninth when Amoros again strode to the plate. "Amoros smashed a sizzling grounder toward second, but O'Connell, moving at top speed, made a brilliant backhand stab of the ball and threw to second for the force," an AP reporter wrote. "No wonder O'Connell looked out at the visiting newspapermen [after the game] and shouted 'Who's choking now?'"

The next day, the Braves played a protracted doubleheader against Philadelphia, winning 3-2 in 13 innings in the first game and 4-3 in a 12-inning nightcap. Danny went four for 10, with a double, a walk, a hit-by-pitch and three runs scored. The Braves' lead increased to two games over Brooklyn. It would never be as big again.

Neither team played inspired ball down the stretch. The Dodgers publicly quarreled among themselves. At one point, several players suggested veteran left fielder Sandy Amoros be benched for making a critical late-inning error that lost a game. The suggestion was sharply rejected by manager Walt Alston. The Braves, meanwhile, seemed to many observers to be playing scared.

"The Braves were so jittery the last part of the year they couldn't even hold the ball when the played catch between innings," a veteran umpire confided to a reporter just after the season ended. Between innings of one game, he said, he asked O'Connell an innocuous question, to which Danny replied "No, of course not," then—according to the anonymous ump—shot him a startled look and asked "What? Did you say something?"

Haney managed as frustratedly as a kid holding a nickel in a store full of six-cent candy bars. He fined Thomson $100 for trying to steal home without a signal from the bench, then rescinded the fine the next day after the left fielder threw out two runners at the plate. He benched Thomson, Adcock and O'Connell for not hitting; announced he would platoon players according to the other's team's pitcher; then proclaimed Adcock and O'Connell would play against everyone. "He said he would play them until the end of the season," the Associated Press reported, "'because we have to go with our best. The best pitching and fielding in the world can't win us games if we don't score runs.'"

Despite any jitters on the field or in the dugout, Braves officials confidently announced they would accept up to 10,000 mailed requests for World Series tickets on September 16. By September 18, they had received more than 30,000. The club also added 1,500 temporary seats to County Stadium so it was set to accommodate up to 44,600 spectators.

As the season's final weekend began, Milwaukee controlled its own fate. The Braves were up one game over the Dodgers going into a three-game series against the fourth-place Cardinals in St. Louis, while Brooklyn hosted the seventh-place Pirates. If the Braves swept the Cards, it didn't matter how the Dodgers fared. "We've got to have help," acknowledged Brooklyn manager Alston. "If the Cardinals win once, we'll be all right."

With two days off before the final series, the Braves arrived fairly fresh at St. Louis' Park Plaza Hotel the night before the first game. Also staying at the hotel was former Illinois Gov. Adlai Stevenson II. Stevenson, who was a bit more than a month away from losing his second try at defeating Dwight Eisenhower for the U.S. presidency, drew a throng of spectators as he walked through the hotel lobby. Among the crowd were Braves outfielder Andy Pafko and shortstop Johnny Logan. Pafko mentioned he'd once seen a president, and when Logan asked which one, he replied "Herbert Hoover." "Go on," guffawed Logan, "you're not that old." Pafko, who with Spahn and catcher Del Rice were the only Braves who had ever played in a World Series, explained he had seen Hoover at the '52 Series when Pafko was with the Dodgers. "You must be talking about the head of the FBI [J. Edgar Hoover]," Logan insisted. "No," Pafko explained, "that's his brother." (He wasn't.)

Despite being on the road, the Braves were hardly in enemy territory. St. Louis fans, like those of most National League teams, generally hated Brooklyn because the Dodgers were both cocky and successful. The *St. Louis Post-Dispatch* editorialized that "rooting for the Braves reflects no disloyalty whatsoever to our Cardinals." Even the St. Louis weather was welcoming with fair skies and temperatures in the low to mid-70s. In Brooklyn, it rained hard enough to postpone Friday night's game and force a doubleheader for Saturday.

The *Post-Dispatch* pointed out that the Braves and Dodgers were well aware that winning the pennant would almost certainly mean a minimum of $5,000 ($57,600 in 2024) more per player than finishing second. "So it's the pennant even more than the world championship where there's the biggest difference in the buckerinos for which the professionals play," the paper concluded.

Any economic anxiety Danny O'Connell felt on arriving at Busch Stadium was quickly replaced by devastation when Haney decided to start Jack Dittmer at second base. While O'Connell's hitting in September had been abysmal, Dittmer's had been only slightly better—and Danny's fielding had maintained its excellence.

Haney's decision came back to bite him in the first inning. With a runner on first and one out, Stan Musial hit a slow roller to Dittmer, who tossed a soft underhand throw over the head of pitcher Bob Buhl, who was covering first base. Both runners were safe. The next hitter walked, loading the bases, and Cardinals star third baseman Ken Boyer quickly unloaded them with a ringing double that gave St. Louis a quick 3-0 lead.

In the eighth inning, with St. Louis still ahead by a run and Henry Aaron on first, Haney ordered Eddie Mathews—he of the 512 lifetime home runs—to bunt. Mathews' effort resulted in Aaron being forced out at second, and the Braves went on to lose 5-4. "I didn't want a double play," Haney explained after the game. "We had more power coming up and you can't win it until you tie it." St. Louis manager Fred Hutchinson claimed the botched bunt wasn't the deciding moment anyway. "The one play that hurt them the most, no doubt, was Dittmer's throwing error."

The loss cut Milwaukee's lead to one-half game. If the Braves won both of their remaining games, the Dodgers would have to win both ends of their Saturday doubleheader and Sunday's game just to tie for first and force a three-game playoff.

For Saturday's game, Haney sent to the pitching mound an Oklahoma cattle rancher who, by the time he retired from his other occupation as a pitcher in 1965, would be among the greatest left-handers of all time. Warren Edward Spahn was told by his first major league manager, Casey Stengel, in 1942 that he lacked enough guts to pitch in the majors because he refused to throw at hitters' heads. Thus admonished, Spahn went off to World War II as an enlisted man and came back in 1946 with a Purple Heart, a Bronze Star and a battlefield commission to the rank of lieutenant. By the time Spahn retired, he had won 363 games, the most by a left-hander in baseball history.

On Sept. 29, 1956, he endured what he called at the time "the most heart-breaking moment I had in 21 years of baseball." It came in the bottom of the 12th inning of a nail-biter. The Braves jumped out to a 1-0 lead in the first inning when Bill Bruton homered. Spahn, meanwhile, did not give up a hit to the Cards until the sixth inning when, with two outs, back-to-back doubles from Don Blasingame and Alvin Dark tied the score.

Spahn gave up only one more hit over the next five innings. But the Cardinals' pitcher, Herm Wehmeier, was almost as good. Wehmeier, for whom the term "journeyman" might have been invented, had a 92-108 record over his 13-year career and a most unflattering 4.80 earned run average to go along with it. But on this particular day he scattered nine hits over 12 innings and allowed no more runs after Bruton's first-inning homer

The Braves came close in the ninth—twice. Eddie Mathews led off with a deep drive to centerfield. Bobby Del Greco, a fleet-footed 23-year-old whom the Cards had picked up from the Pirates early in the season, caught the ball on the dead run before he smacked into the wall at the 422-foot mark. After a single by Adcock and a strikeout by Thomson, Jack Dittmer launched a 380-foot drive that Del Greco snared waist-high after a long sprint.

(It was Dittmer's last at-bat as a Brave. He was traded to Detroit in the off-season, played 16 games with the Tigers and then spent the last two years of his career in the minors. He retired to Elkader to run the family car dealership and as late as 2005 was still complaining bitterly about failing to beat out O'Connell for the Milwaukee second base job. He died in 2014 at the age of 86.)

In the bottom of the 12th inning, with one out, Stan Musial doubled to right. Spahn intentionally walked Boyer, the Cards' All-Star third baseman, to set up the force play. That brought Rip Repulski, a hard-hitting outfielder, to the plate. Repulski hit a sharp grounder to Eddie Mathews. Danny O'Connell, who had entered the game in the 12th as a defensive replacement at second base—and whom many still considered the best defensive third baseman in the league—watched in horror with his teammates as Mathews—who led National

League third basemen in errors during the season—had the ball bounce off his right knee and skip into foul territory near the stands. Musial scored from second base. The Braves lost 2-1.

A stunned Spahn, tears streaming down his face, trudged off the mound, pausing only to angrily hurl his glove at an AP photographer taking a picture (Spahn later apologized). Mathews said "All I was trying to do was to get in front of it, to block it."

The Dodgers, meanwhile, were winning both games of their doubleheader against Pittsburgh. In the first, Sal Maglie threw a complete-game six-hitter, and in the second Clem Labine threw a complete-game seven-hitter. Now Brooklyn was one game up, and Milwaukee not only had to win on Sunday, the Dodgers had to lose to compel a playoff. The Braves won, 4-2. Danny started in place of Dittmer, went 0-3 but walked twice. The Dodgers, however, won too, jumping out to an early 7-2 lead and holding on for an 8-6 victory. It had taken until the last day of the season, but the 1956 National League pennant race was over.

"We lost it ourselves," Haney philosophized. "You could name 10 or 15 games that meant the difference, but to pick out one game would be ridiculous." Other Braves officials reacted with dark humor. Publicity director Donald Davidson and general manager John Quinn went to a top-floor bar at a nearby hotel to drown their sorrows. "John looked out the window," Davidson recalled, "and said to me 'Do you want to jump first or do you want me to push you?'"

Danny O'Connell went home to New Jersey to officiate high school and other amateur basketball games and pick up speaking fees here and there. For finishing second, the Braves players got $1,598.32 from World Series receipts ($18,400 in 2024). For winning the pennant but losing to the Yankees in the Series, the Dodgers got $6,934.34 ($79,850.)

Danny's season numbers were a mixed lot. His .239 batting average was considered weak for the era, when batting averages were deemed, with home runs and RBIs, the most important of offensive statistics. But added to his 119 hits were 76 walks, seventh-best in the league. His on-base percentage of .342 was third on the club only to Mathews and Aaron, and 25th in the league. On defense, O'Connell played 138 games at second base, four at third and one at shortstop. He was third among regular N.L. second baseman in assists, second in double-plays turned and second in fewest errors. His .985 fielding average broke the team record he had set the year before, and was second in the league only to Red Schoendienst of the Giants, whose .993 mark set a league record for second basemen.

Braves officials had lukewarm praise for O'Connell even while fueling speculation he would be traded for everyone from Schoendienst to a 24-year-old Naval reservist named Mel Roach, who at the time had six big-league at-bats and zero hits. "Remember the name," wrote the *Sentinel's* Red Thisted, arguably the most clueless of Milwaukee sportswriters. "Roach."

General manager John Quinn told reporters "We still want to trade, but we're not panicky. For one thing, we're not really desperate for a second baseman. O'Connell wasn't as bad last year as some people think...He got on base quite often. Besides, he did a real good job in the field."

And with four full major league seasons under his belt and a growing realization he was likely not going to be a star, Danny reacted calmly to the trade rumors and the he's-not-that-bad comments—while throwing in a bit of rah-rah optimism.

"If I am traded to another club," he said, "that's the sort of thing all ballplayers take in stride. That's part of the game. However, I certainly hope to stay in Milwaukee because I think this team will win the pennant in 1957. Coming through this tough pennant race this year did a lot for us, in giving us the experience and knowledge of how it feels to play under pressure. I believe all of us are more like veterans now."

CHAPTER 11 NOTES

The point is *Los Angeles Times*, Jan. 9, 2021, p. D8.

But beyond the Danny Peary (ed.) *We Played the Game*, p. 318.

As players' salaries *Los Angeles Times*, Jan. 4, 1979, p. 45.

"Players never talked" Peary, op. cit., p. 489.

When he spoke *The (Brooklyn) Tablet*, June 4, 1955, p. 14.

"Danny O'Connell" *The (Paterson NJ) News*, Jan. 16, 1956, p. 26.

"I was glad" *The (Paterson NJ) News*, Jan. 22, 1956, p. 28; *The (Paterson NJ) Morning Call*, Jan. 25, 1956, p. 17.

"Mom had very" Author's interview, April 11, 2022.

Still, Vera was Author's interview, July 30, 2022.

In later years, Ibid.

"What really gets" *The (Paterson NJ) News*, Jan. 4, 1956, p. 23.

A month later, *Milwaukee Sentinel*, Feb. 15, 1956, p. 7.

For the third *Green Bay (Wisc.) Press-Gazette*, Oct. 2, 1955.

But in January *Milwaukee Sentinel*, Jan. 18, 1956, p. 3.

Dittmer, meanwhile, *Milwaukee Journal*, Jan. 21, 1956, p. 33.

And Danny, who *Milwaukee Sentinel,* Feb. 5, 1956, p. 35.

Haney also wanted *San Francisco Chronicle*, March 25, 1958, p. 2H.

Whether it was *Milwaukee Sentinel*, April 1, 1956, p. 3.

Off the field Ibid; *The Sporting News*, March 28, 1956, p. 8.

In the final *The Jersey (Jersey City NJ) Journal*, April 12, 1956, p. 34.

During spring training *The Sporting News*, April 11, 1956, p. 17.

The Braves' major *Milwaukee Sentinel*, June 13, 1956, p. 25.

Despite their soggy *Milwaukee Sentinel*, May 15, 1956, p. 7.

But in his *Milwaukee Journal,* May 15, 1956, p. 17.

They were the *Stevens Point (Wisc.) Journal*, June 6, 1956, p. 6.

Leading off the Years later, Danny was asked by *a Sports Illustrated* writer if the three-triples game ever came up when he ran into Roberts at various events. "Oh yeah," O'Connell replied, "all the time. I'm usually the one who brings it up."

The Braves brass Bob Buege, *The Milwaukee Braves: A Baseball Eulogy*, p. 116; Charlie Grimm, *Baseball, I Love You!: Jolly Cholly's Story, p. 219.*

The post-mortem William Povletich, *Milwaukee Braves: Heroes and Heartbreak*, p. 54.

While the players' *Kenosha (Wisc.) Evening News*, June 18, 1956, p. 11.

Of course since *Milwaukee Sentinel*, June 3, 1956, p. 21.

The Pirates were *Oshkosh (Wisc.) Northwestern,* June 3, 1956, p. 14. In early August, Danny, Joe Adcock and Fred Haney were invited to speak to a civic club lunch of about 300 while the Braves were in Pittsburgh. According to *The Sporting News*, Danny puckishly mentioned his flap with Kline and the Pirates and his prediction they would finish no better than sixth. "I'm going to say only nice things about the Pirates and Pittsburgh," he said. "I may want to come back here and manage the Pirates one day." By the way, Pittsburgh finished seventh.

The Braves, meanwhile, *Milwaukee Sentinel,* June 19, 1956, p. 29. The Braves' 4-2 loss to the Phillies to end the streak saved Milwaukee restaurateur Gene Webb a few bucks. Webb, owner of a chain of 13 lunch counters, had been broadly hinting since 1953 that he would give away hamburgers if the Braves ever won 12 in a row. Thirty years after his death in 1957, the chain made good on his promise when the Braves' major league successors in town, the Milwaukee Brewers, won 12 in a row. Webb's restaurants handed out 168,194 free burgers over a three-day stand in 1987.

O'Connell fared even *Milwaukee Sentinel*, July 2, 1956, p. 8; *Milwaukee Sentinel*, July 4, 1956, p. 2.

But what kept *Milwaukee Journal*, Aug. 9, 1956. p. 45.

Besides, Danny wasn't *The Rhinelander (Wisc.) Daily News*, July 6, 1956, p. 6.

O'Connell hit just *Milwaukee Journal*, July 29, 1956, p. 44.

"That'll cost you" *The Sporting News*, July 25, 1956, p. 8.

Haney apparently didn't *Wisconsin State Journal (Madison Wisc.)* Sept. 6, 1956, p. 25.

If the Braves *The (Madison, Wisc.) Capital Times*, July 24, 1956, p. 16.

Perini's happiness took *Kenosha (Wisc.) News*, Aug. 4, 1956, p. 6.

And for the *The Sporting News*, Aug. 8, 1956, p. 3.

Salvatore Anthony Maglie Roger Kahn, *The Era,* p. 330.

The next day *The (Passaic NJ) Herald-News*, Sept. 13, 1956, p. 41.

But redemption came *Stevens Point (Wisc.) Journal*, Sept. 13, 1956, p. 6.

"The Braves were" *Buffalo Evening News*, Oct. 3, 1956, p. 70.

Haney managed as *Portage (Wisc.) Daily Register and Democrat*, Sept. 21, 1956, p. 6.

As the season's *St. Louis Post-Dispatch*, Sept. 28, 1956, p. 14.

With two days *St. Louis Post-Dispatch*, Sept. 28, 1956, p. 4.

Despite being on *St. Louis Post-Dispatch*, Sept. 29, 1956, p. 4

The St. Louis *St. Louis Post-Dispatch*, Sept. 28, 1956, p. 19.

In the eighth *St. Louis Post-Dispatch*, Sept. 29, 1956, p. 6.

A stunned Spahn Povletich, op. cit., p. 63.

"We lost it" *St. Louis Post-Dispatch*, Oct. 1, 1956, p. 32; Povletich, op. cit., p. 63.

Braves officials had *Milwaukee Sentinel*, Oct. 21, 1956, p. 11. Over a seven-year career, Roach got into 227 games in the major leagues and hit .238.

General manager John *Milwaukee Journal*, Dec. 12, 1956, p. 67.

And with four *The (Paterson NJ) News*, Oct. 5, 1956, p. 34.

CHAPTER 12

"THIS IS MY YEAR TO PRODUCE"

CHANGING SCENERY

The Milwaukee Braves lost the 1956 National League pennant by one game, and it was *not* Fred Haney's fault. At least according to Fred Haney.

True, the Braves' fuss-budget manager consistently used the pronoun "we" when discussing the team's heart-breaking finish. "There's no one else to blame...We lost it ourselves," he told reporters after the season's final game in St, Louis. "We came here a game ahead with three to play. All we had to do was win three and we'd got it." But the Braves lost two of the three—and the pennant to Brooklyn.

In a closed-door locker room post-game post-mortem with his players, Haney made it bitterly clear that by "we," he really meant "they." They hadn't worked hard enough or performed well enough. "Well," he told them, "have fun this winter, men. Have lots of fun, because next spring, you're going to see the toughest so-and-so you've ever seen. Maybe you'll hate me for a while, but you'll love me when those World Series checks are passed out."

As the off-season trudged along, Haney honed in on the shortcomings of individual players. At 22, Henry Aaron had hit .328. That was good enough to lead the league, but not good enough for Haney, who insisted Aaron was easily capable of hitting .350 or .360. Third baseman Eddie Mathews hit 37 home runs. It should have been at least 40, Haney noted. But the sharpest and most persistent criticisms were aimed at left field and second base. Often injured since joining the Braves, Bobby Thomson did manage to get into 142 games in '56, hit 20 homers and drove in 74 runs. But he hit only .235. Danny O'Connell hit .239, with only two homers and 42 RBIs.

Milwaukee writer Bob Wolf described O'Connell and Thomson as "the unfortunate results of the two deals of three seasons ago. When the Braves got

Thomson from the Giants and O'Connell from the Pirates, they thought they had plugged the only two weak spots in the lineup. It didn't work out that way."

The public assessments of O'Connell's failings by Braves officials were both pointed and perplexing. Ignoring the facts that Danny hit .313 in the games when he led off the batting order and posted the third-highest on-base percentage on the club, general manager John Quinn lamented to *The Sporting News* that the Braves had suffered because "the big thing of course is to have a leadoff man who can get on, and that's where we had trouble." Quinn also ignored the fact that while the Giants' Red Schoendienst, generally considered the best second baseman in the National League, reached base 190 times in '56 through hits, walks or being hit by pitches, O'Connell did it 199 times.

Twenty pages over in the same edition of the weekly newspaper, manager Haney acknowledged "Defensively, O'Connell played good ball for us. But he didn't hit much...In the leadoff spot, of course, Danny drew a lot of walks. That's his job, to get on base, but he was so intent in doing this that he often took pitches when he should have been swinging." In a different interview, however, Haney said it was his fault O'Connell took too many pitches. "I took 20 points off his average by making him the leadoff man, having him take pitches trying to get on base...Now that Danny is experienced as a leadoff man, I can put those 20 points back on his average by letting him hit more often."

O'Connell, meanwhile, rhetorically scratched his head and shrugged. "I drew a lot of walks last season as leadoff man," he told a Paterson service club in early January. "Everybody says a walk is as good as a hit, but the man who sends out the contracts doesn't think so."

Despite his "disappointing" showing in '56, the Braves offered him "close to $14,000" ($156,600 in 2024) for 1957, he told a local newsman, which was $1,000 more than the previous season and which Danny deemed "completely fair." It was more than twice the majors' minimum $6,000 for 1957 and nearly four times the $3,650 ($40,800) that was the median income of the average American male for the year, which in turn was $250 more than 1956. (The median income for working women - $1,100—remained unchanged from the year before.)

Less "completely fair" in Danny's eyes was the Braves' very public search for someone to replace him. In January, Quinn flatly said Milwaukee was looking for a second baseman who would hit .270 or better. "If O'Connell could add 30 points to his batting average I think nothing more could be desired," Quinn said. But, he acknowledged, they were nonetheless shopping around.

A month before, the Braves had come close to dealing Danny and Bobby Thomson to the Giants for Red Schoendienst. But New York also wanted a Milwaukee pitcher, either Bob Buhl or Ray Crone, and $50,000 ($559,000 in 2024), and Quinn dithered. Braves scouts had reported Schoendienst, at 34, may have been nearing the end of the trail in 1956. Red had suffered from calcium deposits in his right shoulder that kept him out of 22 games in 1956 and off the All-Star team for the first time since 1948.

Trading Buhl, an 18-game winner in '56, was too steep a price to pay, and Crone was a durable and promising 25-year-old who had won a total of 21 games over the '55 and '56 seasons. Quinn ruefully remembered swapping pitcher Johnny Antonelli to the Giants for Thomson in 1954, and Antonelli helping lead New York to a World Series win. So the Braves backed out. "We offered them the pennant," said Charles "Chub" Feeney, the Giants' vice president, "and they wouldn't take it."

But speculation about a future deal lingered, and it rankled the generally affable O'Connell. In early March, Danny said a trade "would probably be good for both clubs...The Giants would get help and Schoendienst could help the Braves win the pennant." He added that the Braves' disposal in February of Jack Dittmer, Danny's rival for the second base job since 1954, "means one of two things. Either the Braves think I can do the job or they're going to make that trade for Schoendienst."

Ten days later, O'Connell was more defiant. "I'm not saying I'm a better second baseman than Schoendienst," he said. "Red has been one of the best for years. But I think I can play second base for a pennant winner too...Everybody had to find some reason why the Braves didn't win last year, so they pick on second base and left field because Bobby Thomson and I had the lowest averages...When they traded Jack (Dittmer), I figured that was their way of telling me I had the job. Well, I still have it and somebody is going to have to take it away from me."

There was a surfeit of candidates to do just that, even without a trade. Manager Haney suggested the Braves' incumbent shortstop, Johnny Logan, might be a suitable second baseman if he was willing to move. That would give second-year shortstop Felix Mantilla a chance to take over for Logan, with O'Connell moving into Mantilla's role as a backup utility player. Logan suggested it was a dumb idea. "I think Danny O'Connell was at least 75 percent improved on defense last year," he said, "... and I think O'Connell is capable of boosting his average 30 points. He should hit .280."

Absent Dittmer, Danny's in-house rivals included Mantilla, who had played second only in winter ball; Dick Cole, a seldom-used utility player whom the Braves picked up in a trade with the Pirates for overweight and chronic complainer Jim Pendleton, and rookie Bobby Malkmus, a balding 26-year-old speedster who had hit decently in the minors. Malkmus was a mouthy chap who proudly pointed out he did not smoke, drink or curse and liked to read the Bible in the clubhouse. "I feel I'm just as good as O'Connell," he said. "It's just he's got more experience. But I feel that I have more power." Malkmus subsequently went one for 16 in spring training games and won a ticket to the Braves' Triple A team in Wichita.

Haney had promised his players a grueling spring training, and he was true to his word. "Haney seemed to think that all we needed was some toughening up," Aaron recalled in his autobiography, "so when we reported to Bradenton, it was boot camp. We ran sprints and did push-ups and sit-ups...To us, it made Haney seem more like a drill sergeant than a field manager."

The manager pounded them through three-hour drills in fundamentals from bunting to sliding to shoe-tying. Mental or physical errors during intra-squad games resulted in a sharp blast from a Boy Scout whistle wielded by coach Bob Kelcy—and a lap around the field by everyone. There were so many laps, Aaron claimed, "I swear that by the time we broke camp I knew every blade of grass around that fence by its first name."

O'Connell had already survived a nightmarish spring training run by Haney in Cuba while playing for the Pirates in 1953. Moreover, Danny was mad: at the seemingly endless trade talk, at bearing the burden of blame for the team's '56 failure, and at himself for failing to play up to his own expectations. "I'm getting sick and tired of hearing how the Braves could win the pennant easy with a guy like Red Schoendienst," he said. "I realize I've got to produce or I won't be with the club next year. This is my year to produce."

So despite jamming a finger on his glove hand and nursing the sore digit for a week or two, Danny produced big-time through the spring. He hit over .300 "and is fielding spectacularly," AP reported. Writers for *The Sporting News* named him the most improved player on the team. "Danny O'Connell looked better this spring than any other time since coming to the Braves," Haney said just before the season began, "and there is every reason to believe he is headed for a fine season."

Others were less certain. "Haney knows as well as anybody and better than most that O'Connell at 28 is not going to pick up any second-wind burst of speed," *Milwaukee Journal* reporter Cleon Walfoort wrote in a long and thoughtful pre-season piece. "He knows he makes the double play as well as he is ever likely to, which is good enough...What Haney can't guess is whether the second baseman with whom he must try to win the pennant is going to hit .225 again—or much nearer his career high of .294." Walfoort noted O'Connell was six years younger than Schoendienst "and still a solid ballplayer. The gamble is that the club will be stronger with him than without him...It's as simple as that."

As the season began, O'Connell wasn't the only Brave feeling the heat. The frustration of finishing an oh-so-close second the previous season was accompanied by a fear among more than a few players that it could happen again. "We had shown that we were capable of choking," Aaron recalled, "and deep down, everybody was afraid it might happen again."

In addition to the "choke again?" question—and despite Haney's onerous spring training regimen—the Braves also faced doubts about their toughness. Some of the doubts were from predictable sources. Jackie Robinson, who had decided to retire in the off-season after gaining a lot of weight and being traded to the hated Giants, told a dinner audience in Chicago the '56 Braves had suffered from "two or three players visiting night clubs and bars during early-morning hours." Carl Furillo, the Dodgers' acerbic right fielder, sneered that the Braves "aren't hungry enough. They're the same club that couldn't hold an eight-game lead last year." Other scolds were closer to home. "We've got to get more serious about this thing," Milwaukee team owner Lou Perini said. "The boys will have to be more mean on the field. That's all it takes—more determination."

"The boys" responded with shrugs and scorn. "I never saw anything like that on our club," O'Connell said in response to Robinson. "But if he's got any sense, he should name names so we could defend ourselves." As for Furillo, Danny joked "Sounds like he's worried. And who [on the Dodgers] wouldn't be? They'll be fighting it out with Pittsburgh for fourth place." With uncharacteristic prudence, O'Connell kept quiet about the Milwaukee owner's remarks.

Whatever trepidation Braves players were feeling didn't show up at the box office. More than two weeks before Opening Day, the team sold a hefty 1.1 million tickets, on its way to a fourth straight year of over two million and a fifth straight year of leading the majors in attendance. Tickets for the home opener sold out in two hours.

The Braves rewarded the fans' faith with a lightning start, winning 13 of their first 16, going two games up on Brooklyn and three on St. Louis. Leading off in the lineup just ahead of Aaron, Danny hit a crisp .283. In a game against New York at the Polo Grounds, his 455-foot triple ignited a 10th-inning rally. The next day, he singled and homered to drive in the deciding runs against the Pirates.

In another game against the Giants, the *Sentinel* reported "O'Connell turned in some daring base running - and he is no speedster - when he made it to second on Aaron's fly to Mays in right-center. You don't run much on Mays' arm." On defense, Danny erred only once in his first 74 chances. In a game against Cincinnati, "O'Connell made a dazzling, diving stop of (Roy) McMillan's bid for a single in the fourth. Then he leaped high in the sixth for McMillan's liner and turned it into a double play."

"One of the brightest features of the Braves' play in the first month of the campaign was the showing of Danny O'Connell at second base," Bob Wolf wrote in *The Sporting News*. "... Perhaps the most encouraging sign was that agitation for the purchase of Red Schoendienst from the Giants had just about subsided. Milwaukee fans were finally expressing a certain amount of satisfaction with his play, and rightly so."

And then the roof fell in. In a game on May 6 against the Dodgers, Danny was hit on the left elbow by a Don Drysdale fastball. Although it most certainly hurt like hell, there was no serious injury and O'Connell stayed in the game. But it was an omen of bad things to come, for both Danny and the Braves. Milwaukee lost the game in 14 innings (a 21-year-old lefthander named Sandy Koufax pitched a scoreless 14th for the fifth win of his career.)

The Braves then lost 12 of their next 22 to end the month 2.5 games behind the Redlegs and a half-game behind the Dodgers. O'Connell went 17 for 80, dropping his average 48 points to .235, and his fielding sagged as well. After being benched for two games in favor of Dick Cole (who went none for five), Danny returned to the lineup in the second game of a doubleheader against Chicago, only to botch a double-play ball in the ninth inning that led to a Cubs win. After making only one error in his first 30 games, he made four in his next 10.

Whatever O'Connell's problems were, a lack of trying wasn't among them. "I'd like nine ballplayers who want to play ball when I'm pitching," Warren Spahn snapped at a reporter, "and O'Connell is one of them." Milwaukee management disagreed. "Nobody can say that O'Connell didn't get off to a good start," Quinn said, as if defending his decision not to deal for Schoendienst before the season started. "Maybe a week out of there will make the difference. But that will be entirely up to Fred Haney."

Haney, meanwhile, had his own problems. Earlier in the season he had been hospitalized for several days with acute gastritis. "Our manager is a little shaky," a Braves player confided to a reporter, "and it's being reflected in the way he keeps changing our lineup every few days. It shows his lack of confidence and results in our losing confidence too."

At the beginning of June, Cole was sent down to make room for Bobby Malkmus, who had been hitting .304 at Wichita. "Hitting is the only thing that will stand in my way," Malkmus said when he arrived, "and I know I can hit as well as any other second baseman on the club." He proved it by going two for 19. After five games, O'Connell was re-inserted in the lineup, hitting seventh instead of leadoff. "I hope the five days' rest will bring O'Connell back to his early-season form," Haney said.

It didn't. Danny went none for five in his first game back—and had an expansive, emotional and public rhetorical explosion. "Every time I pick up the paper I read about how the club is doing so poorly because of weak spots in left field and second base," he told the *Sentinel's* Lou Chapman. "It's been like that for three years now and I think it's unfair. What's more, it isn't true. I don't think Bobby Thomson and I have been so bad that we two alone are responsible. I think we are where we are today [which was in fourth place, two games out] because nobody on the club has been terrifically outstanding." Honest as always, O'Connell acknowledged there were better second basemen in the league than himself. "But I'm not the worst in the league and if you'll check the records, you'll see I've been on base an average of one-and-a-half times a game. But I've been stranded there."

Not everyone in the Milwaukee press had tar and feathers in their hands. "I don't know Bobby Thomson or Danny O'Connell from a bale of hay," wrote Lloyd Larson of the *Sentinel.* "But I'm sure they are just average human beings who must be beaten to death by everything they hear and read...No man can relax and do his best with a gun in his back."

Danny wasn't the only highly stressed O'Connell in Milwaukee. His wife was four months pregnant, with a 17-month-old toddler, living in temporary quarters in a still-unfamiliar city 900 miles from the comfort and support of parents, friends and siblings. Danny was sometimes away from home for days at a time when the team was on the road. "Danny rarely speaks baseball at home," Vera said in a 1963 interview. "He leaves his job at the ballpark." But in mid-1957, she was surrounded by a sea of opinion that her husband was not only a failure at his profession, he was failing his colleagues, his employer and the entire populace of the city.

"I don't recall my mom ever talking about my dad's performance on the field," eldest daughter Maureen O'Connell Hurley said. "She understood the game, but she wasn't a huge fan. But looking back on it, I have to believe that there were times when he was doing poorly that she shared in the misery."

The O'Connells' Milwaukee misery ended in Philadelphia on June 15. It was a Saturday, with temperatures in the low 80s and humidity levels in the Turkish bath range. The day before, a violent local storm had resulted in three people killed by lightning. In Washington, D.C., the Senate had passed President Eisenhower's $3.6 billion ($40.3 billion in 2024) foreign aid bill without cutting a penny. The House had temporarily stymied an attempt by

Southern lawmakers to derail the President's civil rights bill. Ike, meanwhile, played golf at a private Maryland country club that had no African American members.

The Braves spent the afternoon at creaking Connie Mack Stadium beating the Phillies 7-2. Danny, hitting seventh, went two-for-four, with a double and a run scored. He was also hit by a pitch. Bobby Thomson, hitting just ahead of O'Connell, went four-for-five with two RBIs.

As the game was ending, Milwaukee general manager John Quinn was in his Philadelphia hotel suite and on the telephone with Giants vice president Chub Feeney. The two had been negotiating privately for two weeks. Now, a few hours before the season's trading deadline imposed by MLB rules, the deal they had failed to consummate in January was done: Red Schoendienst was a Brave; Danny, Thomson and pitcher Ray Crone were on their way to New York.

Milwaukee was convinced, Quinn insisted, that earlier fears Red was over the hill had been assuaged by the fact he was having a very good year. In a three-game series against the Braves two weeks before the trade, for example, Schoendienst had gone seven-for-14 with four homers, five RBIs and five runs scored. New York sportswriters generally thought it was a good deal for both clubs. Crone had promise, while Thomson and O'Connell were proven vets. Schoendienst could help the Braves win the pennant while he could do little to improve the lot of the sixth-place Giants.

New York fans were less impressed. "We got two bums and a fair pitcher for one of the great stars of the game," one fan groused. "We got robbed," said another with a more fatalistic-but-philosophical outlook. "But if we can't win the pennant, let's do everything we can to see the Dodgers don't win it either." As for Danny, he told reporters he was surprised by the trade because of its last-minute nature. "I'm sorry I let the Braves down as much as I did," he said, "although at the same time I feel I was blamed for some of the things that happened for which I wasn't responsible. I wasn't as bad as some people make it out to be."

It's tempting at this point in the story to report that Red Schoendienst was a flop in Milwaukee, the Braves blew the pennant and Danny O'Connell and the Giants became the toast of the Big Apple. Only baseball is often just like real life, and real life has a way of falling short of what should be and settling for what is.

The truth is that Schoendienst, whose sterling career would eventually earn him a plaque in Cooperstown (and whom one writer described as looking and acting like "Huckleberry Finn in a baseball uniform"), became hailed as the Milwaukee messiah, leading the Braves not only to the 1957 National League pennant, but also a thrilling seven-game World Series victory over the Yankees.

Schoendienst hit .309, led the league with 200 hits, led NL second basemen in fielding, made his 10th All-Star team, finished third in the Most Valuable Player vote and steadied the other Braves' players. "We all look up to him," said Eddie Mathews. "He's the old pro. He settles you down...His value to the club is immeasurable." Manager Haney, who gladly let Schoendienst essentially run the team when it was on defense, added "This is not intended as a rap on Danny O'Connell, who's a nice boy and a fine ballplayer. But the boys seem more confident with Red at second."

As for Danny, he played considerably better in '57 as a Giant than as a Brave. In roughly two-thirds of a season, his batting average climbed 35 points, to .266. Seven of his eight home runs came as a Giant, as did eight of his nine stolen bases. Despite appearing in only 95 games, he was third on the club in runs scored, third in doubles, sixth in hits and fourth in on-base percentage. He was versatile on defense, playing in 62 games at second, 30 at third and three at both in the same game.

"I feel I'm wanted here," O'Connell said at the end of June. "It's tough to play for somebody when you get the idea you're not wanted...It won't make any difference to me whether I play second or third, wherever they think I can help out most, that will suit me." Danny's attitude suited both his new teammates and his manager. Two weeks after joining the team, Giants players voted to make him their alternate player representative. Manager Bill Rigney praised his versatility and his hustle. "This O'Connell gives everything he has until the last out," Rigney said. "We made no mistake in getting him in that trade."

In terms of cosmic issues like winning pennants, it's possible the Braves would have won without making the trade. Their .604 winning percentage at the time Danny departed, extended over a full season, would have meant a five-game margin over second-place St. Louis instead of the eight by which they actually won. But if nothing else, the trade provided O'Connell's career with some memorable vignettes. For one thing, he hit just in front of Henry Aaron in the lineup with the Braves and just in front of Willie Mays with the Giants—the two best players during Danny's career and two of the best of all time—in the same season.

He also had the opportunity to play for two different teams against two other different teams on games that began on the same date. On April 28, Danny played for Milwaukee against Cincinnati, going one for three with a double. On August 16, he played for the Giants against the Phillies in a game that originally began on April 28, but was suspended because of rain. Taking Schoendienst's place in the original New York lineup, he walked in his only appearance.

And then there was the oddball play of the sort that seemed to come along at least once in every O'Connell season. Playing the Redlegs on September 10, Danny was on second and Mays on first when they attempted a double steal. Cincy catcher Ed Bailey fired to third and O'Connell was caught in a rundown. But third baseman Don Hoak inexplicably threw the ball to first. Danny steamed into third—and didn't stop. A shocked George Crowe, the Redlegs' first baseman, threw home, but too late to get the sliding O'Connell. Mays ended up at second and O'Connell ended up being credited with two stolen bases on one pitch. "I didn't want to ask them what they were doing out there," an exasperated Cincinnati manager Birdie Tebbetts said after the game, "because I was afraid they would tell me."

The trade's biggest benefit for the O'Connells was it brought them home to the Paterson area. "We doubt if Danny regrets very much the trade that brings him close to home in the uniform of the Giants," columnist Bob Whiting wrote in one of Danny's hometown papers, *The Morning Call*. "… It is always pleasant—and much cheaper—for a ballplayer to have his [in-season] house near his permanent home. It cuts down on house-hunting and gives him a sense of security. Danny always wanted to play for the Giants, and he should be pleased even though there is no question World Series dough was more likely to come his way as a Brave rather than as a Giant."

Whiting was right. The Braves players voted 30 full shares of $8,924.36 (about $99,800 in 2024) for winning the Series. Schoendienst got a full share for playing two-thirds of a season. Rookie John DeMerit, who got into 33 games, received $2,974.78 ($33,271). Bob Taylor, a catcher who played seven games, got $1,000 ($11,184.)

But O'Connell, Thomson and Crone got zilch. Major League rules prohibited traded players employed by other teams at the end of a season from sharing in Series money earned by their previous team. The rationale for the rule was that it would discourage traded players from dogging it so their old clubs could succeed. Worse, since the Giants finished sixth and only the top four teams in each league shared in Series receipts, Danny got nothing in post-season loot for the first time since 1954.

And the often cruel and capricious gods of baseball weren't done yet with the O'Connells in 1957. They were about to move Danny and Vera a continent away from home.

The New York Giants were owned by a 54-year-old moon-faced fellow who looked a bit like the actor Orson Welles and had an inordinate fondness for both baseball and liquor, although not necessarily in that order. Horace Stoneham had inherited the Giants in 1936 from his father Charles. The elder Stoneham was a morally challenged stockbroker who bought the team in 1919 with the help of Arnold Rothstein, best known in baseball circles as the gambler who fixed that year's World Series.

Charles Stoneham became very rich on Wall Street, then very poor in 1929, the year in which Danny O'Connell was born, the stock market crashed and the Great Depression began. By the time Horace inherited the team, the club was pretty much the extent of the Stoneham family fortune. This was in contrast to many other major league club owners, whose deep pockets were rooted in family wealth—Boston Red Sox owner Tom Yawkey inherited $20 million in 1925 (worth $359 million in 2024 dollars)—or in other business interests—the chewing-gum-rich Wrigley family ran the Chicago Cubs basically as a hobby.

Born in the mid-1880s, the Giants had one of baseball's proudest pedigrees. But by 1957, the team had fallen on hard financial times, despite having won two pennants and a World Series during the decade, having the huge metro New York population from which to draw fans and featuring Willie Mays, arguably the most watchable player on the planet.

In both 1956 and 1957, the team was last in the National League in attendance, and outdrew only the pitiful Washington Senators among the majors' 16 franchises. A standing joke was that when someone called the Giants ticket office to inquire what time that day's game started, the response was "What time can you be here?" Stoneham contended the Giants' net profit for 1956 had been a paltry $26,000 (about $300,000 in 2024.)

A big part of the problem was the Polo Grounds, the Giants' cavernous and decrepit home field. The stadium had been shoehorned onto an odd-shaped parcel of land in upper Manhattan in 1890, rebuilt after a fire in 1911, and expanded in 1923. It was shaped like a bathtub to fit the site. As a result, the left and rightfield walls were only short distances from home plate while the centerfield wall was in a different time zone, thus making it more suitable for playing football or parking dirigibles than baseball. The stadium also lacked parking and was surrounded by a deteriorating neighborhood. Worse, Stoneham owned the ballpark but not the land it stood on, making improvements problematical even if he could have afforded them.

From his often-lonely stadium office, the Giants owner had watched other franchises move to greener pastures, starting with the Milwaukee Braves in 1953. Faced with a situation similar to Stoneham's, the Braves moved from Boston and drew 1.8 million in their first year—about six times what they attracted in their last year in Beantown. Prior to the Braves moving west, no major league team had changed cities since 1903, when the Baltimore Orioles moved to New York and became the Highlanders and then the Yankees.

But the Braves sparked a mini-stampede. In 1954, the woeful St. Louis Browns, a charter member of the American League, moved to Baltimore and tripled their customers. In 1955, the Philadelphia Athletics moved to Kansas City, Missouri, and quadrupled their attendance. So it was hardly surprising that Stoneham pricked up his ears when Brooklyn Dodgers owner Walter O'Malley began whispering about a mutual change of scenery.

Like Stoneham, O'Malley was 54. The son of a New York Democratic Party operative and city official, O'Malley was a lawyer by education and a wheeler-dealer by avocation. He began with the Dodgers as the team's legal counsel in the 1930s, bought a quarter-interest in the club in the 1940s and by 1950 had pushed out Branch Rickey as Brooklyn's president and general manager and taken over completely. A gravel-voiced cherub with a cigar constantly in or near his mouth, O'Malley was said to love money to the extent that "his idea of a beautiful figure is $1,000,000."

Unlike the Giants, the Dodgers excelled on the field *and* off it in the 1950s. The team won four pennants and a World Series, and lost two other pennants by only a game. They regularly drew a million or so fans. By 1955, television and radio revenues topped $780,000 a year ($9.1 million in 2024). That covered the payroll with $250,000 ($2.9 million) to spare. "We were in the black before Opening Day," recalled Buzzie Bavasi, the club's vice president. "We never told that to anybody. I mean, you don't exactly advertise a gold strike, do you?"

But the Dodgers had outgrown Ebbets Field, their home park in Brooklyn's Flatbush neighborhood. Opened in 1913 on the site of a garbage dump and named after the team's owner at the time, the stadium had virtually no parking, seated fewer than 35,000 and was in dire need of a facelift. O'Malley had already sold the field in 1956, taken out a five-year lease and began making noises he would move the Dodgers unless he got the city's cooperation to build a new stadium in Brooklyn.

How sincere O'Malley was about staying in Brooklyn is debated to this day. In fact, he had already visited Los Angeles to meet with local officials and scout the political and economic landscape. He also knew that other team owners would balk at only one franchise on the West Coast because travel costs would be too expensive and scheduling too big a headache. So he talked Stoneham, who had been thinking about moving the Giants to Minneapolis, into moving to San Francisco instead.

On May 28, 1957, while Danny O'Connell was still with the Braves, National League owners voted unanimously to allow the Giants and Dodgers to head west, as long as both of them did so. In August, the Giants board of directors voted to move. When Stoneham was asked after the decision was announced if he knew he was breaking the hearts of legions of young Giants fans, he replied "I feel bad about the kids, but I haven't seen many of their fathers lately."

Shortly after Stoneham's announcement, the *New York Daily News* reported that "a host of Paterson fans...are buying up tickets by the hundreds for the team's last New York baseball contest Sept. 29 on the probably accurate premise that they'll never see Danny play again." The last Giants home game at the Polo Grounds took place on a pleasantly cool and sunny Sunday, before a crowd of 11,606. Manager Bill Rigney sentimentally started all of the players who were still with the team from its 1951 and 1954 pennant winners. Danny, who went zero for four, and shortstop Darryl Spencer, were the only exceptions. The Giants lost to the Pirates 9-1.

Jack Mann of *Newsday* wrote an elegantly edgy eulogy. "It was a real nice funeral...Bob Friend and the Pirates buried the body...The Giants were feeble at the plate and dogged it in the field...But there was Willie. He threw out a man at the plate with the kind of throw only Mays can make, and he legged a routine grounder into a hit as if it mattered." Mann asked the Giants' press box attendant, Gus Bache, if he was going to San Francisco with the team. "Naw," snorted Bache, who had started with the Giants in 1905. "What the hell would I do out there?" Mann concluded his piece "… And Gus went and put the record books away in the cabinet, as if there were a tomorrow."

Danny was seemingly unfazed, at least publicly, by the move, telling reporters he didn't care where he played—as long as he played. He said that the O'Connells would remain New Jersey residents, "although all he heard about the San Francisco area has been favorable." And almost certainly to the chagrin of Giants executives working to sell tickets to a new fan base, the ever-candid O'Connell predicted the '58 Giants might not be much of an improvement over the sixth-place '57 model. "I know we can stay ahead of the Cubs and Pirates," he said, "but it's going to be rough getting past the other five clubs."

Privately, O'Connell both beamed and fretted over the arrival of the family's newest rookie. On November 30, Vera gave birth to their second child, Nancy Elizabeth O'Connell. With another player on the family bench and in the absence of the heretofore reliable share of World Series receipts, Danny wrangled a sweet deal with the city of Hoboken's parks department. In return for conducting a 10-week baseball clinic for the city's youth, O'Connell was paid $1,025 (about $11,500 in 2024). He was also more and more in demand as an after-dinner speaker. "I know a lot of men with reputations as speakers who can't come near O'Connell when it comes to putting a dinner crowd in stitches," Giants teammate and old Army buddy Johnny Antonelli told an AP reporter. "He's a very charming, funny guy."

At one event, for example, O'Connell spotted National League umpire Augie Donatelli in the audience. "Ladies and gentlemen," Danny began, paused, and then added, "and Mr. Donatelli." He even carried a black leather notebook full of jokes he could adapt to various audiences. Speaking to a Kiwanis Club in Hoboken, he cited a recent newspaper story that reported someone was struck by a car every 20 minutes in the city. "If I were that guy, I'd move out of Hoboken," he deadpanned.

If the event was for a church, a non-profit group or a youth sports organization, O'Connell waived any speaking fee. He professed to love giving batting or fielding tips to kids—at least most of the time. At one event, the first question a youngster asked was which of the Braves had been the nightclub frequenters alluded to by Jackie Robinson at the start of the season. A startled O'Connell said he didn't know, but complimented the kid for asking the question. And when queried by a reporter as to what question aspiring young ballplayers asked the most often, O'Connell had a quick reply: "They want to know how much money I make."

CHAPTER 12 NOTES

True, the deeply *Chippewa (Wisc.) Herald-Telegram*, Oct. 1, 1956, p. 8.

But in a *The Sporting News,* Jan. 23, 1957, p. 4.

One Milwaukee writer *The Sporting News*, Oct. 3, 1956, p. 6.

The public assessments *The Sporting News*, Jan. 23, 1957, p. 24.

Twenty pages over *The Sporting News*, Jan. 23, 1957, p. 4; *The (Long Branch, NJ) Daily Record*, March 9, 1957, p. 8.

O'Connell, meanwhile *The (Paterson NJ) News*, Jan. 4, 1957, p. 24.

Less "completely fair" *Racine (Wisc.) Journal-Times*, Jan. 18, 1957, p. 15.

But speculation about *Wisconsin State Journal (Madison, Wisc.),* March 4, 1957, p. 20.

Ten days later *The Sheboygan (Wisc.) Press*, March 15, 1957, p. 15.

There was a *Milwaukee Sentinel*, Dec. 9, 1956, p. 11.

Absent Dittmer, Danny's *Oshkosh (Wisc.) Northwestern*, Feb. 26, 1957, p. 14.

Haney had promised Hank Aaron with Lonnie Wheeler, *I had a Hammer: the Hank Aaron Story*, p. 184.

The manager pounded William Povletich, *Milwaukee Braves: Heroes and Heartbreak*, p. 65.

O'Connell had already *The Wisconsin Rapids (Wisc.) Daily Tribune*, March 3, 1957, p. 6.

So despite jamming *Janesville (Wisc.) Daily Gazette*, April 10, 1957, p. 15; *The Sporting News*, April 17, 1957, p. 15; *Milwaukee Sentinel*, April 13, 1957, p. 31.

Others were less *Milwaukee Journal*, March 31, 1957, p. 49.

As the season Aaron, op. cit., p. 172.

In addition to *Green Bay (Wisc.) Press-Gazette*, Jan. 14, 1957, p. 18; *The Hackensack (NJ) Record,* April 15, 1957, p. 21; *The Sporting News*, March 27, 1957, p. 7.

"The boys" responded *Green Bay (Wisc.) Press-Gazette*, Jan. 14, 1957, p. 18; *The Hackensack (NJ) Record,* April 15, 1957, p. 21.

In another game *Milwaukee Sentinel*, May 1, 1957, p. 21; *Milwaukee Sentinel*, April 28, 1957, p. 95.

"One of the" *The Sporting News*, May 22, 1957, p. 7.

Whatever O'Connell's problems *The (Wisconsin Rapids, Wisc.) Daily Tribune*, May 24, 1957, p. 7; *Milwaukee Sentinel*, May 31, 1957, p. 8.

Haney, meanwhile, had *Milwaukee Sentinel*, June 7, 1957, p. 5.

At the beginning *Milwaukee Sentinel*, June 2, 1957, p. 50; *Milwaukee Journal*, June 7, 1957, p. 24. Malkmus' entire big-league career consisted of 268 games over parts of six years, in which he hit a total of eight home runs and batted .215.

It didn't. Danny *Milwaukee Sentinel*, June 9, 1957, p. 17.

Not everyone in *Milwaukee Sentinel*, June 2, 1957, p. 23.

Danny wasn't the *The (Paterson NJ) News*, May 24, 1963, p. 24.

"I don't recall" Author's interview, April 11, 2022.

New York fans *Milwaukee Journal*, June 19, 1957, p. 50; *Milwaukee Sentinel*, June 16, 1957, p. 13.

Schoendienst hit .309 *Janesville (Wisc.) Daily Gazette*, Aug, 8, 1957; *(Omaha Neb.) Evening World-Herald*, Sept. 6, 1957, p. 26.

As for Danny The Braves who were traded with O'Connell, Thomson and Crone, did not fare as well. Thomson hit .236 for Milwaukee and .242 for New York. Crone was 3-1 with a 4.36 Earned Run Average for the Braves, 4-8 with a 4.46 ERA for the Giants.

"I feel I'm" *New York Daily News*, June 28, 1957, p. 68; *The Sporting News*, Sept. 4, 1957, p. 9.

And then there *The Sporting News*, Sept. 18, 1957, p. 29.

The trade's biggest *The (Paterson NJ) Morning Call*, June 18, 1957, p. 20.

The New York Giants In his 2021 biography of Stoneham (*Forty Years a Giant: The Life of Horace Stoneham*), author Steven Treder maintains Stoneham "served as his own GM," and that "every Giants team from the mid-1940s to the mid-1970s was built, or torn down and rebuilt, by Horace Stoneham himself." (p. ix). Treder also details Stoneham's alcohol addiction, quoting Leo Durocher as telling actor friend Spencer Tracy "you can't believe what I put up with. The boss is a full-time drunk" (p. 181). How much the latter affected the former is wisely left to the reader to determine.

A big part They never actually played polo at the Polo Grounds, at least not at the ballpark we're concerned with. The name came from a field some distance away that was the original home of the Giants and which had been the site of polo games.

Unlike the Giants Roger Kahn, *The Era*, p. 285.

On May 28, 1957 Steve Bitker, *The Original San Francisco Giants*, p. 4.

Shortly after Stoneham's *New York Daily News*, Aug. 18, 1957, p. 225.

The last Giants After the move to San Francisco, the Giants came back as visitors to the Polo Grounds in 1962 and 1963 to play the expansion team New York Mets. The Mets moved to a new park, Shea Stadium, in 1964.

Jack Mann of *Newsday*, Sept. 30, 1957, p. 66.

Danny was seemingly *The (Paterson NJ) Evening News*, Feb. 6, 1958, p. 33; *Newark Star-Ledger*, Feb. 7, 1958, p. 22.

Privately, O'Connell both Associated Press, May 26, 1958.

If the event *Tampa Tribune*, Jan. 26, 1958, p. 17.

CHAPTER 13

"DON'T GET EXCITED BOYS. I PROMISE NOT TO BREAK BABE'S RECORD.

BASEBALL ON THE COAST

The westward emigration of the Giants and Dodgers after the 1957 season put America's most famous clown out of work.

For 36 years Emmet Kelly had entertained millions around the world as a circus performer, much of that time in the persona of a sad-faced Depression-era hobo dubbed "Weary Willie." But in 1956, Kelly parted company with the Ringling Brothers Barnum and Bailey Circus—and Walter O'Malley snapped him up.

The Dodgers' owner hired Kelly to entertain fans at Ebbets Field during the 1957 season before games and between innings, making him a forerunner of modern-day costumed performers like the San Diego Chicken and the Philly Phanatic. But Kelly declined to shamble along when the Brooklyn club moved to Los Angeles. He described the Dodgers' new home, the L.A. Coliseum, as "too big for one clown."

In baseball terms the Coliseum was hilarious with or without clowns. Like the Giants, the Dodgers were playing in temporary quarters in their new cities while new ballparks were being constructed. But the Giants' Seals Stadium was an excellent-though-small venue that had actually been built for baseball. The Coliseum, in the words of Shirley Povich of the *Washington Post*, "was designed for things like lion-feeding or chariot racing."

Opened in 1923, the Coliseum seated more than 100,000. Despite its enormous size, however, the stadium had a relatively small playing field more suitable for football games and track and field events than baseball. Squeezing a baseball field into it meant there was virtually no foul territory along the first base line, while along the third base line there was enough foul ground to accommodate a small European country. "The Coliseum was a weird place to play baseball," Dodgers pitcher Stan Williams recalled." Everybody sitting off to one side would think a ball hit 100 feet foul was a home run." Some of the seats were so far away from the field, a *Los Angeles Times* reporter described it as "like looking in at some sort of pinball game...It takes all night and a couple of days for the sound of the crack of the bat to get there."

Worst of all from a baseball afficionado's perspective, while it was a distant 440 feet from home to the right centerfield fence, it was only 252 feet to the left field bleachers. (Or 250 feet, or 251 or 258. Judging from press reports at the time, apparently no two tape measures in late-1950s California agreed with each other.) Whatever the exact distance, there were dire predictions that a deluge of "Chinese" homers—an ancient and derogatory baseball term for balls that barely cleared the fence—would result in someone breaking the single-season mark of 60 homeruns, set by the immortal Babe Ruth in 1927 and among the most revered of baseball statistics.

As a countermeasure to the lack-of-distance problem, Commissioner Ford Frick ordered construction of a 42-foot-high screen in left. Sportswriters alternately guffawed and shuddered. "The left field screen," the *Post's* Povich summed up, "is a horror." And Danny O'Connell, of all players, would be the first to make a mockery of Frick's fence and seemingly add credibility to fears about the looming fall of Ruth's record.

After beating L.A. in the first Major League game played on the West Coast on April 15 (with Danny scoring the first run), the Giants lost the next game to the Dodgers then bounced back the following day to win 7-4. Manager Rigney, who had a history of ulcer problems, was rushed to the hospital in mid-game with severe stomach pains. He thus missed a sparkling performance by O'Connell, who singled, walked, stole a base, scored two runs and made a spectacular bare-handed grab of a drag bunt, throwing out the batter on the dead run and finishing with a somersault to land on his feet.

The Giants drew a total of 58,703 for the first three games in their new home. In New York the previous season it had taken seven games to reach that total, and that was in a ballpark that had almost 2.5 times the number of seats as snug Seals Stadium.

The two teams then journeyed south to Los Angeles to open the Dodgers' home season. Before a record-setting crowd of 78,672 (or 18,770 more than the

1957 Dodgers drew to their first three games in Brooklyn,) the Giants lost 6-5 when rookie third baseman Jim Davenport failed to touch third base during a ninth-inning rally. San Francisco left fielder Hank Sauer hit two home runs. But both were legitimate 340-foot-plus shots to the right of the screen. And Sauer was a legitimate slugger, who would compile 288 homers over a 15-year career.

The Giants bounced back to win 11-4 the following day, and although a total of five homers were hit by both teams, only one was slightly dubious in terms of its distance over the left field screen. It took a couple of at-bats by O'Connell the next day, in the third game of the series, to remove the "slightly."

Danny led off the third inning of a scoreless tie against the Dodgers' menacing Don Drysdale. A friendly fellow with a good sense of humor off the mound, Drysdale was a beast on it. He was equipped with a blazing fastball and an on-field temperament that helped him lead the league four times in hit batters and retire among the 10 best, or worst, pitchers of all time in that department. "He probably would have knocked his mother down if he thought it would give him an advantage, but that was Drysdale," the Giants' Jim Davenport recalled. "If you got a hit off Drysdale," Sauer said, "he'd knock you down the next time up. He'd as soon knock you down as look at you."

On Drysdale's fourth pitch to him, Danny lofted a flyball just over the Frick-ordered leftfield screen. The following inning, he did it again, this time with a runner on. Drysdale was so angry he knocked down the Giant who followed O'Connell to the plate, pitcher Ray Monzant, three times but missed him each time. Monzant retaliated by knocking down Gil Hodges, the first Dodger to come to the plate the next inning. The umpires issued warnings of ejections to both teams, tempers cooled, and the Giants won easily, 12-2.

By the time O'Connell batted again, Drysdale was no longer pitching. But after the game, O'Connell was asked if he feared retribution the next time he faced the Dodgers' big right-hander. "Naw," he laughed. "Pitchers don't knock me down very much. I'm not that good a hitter." He also jokingly reassured reporters he was no threat to the Great Bambino. "Don't get excited boys," he said, "I promise not to break Babe's record." The "boys," noting that O'Connell had hit precisely 33 home runs in his entire career to that point, did not get excited.

But seven years later, Drysdale was still shaking at the memory. "I might have committed suicide if we had stayed in the Coliseum," he said in 1965 from the comfort of spacious Dodger Stadium, to which the team moved in 1962. "… The worst day of all was when Danny O'Connell hit two balls over the screen and both landed in about the second row of the left field bleachers. Danny is still laughing about it."

As it turned out, no one threatened the Babe's record at the Coliseum, and the home-run-heaven scenario never materialized during the four seasons the Dodgers played there. Pitchers learned to keep the ball outside to right-handed pull hitters and hitters learned that trying to hit it over the screen resulted in more pop flies than four-baggers. It also helped that there were few really good hitters on the home-team Dodgers from 1958 to 1961.

But his two-homer game was only part of Danny's great start to the 1958 season. By the end of April, he was getting on base with regularity, had played in every game and had yet to make a fielding error. Plus, he had two home runs, which was twice as many as his teammate Willie Mays. Most important of all, the Giants were where almost no one expected them to be—in first place.

If anyone had envisioned before the season that the Giants would be a good team in 1958, they had kept it to themselves. "The Knights of the Keyboard," as the legendary curmudgeon Ted Williams sneeringly referred to sportswriters, almost all picked San Francisco to finish no better than fifth. Las Vegas bookies set the odds of the team making it to the World Series at 50 to 1. The prevailing theory was that the Giants were pinning their hopes on too many rookies, and the pitching staff was understocked with talent. "On any given day," one writer concluded, "the Giants consist of Willie Mays and eight other guys."

It was true the lineup regularly featured four freshmen: Jim Davenport at third base, Orlando Cepeda at first, Willie Kirkland in rightfield and Bob Schmidt catching. But for much of the season, the rookies, particularly Davenport and Cepeda (who won Rookie of the Year honors and went on to have a Hall of Fame career) performed better than expected, as did the pitching.

At the end of May, the Giants were leading the league in wins, homers, batting average and sourdough bread consumption. For his part, O'Connell was hitting a respectable .276 and had made only two errors. He played in all but three of the first 44 games, and reached base at least once in 26 of the 41 in which he played. Batting second in the lineup most of the time, he was adept at moving runners into scoring position. He also excelled at "little ball" -- doing things that didn't show up in the box scores or on the stat sheets but helped win games.

In a game against the St. Louis Cardinals in late April, Danny came up in the ninth inning with Davenport on first and the Giants trailing by a run. O'Connell singled, moving Davenport to third. The next hitter, Mays, grounded to Cards third baseman Ken Boyer, who threw home to get Davenport trying to score. But catcher Ray Katt dropped the throw. While Katt pondered his error, O'Connell kept running. Danny slid into third safely, and scored the winning run a moment later on a ground ball by Darryl Spencer. "Danny got the big hit," Spencer said after the game. "He really kept the pressure on them."

A few days later against Chicago, the Cubs had a runner on first with one out when the batter hit a soft popup to O'Connell at second base. Danny dropped it on purpose, picked it up, stepped on second and threw to first for an inning-ending double play. Cubs manager Bob Scheffing charged from the dugout to protest, claiming the infield fly rule should have been called. As all baseball fans know (as well as other people with apparently way too much free time on their hands), the rule allows umpires to call the batter automatically out in such situations, meaning the runner at first did not have to progress to second, and was thus still safely on base. But what the wily O'Connell knew and Scheffing had apparently forgotten was the rule applies only when there are runners on first _and_ second or the bases are loaded. "After the game," the Associated Press reported, "Scheffing called the play a brilliant piece of thinking by O'Connell."

And in late May, Milwaukee Braves ace pitcher Warren Spahn retired the first 19 Giants he had faced in a game in Milwaukee when O'Connell came to the plate in the seventh inning. Danny coaxed a walk, breaking up Spahn's perfect game. He went to third on a Mays single and scored on a groundout. In the ninth, O'Connell singled to left, and Mays followed with a game-clinching homer. "This baseball is a crazy game," Spahn philosophized about issuing the walk to Danny. "O'Connell hits the ball where he wants to pretty good...so I tried to anticipate where he'd try to hit it...I tried to work the corners [of the plate], and he just wouldn't bite."

The *Examiner's* Walter Judge, who heretofore hadn't exactly been O'Connell's biggest fan, threw a somewhat limp bouquet in Danny's direction. "... The heavy-bearded O'Connell is the [Giants'] No. 1 Big Man," Judge wrote in late May. "Danny doesn't have the ability of ballplayers like Willie Mays or Darryl Spencer, but neither tries harder. Danno isn't baseball's best second baseman, but you couldn't tell it from the way he has been playing." Another Bay Area columnist, John Connolly of the *San Rafael Daily Independent-Journal*, also jumped on the O'Connell bandwagon. Danny, Connolly wrote, was "a player with a great heart and just enough ability to stay in there. He is strictly a clutch batter, a team player, and I believe his fighting heart is contagious to others on the squad."

Manager Rigney echoed both writers. "O'Connell is playing better ball than I've ever seen him play before, and that means really good," Rigney told an AP writer. "He's making the double plays. I don't know what he's hitting. All I know is that he always seems to be rapping an important one. O'Connell doesn't give you 100 percent, he gives you 110 percent."

On June 4, a headline in *The Sporting News* rhetorically asked "Can Giants Capture Pennant? Why Not?" The reasons gradually became apparent as the season wore on. The team's torrid early-season hitting cooled off and the thinness of the pitching staff began to surface as the innings piled up and arms grew weary. The fidgety Rigney was quick to bench players who encountered even short slumps, and overused some pitchers while underusing others. But a key reason for the Giant's ultimate demise in '58 occurred just three days after the *Sporting News* story ran.

On June 7, during a home game against Cincinnati, O'Connell led off the bottom of the first inning with a walk. Spencer followed with a weak grounder to Reds pitcher Joe Nuxhall, who whirled and fired to shortstop Roy McMillan, who was covering second. Trying to break up the double play, Danny slid hard into the bag. McMillan's knee came down accidentally but emphatically on O'Connell's ribcage. Gasping for breath, Danny tried to stand but got no further than his hands and knees. Teammates carried O'Connell, in agony, off the field, and he was whisked via ambulance to the nearest hospital.

Because it was the nearest hospital, however, didn't make it the most competent. After X-rays determined no ribs were broken, O'Connell was sent home. A few hours later, he was back, with stabbing pain in his chest. This time the diagnosis was a mass of torn muscle and cartilage. After a night in the hospital, Danny was discharged with instructions to do nothing until he was at least relatively pain free. Giants officials announced he would "probably miss a day or two." They were off by three weeks.

For the rest of June and into the first week of July, O'Connell pulled his No. 19 uniform jersey over an assemblage of tape and padding wrapped around his chest and alternately cheered and fretted in the dugout while the team floundered. On the day O'Connell went down, the Giants were 30-20 and in first place. When he returned, they were 39-36 and in third place. To save you the math, they went 9-16 in his absence.

Danny's return to the starting lineup on July 4 was inauspicious. He went 0-2 and dropped a pop fly in his only fielding chance in the first inning, and left the game early. "It felt as though I was playing my first major league game," he said in a post-game interview. "My legs were wobbly, and my eyes were bouncing around in my head like marbles in a shoebox. I'm just not quite in shape yet." In fact, he had put on five pounds while recuperating, and Rigney benched him for a few games while he lost the extra weight. And while he had gained weight during the layoff, he lost something too—his batting eye. By the end of July, his average had plunged to .234.

But he continued to find ways to contribute. In a game against Milwaukee, he scored the game's only run in the first inning, then threw out the potential tying run at the plate in the ninth. In a game against the Phillies, he walked to open the sixth, went to third on a double by Willie Kirkland, and scored on a groundout. In the ninth, he started a double play that ended the game. The Giants won, 1-0. In another game against Philadelphia, O'Connell led off the ninth in a 2-2 tie with a walk and moved to second on a sacrifice. With two out and Danny still on second, Kirkland grounded weakly to first base. But the Phillies pitcher covering first dropped the ball. Danny never stopped running from second and beat the throw home. The Giants won 3-2. And the following day against Cincinnati, he laid down a perfect squeeze bunt to drive in a run and started two double plays.

"Danny's got no batting average to speak of," Rigney said after the

Cincinnati game, "but somehow, whatever he does counts big...He gets little dunkers, or walks, or he gets hit by a pitch, or someone makes an error, and he's usually on to score the tying or winning run." In another interview, Rigney praised O'Connell's play at second base as "right out of a book...All I know is that we keep right on winning when I put O'Connell out there."

The San Francisco sporting press corps also continued to praise Danny's play. "O'Connell, although not flashy, is a steady, consistent and persistent performer without whom the Giants could not possibly today be in contention for the National League championship," pronounced the *Chronicle's* Bob Stevens. "Their key player has actually turned out to be the rugged, blocky O'Connell, the man with the perpetual 5 o'clock shadow."

On July 31, the Giants were still only a game behind the Braves. But O'Connell had almost completely stopped hitting. From July 23 through August 5, a 16-game stretch, Danny went a miserable five for 40. And as the Giants faltered and the Braves began to saunter out of sight in the pennant race, the jittery Rigney decided that all O'Connell's "dunkers" at bat and double plays in the field weren't enough. On August 6, in a loss to St. Louis, the manager employed 15 position players. None of them was named O'Connell.

For the rest of the season, Danny would start games, only to be removed for a pinch hitter, or be inserted late as a defensive replacement. By the end of August, O'Connell had endured the indignity of watching outfielder-first baseman Whitey Lockman, who at 32 couldn't outrun a receding glacier and was hitting even worse than Danny, start at second base for the first time in Lockman's 13-year big league career.

Even so, O'Connell tried to contribute in other ways. One afternoon at Chicago's Wrigley Field, he volunteered to pitch batting practice. With a stiff wind blowing out to left field, Danny threw six pitches to Mays, all of which Willie deposited over the ivy-covered outfield wall. "Get O'Connell out of there," Rigney yelled. "Get somebody in there who can throw a curve, or we'll run out of baseballs."

In September, with the Giants relegated to also-rans in the pennant race behind both the Braves and the surprising Pittsburgh Pirates, shortstop Darryl Spencer was shifted to second base and Andre Rodgers, a former cricket player from the Bahamas and a great favorite of club owner Horace Stoneham, was brought up from the Giants' Triple-A Phoenix club to play short. A decent hitter with good power and an iron fielding glove, Spencer proved as inept at playing second as he was at short, eventually leading the league's infielders with 34 errors. Rodgers, who had been tearing up the Pacific Coast League before his call-up, hit an anemic .206 with the big club. O'Connell, meanwhile, sat out 11 of the Giants' last 13 games. In fact, in 33 of the team's last 55 games, he either didn't play at all or had two or fewer plate appearances. The Giants went 26-29 in those games, and finished third.

O'Connell still started more games at second than any other Giant. In 107 games, he hit a puny .232. But as mentioned earlier, in baseball there are always different stats to look at, and different ways to look at stats. He was fourth on the team in on-base percentage, third in bases on balls and second in sacrifices. Of the regulars, he struck out less often than everyone except Mays. (To be fair to Mays, it should be pointed out that Willie did make up for the fact O'Connell had outhomered him 2-1 in April. Willie ended the season with 29 home runs, Danny with 3.)

O'Connell was second in the National League in fielding percentage at second base - once again behind the Braves' Red Schoendienst, this time by one-thousandth of a percentage point, .987 to .986 - and second in percentage of walks per at-bat to the Cardinals' Joe Cunningham. And most important, When O'Connell was in the lineup, the Giants' record was 62-45, for a winning percentage of .579. When he wasn't, the club was 18-29, a .382 percentage. As Rigney had pointed out earlier in the season "we keep right on winning when I put O'Connell out there."

If there was a consolation prize for the San Francisco club, it was at the box office. The Giants drew 1.27 million to the snug confines of Seals Stadium in '58. That was almost double what they had drawn in their last year in New York, a feat all the more impressive in light of the fact that New York's Polo Grounds had more than twice the seating capacity of Seals Stadium.

The players' wallets were somewhat consoled by the shares of World

Series receipts that came from finishing third. To split the Giants' players' and staff members' shares down to the penny, those whose last name began with A through J got exactly $1,031.14 (about $11,200 in 2024), while those in the K to Z group got $1,031.13. Team trainer Frank Bowman thus got a penny more than Willie Mays and Danny O'Connell.

Danny also got to be on two baseball cards, although that fed his ego and not his bank account. One was part of a 66-card set issued nationwide by the Hires Root Beer Company. One card came with each six-bottle carton. Danny was No. 19 in the set, which coincidentally matched his Giants uniform number. The Hires cards came with detachable tabs. If you taped a dime to the tab and mailed it to Hires headquarters along with two bottle caps, the company sent you a "How to Play Baseball" booklet and a "valuable membership card." Just who considered it valuable and why remains a mystery.

Because many kids actually sent in the tabs, a '58 Hires card with the tab still on it is nowadays hard to find, which naturally adds to its value. A Danny O'Connell card in mint condition and with the tab still there can fetch $225. A Willie Mays card in the same condition goes for $2,000. Either way, that buys a lot of root beer.

O'Connell's other 1958 card was part of a 494-card set issued by Topps. The '58 season set was Topps' biggest yet, in both sales and number of cards. The cards were issued in six series, and Danny was No. 166, in the second set. His photo on the front shows him poised to throw. The back avers that "Danny is a fine defensive infielder," and bears a cartoon of him fielding a grounder behind his back and saying, "just like a vacuum." The back info also relates that "he loves to break up games with timely hits," which both raises the question of which big league players didn't like to break up games with timely hits and proves how hard it was to find something positive to write on 494 different cards.

The Topps cards typically sold for 5 cents (about 54 cents in 2024), which got you six cards and a slab of pink bubblegum coated with a suspicious-looking powder. The company said it was a mixture of powdered sugar and cornstarch and was supposed to keep the gum from sticking to the cards. I have my doubts. Just how many nickels Topps collected in 1958 is unknown since the company declined to release sales figures. But it was a lot. Baseball card collecting exploded in 1958. It wasn't clear why. There was speculation it had something to do with the Giants and Dodgers moving to California, thus sparking new interest in cards throughout the Western U.S. Or maybe kids got tired of trying to master the must-have toy of the year—the Hula Hoop.

Whatever the reason, Topps announced late in the summer it was issuing an unprecedented sixth series—22 "Sport Magazine All-Stars"—to meet the demand for new cards (and of course to increase sales even more.) The *Cincinnati Enquirer* reported card collecting "is the craze among the small fry in our town and elsewhere. Bubble-gum sales figures are skyrocketing to all-time records as a result." The *Enquirer* quoted a local wholesaler as saying Topps was limiting the number of cards it would sell to him to ensure there was at least some supply in all parts of the country.

A New Jersey distributor estimated he had moved 300,000 packs over the summer, and "could have easily sold double that amount." Retailers reported parents buying up 24-pack boxes, a phenomenon they had not seen before. Store owners were also impressed by how efficiently kids' grapevines worked when cards did arrive. "We get in a shipment," a pharmacy owner marveled, "and in two hours we're jammed."

The youthful consumers also established their own card-based economy. *New York Times* business writer Carl Spielvogel noted—with a touch of amused sarcasm—"this sometime medium of currency and exchange has served as a business training ground for many American lieutenants of industry." Spielvogel reported the going rate in the June market in the New York borough of Queens for a Mickey Mantle card "called for the surrender of thirty-five other pitchers and fielders." (A '58 Mantle in near-mint condition in 2024 could fetch $90,000-plus.)

Not everyone was pining only for baseball's luminaries. In the New York City suburb of Mamaroneck, a youngster took out a "Kids Section" classified ad offering 10 unspecified cards for just one of first baseman Ed Bouchee of the Phillies. The kid was doomed to disappointment. Although Bouchee, the 1957 *Sporting News* Rookie of the Year, was listed on 1958 Topps checklists as Card No. 145, it was never issued. Before the season began, Bouchee had been arrested in Spokane, Washington, for exposing himself to several young girls. He was suspended until July, and Topps scrubbed him from its lineup.

(Bouchee, by the way, received counseling, played in the majors until 1962, was never rearrested, and died at the age of 80 in 2013.)

As with any fad, craze or highly publicized popular trend, there were those on the fringes of sense and sensibility. In Madison, Wisconsin, a 10-year-old boy confessed to battering through a basement window at the home of a chum in order to steal his pal's card collection. Enraged when he couldn't find it, he started a fire in the kitchen. On the other end of the spectrum, there was the usual tsk-tsking from the older generation about the foibles of the young.

A *Minneapolis Star-Tribune* editorial writer lamented that boys were wasting their youth on baseball cards. "For a boy to know what Al Dark's batting average was in 1957 does not strike me as knowledge that will ever fill the nation's needs, or even his own," he complained. He suggested, with apparent sincerity, that America would be better served if companies like Topps would issue cards featuring U.S. presidents or noteworthy mathematicians. Still, he conceded, at least baseball cards were a lesser vice than comic books.

Having once again been immortalized on baseball cards and survived another season at the top level of his chosen profession—and with no certainty it wasn't his last—Danny spent the fall and winter making money where he could. Two relatively modest paydays were provided through the largesse of his teammate and pal Willie Mays. The first of these was on a nationally televised game show based on one of the goofiest premises in the long and goofy history of TV game shows.

Brains & Brawn was a Saturday night show in which a "noted intellect" was paired with an accomplished athlete against a similar duo. "The Brain" answered questions to accumulate points while "the Brawn" competed in skills tests relevant to their sport. In early October, Mays was paired with Sally Kirkland, the fashion editor for *Life* magazine. Their foes were Boston Red Sox star Jackie Jensen and an English fashion historian, James Laver.

Since part of the athletic skills competition was a home run derby, Mays needed someone to pitch to him. Recalling the afternoon in Chicago when O'Connell had pitched batting practice and served up so many fat pitches, Willie asked Danny to do the honors on the TV show. Danny must have been up to the task, as Mays defeated Jensen. Diligent searches of newspapers, obscure websites and ancient TV Guides, however, did not reveal how the Sally Kirkland/ James Laver bout came out. The show's premise proved too incomprehensible even for game show viewers, and was quickly canceled.

Almost as incomprehensible to a lot of baseball fans was O'Connell's presence at Yankee Stadium on Oct. 12. The occasion was an "All-Star" exhibition game between a 14-player National League squad led by Mays against an American League team led by Mickey Mantle. Nine of the 28 players would eventually enter the Hall of Fame. Two days before the game, Mays added Danny to the NL roster as a substitute for Chicago Cubs outfielder Lee Walls.

Danny's statistical credentials as an All-Star were suspect, but his selection was probably due to a combination of factors: A) he could competently play second, short and third; B) he was Willie's friend; C) he had just helped Mays win on the TV show, and D) he lived just across the Hudson River from the stadium and could make it to the game pretty easily. Almost all of America's baseball fans paid little to no attention to the game. The attending crowd of about 22,000 was only half what the game's promoters had hoped for, there was no television or radio coverage, and most newspapers gave it only a few paragraphs. This was just as well for O'Connell, who in his only appearance, as a pinch-hitter, struck out.

Danny also picked up another $1,000 (about $11,000 in 2024) for once again running baseball clinics for the city of Hoboken, and did a little after-dinner speaking. In answering audience questions, O'Connell frankly acknowledged that once again he would be fighting to hold on to his job in 1959.

This time around, Danny wasn't mentioned as a potential trade candidate as much as he was talked about as being replaced in the starting lineup. That was more ominous, since it meant few other teams were even interested in him. One of the hot rumors at MLB's winter meetings in Washington, D.C., was that the Giants were negotiating with the Cardinals to trade Darryl Spencer and at least one other player for St. Louis second baseman Don Blasingame. "The Giants are badly in need of a second baseman," AP reported. "Last season they struggled along with Danny O'Connell and Eddie Bressoud [Danny's replacement most of the time when he was injured] most of the way. Each barely hit above his weight...the Giants feel the swift and spirited Mississippian [Blasingame] would fit perfectly into their setup." A week later, UPI quoted Rigney as saying he was eager to land Cincinnati second baseman Johnny Temple.

At least the uncertainty helped cement a decision the O'Connells had already made. For the upcoming season, Vera and the kids would not accompany Danny to wherever it was he might end up playing. In the Giants' first season on the West Coast, the O'Connell family had headquartered in a first-floor apartment in a complex in Burlingame, about 17 miles south of San Francisco. "I remember the place had a sliding glass door, which I had never seen before, and it led to a common lawn," Danny's oldest daughter Maureen recalled. "We liked it because it had a big swimming pool, but Mom didn't."

For Vera, a Jersey girl who had rarely left her home turf before marrying Danny, California might as well have been Alaska. "She went out sometimes with the other [players'] wives, Willie Mays' wife and Darryl Spencer's—she really liked Darryl Spencer's wife—and they would all order martinis and Vera wasn't even sure what was in them," Vera's daughter-in-law Leslie O'Connell said. "She told me Burlingame was the least favorite place she lived during Danny's career...She said she just felt so far from home."

"Home" for the O'Connells in late 1958 was a small house in Fair Lawn, New Jersey, about four miles northeast of Danny's hometown of Paterson and 12 miles northeast of Vera's hometown of Upper Montclair. For the upcoming '59 season, it was decided Vera and daughters Maureen and Nancy would stay there, close to family and friends.

And there was a more compelling reason for them to stay put than just Vera's antipathy for the West Coast: She was pregnant, with the new arrival scheduled for late May or early June. If Danny was nervous about the looming arrival of another mouth to feed, however, he didn't show it. When a local reporter asked him if he was hoping for a boy this time around, O'Connell smilingly shrugged. "It doesn't matter at all," he said. "The kid probably won't start working for a few years anyway."

The big question the O'Connells faced as 1959 began was where—and whether—Danny himself would be working.

CHAPTER 13 NOTES

The Dodgers' owner *Santa Barbara (Ca.) News-Press*, Mar. 19, 1958, p. 22.

It was almost Steve Bitker, *The Original San Francisco Giants,* p. 33.

Opened in 1923 Danny Peary (ed.), *We Played the Game,* p. 393; Los Angeles Times, April 19, 1958, p. 24.

Worse, it was Bitker, op. cit. Frick had been a ghostwriter for Ruth. As commissioner, he was basically a waste of space, dealing with most controversial matters by deferring to one or both of the leagues to deal with it. But in 1961, he gained infamy for the bone-headed "asterisk" decision that decreed any breaking of the Babe's single-season homer record had to be accomplished in 154 games or less, which was the season's length in Ruth's day. Sanity has since prevailed and the decree rescinded.

Danny led off Ed Attanasio interview of Jim Davenport for the Society for American Baseball Research (SABR) Oral History Project, Oct. 1, 2003; Peary, op. cit., p. 393.

By the time *The (Paterson NJ) Morning Call,* April 22, 1958, p. 15; Associated Press, April 21, 1958.

But seven years *San Francisco Chronicle,* March 29, 1965, p. 48.

In a game *San Francisco Examiner,* April 25, 1958, p. 35.

A few days later *Redding (Ca.) Record-Searchlight,* April 28, 1958, p. 10.

And in late *Rhinelander (Wisc.) Daily News,* May 24, 1958, p. 6.

The *Examiner's* Walter *San Francisco Examiner,* May 22, 1958, p. 33; *San Rafael (Ca.) Daily Independent-Journal,* June 2, 1958, p. 10.

Manager Rigney echoed Associated Press, May. 26, 1958.

Danny's return, on *San Francisco Chronicle,* July 6, 1958, p. 40.

"Danny's got no" *Dayton (Oh.) Daily News,* July 30, 1958, p. 12; *The Biloxi (Ms.) Daily Herald,* July 26, 1958, p. 17.

The San Francisco *San Francisco Chronicle,* July 29, 1958.

Even so, O'Connell *Bangor (Me.) Daily News,* August 16, 1958, p. 17.

Whatever the reason *Cincinnati Enquirer,* June 11, 1958, p. 5

A New Jersey *Asbury Park (NJ) Press,* Aug. 3, 1958, p. 3.

The youthful consumers *New York Times,* June 18, 1958, p. 66.

As with any *Wisconsin State Journal,* June 23, 1958, p. 9.

A *Minneapolis Star Tribune* *Minneapolis Star-Tribune,* July 12, 1958, p. 4.

For a change *Meriden (CT) Record,* Dec. 2, 1958, p. 4.

At least the Author interview of Maureen O'Connell Hurley, April 11, 2022.

For a Jersey girl Author interview of Leslie O'Connell, Feb. 15, 2022.

And there was *Paterson (NJ) Evening News*, Jan. 20, 1959, p. 24.

CHAPTER 14
"TIME IS UP FOR THE VETERAN"
DANNY'S GAMBLE

On a pleasant, partly cloudy mid-February afternoon at downtown Phoenix's Municipal Stadium, a 30-year-old baseball player "with a perpetual five o'clock shadow and a ready quip" sat in a training room with a sweat-stained towel around his neck and growled. "Nobody," he told a reporter, "is going to take second base away from me."

In the 1958 season, Danny O'Connell had played in the fewest baseball games of his 12-year career as a professional. All winter he had worked on staying in shape, reporting to the Giants' '59 camp four pounds lighter than the year before and 10 days earlier than required. He felt no lingering effects from the nasty rib injury he had suffered the previous June.

But all winter he had also read and heard that his job as San Francisco's everyday second baseman had already been given to Darryl Spencer, his road roommate and best friend on the club. So on this particular afternoon, after some informal batting practice and a workout with two or three other early arrivals, O'Connell wasn't quite as breezy as usual when he agreed to chat with Bob Stevens of the *Chronicle*. Stevens had been covering baseball for the paper since 1940, and was more knowledgeable and less provincial than most of his ink-stained Bay Area brethren. He too had shown up early for spring training.

When Danny signed his 1959 contract the month before for an estimated $1,500 (about $16,000 in 2024) less than his $14,500 (about $158,000) salary of 1958—a 10.3 percent cut—Stevens reminded Giants fans that "until he was inadvertently stepped on and suffered painfully torn rib muscles, O'Connell was enjoying one of his top seasons. The Giants won with him, (and) began fading into the shadows created by accumulated defeat without him."

Now, sitting in the training room after that first workout of '59, Stevens asked Danny if all the speculation about losing his job depressed him. "No,"

Danny replied. "It made me mad. It seemed every week a story would come out saying something about the new second base-shortstop combination the Giants were going to use this year." In reporting the conversation, Stevens sympathetically noted that the Giants' announced plans to move Spencer from his shortstop position to second "leaves O'Connell standing mutely on the fringe of regular employment and protesting with the only weapons he has at his command—hustle and determination."

Danny wasn't exactly mute. "I'm going to prove them wrong," he told an AP reporter. "... I hope to show them some hitting this spring training so they'll have to put me somewhere - if not second, perhaps third. I'm still figuring on being in the starting lineup on Opening Day, unless it's already set, and I don't think it is."

But it was. Giants owner Horace Stoneham was a hands-on boss when it came to players, and Stoneham was fixated on the potential of a well-muscled 6'3" 200-lb. Bahamian who had never even seen a baseball until he was 17. Andre Rodgers had been a wizard at cricket in his home country, but agreed to give baseball a try when a Giants scout came calling in 1952.

A natural athlete, Rodgers tore through the minor leagues and in 1957 made it to the Giants. In July, he injured an ankle and was sent to the club's top minor-league team in Minneapolis. The following year he was assigned to their new top farm team in Phoenix, where he smacked Pacific Coast League pitching for a .354 average and 31 homers. He joined the big club in September but hit only .206 in 22 games.

Still, Stoneham was convinced the 25-year-old Rodgers was destined to be the next Ernie Banks, the Chicago Cubs' slugging shortstop who on his way to the Hall of Fame won back-to-back Most Valuable Player awards in 1958 and 1959. Giants manager Bill Rigney disagreed with his boss. "Andre Rodgers never quite did the things we hoped he could do," Rigney recalled years later. "Horace and I always had a big debate over who should play shortstop."

But Horace signed the checks, which meant Rodgers was going to be the Giants shortstop for 1959. Spencer, the incumbent shortstop who definitely was a better hitter than either Rodgers or Danny O'Connell but on defense couldn't catch a cold, was moved to second. Danny was assigned a seat on the bench—at the far end as it turned out.

Used sparingly in spring training games, O'Connell obligingly worked with his pal Spencer, teaching him the nuances of playing second. "I was making little mistakes, coming off the bag with my wrong foot," Spencer told a reporter, "but Danny has me straightened out." "Don't forget," O'Connell chimed in over Spencer's shoulder, "if you don't make it, I'm right behind you to take over."

As in 1958, the Giants were feted with a festive pre-season parade through downtown, complete with balloons and a half-ton of confetti that for some reason had been imported from Los Angeles. As the convertible containing O'Connell and Spencer passed the Internal Revenue Service building on McAllister Street, Danny stood, doffed his hat, bowed low toward the building and shouted "there's where it goes!"

Where Danny went—and stayed once the season began—was the bench. On Opening Day against the Cardinals, he watched Rodgers triple, walk and drive in a run. But Rodgers also made two errors. The next day, he made another one. And the day after that, and the day after that and so on for the first eight games of the season. By the 66th game, Rodgers had committed a hefty 21 errors. On June 30 he fumbled a routine grounder with two out in the eighth inning of a game against the Dodgers. The official scorer inexplicably ruled it a hit—the only one given up in the game by Giants pitcher Sad Sam Jones. After making another error the next game, Rodgers was benched. Even Stoneham had seen enough, and at the end of July, he was sent back to Phoenix.

But Spencer stayed at second and O'Connell stayed nearly invisible. To replace Rodgers, Rigney installed Eddie Bressoud at shortstop. Bressoud was a mediocre hitter but a dependable fielder. O'Connell, meanwhile, didn't even get into a game until April 22, and didn't start one until May 27, when he filled in for Jim Davenport at third base.

By August 1, Danny had appeared in a grand total of 10 games and had a total of 27 at-bats. Most of his appearances were to give Davenport or Spencer a day off or fill in for the defensively-challenged Spencer late in a tight game. (Spencer hit a respectable .262 with 12 homers for the season, but was second among N.L. second basemen in errors with 24, and had the next-to-worst fielding percentage.)

The highlight of O'Connell's season came on July 5, in the second game of a double-header against the Cardinals. Leading off and playing third, Danny singled in the first and scored on a Mays homer. He singled again leading off the third inning and scored on a single by Spencer. In the seventh, he reached on an error and came around again to score. The Giants won 4-2 to maintain a first-place tie with Milwaukee.

That was it for the highlights. The lowlights were numerous. One was the indignity that followed a season-ending injury to Davenport on August 17 after "Davvy" banged into Cincinnati catcher Ed Bailey trying to score and tore ligaments in his knee. Instead of using O'Connell, a panicky Rigney inserted Jackie Brandt, a 25-year-old outfielder with zero big-league games' experience at third base, into Davenport's slot. It did not go well. Rigney also tried Jose Pagan, a rookie shortstop who had been called up to take Rodgers' place on the team. Finally, he gave O'Connell a chance in September, with the Giants locked in a tight race with both the Dodgers and Braves.

That did not go well either. Danny was covered with rust from inactivity. In 12 games he went one for 18. The lowest of low points came September 13, when he was lifted for a pinch-hitter with the bases loaded—in the second inning. Salt was poured in O'Connell's wounded pride when the pinch-hitter, Dusty Rhodes, lofted a sacrifice fly that plated the game's only run. And that was after Danny had committed a first-inning error. After the game, Rigney admitted it was the earliest he had ever yanked anyone for a pinch-hitter. "But this year I've done a lot of things I've never done before," he said.

One of the things Rigney had done before was cheat—or at least be part of a team that resorted to ethically dubious maneuvers. In 1951, Rigney had been a backup infielder on the New York Giants when Leo Durocher, his predecessor as the Giants' skipper, okayed an elaborate system that involved planting a guy with a telescope in the team's centerfield clubhouse at the Polo Grounds; stealing the other team's pitching signs, then relaying them via a wire strung from centerfield to the Giants' dugout. There it was attached to a buzzer—one buzz for a fast ball, two for a breaking pitch. Someone in the dugout then relayed the signal to the batter.

Knowing what was coming was a valuable bit of information. After installing the buzzer system, the Giants won 36 of their last 45 games and overcame a 13.5-game lead by the Dodgers to win the pennant after a three-game playoff capped by Bobby Thomson's dramatic ninth-inning "Shot Heard 'Round the World" home run in the third game.

In 1959, Rigney approved a simpler stratagem that installed a fellow in the Seals Stadium scoreboard, who would use a telescope to get the sign put down by the opposing team's catcher, then relay it to the hitter by closing one or both of two slats on the scoreboard, depending on the pitch. Rigney's team used it in two games against the Braves, and then dropped the idea after relief pitcher Al "Red" Worthington, a born-again Christian, threatened to expose what he considered immoral behavior. Actually, it was unethical but not strictly illegal under baseball rules. Every team tried to steal signs, but usually through more conventional means such as relying on the sharp eyes of a coach or baserunner to pick up signals from the opposing catcher.

In any event, the Giants, who led by two games with eight to go in '59, got out of the scoreboard and promptly dropped three straight to the Dodgers (none of which Danny played in) and wound up finishing third, behind both Los Angeles and Milwaukee. Those two teams tied for first; the Dodgers won two straight games in a best-of-three playoff, and went on to win the World Series against the Chicago White Sox.

It was a dispiriting end to a miserable season. O'Connell's stats were microscopic. Getting into only 34 games and getting only 58 at-bats, he hit .190, with three doubles, five walks, six runs scored and zero homers, triples, stolen bases or runs batted in. He made four errors in 80 chances for the worst fielding percentage of his career.

Worse, he suffered through the season alone. While Vera and the kids stayed in New Jersey, Danny stayed at the comfortable but hardly ostentatious Benjamin Franklin hotel in San Mateo, about 20 miles south of Seals Stadium. On May 29, while Danny was playing against the Cardinals in a rare start in San Francisco (and going zero for four), Vera was giving birth to Daniel Francis O'Connell IV at St. Francis Hospital in Montclair, New Jersey. "My mom certainly understood," Danny the fourth said in a 2022 interview. "Everyone did. But it still had to have been rough for both of them for him not to be there."

Despite his meager contribution on the field, O'Connell's teammates voted him a full share ($1,338.34, or $14,480 in 2024) of the team's third-place share of World Series receipts. It was an indication of how much O'Connell was liked by the other players. They nicknamed him "Buzzy" because like a bee he seemed to be continually in motion—and also seemed to be continually making noise, whether it was singing in the shower, telling jokes or chirping at umpires from the dugout. The fact he remained on the major league roster for the full year indicated how Giants management at least appreciated the fact he never publicly griped about not playing, was a positive influence in the clubhouse and remained a first-class bench jockey, riding the opposition with good-humored razzing that helped keep the other players loose in a tight pennant race.

Back in Jersey, Danny refereed high school and other amateur basketball games. With the arrival of their first son in mid-1959 adding to their two daughters, the O'Connells took a gigantic domestic step late in the year. They bought a home in the middle-class town of Bloomfield, about 10 miles south of Paterson. Only 12 miles from the Lincoln Tunnel and New York City, Bloomfield had a population of around 50,000. Most important to the O'Connell clan, it was only a few miles from Vera's family in Upper Montclair. "My mother always used to joke that they bought it as a 'starter home,'" their son Danny said, "and she wound up living there 50 years."

Danny also once again conducted baseball clinics for the city of Hoboken. But even that took a sour turn. For some reason the city had agreed to pay O'Connell and three other players $4,000 each ($43,400) for the 10-week clinics rather than the usual $1,000. That outraged the 18 women who cleaned Hoboken's City Hall on a year-round basis for annual salaries of $2,700 ($29,213.) The fuss made nationwide news and the city council hastily reduced the ballplayers' fees back to $1,000 each.

All in all—with the singular exception of the birth of his first son—1959 was one crappy year for Danny O'Connell. "Danny told me he has no idea where he will play next season," O'Connell's newspaper pal Joe Gooter wrote in a mid-October column. But Gooter added that O'Connell pointed out with characteristic optimism "I know things have to be better than 1959. They couldn't be worse." He was overly optimistic.

Ty Cobb was 73 years old in the spring of 1960, ailing and just out of a Phoenix hospital after a surgical procedure that would help prolong his life for another 16 months. But Cobb, one of the greatest hitters of all time, felt well enough to visit the Giants training camp. "He appeared to have lost considerable weight," AP reported, "but he was vigorous enough to give Danny O'Connell, veteran infielder, personal instruction in hitting."

Going into the 1960 season, O'Connell needed all the help he could get. For one thing, there was the hangover of Danny's '59 season, which had been horrendous enough to end careers better than his. For another, there was a pre-season contract dispute. The Giants had offered $10,000 (about $106,400 in 2024) for the coming year, a hefty 23 percent cut from 1959. O'Connell sent the contract back unsigned. The Giants waited two weeks, then re-sent it. Danny got the message. This time he signed it.

Then there was the trade San Francisco had made over the winter. In return for Darryl Spencer and outfielder Leon Wagner, the Giants acquired Don Blasingame, the St. Louis second baseman whom they had sought before the '59 season. Blasingame was coming off a year in which he hit a solid .289 with an impressive .361 on-base percentage, and had fielded his position well. There was no question who the new Giants' second baseman was going to be for 1960. For his part, Spencer did not go quietly to St. Louis. "I broke my back for San Francisco," he said. "… We'da won the pennant if Danny O'Connell had played second and I had played shortstop."

The Giants also picked up utility infielder Joey Amalfitano, and it became quickly apparent that he and Andre Rodgers would be the club's backup infielders. O'Connell got only 10 at-bats in spring training games, getting three hits. It didn't help when he fouled a pitch off his left big toe and had to have two holes drilled in the toenail to relieve pressure. "It looks as if time is up for the veteran and popular Danny O'Connell," wrote the *Examiner's* Walter Judge.

Columnist Jack Handley of the *Santa Rosa (Ca.) Press Democrat* astutely noted that Danny had even more at stake than it might appear to the average fan. "If he makes the team," Handley wrote, "his present five-year player pension status will jump to the 10-year category after July [21st]...So O'Connell is battling with a two-fold purpose as his objective: (1) a job with a potential pennant winner, (2) an enhanced pension in the not-too-distant future for Danny Boy."

Baseball's pension system was rooted in the unrest of players at the end of World War II. The brief rise of the Mexican League, a spate of lawsuits challenging the reserve clause and other owner-friendly contract provisions, and the threat of a players union had prodded the game's feudal lords into agreeing to some post-career compensation for their serfs. The system, which went into effect in 1947 and was amended periodically over the years, was financed by annual contributions from players, coaches and managers that were matched by the clubs. In addition, revenues from TV and radio broadcast rights for World Series coverage and a chunk of money from the All-Star Game went into the system.

Payments would begin when a player reached the age of 50 and would transfer to his widow if and when the player died. But to be eligible, a player had to have at least five years in the major leagues, with a significant bump for that very rare player who lasted 10 years. In 1968, for example, a five-year man would be eligible for $643 a month ($5,818 in 2024) while a 10-year veteran would get $1,288 a month ($11,672.)

As the 1960 season began, Danny O'Connell was still a few months short of the 10-year mark. He had begun his run in the big leagues in July 1950. Under a federal law enacted to benefit World War II and Korean War veterans, he received credit toward his pension for the two seasons he lost while in the Army. He needed just a few months more.

But when it came to his baseball career, it seemed O'Connell's middle name was "almost." On April 4, a week before the season began, Danny was released by the Giants. "O'Connell, 32 (he was actually 31), would have been a 10-year man if he had lasted until July 20," the *Examiner* calculated. "Too bad his bat couldn't match his personality."

The next day, Danny told his New Jersey journalist pal Joe Gooter how he had been summoned to a Phoenix hotel room by Giants vice president Chub Feeney and manager Bill Rigney and told the team just had too many infielders. "I felt good and seemed to be coming along," O'Connell said, "but I guess the club had given up on me even before the spring rolled around." He hastened to add he thought the Giants had been "very fair with me. They offered me a chance to go to their farm team in Tacoma, Washington, which is in a good league with nice ballparks. I will receive the same salary specified by my Giants contract even though I'll be playing minor league ball."

O'Connell told Gooter he was weighing his options, which in addition to the Giants' Tacoma offer included trying to catch on with another major league club or accepting an offer to play with the San Diego Padres of the Pacific Coast League, where his old Pirates buddy, Ralph Kiner, was the general manager.

"Certainly I have no intentions of retiring yet," Danny said. "If I am able to land a place with a major league club, fine. If not, I'll go to one of the minor league clubs. I think I would consider retiring if I couldn't move back to the big time in another season. But I believe I can do it. Right now, I'm not sure if I can play baseball or not. I have seen little action for two years, and I would like to find that out for myself."

A week later, he headed to Tacoma.

The major leagues' move west dramatically changed the landscape of the Pacific Coast League. The Dodgers and Giants collectively agreed to pay the PCL a relatively token $946,000 ($10.3 million in 2024) as compensation for usurping the league's two biggest markets. The Dodgers moved their new PCL farm team, the Los Angeles Angels, to Spokane, Washington. Faced with big-league competition, a second L.A.-area team, the Hollywood Stars, grudgingly fled to Salt Lake City.

The Giants, who had traded their Triple-A affiliate in Minneapolis to the Boston Red Sox for the Sox-owned San Francisco Seals, moved the Seals to Phoenix. But after two years beneath a roasting Sonoran Desert sun, the Giants looked to relocate their top minor-league club to the cooler, if quite a bit soggier, Pacific Northwest. They settled on Tacoma, a city of 150,000 about 30 miles south of Seattle, on the condition local officials could have a playing venue ready by Opening Day 1960. They could. Pierce County taxpayers ponied up $840,000 ($8.9 million) through a bond issuance and local lumber magnate and baseball fanatic Ben Cheney kicked in another $100,000 ($1 million.)

The resulting handsome 8,000-seat ballpark—by no coincidence named Ben Cheney Stadium - was built in slightly more than 100 days. Fittingly, it incorporated seats and light standards from San Francisco's Seals Stadium. That park was torn down even as the Giants were moving into Candlestick Park, a windswept and generally miserable stadium that would imprison the team for four decades before it moved into a fabulous waterfront ballpark in 2000.

The new Tacoma Giants were part of a league with a long and storied history. The Pacific Coast League was born in 1903, and by mid-century had established a reputation as "the third major league." Mild weather, easy travel between the league's cities, generally nice ballparks, relatively good salaries and a high-quality level of play made the PCL attractive enough that some players actually preferred it to the eastern-based National and American leagues. Those who didn't included PCL "graduates" like Ted Williams and Joe DiMaggio.

By 1960, the PCL was feeling an economic pinch from competition with nationally televised major league games and the recent incursion of the Giants and Dodgers to the West Coast. But it was still populated by an intriguing mix of rising young players on their way to stardom and fading former big leaguers who nonetheless had some skills still left in their tanks.

Tacoma's 1960 club, for example, included a 22-year-old right-handed pitcher from the Dominican Republic who was on his way to the Hall of Fame. Juan Marichal would become one of the two or three most dominant pitchers of the coming decade. The team also featured a 33-year-old free spirit who had been the hitting hero of the 1954 World Series for the New York Giants. Dusty Rhodes would lead Tacoma in home runs in 1960, then "hang 'em up"—literally—in retiring from the team two years later by nailing his shoes to the clubhouse wall.

And then there was Danny O'Connell. At 31, his playing-days clock was winding down. The few months he was short of earning a 10-year man's major league pension was a Damoclean sword hanging over his family's future financial security. A good season—make that a really good season—with Tacoma would enhance his chances of making it back to the big leagues in 1961. A bad or even ho-hum year would quite likely doom him to winding up his baseball career in the minors, or push him into retirement from the game. Having failed to interest another big-league team to sign him after being cut by San Francisco, Danny was taking a high-stakes gamble he could not avoid.

His season got off to a good start—when Tacoma's season finally started. Heavy rain delayed Opening Day from April 14 to April 16. To dry out Cheney Stadium's new playing surface, soldiers from nearby Fort Lewis used heavy hot-air blowers connected to long hoses and a napalm-fueled fire on the infield.

O'Connell singled in the first inning, which was also the team's first hit of the year. At the end of May, he was hitting over .300, and stayed consistently just over or just under that percentage throughout the season. He also fielded like a talented youngster. "Danny O'Connell has come up with some four-star defensive plays at second base for the Giants," wrote sports editor Dan Walton of Tacoma's *News Tribune*, "but the Tacoma fans haven't seen anything yet." Tacoma manager Red Davis concurred. "Danny is a smart ballplayer," Davis said, "and just wait until he learns more about playing the hitters in this league."

The league's players occasionally learned the hard way about O'Connell's baseball smarts. In a June game against Vancouver, he pulled off the purposely-dropped infield fly trick to turn a double play. In a game against Spokane in August, he innocently asked Willie Davis, a future big-league star with the Dodgers and the fastest man in the PCL, to step off second so O'Connell could whisk off the dirt Davis had just kicked there while sliding in with a double. When Davis obliged, a grinning Danny tagged him out.

"I'd like to have that second sacker of yours, Danny O'Connell, playing for my side," San Diego Padres manager George "Catfish" Metkovich told a reporter. "I know him—played with him in Milwaukee. He plays heads-up baseball." Another old O'Connell teammate praised him from afar. "He'll be back [to the majors,] Pittsburgh Pirates manager Danny Murtaugh told the *New York Daily News*. "He's manager material."

O'Connell even led the league in larynx utility. When the club scheduled several Fan Night events, Danny led the assemblage in "community sing-alongs." During one particularly long rain delay, he climbed onto the dugout roof and entertained the hearty faithful who stuck it out by belting out a few tunes. "Second sacker Danny O'Connell, an Irish tenor, is the sweetest warbler on the Tacoma roster," gushed the hometown paper.

As the season wound down, Tacoma manager Red Davis publicly thanked O'Connell for his leadership. During an interview with *News Tribune* sports editor Dan Walton, Davis said "I'd like to stick in here something about the tremendous help Danny O'Connell was to the team and to me personally. He not only was a terrific performer, but he helped me out with the young players, particularly when I couldn't take another mound visit" because of a rule limiting the number of per-inning trips by a coach or manager.

Tacoma went 81-73, finishing second in the standings. As important, the team attracted 270,024 fans, outdrawing every minor league club in the country except the Buffalo Bisons, who had a bigger population base from which to draw.

Danny, meanwhile, led the team in hitting with a .312 average (seventh in the league), was second in hits and doubles and fourth in runs batted in. He was named to both the mid-season All-Star team and *Look* magazine's post-season All-PCL team. League managers voted him the PCL's best hit-and-run man, and with shortstop Jose Pagan the league's best double-play combination. "He was the keystone of the infield," the *News Tribune* extolled. "… Too, he was the one Giant who could be counted on to advance a base runner, and in many tense situations it was Danny's skillful bat which propelled a desperately needed tally across the plate."

O'Connell had done what he could to show he could still play baseball well. Now he needed a little help. For a change he got it, in part and indirectly from the man who had started him toward the big leagues 15 years before - and who had sold him twice.

If anything frightened Branch Rickey, it was being deemed irrelevant, particularly to the game that had consumed most of his life for the past 60 years. So when Bill Shea asked him in the summer of 1959 to become president of something called the Continental League, Rickey jumped at the chance—or at least as much as 77-year-old men with bad hearts can jump.

William Shea was a former college basketball player who had evolved into a prominent corporate attorney in Manhattan. He was also a baseball fan greatly dismayed at the departure of the Giants and Dodgers after the 1957 season, leaving American's largest metropolis bereft of a National League team. Asked by New York City Mayor Robert Wagner to find a replacement, Shea first attempted to lure an existing National League franchise to the Big Apple, then to convince Major League Baseball to expand by creating new franchises. He failed in both efforts.

Shea had read a long interview Rickey granted *The Sporting News* in 1958 while he was still recovering from a heart attack earlier in the year. In the piece, the "Thomas Edison of baseball" called for the invention of a third eight-team major league to complement the existing National and American leagues. Rickey pointed out that the number of major league franchises had been stuck at 16 since 1903, even as the nation's population had more than doubled.

"The time is ripe for the Majors to expand," Rickey said. "It should be the creation of the present two leagues. It should be formed with their coopera-tion, if possible, and if not, then without their cooperation...but a third league is something we must have soon." Shea agreed. For months he traveled around the United States and Canada, talking to people with pockets deep enough to finance a big league-caliber team. By August 1959 he had lined up enough solid interest to approach Rickey about becoming the new league's leader.

Since being ousted as general manager of the Pittsburgh Pirates after the 1955 season, Rickey had been in restless semi-retirement. But he was still widely respected, even revered, as the builder of baseball dynasties in St. Louis and Brooklyn, the innovator who gave the game everything from minor league farm systems to batting helmets, and the trailblazer who helped spark the Civil Rights Movement by signing Jackie Robinson to a major league contract. He was also still feared by many of the game's oligarchs whom he had bested in various past conflicts. Rickey's involvement with the new league gave it considerable gravitas.

The lords of baseball were well aware of Shea's efforts even before he approached Rickey. They were also well aware that Congress was once again pondering changes to baseball's judicially sanctified exemption from the nation's anti-trust laws. Particularly noxious to the existing team owners was a provision in a pending bill that would impose a limit of 80 players whose livelihoods could be controlled by any one club. Through their farm systems, some teams controlled as many as 300 players. The proposed limit would free hundreds of players to sign with other teams—even clubs in the Continental

League.

So MLB owners pretended to welcome the prospect of new and equal members to their fraternity. "The Major Leagues recognize the desire of certain groups to obtain major league franchises," Commissioner Ford Frick announced after a secret meeting of MLB club owners at the plush Ohio thoroughbred farm of Pirates owner John Galbreath in May 1959, "and since there is no existing plan to expand the present Major Leagues, the two Major Leagues hereby declare they will favorably consider an application for major league status within the present baseball structure by an acceptable group of eight clubs which would qualify under 10 specifications."

The conditions Frick outlined included minimum-sized stadiums of 25,000 seats in cities no smaller than Kansas City, Missouri, which with a population of 440,000 was at the time the smallest big-league city. The new league would have to play a 154-game schedule and adopt MLB's standard contract, which included the infamous reserve clause binding players to a club as long as the club pleased. All of the potential Continental League (CL) franchises—New York, Toronto, Houston, Dallas-Ft. Worth, Minneapolis-St. Paul, Buffalo, Denver and Atlanta—seemingly could meet all the conditions.

By pretending to welcome a new major league, MLB owners hoped to convince Congress there was no need for lawmakers to tinker with the way things were and had been for decades. It worked. No legislation was passed. "The less Congress has to do with organized baseball," said Sen. Ken Keating, R-New York, "the better baseball will be for the fans and the players."

Thus unfettered by sensible legal strictures, MLB owners adopted a new tactic of conquest by absorption. On Aug. 2, 1960, while Danny O'Connell was in Tacoma going one for two with a walk in a 12-1 romp over Seattle, a cadre of Major League owners were meeting with their Continental League counterparts in a Chicago hotel conference room. "There is only one move open," Los Angeles Dodgers owner Walter O'Malley said. "We must compromise. We will take four of your cities and later the rest."

The Continental League owners excused themselves to huddle privately, and then returned to accept the offer. The deal, they figured, would head off a long and costly war, and would assure their respective cities entry into the big leagues. Rickey went home. He would die in 1965, 11 days short of his 84th birthday, after suffering a stroke while giving a speech.

On October 17, the National League announced it would welcome new franchises in New York and Houston, beginning with the 1962 season. The American League eventually decided to double-cross both the Continental League owners and the Dodgers' O'Malley by putting a team in Los Angeles, which had not been among the original CL cities and which infuriated O'Malley, who regarded L.A. as his city. The other new A.L. franchise was given to Washington D.C., to replace the economically crippled existing club there that had been allowed to move to Minneapolis. Moreover, the American League announced it would get the jump on the National League by fielding its new teams in 1961.

What all of these machinations and manipulations meant to Daniel Francis O'Connell III was that there would be 50 more jobs in the major leagues in the coming season. Now all he had to do was land one of them.

CHAPTER 14 NOTES

On a pleasant *San Francisco Chronicle*, Feb. 18, 1959.

When Danny had *San Francisco Chronicle*, Jan. 24, 1959.

Now, sitting in *San Francisco Chronicle*, Feb. 18, 1959.

Danny wasn't exactly *Redwood City (Ca.) Tribune*, Feb. 16, 1959, p. 8.

Stoneham, however, was Steve Bitker, *The Original San Francisco Giants*, p. 55.

Used sparingly in *San Francisco Chronicle*, March 28, 1959.

As in 1958, *San Francisco Chronicle*, April 14, 1959, p. 11.

That did not *Redwood City (Ca.) Tribune*, Sept. 14, 1959, p. 10.

Worse, he suffered, Author's interview, Feb. 15, 2022.

Back in Jersey Author's interview, Feb. 15, 2022.

All in all *The (Paterson NJ) News*, Oct. 17, 1959, p. 14.

Ty Cobb was *The (Allentown Pa.) Morning Call*, March 8, 1960, p. 14.

There was the *Rutland (Vt.) Daily Herald*, April 6, 1960, p. 17. Blasingame hit .235 for the Giants in 1960, and the team, a pre-season favorite for the pennant, finished a distant fifth.

The Giants also *San Francisco Examiner*, March 29, 1960, p. 43.

Columnist Jack Handley *Santa Rosa (Ca.) Press Democrat*, March 14, 1960, p. 12.

Payments would begin The pension example comes from a Feb. 16, 1968 letter to *Cincinnati Enquirer* sports editor Ken Smith from MLB public relations director Joseph Reichler. National Baseball Hall of Fame archives.

But when it *San Francisco Examiner*, April 5, 1960, p. 45.

The next day *The (Paterson NJ) Evening News*, April 6, 1960, p. 13.

"Certainly I have" Ibid.

The resulting handsome If there was any consolation for O'Connell in being cut, it was he never had to play at Candlestick. He also got to be on a Topps baseball card that had been readied for distribution before he was released.

The new Tacoma The city had a PCL franchise in 1905, but it moved to Sacramento after only one season.

O'Connell singled in *The (Tacoma Wa.) News Tribune*, April 26, 1960, p. 17.

The league's players *Spokane Chronicle*, Aug. 6, 1960, p. 8.

"I'd like to" *The (Tacoma Wa.) News Tribune*, May 20, 1960, p. 39; *New York Daily News*, April 28, 1960, p. 90.

O'Connell even led *The (Tacoma Wa.) News Tribune*, July 12, 1960, p. 16.

As the season *The (Tacoma Wa.) News Tribune*, Aug. 23, 1960, p. 24.

Danny, meanwhile, led *The (Tacoma Wa.) News Tribune*, Dec. 11, 1960, p. 57. For the uninitiated, the hit-and-run play is a somewhat risky tactic that is actually named backwards. It involves a base runner taking off for the next base as the pitch is delivered and relies on the batter, who's been alerted via signals that the play is on, to make contact with the pitch. O'Connell was not only adept at the hit-and-run, he was also an excellent bunter.

"The time is" *The Sporting News*, May 21, 1958, p. 1.

So the lords *The Sporting News*, May 27, 1959, p. 8.

By pretending to G. Scott Thomas, *A Brand-New Ballgame*, p. 221.

Thus unfettered by Michael Shapiro, *Bottom of the Ninth*, pp. 213-214. The Machiavellian O'Malley's promise about the majors absorbing all the CL cities was just sort-of true. New York and Houston (1962), Toronto (1977) and Denver (1993) all got expansion teams. Atlanta, Minneapolis and the Dallas-Ft. Worth area got existing MLB franchises that moved from Milwaukee, Washington D.C. and Washington D.C. again. Milwaukee and D.C., in turn, got replacement teams in the form of expansion franchises. Buffalo is still waiting.

"O'CONNELL...FINE NAME"
DANNY'S RETURN

O n Sept. 11, 1960 in Washington State, Danny O'Connell was wondering where his next paycheck would come from. Almost precisely seven months later in Washington, D.C, Danny O'Connell was chatting with the brand-new president of the United States. In between was a tale of perseverance and luck for a baseball player whose career had been marked by plenty of the former and a paucity of the latter.

O'Connell's journey began by taking his fate into his own hands. As a condition of his reporting to Tacoma before the start of the 1960 season, Danny had arranged with the Giants to become a free agent at the end of the season. It was a gamble that allowed him to make his own deal for 1961 but also carried the risk he wouldn't be able to find a job with another major league club, particularly if he had a bad year.

He had a very good year, however, and, as the Tacoma *News Tribune* reported, he "left right after the [season's] wind-up doubleheader on his solo automobile jaunt for New Jersey." But O'Connell was not only going home; he was going job-hunting. "I figured I'd start with the worst clubs and see if I couldn't get somebody to give me a tryout," Danny recalled months later. "When the Philadelphia Phillies [the National League's last-place club in 1960 with a record of 59-95] turned me down, I was afraid it was going to be pretty tough to get anybody to give me a look."

Boston and Kansas City also told him no thanks. The Yankees offered him a job as a player-coach with their top farm team at Richmond, Virginia, for more than he had made with Tacoma. After thinking it over for a day or two, O'Connell turned them down. He knew a bad year in the minors would finish him and even a good one might accomplish nothing more except put him in the same hunt in 1962, when he would be a year older.

But the looming expansion of the American League in the 1961 season gave him a Plan B. On November 17, owners of the existing eight A.L. clubs met at the Savoy-Hilton Hotel in New York City to screen prospective owners of the two new franchises awarded to Los Angeles and Washington D.C. So Danny went to the Savoy. Unfortunately, that was as far as he had planned his Plan B.

O'Connell wandered around, unsure of who he was looking for, and eventually found himself in what was serving as the press room for the meetings. "I was down, and I looked it," he recalled, "and the writers helped me. They said a guy named Quesada was in as the new Washington owner and suggested I see him."

Elwood Richard "Pete" Quesada was indeed the new principal owner of the new Washington Senators. A decorated former Air Force general and aircraft industry executive, Quesada had recently stepped down as chairman of the Federal Aviation Administration to get into the baseball business. He and a group of nine D.C.-area businessmen had out-talked two other groups to win rights to a team replacing the existing Washington club that was moving to Minneapolis. Only Danny couldn't find Quesada at the Savoy, and subsequently couldn't get him on the phone.

Thwarted but undaunted, O'Connell launched Plan C. This took him 10 days later to Louisville Kentucky, where baseball executives were convening for the annual minor league meetings. For the better part of two days, Danny tried in vain to arrange a meeting with Ed Doherty, the longtime president of the Triple-A International Association who had been named general manager of the new Washington Senators.

Daunted but not defeated—and lucky for a change—O'Connell ran into Rosy Ryan, general manager of the Tacoma team for which Danny had labored the previous season. He asked Ryan for a favor: Would he put in a good word for Danny with Doherty? Ryan not only readily assented, it turned out he was an old friend of Washington's new G.M. Give him a day off now and then, Ryan told Doherty, and Danny O'Connell could still play at the major league level. O'Connell fielded his position well, had an off-the-charts baseball IQ, was a terrific presence in the clubhouse, "and after watching him all season on our club," Ryan said, "I'm convinced he can hit enough if they had to bring him up to the plate in a wheelchair."

So Doherty agreed to meet Danny in the bar of Louisville's venerable Brown Hotel and listen to his pitch. It was simple math, O'Connell explained.

Under the existing stipulations MLB owners had established, each existing team would expose seven roster players who could be drafted by the new clubs—for $75,000 each (about $790,000 in 2024.) Any minor league player under the contractual control of a big-league club could be had for $25,000 ($263,000.) Doherty had already secured two minor league pitchers, paying $50,000 for a duo that would win a combined total of three games for the Senators before fading away.

"I'm a better ballplayer than most of those fellows you're going to pay $75,000 each for in that player raffle," O'Connell told Doherty. "And you can sign me for nothing as a free agent." Coupled with Ryan's hearty recommendation, Doherty was sold. "We didn't even have any blank contracts," he related to a Washington writer. "We signed him in the hotel lobby on a piece of scrap paper." The numbers on the scrap paper were reported to be impressively generous: a salary of $15,000 ($158,000 in 2024) plus a signing bonus of $5,000 ($52,700.)

Elated, Danny flew home. But his joy was tempered by the realization he had yet to earn the money. "I don't know if I'll be a regular or a benchwarmer," he told a New Jersey reporter a week after signing. "I used to gripe about not playing with the Giants, but I won't do that anymore." When another writer jokingly asked him where he'd been playing, Danny quipped "Near Alaska, a place called Tacoma. And it's nice to be interviewed again. First time since I left the [S.F.] Giants. Now I know I'm back in the majors."

But Danny was scared, and that fact shone through a few minutes later in the interview when the writer asked about O'Connell's immediate plans. "I'm looking for a job," Danny replied. "Know anybody who wants a bright young guy? Seriously, I'm concerned about the future. I haven't too much time left as a player and if I don't make it as a manager or coach I've got to find some line. I'm interested in public relations or real estate. I'd almost work for nothing to learn something."

O'Connell packed his concerns along with his glove and cleats in mid-February when he left for the Senators' training camp at Pompano Beach, Florida. He arrived two weeks earlier than he had to, and several pounds heavier than he wanted. "I was scared all the way through spring training," he recalled. "I didn't know if I could make the club. I just wanted to stay, as a utility man or anything else."

He had reason to be concerned. Washington had four other players in camp who had played at least a few games at second base in the majors, and all of them were younger than O'Connell. "Mickey," he told Senators' manager Mickey Vernon, "I'll play wherever you need me." Vernon had his qualms. "I thought maybe he'd play 80 or 90 games filling in here and there," Vernon said in an interview six months later, "and during spring training I began to doubt if Danny could play that many. He was slow rounding into shape."

The 52-year-old Vernon, whose given first name was James, was a rookie manager who had been a marvelous player. For much of the 1940s and 1950s, he was regarded as perhaps the best first baseman in the American League. He twice led the league in hitting, was an excellent fielder and a good base-runner. A seven-time All-Star, Vernon compiled nearly 2,500 hits over a two-decade career. And unlike two of O'Connell's previous big-league managers—the finger-pointing Fred Haney and the neurotic Bill Rigney—Vernon was an easy-going and well-liked fellow. More important for O'Connell, Vernon gave more weight to playing hard and smart than to statistics and sports writers' second-guessing.

"He gives the hitter more confidence than any manager I've ever played for," O'Connell said of Vernon. "We're supposed to be major leaguers and he knows that. He puts a lot of us on our own, when to take a pitch, when to hit and run...and I appreciate his respect for a player's experience."

Danny's confidence was also buoyed by the presence of his family. Vera and the three kids joined him in Florida and would accompany him to Washington—assuming he made the team. The O'Connells would rent out their still-relatively new Bloomfield home for $200 ($2,100 in 2024) a month. One prospective tenant was the New York Yankees right fielder, Roger Maris. The A.L.'s reining MVP was sold on the idea—but Mrs. Maris wasn't. "That's too much money to spend for housing," Patricia Maris said, and went back to the family's home near Kansas City, Missouri. Maris spent the season in a New York apartment he shared with teammates Mickey Mantle and Bob Cerv. (He had a pretty good year anyway—hitting 61 home runs in breaking Babe Ruth's 34-year-old single-season record.)

By April 1, O'Connell had slimmed down, sped up and was hitting .364, or more than 200 percentage points higher than his nearest competitor. "O'Connell has made this ballclub," Vernon announced. "… He has been playing second base, but I know he can play short and third too. He's been around and he's a good man to have on a club like this."

The unanswered question was Danny's durability over a long hot summer in Washington. "O'Connell says he can go the whole season," the *Evening Star* reported. "'Not all 162 games,' he says. 'The way the game is played now, with all the night games and travel, even the young guys need a rest every couple of weeks or so.'" Danny also predicted he and his ragtag cohort of teammates might surprise a few people when the season started. "If we can keep hustling," he said, "no one is going to run over us." And then the season started.

If the new Washington Senators had one thing going for them, it was that they didn't have a tough act to follow. The old Washington Senators, in a word, stank. In 59 years, they won three pennants and one World Series, none of them since 1933. In the ensuing 26 years, the team finished sixth or lower 18 times. Their attendance correlated with their performance: from 1955 to 1960, the Senators annually attracted fewer customers than any other major league club. They were so reliably bad they inspired one of baseball's most oft-repeated quips: "Washington: first in war, first in peace, and last in the American League."

As the old team moved on to Minneapolis (where they would win the American League pennant in 1965), expectations for the new team were not high. More than a few pundits picked them to finish 10th, lower than any team in major league history owing to the fact there were now 10 A.L. teams when there had previously been no more than eight.

Like their predecessors, the new Senators (called the "Nats" in newspaper shorthand) would play their home games in creaky old Griffith Stadium, a steel-and-concrete structure that opened in 1911 and seated maximum crowds of only 27,000 to 29,000, depending on that season's configuration. It was a long poke to left field (388 feet) and center (421 feet) but a fair 320 feet to right.

One of the more time-honored Washington traditions was that every U.S.

president since William Howard Taft in 1910 had thrown out a ceremonial Opening Day first pitch at least once during their White House tenures. Taft's eighth successor was no exception. The 43-year-old John Fitzgerald Kennedy had been chief executive for exactly 80 days when the Senators season opened April 10. "The youngest [elected] president demonstrated more zip on the ball than any of his predecessors," *Washington Post* writer Shirley Povich wryly noted. "The official pitch was a whizzing fastball that cleared the heads of all the assembled Washington and [Chicago] White Sox players except Jim Rivera, the White Sox outfielder who was playing deep."

Despite game-time temperatures in the low 50s and a biting breeze, Kennedy stuck it out the entire game, munching a hot dog, sipping a soft drink and cheering vociferously for the home team. Sitting just above the Senators' dugout, the President—himself a scion of the "Auld Sod"—"spotted an Irish face among" the Senators, New York's *Daily News* reported. "'Who are you?' Kennedy asked. 'Where are you from?' 'Danny O'Connell, New Jersey,' was the proud answer. 'O'Connell,' said JFK. 'Fine name.'"

Hitting seventh, Danny went two for four before being lifted for a pinch-runner in the seventh inning of a game Washington lost 4-3. The game was the only one played in the majors on the 10th. The resulting dearth of fodder for sports pages meant a dramatic wire service photo of Danny barreling into second base to break up a double play appeared in hundreds of newspapers across the country. All in all, it was an auspicious start to the season.

In fact, the first two months of the season brimmed with auspiciousness. On June 15, the Nats defeated the Orioles in Baltimore 5-2, which evened Washington's season record at 30-30 and tied them with the Orioles for fourth place. "The team that was supposed to be just about everybody's patsy is at the .500 mark in mid-June," wrote the *Evening Star's* Bill Fuchs, who grandiloquently described the team as riding "on the pink cloud of success" and being "baseball's surprise story of the year."

Leading off and playing third base in the June 15 game, O'Connell went two for three with two walks, two runs scored and two RBIs. One of his hits was his first homer of the season, a third-inning 315-foot fly ball that just cleared the left field fence and landed in the first row of seats. At game's end, Danny was hitting a not-too-shabby .267 with a glittering .391 on-base percentage. He had played in all but two of the team's first 60 games, splitting time between second base and third as well as occasionally pinch-hitting.

However he got into the game, it seemed he found a way to contribute. In an 8-7 win over the Yankees in May, O'Connell got two hits, walked and was twice hit by pitches. In a June game against the White Sox, he batted for second baseman Chuck Cottier with two outs in the ninth inning of a tie game and drove in the winning run with a single. Two days later against Detroit, he drove in three runs with two doubles and a single and scored twice in a 7-4 win.

"O'Connell could be voted the most valuable player on this club," manager Vernon told *The Sporting News*. "He gets on base for us. He draws more walks than anybody on the club. He hits behind the runner, and he's as useful a hitter as we have on the ballclub"

The team's unexpected success, however, did not arouse great interest in the local citizenry. By mid-June, the new Senators had actually attracted fewer customers than the departed team of the year before. Part of the reason was the drawing power of the personnel. Bad as they were overall, the 1960 team had some genuine stars such as future Hall of Fame slugger Harmon Killebrew and flame-throwing pitcher Camilo Pascual. The '61 club on the other hand was comprised of solid players whose best days were behind them, like outfielder Gene Woodling, who had played on five World Series champion teams with the Yankees, and untested rookies like 21-year-old pitcher Claude Osteen.

A more ingrained part of the attendance problem was the fact that America's capital was just not all that wild about the National Pastime. As one local wit put it, "we like having a baseball team, we just don't like watching it." As the Senators' season progressed, not watching them became more and more understandable.

If people weren't flocking to see Danny O'Connell play in person in 1961, they certainly were buying a hefty number of his baseball cards. Or at least baseball cards in general. The Newspaper Enterprise Association (NEA) estimated 250 million cards would be sold in 1961. United Press International

(UPI) calculated $30 million worth of bubble gum would be sold, much of it accompanied by cards, and extrapolated that figure to represent 168.4 million pieces of gum—and at five cards per pack—842 million cards. While declining to discuss specific numbers, a spokesman for the Topps Company impishly suggested it was easy to know when baseball season had begun: "Our wrappers are lying all over the place with unchewed gum still inside."

The dubious accuracy of news service math notwithstanding, there were a lot of cards sold. "The card business now is so big that it supports another big business," an NEA writer marveled: "Dealers in second-hand and out-of-print baseball cards needed to fill out collections. Their market: not only kids but at least 5,000 full-grown American men and women. In the words of one dealer, 'what's so funny? Some people collect Rembrandts and Picassos. Others collect cards.'" The most valuable card in 1961, dealers said, was the Honus Wagner "T206" tobacco card from 1909. The estimate at the time was there were only six in existence and the card's value was an impressive $250 (about $2,600 in 2024.)

Danny O'Connell's '61 card (Topps No. 318) was only a penny (10.5 cents.) On the front is a closeup head shot. His hair is neatly short and his trademark five o'clock shadow proudly evident. He appears to have either a small wad of chewing tobacco in his right cheek, or he has the mumps. His demeanor is far more serious than most of his previous cards. On the back, three little cartoons report he hit .312 at Tacoma in 1960, once hit three triples in a game and pitched in the minors in 1946. (The last cartoon is wrong.)

Danny's card was one of 587 in Topps' 1961 set. The Brooklyn-based company completely dominated the baseball card business, although there were still a few competitors selling bubble gum. Fleer, the Philadelphia-based company that first gave the world bubble gum in 1928, did put out an 88-card set featuring long-gone players such as Roger Peckinpaugh, a shortstop whose career ended in 1927 and who was unknown even to the fathers of most card buyers. The set did not sell well. Fleer also tried to lure current players whose exclusive agreements with Topps had lapsed, into signing non-exclusive deals that paid the same $125 Topps paid, plus a 5 percent cut of the gross sales. There were few takers. Donruss, a seven-year-old Memphis-based company, limited its efforts to a set of what were correctly called "Idiot" cards that featured cartoonish figures telling lame jokes.

Despite Topps' dominance, its rivals could not be accused of accepting their lot meekly. In March, prosecutors in Queens County, New York, announced they were charging Donald Wiener—the self-proclaimed "Bubble Gum King" who was also president of the Donruss company—with commercial bribery. Wiener was accused of trying to entice a Topps machinist into giving Wiener the specifications for a machine that Topps used to wrap its cards, instead of the laborious hand-wrapping process Donruss used. The machinist went to the cops instead, who arrested Wiener at a New York airport cocktail lounge after he handed the Topps worker $1,500 ($15,800.) Topps officials, figuring the embarrassment Wiener suffered was punishment enough, declined to prosecute, and the charges were dropped.

Topps also introduced a new product in 1961: stamps that depicted various players and could be pasted into collector albums. One kid successfully mailed a fan letter to Yankees pitcher Whitey Ford affixed with a stamp of Yankees catcher Elston Howard instead of an official U.S. postage stamp. Noting the letter's postmark, Ford quipped "Hmmm, Brooklyn. It figures. The kid has larceny in his heart. He'll probably grow up and sell the [Brooklyn] Bridge."

Topps had no intention of relaxing its iron grip on the industry, or on the multitudes of players under its sticky control. By 1961 it employed at least one fulltime scout who roamed the country signing hundreds of potential big leaguers to exclusive contracts. A former scout for the Dodgers, Yankees and Cubs, Turk Karam was aided in his quest by an army of high school, semi-pro and minor league coaches and managers who picked up a buck or two from Topps for tipping the company to prospects. In return for the chance to one day have their photos on a Topps baseball card—and no other company's -- the prospects got exactly $5.

One of Karam's bird dogs sent a tip from Pine Grove, Pennsylvania, a small town about 100 miles northwest of Philadelphia. And in May, 1961, the parents of 19-year-old George Brommer, who had been a multi-sport star at Pine Grove High, were thrilled to receive a letter from Topps maven Sy Berger. Their son, Berger informed them, had been identified by the gum company "as a prospective major leaguer." Since George was not yet 21, Berger needed his folks to sign the binding agreement to put him on a card once he made the big leagues.

Enclosed with the letter was a set of FAQs "most prevalently asked by parents;" a copy of the gift catalog from which major league players could choose merchandise in return for allowing use of their likenesses on cards, and Berger's phone number in Brooklyn, which they could call collect with any questions. "We look forward to having your boy with Topps in our Baseball Program," Berger concluded.

Berger's letter arrived at the Brommer household while George was in Jamestown, New York. After receiving what was described as a "substantial" bonus from the Detroit Tigers in 1960, Brommer, a pitcher-shortstop, was assigned to a Class D club in Montgomery, Alabama. In 1961, he graduated to the Jamestown Tigers, a Detroit farm team in the New York-Penn League, which was a distant successor to the North Atlantic League where Danny O'Connell began his own professional career in 1946.

But a week after his folks got the letter from Topps, George was given his unconditional release without ever appearing in a game for Jamestown. He went home to Pine Grove and became the high school basketball coach. Professional baseball was a tough business—and it was no easy task to appear on a major league baseball card.

Well before the '61 season started, a Senators executive confided his hopes for the fledgling team to a reporter. "If we can hold our own with the rest of the clubs for a while until we can beef up, we'll do all right," he said. "The one thing I hope doesn't happen is a long losing streak."

Beginning on June 16, his hopes were crushed into dust. After winning in Baltimore the previous day to even their season's record at 30-30—and playing better than almost anyone had thought possible—the Nats rolled into Boston for a four-game series. O'Connell led off the first game with a booming double. The Senators went on to score four runs in the first inning and single runs in the next two to take a 6-0 lead. But Danny went hitless the rest of the game, the Red Sox pummeled Washington pitchers for 14 runs, and the Senators lost. They lost the next day too. And then came a Sunday doubleheader of the sort that makes the most stalwart of managers gnash their teeth and rend their garments.

In the first game, the Senators scored five runs in the top of the ninth to take a 12-5 lead. The Red Sox countered in the bottom of the ninth by scoring a run and loading the bases. But there were two outs and two strikes on Sox outfielder Jackie Jensen. One strike away from ending the game, Nats pitcher Dick Sisler walked Jensen, forcing in a run. Then he walked the next hitter, forcing in another run and making it 12-8. Then he gave up a grand slam to Sox catcher Jim Pagliaroni, who to that point in his career had hit a total of seven home runs. Another walk and two more singles, and the Red Sox won 13-12.

Danny watched the debacle from the bench, but started the second game, leading off and playing third. In six plate appearances, he walked three times, singled and stole a base. And he had a field-level view when in the bottom of the 13th inning, the aforementioned Pagliaroni hit another homer to win the game for Boston, 6-5.

The Senators were just getting started. Before beating Cleveland on June 27, the Nats lost 10 in a row, falling from fourth place to seventh. Over the rest of the season, they had additional losing streaks of seven, seven, eight and 14. After compiling a 30-30 record to begin the year, Washington ended it by going 31-70, finishing 47.5 games behind the pennant-winning Yankees. The club was last in the A.L. in hits, runs and batting average. It was also last in attendance, somehow managing to draw 145,533 fewer fans than the 1960 Senators. But they technically did not finish 10th in the standings as had been predicted by a horde of pre-season soothsayers. This was due to the fact Kansas City posted an identical 61-100 record, so the two teams tied for ninth.

If there was anything for the Senators to look forward to in 1962, it was that they'd be moving out of decaying old Griffith Stadium and into D.C. Stadium, a soulless doughnut-shaped taxpayer-financed venue designed for both baseball and football. It cost $24 million ($252.8 million in 2024), was owned and administered by the federal government, was renamed RFK stadium in 1969 after the assassinated U.S. senator and presidential candidate Robert F. Kennedy and in late 2023 was in the process of being demolished due to no teams playing there anymore.

The last game at Griffith Stadium was played on September 21 against the

Minnesota Twins before 1,498 people who clearly had nothing else to do. As one sportswriter put it, the attendance figure "smacked more of a mark-down sale than a baseball crowd." Washington lost 6-3. O'Connell went one for five, By grounding out to short in the ninth inning, he also had the distinction of making the last out ever in the 50-year-old ballpark. For those with a fondness for historical symmetry of a sort, the out came four years, five months and six days after he scored the first run in an official major league game on the West Coast.

The good news for Danny was that his historical footnote was not even close to being a highlight of his 1961 season, In fact, Danny O'Connell had a very good year. While his .260 batting average (four points higher than the league average) was only so-so, his .361 on-base percentage (OBP) was 21st in the American League and 35 points higher than the league average.

He tied with Chicago's Nellie Fox for the most sacrifices in either major league and was seventh in the A.L. in doubles, 14th in walks and—at the age of 32—10th in stolen bases, swiping 15 bags in 20 tries. Hitting mostly from the leadoff spot and with relatively few runners on base when he came up, he drove in only 37 runs. But half of them came with two out, speaking to his ability to come through in the clutch.

Danny led the Nats in hits, doubles, walks and plate appearances, was second in OBP and fourth in total bases. His Wins-Above-Replacement (WAR) score was tops on the team among position players. True, he hit only one home run, which tied him for 114th in the league. But that was still more than 216 other players who got at least one at-bat in the A.L. in 1961.

His defensive versatility also shone, playing 60 games at second base and 74 at third. O'Connell, noted the *Post's* Povich, "has been a fixture in the Senators infield...He solved completely their second base problem, and when the weakness developed at third [due to injuries] he moved to that spot to give the club excellent protection." Despite manager Vernon's pre-season concern about O'Connell's stamina, Danny missed only five games to get some rest. But he did miss 28 games with various injuries that included straining his back chasing a pop fly and banging up a knee in a collision at home plate.

It was during a six-game injury-caused hiatus in late July that O'Connell achieved what was perhaps his greatest milestone. While watching the Senators get thumped 16-5 by the Los Angeles Angels, their expansion counterparts, on July 21, Danny reached the 10-year mark as a major league player. It was an accomplishment reached by only about 10 percent of big-league players before or since.

He put his experience to good use with an assortment of heads-up plays. In the late innings of a tight game against Detroit in June, the Tigers had a runner on first with the weak-hitting pitcher Hank Aguirre at the plate. Convinced Aguirre would be bunting, O'Connell persuaded Vernon to move centerfielder Marty Keough to a spot between the pitcher's mound and first base. Vernon agreed to try it and it worked, with Aguirre grounding into a force out. "It's something new to baseball," an AP reporter noted, "and the Nats deserve credit for giving it a fling." While playing third base in August against the Angels, Danny performed what the *Los Angeles Times* called "the oldest play in baseball" by pulling off the hidden ball trick on old Giants teammate Leon Wagner. It was the only time that play worked anywhere in the majors in 1961.

In another August game, against Detroit, O'Connell bunted down the third base line. Tigers third baseman Bobo Osborne let the ball roll, expecting it to go foul. It didn't, and Danny steamed into second base with a 50-foot double. Albeit the shortest of his 30 two-base hits in 1961, it helped him set a doubles record for an expansion team player that lasted until the Colorado Rockies' Charlie Hayes broke it 33 years later.

While Danny seemed always to be thinking on the field, however, off the field his tongue was occasionally quicker than his brain. While chatting with two New Jersey congressmen in the Senators' dugout before a game in July, O'Connell was asked if he thought the team could finish in the first division. "I don't think so," he replied with customary candor. "We might wind up in sixth place though. I think we could beat out Boston for that spot." Washington's ticket sellers and publicists winced.

But Senators fans - what there was of them - didn't hold it against him. O'Connell was named the team's most valuable player by the club's official booster group, similar to the award he won eight years before with Pittsburgh. "They certainly like me in Washington. I received a silver tray worth $300 (about $3,200 in 2024)," Danny told a Newark reporter. "I don't think I deserved it for hitting .260," he modestly added. O'Connell even got two votes as the A.L.'s

Comeback Player of the Year, even though the award usually goes to a player rebounding from a bad year in the majors rather than a good year in the minors.

Back in New Jersey, Danny worked in the off-season as a "goodwill ambassador" for the Ballantine Brewery. He also refereed high school basketball games. "I'm recognized as one of the best high school basketball referees money can buy," he joked to an interviewer. "make sure you include that...I'm looking forward to officiating a lot of games."

Actually, for the first time since 1954, O'Connell had no worries about next year's contract. Before the '61 season concluded, he'd agreed to a 1962 contract that would pay him $20,000 ($210,600), his highest salary ever. "The Senators were not only beholding to O'Connell last season for his defensive play," Shirley Povich wrote in November. "He proved the most able hit-and-run man on the club, and was their leading bunter...He stacks up as the key man in Mickey Vernon's infield."

It had been a long and winding road, from a minor league clubhouse in Tacoma to hotel lobbies in New York City and Louisville to a big-league training camp in Florida and through a long hot season in an unfamiliar league. But Danny O'Connell knew where he would be in 1962. He also knew he would be 33 years old.

CHAPTER 15 NOTES

He had a *The (Tacoma Wa.) News Tribune*, Sept. 11, 1960, p. 20; *Buffalo Evening News*, March 29, 1962, p. 15.

O'Connell wandered around *The (Washington D.C.) Evening Star*, July 11, 1961, p. 18.

Daunted but not *The (Tacoma Wa.) News Tribune*, Dec. 11, 1960, p. 57.

"I'm a better" *The Sporting News*, May 24, 1961, p. 12; *Washington (D.C.) Evening Star*, July 11, 1961, p. 18.

Elated, Danny flew *The (Passaic NJ) Herald-News*, Dec. 6, 1960, p. 54; *Newark Sunday Star Ledger*, Dec. 4, 1960.

But Danny was *Newark Sunday Star Ledger*, Dec. 4, 1960.

O'Connell packed his *Buffalo Evening News*, March 29, 1962, p. 15.

He had reason *The (Washington D.C.) Evening Star*, Sept. 22, 1961, p. 20.

"He gives the" *The (Washington D.C.) Evening Star*, June 1, 1961, p. 17.

Danny's confidence was *Memphis (Tn.) Press-Scimitar*, Aug. 22, 1961, p. 15.

By April 1 The (Paterson NJ) Evening News, April 1, 1961, p. 14.

The unanswered question *The (Washington DC) Evening Star*, April 1, 1961, p. 14; *Fort Lauderdale (Fla.) News*, April 6, 1961, p. 55.

One of the *The Sporting News*, April 19, 1961, p. 3. Kennedy was the youngest man to be elected president, but not the youngest to assume the office. Theodore Roosevelt holds that distinction, having ascended to the office from the vice presidency at the age of 42, when the incumbent chief executive, William McKinley, was assassinated in Buffalo in 1901.

Despite game-time *The (New York) Daily News* April 11, 1961, p. 55.

In fact, the *The (Washington D.C.) Evening Star*, June 16, 1961, p. 39.

"O'Connell could" *The Sporting News*, July 19, 1961, p. 25.

If people weren't *Altus (Ok) Times-Democrat*, May 25, 1961, p. 6; *Berkshire (Ma.) Eagle*, May 29, 1961, p. 8.

The accuracy of If needed, see Chapter 6 for a refresher on the legend of the T206 Wagner card.

The accuracy of *Altus (Ok) Times-Democrat*, May 25, 1961, p. 6. See Chapter 6 for a refresher course on the Wagner card.

Topps also introduced *The (New York) Daily News*, April 13, 1961, p. 79.

One of Karam's *The West Schuylkill Press and Pine Grove Herald*, May 17, 1961, p. 4.

Well before the *The (Washington D.C.) Evening Star*, Jan. 18, 1961, p. 81.

The last game *The Washington Post*, Sept. 22, 1961, p. C1.

His defensive versatility *The Sporting News*, July 19, 1961, p. 25.

He put his *Lancaster (Pa.) New Era*, June 19, 1961, p. 15; *Los Angeles Times*, Aug. 15, 1961, p. 67.

While Danny seemed *The (Passaic NJ) Herald-News*, July 21, 1961, p. 20.

Back in New Jersey *The (Paterson NJ) Evening News*, Feb. 9, 1962, p. 23.

Actually, for the *The Sporting News*, Nov. 8, 1961, p. 25.

CHAPTER 16
"I WISH I HAD A DOZEN O'CONNELLS"
DANNY'S LAST HURRAH

To Mother Nature, age is a relative measurement. At 33, a California redwood tree isn't even a toddler yet. A 33-year-old gray wolf, on the other hand, has almost certainly been dead for at least 20 years. A baseball player at 33 is much closer to a gray wolf than a redwood tree. "The trouble with baseball," longtime major league catcher Joe Ginsberg once observed, "is that you grow old so fast." At the time of his observation, Ginsberg was 31.

Danny O'Connell was 33 as he arrived at the Senators' 1962 training camp in Pompano Beach for his 10th major league season. This fact seemingly was noted in at least half of the newspaper stories in which his name was included: "the 33-year-old veteran infielder;" "Johnson was moved to third where he may have to fill in at times for 33-year-old Danny O'Connell;" "Danny O'Connell, now 33."

In addition to his advanced age, O'Connell was also a baseball anomaly in terms of his career's longevity. An enterprising Miami columnist calculated that of the 250 players in the American League on Opening Day 1962, only 15—that's 6 percent—had lasted 10 seasons or more as big leaguers. Seven of those would go on to the Hall of Fame. Seven would no longer be in the majors after 1963.

Danny was well aware of the march of time. He asked for and received permission to report a week early to Pompano, "to get my old legs in shape with a lot of running," he told a New Jersey reporter. "That extra week of conditioning can mean a lot to a creaking old guy." His tone took on a bit more bravado with another reporter. "I feel good," he said. "My legs are okay and my back, which had bothered me before, didn't hurt at all last season. I'm used to the American League now and believe I can do my fair share…".

His confidence was evidenced further by the fact that Vera and the three kids were all driving down to Florida with him in the family's new station wagon. This spring would be comfortable. For the first spring in years, O'Connell was at ease with his immediate future. He had already signed a contract "for more money—after being a National League washout—than I've ever got in baseball." That he would make the team wasn't in doubt, and if he wasn't an everyday player, so be it. He joked he planned to play five more years and then turn to coaching. "I love this game," he said, "and want to be in it as long as I can."

His Washington bosses were effusive in their gratitude for his 1961 performance and in their assurances he had a future with the organization. "Danny brings a lot to the club," manager Vernon said. "His steadiness picks up the whole infield...I wish I had a dozen O'Connells. We'd be high in the first division."

General manager Ed Doherty said the Nats so valued O'Connell they had given him a $5,000 ($52,000 in 2024) raise, "and I hope he's with us for many seasons to come to impart some of his hustle, desire and good baseball sense to some of our younger players even when his active days on the diamond are over." Team president and principal owner Pete Quesada was more specific. "This may be Danny O'Connell's last year as an active player," he said. "If he decides to retire and wants a shot at managing, I think it's possible we find him a job in the minors. I rate him a smart and imaginative baseball man, and eventually he may become a big-league manager."

And lest his head swell bigger than his cap size, there were always old pals to remind him the playing clock was ticking. Taking his swings during batting practice before an exhibition game against Pittsburgh, Danny heard a familiar voice behind him. "My my," the voice said, "the American League is really hard up when they have to use old men like this to play." O'Connell turned to see a former teammate—and the potential personification of his own future. Danny Murtaugh had retired in 1951 as a player, managed in the minors, coached in the majors and taken over as skipper of the Pirates in mid-1957, leading them to a World Series win in 1960. It was a career path that O'Connell's own feet might travel when they got too sore and slow to run the bases.

But this was spring training, with every team in first place, every pitcher undefeated, every hitter perfect at the plate. So it's highly likely that at that moment, Danny was focused on the present. He gave Murtaugh a look of mock pity. "You never really recovered," Danny said, "from that [Sal] Maglie pitch that hit you in the head, did you?" Murtaugh ruefully rubbed the side of his noggin. "No," he answered, "and me a .190 hitter."

While Danny was running his legs into shape, he also ran his mouth—right over a good friend. On March 22, O'Connell was chatting with Joe Reichler, an Associated Press writer, when the subject somehow made its way around to sign-stealing. Danny might have told Reichler about the '59 Giants very briefly (two games) using the Seals Stadium scoreboard to steal signs, until the born-again relief pitcher Al Worthington balked at what he deemed cheating and threatened to reveal all. If O'Connell did talk about his first-hand experience with the Giants, Reichler didn't write about it. But he did write about a much juicier scheme Danny didn't witness but had heard about.

Under a pledge of anonymity from Reichler, O'Connell told the reporter what he knew about the '51 "miracle comeback" Giants' system of using a telescope from the centerfield clubhouse to steal signs and relay the information to a buzzer in the home team's dugout. Worse, he suggested that Bobby Thomson—his frequent golf buddy and roommate with both the Braves and Giants—knew what pitch was coming when he hit his historic homer. "You might say that the 'Shot heard round the world' [as Thomson's home run had come to be called] was set off by a buzzer," Danny said.

Reichler's story the next day appeared in hundreds of papers across the country. It was often accompanied by another AP story, this one out of Phoenix where the Giants held spring training. The second story quoted anonymous sources as confirming O'Connell's tale of Thomson and the '51 Giants, as well as revealing the '59 caper in San Francisco. "It was perfectly legal to steal signs in 1959 and before, any way you could," an unidentified Giant said.

Reichler hadn't bothered to contact the retired Thomson for his story, but the next day Thomson angrily denied the whole thing, as did every other member of the '51 Giants who was asked. "I think the player who talked to the press about this thing should have been man enough to attach his name to the story," Thomson said.

The tempest rather quickly shrank to teapot status. Ford Frick, baseball's waste-of-space commissioner, harrumphed that he would order a forfeit of any game in which he had firm evidence of such behavior, but since he didn't, he wouldn't do anything. He might not have been able to anyway, since there was no specific MLB rule against sign-stealing. Also dampening the scandal was the reluctance of Ralph Branca—the Dodgers pitcher who threw the fateful pitch to Thomson and whose life was forever tarred by it—to make a big deal out of it. In time, in fact, Branca and Thomson became friends who made money signing baseballs together at sports collectible shows.

Although he eventually learned O'Connell was Reichler's source, Thomson didn't hold a grudge toward Danny any more than Branca had toward Thomson. "My dad and Bobby Thomson remained friends," said the O'Connells' oldest son, Daniel F. O'Connell IV. "Even after his wife Winkie died, my mother and Bobby corresponded and kept in touch. I remember seeing Christmas cards from Bobby Thomson."

Just why Danny told Reichler—in effect, betraying a friend's secret - remains baffling. Maybe he simply admired the ingenuity of the scheme and didn't consider it cheating as much as taking advantage of an opportunity. Danny was a gamer. He enjoyed competition not from a lust to win but for the love of competing, whether it was at baseball, golf, pinochle or ping pong. To compete was to use every tool in the box to gain an edge—pulling the hidden ball trick or whistling show tunes during card games as a way of distracting the other players. Or maybe the reason was much simpler, contained in a self-assessment O'Connell gave to a reporter 10 months later on an entirely different topic. "I love to talk," Danny said.

When he wasn't gabbing, he was hitting. As the Senators broke camp and headed north for Opening Day, O'Connell's spring training average stood at a lofty .451. "[First baseman Dale] Long has been crushing the ball, and O'Connell's hitting well over .400," manager Vernon said. "… If we can get some pitching, we should be all right."

Long and O'Connell, along with outfielder Willie Tasby, were the only holdovers from the '61 Nats opening day lineup to also start the first game in Washington's brand-new D.C. Stadium, against the Detroit Tigers on April 9. The novelty of a new ballpark attracted a near-capacity crowd of 44,383, despite on-and-off rain that made the stadium's freshly laid sod so soggy the Senators donned long-cleated football shoes to ensure better traction.

Among the throng was President Kennedy, who once again threw out the ceremonial first pitch. The President huddled in the umpires' dressing room during a 30-minute first-inning rain delay, peppering the umps with questions, such as how much did Ted Williams complain about strike calls. He didn't, the umps told him. Kennedy also ducked a hard-hit foul ball that bounced off the roof of the Senators dugout behind which he was sitting. And he kept the Laotian ambassador to the United States cooling his heels at the White House all afternoon for a scheduled meeting when Kennedy opted to stay for the entire game.

Of more historic significance—because after all seven presidents before JFK had thrown out opening-day balls—was that the Senators' starting pitcher, Bernie Daniels, was the first African American to pitch an opener in the nation's capital. Daniels threw a splendid complete-game five-hitter. O'Connell, playing third and batting second, went two for four with a double. The Nats won 4-1.

It pretty much went downhill from there for all concerned. Daniels finished the season with a 7-16 won-lost record, giving up nearly five earned runs per nine innings pitched and walking more batters than he struck out. Washington won again the next day and then lost 13 straight on its way to a season record of 60-101-1, claiming the 10th place finish that had eluded the club in 1961.

And time caught up with Danny O'Connell, although not immediately. He began the season as hot at the plate as he had been in spring training. Over the first four games, Danny was eight for 16. That included two doubles and a home run, tying his entire long-ball output in 1961. Then he went zip for 16 in the next four games. Then he mostly sat on the bench for the rest of April, starting in only one game and pinch-hitting in three.

May was a Hyde-and-Jekyll affair. Over the first 12 games, Danny didn't play in seven and went two for 15 in the other five. O'Connell couldn't see what was wrong—literally as it turned out. After a couple of weeks resisting the advice of team physician Dr. George Resta, Danny donned glasses. "I never realized I needed them until I put them on," he marveled. "Man what a difference...The ball is bigger and clearer. I don't see how I did without them."

Over the last 17 games of May, O'Connell blistered the ball, going 24 for 59, a .409 clip. A 10-game hitting streak during that period included an eighth-inning home run to deep left field against Cleveland. It was the 39th and last of Danny's career. Naturally the Senators lost 2-1.

But his big hit came on a sultry Wednesday night in Chicago. The Nats were facing White Sox pitcher Early Wynn, who was seeking his 295th career victory on the way to the Hall of Fame. At 42, Wynn was nearing the end of his playing days. But he still had the respect hitters accorded anyone who threw hard and had a well-earned reputation as being meaner than an entire kennel full of junkyard dogs. Danny was getting a rare start at second base because Chuck Cottier, the incumbent, was deep in a slump.

In the first inning, Danny whacked a Wynn fastball into left field for a single. In the third inning, he did it again, and when Sox left fielder Floyd Robinson kicked the ball, Danny slid safely into second. "That was hit No. 1,000 for me Nellie," O'Connell told Sox second baseman Nelson Fox, who was also bound for the Hall of Fame. "You're about 1,400 behind me," Fox replied with a grin, "but I'll stop the game and get the ball if you want." Danny, however, was never big on souvenirs. "Don't bother," he told Fox, "I'll have them stop the game and get the ball when I get to 2,000."

Now, to put 1,000 hits in perspective, it should be noted that through the 2022 season, 1,345 major league players besides O'Connell had achieved at least a thousand hits or more since 1876. But it should also be noted that during that 146-year span, 18,926 players—that's 93.3 percent—did *not* reach that plateau.

Still, 1,000 hits was not then, nor is it now, considered huge news, and Danny's achievement had been rendered even less newsworthy earlier in the day by the St. Louis Cardinals' Stan Musial. Playing in San Francisco, the 41-year-old Musial rapped out the 3,430[th] hit of his career, breaking the all-time National League mark held by Honus Wagner. As mentioned earlier in this chapter, age is a relative measurement.

As something of a consolation prize, Washington writers named Danny the Senators player of the month for May, for which he was awarded a new suit. He was hitting .321 as June arrived, with a .393 on-base percentage. "Unless the Fountain of Youth is real, Danny will never hit 2,000," *Evening Star* columnist Merrell Whittlesey wrote. "But he is one of baseball's deep thinkers, and with a break he figures to be in the game for years. O'Connell studies hitters, he studies pitchers...If he ever realizes his managerial ambitions, his ball club is not going to play by the book."

Age being relative, however, Stan Musial was a young 41, and Danny O'Connell suddenly became an old 33. His back hurt; his knees were bothering him; the magic of the glasses slipped away. Manager Mickey Vernon, on his way to employing six different players at third base and six at second through the season in a desperate effort to stop losing, played Danny sparingly. O'Connell started 15 games in June; three in July, four in August and five in September. At season's end, he had played in 84 games, but only 53 as a starter. His .263 batting average was respectable, his eight-for-23 (.347) stint as a pinch hitter good enough for fifth-best in the American League. And even with a bad back and bum knees, Danny stole five bases in six attempts.

It may have offered small comfort, but the Topps Company had several parting mementoes for Danny, or at least featuring him. There was the usual baseball card, this one bearing a photo of a lean and smiling O'Connell posed with a bat over his shoulder. On the back the cardholder is informed that "Danny made a dramatic comeback last year" and "had his best big-league season since 1954." An accompanying drawing bears the always-included recounting of Danny's 1956 record-tying three triples in one game.

But Topps didn't stop there. Danny's likeness was on stamp No. 99 of the company's 201-stamp set for 1962. And his smiling face was on a Topps-issued pint-sized facsimile of a one-dollar bill that featured the infielder rather than George Washington. The bill was part of a "Topps Bucks" set of 96 that came in denominations of $1, $5 and $10, with the bigger stars on the bigger bills. The stamps sold two for a penny, while the bills were a penny apiece. Finally, there was a plastic coin with a paper likeness pasted on it that incorrectly identified him as a shortstop. The token, part of a 265-coin set, was issued by the Salada-Junket company in boxes of pudding mix.

Even so immortalized, there was a generally anti-climactic feel to Danny's career-ending season. But there was still a sprinkling of "only O'Connell" moments. During a stiflingly hot late July game against the Yankees, the Senators were chafing at the miniscule strike zone of Ed Hurley, the home plate umpire. Hurley's nickname around the league was "Three-Hour Ed" because his seeming reluctance to call strikes stretched games to what in the 1960s were considered unendurable lengths. By the fourth inning, Danny—who was injured and couldn't play anyway—could take no more. "It's nine o'clock already!" he shouted from the dugout. The umpire took umbrage; O'Connell was tossed from a game for only the third time in his big-league career—and happily toddled off to the cool clubhouse for a shower.

Then there were the tricks. True, Danny couldn't consistently score from second base on a single to right any more, and grounders to his left while playing third were increasingly out of his reach. But as a Miami columnist put it at the start of the season, "Danny specializes in trickery."

In a game against the White Sox in July, Danny pinch-hit in the eighth inning with runners on first and second and none out, and the Nats trailing 3-1. While in the on-deck circle, O'Connell practiced his bunting technique. "At bat," the *Evening Star* admiringly reported, "[O'Connell] took a look at George Case, the third base coach, who gave the bunt sign. Danny nodded in the affirmative. The White Sox infield played in for the bunt...(but) Danny crossed up the Sox by swinging away on his patented hit to right and sliced a single...". A run scored and the Senators went on to score five more times for a 7-3 win.

Against the Minnesota Twins in September, O'Connell was playing third in the 10th inning of a 7-7 tie. The Twins had a rookie pinch-running at first base with one out when the hitter lofted a deep but routine fly ball to right field. The right fielder made the catch, and the rookie, who was almost to second, dutifully started to jog back to first. Only Danny started clapping his hands and shouting while seeming to head for the dugout, as if the fly had been the last out of the inning. The Twins runner shruggingly trotted toward his own dugout and was easily doubled off first. "We sure miss him in the [everyday] lineup," manager Vernon said of O'Connell after the game. "He never misses a sign. Some of the guys will be sitting on the bench talking, but Danny is always with the ball game."

But the most fun Danny had in the '62 season had to come from tormenting one of the very few people in baseball O'Connell didn't like. Bill Rigney, who was fired in mid-1960 as manager of the Giants, was signed on as the first manager of the Los Angeles Angels, who with the Senators became the American League's first expansion clubs in 1961. O'Connell had never forgiven Rigney for not playing him for most of the 1959 season, and worse, for inserting an outfielder, Jackie Brandt, at third base while Danny languished on the bench. Rigney had also annoyed O'Connell when he removed him for a pinch hitter in the second inning of a game in '59. So Danny delighted in excelling against the Angels. In 11 games against L.A., O'Connell hit .517. His 15 hits included three doubles and a triple, as well as five walks, six RBIs, three runs scored, two sacrifice flies and a stolen base.

In a May 23 game, O'Connell really irritated the Angels when he bunted for a single and stole second with the Senators already leading 7-1 in the bottom of the third. This, in the Angels' minds, violated an unwritten baseball rule about not piling it on with a big lead. Angels pitcher Tom Donohue was so infuriated, "he made half a dozen needless throws to second with O'Connell standing not more than a step off the bag, coming a little closer to hitting O'Connell each time. Donohue finally threw one into centerfield and Danny romped to third."

Sometimes even when he failed against L.A. in '62, Danny succeeded. In August, he came to bat as a pinch-hitter in the eighth inning of a 2-2 tie with the Angels, with the bases loaded. Danny hadn't been to the plate in the Nats' previous 15 games, but he was by far the team's best bunter, so Vernon put on the squeeze play. Only O'Connell missed the pitch and the Senators runner who had charged in from third was a dead duck. But the other two runners moved up to second and third on the play. A red-faced Danny fouled off the next two pitches, then whistled a single into centerfield, scoring both. Washington won 4-2. After the game, a straight-faced Vernon said he figured it might just turn out that way when he called the squeeze in the first place, "and that's what happened."

Los Angeles did get a small measure of revenge against Danny. As a gag, the Angels routinely posted in the visiting club's dugout a lineup of opposing players they deemed members of the "All-Ugly Team." On a trip to L.A. in July, O'Connell found he had been designated the Uglies third baseman. "I don't know why they had to pick on me," he said in faux dismay. "I think Steve Boros of the Tigers belongs on the team ahead of me."

But fun moments aside, it was clear to O'Connell that the game itself was becoming less fun as a player. "I think I could continue to play, at least for another season, but of course I'm not getting any younger," Danny told his New Jersey newspaper pal Joe Gooter in October. "I would like to be a manager because it would give me a chance to stay in baseball. Someday I would like to be manager of a big league team, especially if I can make the grade with a minor league club first." He also told Gooter he'd met with Senators president Pete Quesada even before the season was over to talk about Danny retiring and beginning a new career in management

Quesada was encouraging but non-committal. The best he could do, he told Danny, was to give O'Connell permission to nose around after the season for job opportunities with other organizations while the Senators sorted out their plans for 1963. When that was done, there might well be a job somewhere with Washington. That sounded encouraging to the ever-optimistic O'Connell. He and Quesada got along well, and Nats general manager Ed Doherty was a big O'Connell fan. With the Luck O' the Irish, what could go wrong?

Danny was downcast. "I didn't know jobs were so scarce," he said in late November after spending three fruitless days job-hunting in Rochester, New York. The city was the site of the 1962 minor league meetings. "Danny, who will be 34 next month, has a sharp baseball mind and has long had manage-rial ambitions," *The Evening Star* sympathetically noted. "However, Danny wanted to start a bit higher than the low minors, which was his best offer at the meetings."

Actually his best—and only—offer was not to manage but to play, and for a not-too-shabby $25,000 (about $261,000 in 2024 dollars). The trouble was the offer came from a team some 6,700 miles away from New Jersey—in Japan. A handful of Americans had played in Japanese leagues as early as the 1930s, most of them players from Hawaii or African American expatriates from the Negro Leagues. But the first truly big-name U.S. players arrived in 1962. Don Newcombe, star pitcher of so many great Brooklyn Dodger teams in the '50s, and future Hall-of-Famer Larry Doby, who like Danny was from Paterson and who broke the American League color barrier in 1947, each received $30,000 ($313,000) to play one season in Japan.

To Danny, who had enjoyed his visit to the country in 1952 while in the Army, the offer from the Chunichi Dragons might have been tempting. But Vera O'Connell would have none of it. She had been willing to bundle up small children and endure a season in the wilds of California, but that was the limit. Danny turned down the offer.

While in Rochester, O'Connell applied for a job with the Triple-A Buffalo Bisons as a player-coach, to no avail. The fact was America's minor leagues were in trouble. At the peak of the post-war baseball boom in 1948, there were 448 minor league clubs in 59 leagues throughout the country. By 1962, there were only 134 teams in 20 leagues. Major league expansion, the ubiquity of televised big-league games and the rising popularity of other professional sports all contributed to the slow suffocation of minor league baseball—and the dwindling number of minor league managing jobs.

Deepening Danny's dilemma was the departure of his two highest-ranking boosters in the Senators food chain. In late September, team president Quesada fired Ed Doherty, the general manager who had given O'Connell new life as a major leaguer by signing him on a piece of scrap paper in that Louisville hotel lobby.

Doherty's replacement, who wasn't named to the job until late November, was George Selkirk, a former New York Yankee outfielder who had labored for a decade as a minor league manager. Selkirk, who described himself as an "old-fashioned" baseball man, was a very good player who nonetheless was forever fated to be best known as the man who replaced Babe Ruth in rightfield for the Yankees. He had also been stuck with one of the goofier nicknames in baseball circles: Selkirk was called "Twinkletoes" because of the way he ran on the balls of his feet.

On December 8, Selkirk said O'Connell would be given "serious consideration" for a minor league managerial post. He said it while giving Danny his unconditional release. Within a few weeks of Danny's release, Pete Quesada, who like Doherty had always been an O'Connell fan, resigned as the Senators' president and sold his interest in the club to a three-man group headed by a

North Carolina investment banker.

But O'Connell had not fared as badly in Rochester as he figured. During the meetings, the minor leagues had formally accepted a lifeline from the majors in the form of a restructuring of the minor league system. In addition to a badly needed infusion of cash, leagues were consolidated into more efficient groups. Major league clubs also agreed to turn some struggling minor league franchises into "pool clubs" that would be supplied with players from several MLB teams rather than have any one major league club bear the expense of the players' salaries alone.

One of these was in York, a southern Pennsylvania town with a population of about 50,000 and situated about 50 miles north of Baltimore. The York White Roses were a club in the Double-A Eastern League. Under the new restructuring, the Senators agreed to take over administration of the team and supply it with at least seven players, with the rest coming from other big-league clubs. In early January, Washington announced one of the players would also manage the White Roses. His name was O'Connell.

CHAPTER 16 NOTES

In Nature, age *Miami News,* June 20, 1962, p. 26

Danny O'Connell was *The (Tacoma Wa.) News Tribune,* March 4, 1962, p. 33; *The (Washington D.C.) Evening Star,* March 30, 1962, p. 39; *Pittsburgh Post-Gazette,* March 12, 1962, p. 22.

In addition to *Miami News,* June 20, 1962, p. 26.

Danny was well *Newark Star-Ledger,* Feb. 10, 1962; *Paterson (NJ) Sunday Eagle,* Feb. 4, 1962.

His self-confidence was *Newark Star-Ledger,* Feb. 10, 1962; *Minneapolis Star Tribune,* March 3, 1962, p. 13.

His Washington bosses *The (Tacoma Wa.) News Tribune,* Feb. 27, 1962, p. 18; *The Sporting News,* Jan. 24, 1962, p. 28.

General manager Ed *The (Tacoma Wa.) News Tribune,* April 3, 1962, p. 20; *The (Washington D.C.) Evening Star,* Aug. 12, 1962, p. 25.

And lest his *Pittsburgh Post-Gazette,* March 12, 1962, p. 22.

While Danny was For a meticulously researched and superbly written account of the 1951 stolen sign saga, see Joshua Prager's *The Echoing Green: The Untold Story of Bobby Thomson, Ralph Branca and the Shot Heard Round the World* (Vintage Books, 2008.)

Under a pledge *Daily Palo Alto (Ca.) Times,* March 23, 1962, p. 22.

Reichler's story the *Daily Palo Alto (Ca.) Times,* March 23, 1962, p. 24.

Reichler hadn't bothered *The Bridgewater (NJ) Courier News,* March 23, 1962, p. 36.

Although he eventually August 28, 2023 email to author from Daniel F. O'Connell IV. In 2003, Thomson revealed to author Joshua Prager that O'Connell had confessed to him he was Reichler's source for the story. See Prager's excellent *The Echoing Green* for details.

Just why Danny *York (Pa.) Dispatch,* Jan. 19, 1963, p. 12.

May was a *The (Long Beach Ca.) Press-Telegram,* May 30, 1962, p. 36; *The (Washington D.C.) Evening Star,* May 29, 1962, p. 36.

In the first *The Sporting News,* June 2, 1962, p. 26.

As something of *The (Washington D.C.) Evening Star,* May 30, 1962, p. 41.

Despite the generally *Newsday (Suffolk County Edition)* Aug. 1, 1962, p. 17.

Then there were *The Miami News,* March 17, 1962, p. 32.

In a game *The (Washington D.C.) Evening Star,* July 18, 1962, p. 32.

Playing the Minnesota *The (Washington D.C.) Evening Star,* Sept. 9, 1962, p. 79.

In a May *The (Washington D.C.) Evening Star*, May 24, 1962, p. 65.

Sometimes even when *The (Washington D.C.) Evening Star,* Sept. 1, 1962, p. 10.

Los Angeles did The (Washington D.C.) Evening Star, July 17, 1962, p. 11.

But fun and *Paterson (NJ) Sunday Eagle*, Oct. 21, 1962, p. 26.

Danny was downcast. *The (Washington D.C.) Evening Star*, Dec. 9, 1962, p. 37.

On December 8, Ibid.

CHAPTER 17
"HEY, DID YOU SEE THAT HOMER I HIT?"
BASEBALL FROM THE SIDELINES

Danny had never been to York Pennsylvania and wasn't sure he wanted to go. Despite all his pronouncements in the previous couple of years about how he wanted to manage, he knew he was taking on a job at which he had no experience. Unlike players, whose success or failure is measured by their performance as individuals, the careers of managers are dependent to a substantial degree on the performances of the players they manage. One of the oldest saws in baseball is that it's easier to fire a manager than 25 players.

Then there was the status thing. For nine of the last 10 years going into 1963, O'Connell had been a big-league player, one of a few hundred American men who got to play a game at its highest level for pretty good money, substantial name recognition—and their pictures on baseball cards. Minor league managers generally got significantly less money to scold, cajole, strategize, commiserate and take the blame, all with the hope of someday getting to do the same job in the major leagues. Finally—but not lastly—there was family. York was 180 miles from Bloomfield. The plan was for Vera and the kids to drive to York on weekends when the White Roses were playing home games, but that left a lot of spring and summer days and weeks of separation.

Danny put a good face on his misgivings. "I think I'm going to like managing and from what I hear I'm going to like York," he said in a long piece that ran in the *York Dispatch* a few days after he was named manager. The article was accompanied by a four-column photo of Danny siting on a couch with his family, all of whom were described as "attractive:" "attractive family;" "attractive wife" "attractive children." (The reporter apparently didn't care for the couch.) The piece described O'Connell as an "amiable New Jersey Irishman (who) is believed to be the first (York) manager ever to come directly from a major league club." It also quoted Danny as saying "Of course you can't beat playing in the majors, but I figure my playing days are about over."

In another interview, O'Connell said he planned to be an active manager. "I've got plenty of ideas about managing, and I'm going to try everything that comes to mind," he said. "I believe a manager should keep doing things...The more he does, the more he'll have the opposition on its heels."

But here and there were hints of his pensiveness about going from individual player to dugout maestro. In an interview with a New Jersey columnist not long before leaving for the White Roses' training camp in Pensacola, Florida—where he had trained as a teenager with the Dodgers' minor leaguers 16 years earlier—O'Connell said that he intended to pencil himself into the lineup for perhaps 100 of the team's 140 games. He also joked that "managing might be okay, but I'd like someday to return to the majors as a coach. Those guys have it made. No worries...just coach and possibly get a share of World Series money to boot."

A few days later, after giving a "meet the manager" speech in York to a civic group, Danny was more serious in a conversation with a reporter. "Guys manage in the minors 15, 20 years," he said. "Managing is not really an obsession. But I like baseball and always wanted to stay in the game...I've got a lot of ideas on managing...There are a lot of things I'd like to try. I hope I don't lose my nerve."

If Danny's customary candor might have bothered local fans, however, his equally customary sense of humor charmed the local press. In a spring training doubleheader against another Senators farm club, the Roses won both games. In the second game, Danny hit a 390-foot homer, doubled, walked and scored from second on a single to right. The *York Dispatch* giddily noted that "O'Connell, who the York fans will positively enjoy because of his humorous and care-free attitude, quipped following the second game, 'I don't know about winning two games like this, these guys are all liable to get big heads. Hey, did you see that homer I hit?'"

O'Connell had started fast in most of his big-league seasons as a player and his debut as a manager proved no different. Opening on the road, the White Roses won their first four games before their home opener on April 23. With Danny playing third base and leading off, York won 6-0 over the Binghamton

(New York) Triplets. O'Connell went one for two with a walk, a ground-rule double and an RBI. The double was a one-bouncer over the centerfield fence— only Danny didn't realize it until the infield umpire put a bearhug on him as O'Connell steamed around second base. "There's no such thing as too much hustle," he later explained with a sheepish grin.

The game was played under somewhat less than ideal conditions: strong, frigid winds and temperatures in the mid-40s, which helped explain the turnout of 777 customers instead of the expected 3,000. Then again, neither York nor the Eastern League in which its team played had ever been rock-solid bastions of baseball. Since its first team in 1884, York had seen five franchises come and go, spaced by intervals of years. Moreover, Calvin Coolidge was president the last time the town had seen a pennant winner (1925.) The six-team Eastern League, while long-lived, was hardly stable either. From its birth in 1938 through the 2023 season, the league had fielded teams in 52 different cities scattered across 12 states and two Canadian provinces, from the Akron Rubber Ducks (seriously) to the York White Roses.

And the league was hardly a reliable launching point for 34-year-old player managers who hoped to quickly be back in the majors. The other five Eastern league managers in 1963 would average nearly 16 years as minor league skippers over their careers. Two—Earl Weaver and John McNamara—would go on to have successful major league managing stints. But it took McNamara 23 years as a player and manager in the minors to make it, and Weaver 19. The other three—Johnny Lipon, Buddy Kerr and Eddie Popowski—would manage a cumulative total of 58 big-league games as fill-in skippers.

However much his future bothered O'Connell, it didn't seem to greatly affect him in the moment, and as the season got rolling, so did he. By May 9, he was hitting .423 and had the White Roses only two games out of first. After one game, O'Connell dutifully filed the nightly report required by Senators general manager George Selkirk from each of the team's farm clubs. "He closed his wire with 'O'Connell went three for three,'" the *Washington Evening Star* noted. The paper added "Selkirk said he had a hunch that when O'Connell had 0-for-5 nights Danny wouldn't bother to mention it." A few days later, *Evening Star* columnist Morris Siegel wrote that "except for pitcher Bob Baird, the best-looking prospect on Washington's farm team at York, Pa., is third baseman-manager Danny O'Connell, 34, hardly eligible for rookie honors …".

A proponent of "little ball"—advancing runners, bunting, coaxing walks—Danny practiced what he preached. In a late-April game against Binghamton before a home "crowd" of 428, O'Connell doubled, walked, and drove in one run with a bunt and another with a sacrifice fly. He even pitched in with the pitching. With York losing 11-5 to the Charleston (WV) Indians, Danny took the mound himself to save his tired bullpen. The first pitch he threw was deposited in the bleachers by the Charleston hitter, but O'Connell thereafter pitched two shutout innings. (York still lost, 12-6.)

As usual, Danny cooled off at the plate. On May 21, he was hitting only .266. But he still led the club with a lofty .430 on-base percentage, thanks in large part to drawing 25 walks while playing third base or shortstop in 26 of the team's 28 games. More importantly as manager, he had steered York to a surprising 15-13 record, good for second place. On May 22, the White Roses had the day off. Their manager spent the evening about 90 miles south of York, watching a ball game. He wouldn't come back.

George Selkirk was mad as hell, and he wasn't going to take it anymore. He had just watched the Washington Senators, for whom he had been general manager for about six months, lose the 10th game of their last 11. They languished in last place, already 11.5 games out of first with the season only 39 games old.

Selkirk was tired of "mound-kicking, helmet-throwing signs of frustration" by Nats players, the press reported. "Too many of them are more concerned with their own base hits than winning a ball game," he said. Thus angered, Selkirk on May 22 followed the time-honored practice of general managers since they covered baseballs with wooly mammoth hide: He fired the manager. "It was not a pleasant task to replace [Mickey] Vernon," Selkirk said, "but we reached the point where I believe new blood was needed. I expect Gil will get our club hustling, but I don't anticipate he'll achieve the impossible."

The "Gil" to whom Selkirk referred was Gilbert Ray Hodges, who on May

21 was a 39-year-old injured first baseman for the lowly New York Mets. On May 22, he was an ex-first baseman, and along with Danny O'Connell was a guest in Selkirk's box at D.C. Stadium, where they watched the Nats lose 9-3 to the White Sox. Hodges was there as Washington's new manager, Danny as the new first base coach.

Prior to his employment with the Mets, Hodges had been a Dodger—and one of the best. In 18 seasons, Hodges compiled 1,921 hits, a lifetime .276 average and 370 home runs, at the time of his retirement the most ever by a National League right-handed hitter. He held the league records for grand slams in a career and sacrifice flies in a season; was an eight-time All-Star; played on six pennant-winning teams and won three Gold Gloves for fielding at first base.

Hodges was a quiet, congenial fellow, which was a good thing because he was also a very strong 6'1" and 200 lbs. with hands seemingly powerful enough to crush bowling balls. Just why he was the Nats' new manager, however, was something of a mystery because like O'Connell, he had no managerial experience prior to the 1963 season. To many, Hodges seemed like just too nice a guy to be a big-league manager.

But Vernon had been a favorite with Senators fans—what there were of them—as a player and manager, and Selkirk may have figured it would sit better if he replaced him with a big name. That may also have been the reason O'Connell found himself in the first-base coaching box for the Senators on May 23 in Baltimore. Danny replaced George Case, who was fired along with Vernon. During his 11-year playing career in the 1930s and '40s, mostly with Washington, Case was deemed the fastest man in the big leagues, and led the American League six times in stolen bases. That made him very popular with D.C. fans.

As a coach, Case's principal sin was that he was Vernon's best friend on the club. Selkirk wanted to ensure his new manager would encounter no hard feelings among his coaches, while at the same time placating Senators fans. Danny was still quite popular in Washington, and as the press pointed out "returns to the Senators with an excellent rating for his few weeks as manager" of York. Just in case he might be blamed for Case's ouster, Hodges made it clear, without being too pointed about it, that it was Selkirk's idea and that he intended to keep the rest of the staff he inherited from Vernon.

O'Connell and Hodges had always been friendly rivals as players, and Danny—in keeping with his voluble nature—soon became one of Gil's most public boosters. "Coach Danny O'Connell testifies to the new spirit of the Senators," *The Sporting News* reported in July. "Hodges' No. 1 aide [O'Connell] declared 'Not in three years has the club ever talked it up so much on the bench. You hear baseball talk around the club instead of small talk. They've got a new urge—to win.'"

Urges aside, they didn't. The club's .347 winning percentage under Hodges in '63 was actually a bit lower than the .350 it had been under Vernon in the first part of the season. And with a pathetic team batting average of .227, a newspaper wit cracked that "Danny O'Connell must be the loneliest guy in the world. He coaches first base for Washington, and how often do the Senators get a man on base?"

If Danny was lonely on the field, however, he had plenty of company off it. Vera found an apartment in Washington and she and the kids joined him for most of the season. "Danny phoned me from York," she told a reporter in a rare interview a few days after the announcement. "He was happy as a big kid. We were delighted the promotion came as soon as it did." Vera said the family would return to Bloomfield when the Nats were on the road. Asked if the O'Connells would regularly help boost attendance at D.C. Stadium, Vera said "only on nice Sunday afternoons. Washington plays many night games and I'm just an old-fashioned mother. I believe in their getting to bed at an early hour."

Danny's 1963 season highlight probably came a day or two after the season ended when he won the club's annual player-press golf tournament. Back in Jersey, O'Connell was in constant demand as a speaker, particularly for youth sports groups: the Watchung Hills Tri-Boro Pony Baseball League (of which Danny's former teammate Bobby Thomson was commissioner); the New Jersey Sunday Softball League, the St. Mary's Little League. O'Connell's message was invariably that the kids shouldn't "drink or smoke and (should) hit the books hard, because later in life education would be their stand-by."

He also said all the right things to the press. "Danny believes better things are in store for the [Washington] club as the future develops," longtime newspaper pal Joe Gooter wrote. "Of his manager, he says, 'Gil Hodges did a good job of breaking in and everybody feels he will make a good boss. He means business.'" O'Connell told Gooter he missed neither playing nor managing. "Coaching is the best job in baseball as far as I'm concerned."

It's entirely possible that Danny believed what he told Gooter about his love of coaching, at least while he was saying it. But the cold fact is that coaching first base is about as anonymous a job as there is in pro baseball. Danny's name showed up in the papers in cameo roles at least as often as it did as the featured player, such as in a story about Dona Shortway, "a short happy-go-lucky bowler, softball player and basketball star who happens to be engaged to Washington Senators coach Danny O'Connell's younger brother Bob."

So his pulse must've quickened at least a bit when he read during 1964's spring training that Hodges was holding auditions for third base after Don Zimmer, who had been penciled in as the starter, fractured his wrist. "There's just a possibility—a slim one—that this could mean a diamond comeback by Danny O'Connell," the Associated Press speculated.

Nothing came of it. Danny stayed in the first base coaches' box for the '64 season, in which the Senators climbed to the giddy heights of ninth place. Those who noticed he was there approved of his performance. "O'Connell is the holler-guy type, but with it he is a shrewd baseball man," *The Sporting News* observed. "Danny often does a great job in upsetting the opposition and he certainly keeps the umpires on their toes—by stepping on them."

Following the '64 season, Danny took on the first real fulltime job he'd had outside of baseball, as a sales rep for the Lee Company, a waterworks supply and equipment firm based in Denville, New Jersey, about 25 miles northwest of Bloomfield. He had already signed a contract with Washington for the 1965 season, and sometime in December, the Senators asked O'Connell to make a two-week scouting trip to Japan a few weeks before spring training opened. So it came as a surprise when on January 19, two days before his 36th birthday, Danny O'Connell quit baseball.

It certainly surprised the Senators. The week before his retirement announcement, O'Connell went to Washington to meet with Selkirk. "When I told him I was considering retiring," Danny said later, "he told me not to make a hasty decision. He told me to think it over, but he and Gil Hodges understood. I'm leaving on a friendly basis...In fact, he said if things don't work out in the new venture I should come back and see him...It was a tough decision to make, and the move came rather unexpectedly."

Explaining in various interviews why he was leaving behind a game that that had gripped him for three decades—or 83 percent of his life so far - took a bit of doing. Boiled down, and sometimes reading between the lines, it appeared he quit for love. And money. And something else.

Love as a reason was easy to explain. Daughter Maureen had just celebrated her ninth birthday. Daughter Nancy was seven, son Danny IV five. As the kids grew older, the family's housing logistics grew more complicated. In an interview 18 months before Danny quit, Vera estimated the couple had at least 25 addresses during their nine-year marriage to that point: apartments in spring training, apartments in the various cities where he played, apartments or houses in New Jersey. The result was the family stayed home more often during the season. Even when they went along, there were logistical problems. "I remember one year they took us out of school in the spring and my mom home-schooled us," Maureen said. "Later I told her, 'Mom, you were ahead of your time,' and she replied 'well it was either being with your dad for an extra couple of months or without him.'"

"Last year I didn't see them for seven weeks during spring training," O'Connell said in an interview following his retirement announcement, "and then too infrequently during the season. They are more important to me than money... After 19 years away from home every baseball season, I finally (am) able to hold the same address all the time."

The money reason was also easy to explain, although O'Connell referred to it as "security." "There is little security in baseball," he said, "especially as a coach. And remember, I was released twice from jobs in the last four years [in 1960 with the Giants and 1963 with the Senators.]" Moreover, Danny as a coach was making about half what he had made in his last two years as a player. "We had to pay $200 a month rent on an apartment ($2,031 in 2024) in Washington," he added, "and that doesn't help the mortgage back home."

O'Connell's "new venture" was in a field about which he knew nothing.

The Lee Company sold water-system building materials and supplies and rented equipment to utilities, municipalities and commercial construction companies. How Danny got the job was much more interesting than what he was going to do in it.

"Don't let anyone tell you the banquet circuit doesn't pay off," he told an interviewer. "I've been attending banquets (at the request of) Howard Lee, the president of the Lee Company, for about 10 years, you know, the Little League affairs in Denville and at the Rockaway River Country Club. They were all for free, I didn't get paid for those appearances." Lee, a self-described "rabid sports fan," told Danny if he ever left baseball, he had a job waiting. After O'Connell worked for the company following the 1964 season, Lee offered to make the job permanent. "We played golf," Danny added about his new boss, "and I beat him, but I guess I'll have to let him win now that I'm working for him."

But love and money weren't the whole story. There were hints Danny felt baseball had let him down, or that he had maybe made a mistake in taking a job as a coach for Gil Hodges, or that he hadn't calculated how long it might take after he quit playing to realize his dream to be a big-league manager. "That was my ultimate goal in baseball," he said, "but it's tough. The modern trend is to get a big name like Yogi Berra for your manager."

O'Connell's reference was to the fact that the New York Yankees had named Berra their manager in 1964 even though he had no managing experience. Danny left unsaid that the Senators had done the same thing with Hodges in 1963. And it was true that two other major league teams—the San Francisco Giants and Baltimore Orioles - had former All-Stars as managers who had gone straight from the playing field to jobs as field bosses. But that left 16 skippers who had paid their dues in the minors, and O'Connell was no longer willing to take that route. He'd been to York. "I'm not thinking about baseball at all, not even a scouting job," he claimed. "I'm too busy getting myself established as a sales representative."

He simultaneously claimed that "I have no regrets, nosiree" while adding "it was a tough decision to make to retire from baseball. I loved every minute of it while I was in it." Then he thought of something that might have given him just the slightest moment of reconsideration—or else he was just goofing around. "Say," he said, "come to think of it, this will be first time in 20 years that I'll be in New Jersey in April. When does it get warm here?"

Ten months later, Danny sat down with columnist Joe Gooter to talk about his first professional baseball-barren summer since 1946. "The veteran thought he would miss baseball much more than was the case," Gooter wrote. "Looking back on his first season away from the diamond scene, O'Connell says 'Naturally a lot of the excitement's gone, but I certainly don't miss going all over the country in airplanes and being away from home. I like my job and think it offers me the sort of future I can look forward to. I might be tempted to go back into baseball if a major league club offered me a manager's spot or wanted to give me an extra-big salary to coach,' he said, 'but I don't expect either to happen.'"

Neither offer did. And as much as Danny seemed to enjoy his job with the Lee Company, his children weren't exactly sure what his job was. "My father was not a plumber, didn't know anything about plumbing or any handywork around the house for that matter," Danny's oldest daughter Maureen recalled with a laugh. "I don't remember him fixing a lot of things around the house. I'm pretty sure his job was in the capacity of him having such a winning personality and being a pretty well-known figure in the area, a celebrity salesman...He liked being around people telling stories and laughing."

O'Connell occasionally watched a ball game on television, and played golf regularly with Bobby Thomson, who lived not far away. The family sometimes patronized a bowling alley owned by Yogi Berra, Danny joked, "but I never see Yogi. I think he just comes in to collect the money." In fact he rarely saw other faces from his baseball past, which made a late 1967 visit from Don Zimmer stick out in family memories. Zimmer, who would spend 65 years in professional baseball, knew O'Connell from Zimmer's days with the Dodgers, and had followed Danny as the Senators third baseman. In addition to his longevity in the game, Zimmer had the distinction of having been once put into a two-week coma by a beaning in the minor leagues, which also resulted in him having a metal plate installed in his head.

In late '67, Zimmer had just finished a season as player-manager of the Buffalo Bisons. "He and my dad went out to dinner," Maureen said. "My mother believed that he was trying to convince my dad to come back to baseball. He [Danny] never confirmed that to her, or had a conversation with her about it, but she always wondered whether it was something he was tempted to do."

If Danny was tempted, he did not succumb. The family was reasonably secure financially and as *The Morning Call* pointed out "He figures to reap handsome dividends from baseball's pension plan." His fourth child, John, (named after Danny's uncle, who was a longtime and well-liked Paterson policeman and well-known local bowler) had been born not long before Zimmer's visit, adding to Danny's responsibilities. O'Connell was still in demand as an after-dinner speaker. He liked playing golf with prospective plumbing customers. Life was okay without baseball.

But he had one more game in him. In August 1968, Danny was invited to play in an Old Timers Game in San Francisco. The three-inning exhibition pitted members of the 1958 Giants against their Los Angeles Dodgers counterparts to commemorate the first game the two teams had played against each other on the West Coast. Two players for each club were still active major league players—Willie Mays and Jim Davenport for the Giants and Don Drysdale and catcher John Roseboro for the Dodgers. To minimize the chance of injury, Drysdale played right field for L.A. instead of pitching, and Mays played first base instead of center field.

Danny played second base and hit second for the Giants. In the second inning, he doubled, then scored on a single by 41-year-old Hank Sauer, who in turn scored on a double by Mays. In the top of the third inning, Drysdale singled and went to second on an error. Standing at second with the ball, Danny pretended to throw it to Mays at first, who pretended to catch it. Drysdale strayed off second—only to be tagged out. Danny O'Connell ended his baseball life with a Hall-of-Fame-worthy Danny O'Connell play: The hidden ball trick.

CHAPTER 17 NOTES

Danny put a *The York (Pa.) Dispatch,* Jan. 19, 1963, p. 12.

In another interview *Washington Daily News*, Jan. 18, 1963, p. 42.

But here and *The (Paterson NJ) Evening News*, March 6, 1963, p. 39;

A few days *Lancaster (Pa.) Sunday News*, March 10, 1963, p. 33.

If Danny's customary *The York (Pa.) Dispatch*, April 10, 1963, p. 20.

O'Connell had started *The York (Pa.) Dispatch*, April 24, 1963, p. 17.

However much his *The (Washington D.C.) Evening Star*, April 22, 1963, p. 21; April 28, 1963, p. F3.

Selkirk was tired *The (Washington D.C.) Evening Star,* May 23, 1963, p. 21; *The (Passaic County NJ) News Herald,* May 23, 1963, p. 33.

Prior to his Despite being one of the best players of the 1950s, Hodges was not elected to the Hall of Fame until 2021—49 years after his sudden death from a heart attack in 1972, at the age of 47.

As a coach, *The (Washington D.C.) Evening Star*, May 23, 1963, p. 21. Case was retained by Selkirk as a scout and eventually became one of his most valued aides; Vernon was kicked upstairs to a job in the Nats' front office.

But O'Connell and *The Sporting News*, July 20, 1963, p. 12.

Urges aside, they *The (Paterson NJ) News*, June 22, 1963, p. 12.

If Danny was *The Newark Star-Ledger*, May 25, 1963.

Danny's 1963 season *The Bridgewater (NJ) Courier-News*, Oct. 22, 1963, p. 25.

He also said *The (Paterson NJ) Morning Call*, Oct. 3, 1963, p. 21.

It's entirely possible *The (Passaic County NJ) Herald-News,* March 12, 1964, p. 34.

So his pulse *The (Paterson NJ) News*, March 10, 1964, p. 29.

Nothing came of *The Sporting News*, Nov. 2, 1964, pp. 23-24.

It certainly surprised *The (Paterson NJ) News*, Jan. 20, 1965, p. 40; *The (Paterson NJ) Morning Call*, Jan. 20, 1965, p. 18.

The love-as-a-reason Author's interview of Maureen O'Connell, April 11, 2022.

"Last year I" *The (Paterson NJ) News*, Jan. 20, 1965, p. 40; *The (Paterson NJ) Morning Call,* Oct. 17, 1965, p. 49.

The money was *The (Paterson NJ) Morning Call*, Jan. 20, 1965, p. 18.

"Don't let anyone" *The (Paterson NJ) News*, Jan. 20, 1965, p. 40.

But love and *The (Paterson NJ) Morning Call*, Jan. 20, 1965, p. 18.

O'Connell's reference was Ibid.

He simultaneously claimed *The (Paterson NJ) News*, Jan. 20, 1965, p. 40.

Ten months later *The (Paterson NJ) News,* Oct. 17, 1965, p. 49.

Neither offer did. And Author's interview of Maureen O'Connell, April 11, 2022.

In late '67 Author's interview of Maureen O'Connell, April 11, 2022.

If Danny was *The (Paterson NJ) Morning Call*, Jan. 20, 1965, p. 18.

CHAPTER 18

"ALWAYS A MAJOR LEAGUER"

NINTH INNING

It rained hard the night Danny O'Connell died. Temperatures were reasonable for the date, the former of which ranged in the mid-to-high 60s and the latter being Oct. 2, 1969. But it rained off and on all day, turning the golf course at the Upper Montclair Country Club into a water park.

Even so, and after due deliberation, the sponsors of the 7th Annual Paterson Diocesan Golf Tournament decided to steam ahead. Among the tourney's 173 entrants were a number of sports celebrities, such as former Notre Dame University star quarterbacks Frank Tripucka and Angelo Bertelli—and former major league baseball player Danny O'Connell.

It was an event tailor-made for Danny. For one thing, he'd become an active member of several Catholic associations, and the golf tournament and banquet that followed would raise $12,000 (about $103,000 in 2024) for one of them, the Catholic Youth Organization (CYO.) For another, Danny loved to play golf, even if it was ostensibly a work day and he wasn't likely to sell much plumbing equipment on the greens or at the dinner table. Finally, the country club was conveniently located only a five-to-10-minute drive from the O'Connell home on Fairway Street in Bloomfield.

Five years removed from baseball, the game was nonetheless almost certainly on his mind as he perused that morning's paper. October 2 was the last day of the 1969 major league regular season. The biggest story all summer long had been the once-lowly New York Mets, who won 100 games and had clinched the National League's Eastern Division title. They would go on to win the N.L. flag and, improbably, the World Series. The "Miracle Mets" manager was none other than Gil Hodges, Danny's old boss in Washington who had moved to the New York job in 1968 and taken his D.C. coaching staff with him. For years to come, the O'Connell family would play the "what-if" game: "What if Danny had stuck it out with the Senators a few years longer? He would've gone to the Series with the Mets…".

A more bittersweet story for Danny on the sports page that morning was the news that the Boston Red Sox had named Eddie Kasko as the club's new manager, and would pay him somewhere in the neighborhood of $50,000 ($429,000.) The 38-year-old Kasko had played 10 years in the majors as an infielder who could play second base, third base and shortstop, and play them well. He was a pretty good hitter, but not great: lifetime average around .260, about 1,000 lifetime hits, just a handful of home runs. His press references often included the phrase "smart baseball man." To Danny, it all had to sound eerily familiar, except the fact Kasko, after putting in just two years as a manager at the highest minor league level, was going to be a big-league manager and O'Connell wasn't.

Bittersweet and bitter, however, are not at all the same thing, and O'Connell's family devotion, religious faith and generally cheery character crushed any semblance of bitterness. "He was saying how happy he was now, even though the money wasn't the same, to be home with his wife and kids," said Father Paul Longula, who with two priests from Newark spent more than an hour chatting with Danny as the post-golf tournament banquet crowd at the country club dispersed.

In fact, O'Connell's dance card was pretty full without baseball, even if his day job wasn't particularly demanding. He was a member of the Holy Name Society, a Catholic advocacy and good-works organization; vice-president of the lay advisory group at his parish, and on the board of directors for the local CYO. He was a regular in card games at his American Legion post, and he enjoyed "taking a flutter" on horse races through a bookie the family knew only as "Harp." "Mom was sure the cops were going to get Harp, and Dad would be in big trouble," eldest daughter Maureen laughingly recalled. "I know he was still gone a lot even after he retired, but Mom was fine with it—as long as she didn't have to go."

Always the socializer, Danny was in great demand as an after-dinner speaker throughout Northern New Jersey, sometimes for a fee but mostly for free. And at parties, he was generally the life thereof. "All somebody had to do was give him a little push and he would sing something," daughter Maureen said. "He would do 'Danny Boy' every time, 'Climb Every Mountain' and 'Ol' Man River.' That was his repertoire. He didn't always do all of them, but those were his go-to songs."

Sometimes Danny's celebrity could be inconvenient. "When we would order pizza, my mother would give a fake name...because my dad was a local hero and would end up talking to everyone in the restaurant for an hour," daughter Nancy said. "But he often would forget the name my mom gave so he would end up being there for an hour anyway."

With Danny home full-time, Maureen recalled, "there was a little bit of a different cadence to life" in the O'Connell household. Vera remained the chief disciplinarian, although when Danny stopped whistling and raised his thick dark eyebrows, the kids generally stopped whatever it was they were doing that had occasioned the eyebrow-raising. "He had a temper sometimes," Maureen said, "but it came and went quickly. He was pretty happy-go-lucky most of the time."

He also hadn't left his sharp sense of humor in the dugout. Once, the O'Connell kids recalled, one of Danny's closest friends dropped by—and wouldn't go home. O'Connell excused himself and went upstairs. He came back wearing his pajamas, with the fly held closed by a safety pin, and announced he was going to bed. Vera was appalled at the time, but it became the basis of a running family joke: When it was time to leave someplace, one of the kids would say "well, it's time to put our pajamas on and get the safety pin."

The O'Connells' three-bedroom 1.5-bath house was not festooned with memorabilia from his career. There wasn't room. Danny had a few photos on his dresser and a large painting of himself in a Giants uniform with a bat cocked over his shoulder, most likely a gift for appearing in Old Timers games. That was about it for mementoes of his past life. But if O'Connell had taken himself out of baseball, the game hadn't taken itself out of him.

Eldest son Dan recalled going to various youth group events with his dad "and he would say a few things and they would talk him into getting him into a batting cage or something like that, and he would just hit bullet after bullet, and I remember thinking 'That's my dad in there!' And it was interesting too that before, he would be joking and lovable, and then he got in that cage and man, it was serious business." Nancy remembered that when Danny took them to an amusement park or carnival, "if there was a booth where my dad needed to knock something down by throwing a ball, I was going home with a stuffed animal! He would rip the ball and I remember being so amazed and so proud."

At the banquet, O'Connell regaled the priests with baseball yarns. He told them how Willie Mays would have a dinner at his home for the team after the season, "and never failed to get a laugh when the main course was served by two white butlers in tuxedos." Danny's stories, Longula wrote in a piece for a Catholic weekly magazine, were invariably self-deprecating when describing his own accomplishments. "But he valued one thing," Longula wrote. "He had never been unfaithful [to Vera] all the time he was in baseball."

Longula left the country club that night before O'Connell. "It was raining something fierce," he wrote. "… I couldn't see 15 feet in front of me…The rain was slamming like gravel against the windshield and the fog so thick that the car headlights made you think you were driving into a world of white fluffy cotton."

About 11:45 p.m., the family station wagon Danny was driving left the road at an intersection and rammed into a utility pole. O'Connell's skull was fractured, and he was pronounced dead on arrival at Passaic General Hospital. The accident occurred maybe 10 minutes from home, and 110 days short of O'Connell's 41st birthday. But as it turned out, the lousy weather had little or nothing to do with the crash: An autopsy revealed Danny had suffered a massive heart attack before hitting the pole.

Earlier in the evening, O'Connell had called home to say he would be late. Thirteen-year-old Maureen pushed aside her homework—it was a Thursday night—and answered the phone. "My mom said 'ask Dad how the banquet went and did he win anything [in the golf tournament],'" Maureen recalled, "and then I just handed the phone over to Mom." The kids went to bed. Sometime after midnight, Vera awakened Maureen and 11-year-old Nancy. "I've got to go to the hospital," she told them, "because Dad's been in a car accident." The next morning, she gathered the children together in hers and Danny's bedroom and told them Dad was gone. "There was of course shock," Maureen recalled, "and then it was all a bit of a blur."

Vera, who had lost her own mother the year before, reacted with her usual equanimity. She told the kids they should be thankful they had been blessed with as good a father as Danny had been, that he was in a better place and would always be with them—and to be happy that at least no one else had been injured in the accident.

The widow had support of her own from her siblings. Her sister Madeline stayed constantly at Vera's side in the first days after Danny's death. "Aunt Maddie became my mom's soulmate and partner, and she was there for us every Christmas and holiday," Maureen recalled. "I vividly remember her coming over the next day [after the accident] and we were polishing the silver and Aunt Maddie said 'oh I wish God had taken me instead' because she never got married or had children, and I remember thinking 'wow, that's pretty unselfish of you Aunt Maddie.'"

Another sister, Mildred O'Brien, lived nearby and the O'Connell kids were sent over to the O'Briens while funeral arrangements were made. Kids being kids, that worried them. Aunt Millie was married to Walter P. O'Brien, a longtime Wall Street stockbroker, with whom she had produced seven children in a relatively short time. Probably as a matter of preserving his sanity, "Uncle Obie" was regarded by the O'Connells as a strict taskmaster, particularly compared to Danny. "I remember as we were growing up we all hoped and prayed nothing would happen to our mom," John O'Connell said, "because we'd have to go live with the O'Briens."

Danny's wake at his pal Frank Halpin's funeral home stretched over two days. The funeral mass at St. Thomas the Apostle Church attracted a standing-room-only crowd. Eulogies arrived from the baseball world as well as Danny's hometown. "In this moment of happiness for me and my family," Gil Hodges said the day the Mets clinched the N.L. pennant by beating the Atlanta Braves in the playoffs, "I am saddened greatly. I have just been told that Danny O'Connell died in an automobile accident a few days ago. I am shocked. Danny coached for me in Washington and was a good friend, a major league player before that, and always a major leaguer. He was a great individual."

Chuck Pezzano, a writer who grew up with Danny in Paterson's Stony Road neighborhood, recalled his lifelong friend as someone who honed his skills at various endeavors by working them from all angles. O'Connell, Pezzano wrote, "was a fine golfer, aided by caddying; a fine bowler, aided by setting up pins, and a fine debater, aided by the practice he got in corner drug store arguments. And he was no slouch when it came to pitching pennies, matching baseball cards and all forms of marbles...It's been a dark couple of days for his family and friends. I feel like the clock has been turned back 30 years and we're at Pennington Park in the dark, afraid to go home because we should have been home hours ago. But Danny is in his final home now, and Heaven is all the richer."

If the wakes, funeral mass and eulogies were cathartic for the grownups, however, they were a bit overwhelming for the kids. "After the second wake," Maureen said, "we asked Mom 'Can we go back to school tomorrow?' We just wanted to return to some kind of normalcy."

A few months after Danny's death, there was a knock at the door of the O'Connell home. When Vera opened it, a small and unfamiliar woman introduced herself as "Harp's wife." A chill seized Vera. Harp was Danny's bookie, and Vera was sure Harp had sent his wife to collect some unpaid debt to ease his embarrassment for dunning a widow.

"But she came in and had an envelope with $5,000 in cash in it (about $40,600 in 2024)," John O'Connell said. "She offered it to my mother and said 'you're a widow with four young children, and Harp doesn't know I have this, but take it.'" Vera graciously turned down the offer. But decades later, she saw the woman again at a wake, reminded her about the offer and told her how much it had meant to her at the time. "You should have taken it," Harp's wife replied.

Actually, Vera already had help with the family's finances, indirectly and directly, from other sources—indirectly from a 49-year-old labor negotiator she never met, and directly from her big brother Cliff. The negotiator was Marvin Miller, an economist by education who had been a labor representative for national unions such as the United Auto Workers and United Steelworkers. In 1966, he was elected by the players as executive director of the Major League Baseball Players Association. By the end of his first year in office, Miller had badgered the owners into a much-improved pension plan that by 1968 brought benefits for 10-year players to about $15,600 a year (about $134,00 in 2024 dollars) when they reached 65 and provided a generous 100 percent survivor benefit to their widows.

Exactly how much the O'Connell family received from the pension fund is unknown, but it was a substantial part of Vera's resources. "My mother would drill us to 'watch the All-Star game' because the proceeds from the game went to the pension fund," Dan O'Connell IV recalled. "She was sort of kidding, but she wanted us to make sure the All-Star Game got good ratings to keep the pension fund healthy...In all seriousness, it meant my mom never had to go to work...My mom was there when I came home from school and so my brother and sisters have always been thankful to Major League Baseball for that."

Vera wrote the commissioner of baseball every year to thank him for the pension, although in actuality commissioners had nothing to do with it. But baseball—and the fact Danny O'Connell had persevered to get his 10 years in—did. "If we hadn't gotten the pension," daughter Maureen said, "the four of us would not have gone to college." Other than praising baseball officials and urging the viewing of the All-Star game, Vera was consistently closed-mouth about money matters. But the O'Connell offspring were convinced there was almost certainly a fairly substantial insurance payment to help out. And then there was Uncle Cliff.

Five years older than Vera, Clifford John Sharkey certainly had the financial chops to advise and counsel his widowed sister. A decorated World War II Navy vet, Sharkey got into the banking business after the war. By the time of Danny O'Connell's death in 1969, Sharkey had been president of a savings and loan firm, board chairman of the New Jersey Savings & Loan League and president of the Federal Home Loan Bank Board of New York. "An effervescent outgoing fellow with a hearty sense of humor and a solid background in the business," as a Newark business columnist described him, Sharkey was also an avid sportsman. He golfed, bowled and skied well into his 80s. And he dearly loved his brother-in-law, the baseball player. It was Uncle Cliff who drove Vera to the hospital the night Danny died.

"Uncle Cliff and my father adored each other," Maureen said. "And when my dad died, he stepped up...he helped my mother figure out finances and where to invest. I don't think he lent her any money because I don't think he personally had a lot of money, but he definitely gave her advice on how to manage things...and it must've been pretty good advice, because she never had to go to work and we did okay." John O'Connell recalled coming into the house from playing "and my mom and Uncle Cliff would be sitting at the dining room table going over things...he'd be telling her to switch over from one account to another to make more money."

Vera remained in the Fairway Street house—which she laughingly referred to as her "starter home"—for 47 years after Danny's death. Fairway is a quiet and tidy cul-de-sac, about seven miles south of Danny's boyhood home in Paterson. "We've only been here two years," said the young man who answered the door in the summer of 2022 at the home that once belonged to the O'Connells, "but we've heard lots of stories about them. Everyone who knew them liked them, especially the mother...They tell me she was a really sweet woman, and the kids very nice too." She must have been. "One reason she was able to stay on Fairway into her 80's was the kindness of her neighbors," son John said. "Some have since moved on, but some remain. They watched out for her for many years, which was comforting for us."

A devout Catholic, Vera attended Mass almost daily, albeit with precautions. "Mom was kind of a germaphobe," Maureen said, then thought it over for a moment. "Not kind of, she was definitely a germaphobe. She would go to Mass every day and after everyone did the sign of peace [a gesture that involves shaking hands or lightly embracing the person on one side of you] she'd whip out a little sanitation wipe and wipe her hands down. We'd say 'Mom, it's kind of insulting, these people all know you and you know them. But she couldn't help herself." Danny IV referred to Vera as "a pandemic precursor." Both children's comments were made with slightly exasperated affection.

In 2016, at the age of 86, Vera moved to an assisted living facility within walking distance of the home of John, her youngest son. She died in 2018. Danny and Vera are buried together at the Immaculate Conception Cemetery, a few miles from the Fairway Street residence. Many, if not most, of the cemetery's granite markers bear Italian surnames. But the O'Connells are watched over in the "Irish section," as a friendly caretaker put it, by a reasonably sized if slightly gaudy statue of St. Patrick not too far away from their shared plot. The O'Connells' marker is elegant in its simplicity, bearing only their names and birth and death dates. On Danny's side, an American Legion medallion is stuck in the ground as well.

Eldest daughter Maureen O'Connell Hurley graduated from the University of New Hampshire and earned a law degree from Notre Dame University, where she met her husband John. After practicing law in Chicago, the couple moved to Buffalo, New York. Maureen worked for 31 years at Rich Products Corporation. She retired in 2015 as executive vice president and chief administrative officer. She and John had three children.

Nancy O'Connell Mellin graduated from the University of Delaware with a degree in education, settled in Annapolis, Maryland, where she had a 35-year-career as a teacher. She and her husband Daniel had two children.

Daniel F. O'Connell IV graduated from Notre Dame University with a degree in chemical engineering, and spent most of his working life with Air Products, an international corporation that supplies gases and chemicals to various industries. Dan and his wife Leslie retired to Ocean City, New Jersey. They had four children.

John O'Connell graduated from St. Bonaventure University in New York and became an account executive in the transportation and logistics industry. A bachelor, he lived in Hockessin, Delaware.

"This may sound a little morbid, or selfish, I don't know what the right word is," Danny O'Connell IV summed up for his siblings, "but however stressed out my dad might have been about how well it was all going to turn out, it turned out pretty well for his kids. We're healthy and we've lived pretty good lives. And I think he'd be at peace with that."

CHAPTER 18 NOTES

Danny put a *The York (Pa.) Dispatch,* Jan. 19, 1963, p. 12.

Bittersweet and bitter *The Advocate* (Newark NJ), Vol. 18, No. 44, Oct. 23, 1969.

Always the socializer This and many of the succeeding paragraphs are based on my interviews in person, over the phone and via email with O'Connell's offspring.

O'Connell regaled the *The Advocate,* op. cit.

Longula left the Ibid.

Danny's wake at *New York Daily News,* Oct. 7, 1969, p. 81.

Chuck Pezzano, a *Bergen County Record,* Oct. 4, 1969.

Five years older *The (Newark NJ) Star-Ledger,* May 9, 1967.

EPILOGUE
CARDBOARD DREAMS
AND COMMON HEROES

In the bucolic town of Idaho Falls, which coincidentally enough is in the state of Idaho, there lives a man with a lot of baseball cards.

A whole lot. As in well over four million. As in Guinness-Book-of-Records-for-the-largest-private-card-collection-in-the-world. They are ensconced in scores of file cabinets and white rectangular cardboard boxes, each box holding from 3,200 to 5,000 cards. The boxes and cabinets, in turn, fill a hefty percentage of a three-car garage, which is attached to a handsome two-story house on a one-third-acre lot. The house borders farmland that is still green despite the hot sun of a late June day in 2022.

The cards are only part of Paul Jones' collection of baseball stuff. He also has close to 100,000 photos, paintings, posters, bats, balls, jerseys, bobble-heads and other items, many of them autographed. You could say Paul Jones has a passion for baseball. You could also say Glacier National Park is scenic. Both would be understatements. But to say that baseball, and baseball cards, have made Paul Jones' life worth living would almost certainly *not* be an overstatement.

"I love baseball," the 36-year-old Jones says as he shows a visitor around his basement-level "apartment" jammed with memorabilia. This ranges from a colorful poster of former slugger and baseball bad boy Jose Canseco—who is a friend of Paul's and of whom Paul has 2,000-plus cards—to an autographed jersey from the Chicago American Giants, a Negro Leagues team from the first three decades of the 20th century.

That Paul Jones, who lives with his parents Lorraine and Barry, is amiably showing a stranger his collection, or is even around to do anything at all, is something of a miracle in itself. "They told us when he was born that he would never leave the hospital," says Barry. "Then they told us we would have to put him in an institution because he was missing one of his genes and his brain could shut down any time...That went on for years." Paul was eventually diagnosed with Asperger Syndrome, a rare neurodevelopmental condition whose victims are often deeply withdrawn, socially awkward and uncommunicative. "He was in a shell," Barry Jones says, "and baseball drew him out of it."

The magic began in 1995, while the Joneses were living in Las Vegas. The family happened to encounter Hall of Fame pitcher Rollie Fingers at a book signing. After hearing about Paul's condition, Fingers talked Barry and Lorraine into taking Paul to a baseball game at Cashman Field, home of the Triple-A Las Vegas Stars. Neither Lorraine nor Barry was a baseball fan, but they were willing to give it a try. Paul liked the hot dogs, so they returned the next evening.

This time they bought their son a pack of baseball cards featuring the Stars and coaxed him down to the rail separating the stands from the field, where other kids were getting autographs. Paul stood there, mute and unmoving. Stars manager Tim Flannery happened by. "Want my autograph?" the 11-year big-league veteran asked the 10-year-old kid standing still as a statue. Paul nodded and handed Flannery all his cards. The manager noticed none of the cards were signed, and asked Barry and Lorraine if he could take Paul to the Stars' clubhouse for signatures from the players.

"They handed me over to Flannery," Paul recalled with a smile, "and I came back with all my cards signed, and my mom said 'maybe we should get him some more cards.'" The rest is history. In 2008, Paul was recognized by Guinness as the king of card collections. In 2021, he was named an inaugural inductee to the *Sports Collectors Digest* Collectors Hall of Fame. As of late 2023, he was still collecting cards by the thousands, many of them sent to him by perfect strangers. "He's even in some guy's will to get the guy's cards when he dies," Barry said.

That is nowhere near all there is to the story of Paul Jones and baseball. In addition to amassing his collection through the mail and traveling all over the country to card shops, spring training camps and minor- and major-league ballparks, Paul is quite probably the most famous bat boy in America. Known as "Foul Ball Paul" for once having been struck by an errantly batted spheroid, he has practiced his craft for scores of minor league teams and for major league clubs in spring training. "I'm really good at it," he says without a trace of false modesty. "They all want me." In fact, on the day of my visit the Joneses were preparing to leave the following day for Missoula, Montana, where Paul has been invited to work a game or two for the PaddleHeads, of the Pioneer League.

The cards, however, are at Paul's core. They've taught him math, spelling, geography and history—and infused him with self-confidence. In turn, he treats the cards with the democratic even-handedness of a pure old-school collector. They are harvested without regard to the pictured player's status or the card's level of scarcity or condition. And they are filed alphabetically for storage in a garage file cabinet or cardboard box rather than a safe deposit box or faraway security vault.

"I take them out and look at them all the time," he says. "They're my passion. They make me happy. It's about fun, not money."

A bit more than 2,200 miles east of the Jones residence, it's mostly about money. Over five days in late July 2022, more than 85,000 people push and crowd their way into the Atlantic City (NJ) Convention Center to buy, sell and trade hundreds of thousands of items, almost none of which has any practical use whatsoever. It's the 42nd National Sports Collectors Convention.

Not everything is sports-related. For instance, you can get an otherwise blank card signed by Grover Cleveland, the 22nd and 24th U.S. president ($610) or a baseball signed by Donald Trump Jr. ($350.) But it is overwhelmingly a vast array of sports memorabilia. There is a 1927 check for $9,914.09, made out to and endorsed by Babe Ruth, from Ruth's business manager. The check is for two weeks' salary and some medical bills. It sells at auction for $7,500. A movie poster advertising the 1951 biopic "Follow the Sun," about the legendary golfer Ben Hogan (as portrayed by Glenn Ford) is advertised for $450, next to an early-50s framed magazine ad featuring the real Ben Hogan, in which he is enthusiastically proclaiming that Chesterfield cigarettes have been his go-to smoke for seven years. It has a $175 price tag. A "game used" chunk of the wooden floor the Minneapolis Lakers played on in 1954, autographed by the legendary Laker George Mikan is on offer for $795.

And there are lots of baseball cards. The "vintage" cards come graded and ungraded, in all conditions and for prices that to the non-collector would range from the *"that's a lot of money for a piece of cardboard"* to *"are you frigging kidding me?"* At one booth a 1958 Mickey Mantle that appears to have been flipped into brick walls more than a few times is being offered for $800. At another booth the same year's card, in much better shape, is $350.

There is also a significantly more expensive 1952 Mantle card on display at the heavily guarded 2,500-square-foot Heritage Auctions corral. A month after the show, the card will sell for $12.6 million, shattering the previous record price of $7.25 million set a few months before for a 1909 Honus Wagner. The price the Mantle card fetches is 252 times more than the seller paid for it in 1991, or about 100 times the inflation rate over that period. That should tell you something about the state of baseball card collecting. What this is I'm not exactly sure.

There are new cards as well. For $225, you can buy a Topps "Gypsy Queen" box. Inside are 24 packs with eight cards in each pack, but no gum. It is guaranteed that two of the cards are autographed. If one of the cards is the Angels' superstar Mike Trout and the other is the Phillies' luminous Bryce Harper, you've got yourself maybe a $1,000 box for $225. If the autographs are those of the Pirates' less stellar Hoy Park and the Marlins' Jesus Luzardo (who?) on the other hand, you're the proud owner of $225 worth of baseball cards, for which you paid $225. "It's a roll of the dice," understates the grinning vendor who explains all this to me. "It's the dream, like the lottery, or Cracker Jacks prizes" - if Cracker Jacks sold for $225 a box.

Despite the fact there are 339 vendors at the show, I search in vain at several dozen booths for "commons" - cards of the thousands of lunchpail players who were nonetheless bonafide major leaguers. Most of the dealers tell me they don't deal in commons, other than to occasionally buy a set, pluck out the stars and offload the rest in lots of 50 to 100. There are scores of Wille Mayses, Ted Williamses, Brooks Robinsons, Frank Robinsons, Stan Musials and Henry Aarons, almost always for hundreds or thousands of dollars. While I was talking to one vendor, a fellow interrupted us to say he had thought it over, and he would take the Nolan Ryan for $5,000. Sorry, the vendor replied, I sold it 15 minutes ago for $7,100.

Jack Kerekes of Jack's Cards in Cleveland, however, does it differently, at least at this show. He's selling commons one by one. They're priced, he says, according to whether he deems the card in better than average condition, or whether the players are more memorable than their peers. "The only exceptions are Yankees," he says. "They have a slight premium."

And so in a box of 1960 Topps cards, arranged in numerical order, between a Johnny Klippstein ($3.50) and a Dick Hyde ($2.00), I find a—you guessed it—Danny O'Connell. This is the very card that so vexed me six decades before, when it appeared to exist in every single pack of cards I bought and was purposely put there by the Topps people to taunt me personally.

The O'Connell card is priced at $3.00, but Kerekes lets me have it for $1.50 after I tell him why I want it. "You're writing a book about this guy?" he asks as I hand him $2 and tell him to keep the change. I reply in the affirmative.

"Good luck with that," he says.

In its April 1, 1962 edition, the *Philadelphia Inquirer* ran a full-page piece by sportswriter Edgar Williams headlined "The Unsung." "On virtually every club," Williams wrote, "there is a man of limited talents and modest achievements, who nonetheless is an important factor in his team's scheme of things. He has made the big time because, to borrow a dugout term, he 'puts out 110 percent,' and has the gift of adaptability—meaning that he can do an adequate job at several positions. By comparison with most other players, he is a lightweight on the salary scale and agents do not flock around him with offers of fees to endorse products. But the work is steady, and there is a certain psychic return that derives from being part of a special breed…".

The story offered mini-profiles of seven such players, including Danny O'Connell. Of the other six, two had lifetime batting averages just slightly above Danny's .260: Lee Walls (.262) and Felix Mantilla (.261.) None were within 275 hits of O'Connell's career total of 1,049. But all of them played at least three positions during their careers. More remarkably, all but one— Joe Koppe—had major league careers of 10 seasons or more, and Koppe had eight. I say "remarkably" because as pointed out in the introduction of this book, fewer than 10 percent of the 20,000-plus men who have played in the big leagues since 1876 have lasted at least a decade at that level of their profession.

Williams included an observation by George "Birdie" Tebbetts, who for most of 14 years was a very good big-league catcher and for 11 years a pretty good big-league manager—and who had a degree in philosophy from Rhode Island's Providence College. "There ought to be a junior Hall of Fame for them," Tebbetts said of players like Danny O'Connell. "They pour their life's blood into it. They have to claw and scramble and fight and hustle to make it. It's a matter of pride."

Tebbetts was right about the effort players like O'Connell put into their work, but he left out a more important element. In all the clawing and scrambling and fighting and hustling to make it, they and all the players like them were realizing their dreams. Daniel Francis O'Connell III had a career full of "almosts" and a life cut unexpectedly short. But for at least three-fourths of that life he played baseball, successfully enough to leave evidence of his accomplishments on a dozen different rectangular pieces of cardboard.

And maybe that's the true value of baseball cards. Maybe they're mirrors as well as pictures. Maybe we see our efforts to achieve our own aspirations in the faces of the players, or reflect on how we can achieve them. And maybe it's easier to see that in the cards of "commons" than "stars." At the beginning of his major league career, Danny said he couldn't imagine life without baseball. I look at his cards and can't imagine baseball without players like Danny O'Connell.

SELECTED BIBLIOGRAPHY

Aaron, Hank, with Lonnie Wheeler. *I Had a Hammer: The Hank Aaron Story.* New York: Harper Perennial, 1991.

Acheson, Dean. *The Korean War.* New York: W.W. Norton & Company, 1996.

Andrews, Tom, and Rich Wolfe. *For Milwaukee Braves Fans Only!* Scottsdale, Az.: Lone Wolfe Press, 2011.

Angell, Roger. *Late Innings: A Baseball Companion.* New York: Simon & Schuster, 1982.

Balukjian, Brad. *The Wax Pack: On the Open Road in Search of Baseball's Afterlife.* Lincoln, Neb.: University of Nebraska Press, 2020.

Barzun, Jacques. *God's Country and Mine: A Declaration of Love Spiced With a Few Harsh Words.* Boston: Little, Brown and Company, 1954.

Bilby, Joseph G., James M. Madden and Harry Ziegler. *Hidden History of New Jersey.* Charleston, S.C.: History Press, 2011.

Bitker, Steve. *The Original San Francisco Giants.* New York: Sports Publishing Inc., 2001.

Blau, Marc H. *Baseball in Tacoma-Pierce County.* Charleston, S.C.: Arcadia Publishing, 2011.

Bloom, John. *A House of Cards: Baseball Card Collecting and Popular Culture.* Minneapolis: University of Minnesota Press, 1997.

Bradbury, J.C. *The Baseball Economist: The Real Game Exposed.* New York: Dutton, 2007.

Branson, Douglas M. *Greatness in the Shadows: Larry Doby and the Integration of the American League.* Lincoln, Neb.: University of Nebraska Press, 2016.

Breslin, Jimmy. *Branch Rickey.* New York: Penguin Group, 2011.

Brosnan, Jim. *The Long Season: The Classic Inside Account of a Baseball Year, 1959.* New York: Harper, 2002 edition.

Bouton, Jim. *Ball Four, Plus Five: An Update, 1970-1980.* New York: Stein & Day, 1981.

Boyd, Brendan C. and Fred C. Harris. *The Great American Baseball Card Flipping, Trading and Bubble Gum Book.* New York: Ticknor & Fields, 1991.

Buege, Bob. *The Milwaukee Braves: A Baseball Eulogy.* Milwaukee, WI: Douglas American Sports Publications, 1988.

Casey, Steven. *Selling the Korean War: Propaganda, Politics and Public Opinion, 1950-1953.* New York: Oxford University Press, 2008.

Chernow, Ron. *Alexander Hamilton.* New York: Penguin Books, 2004.

Clavin, Tom and Danny Peary. *Gil Hodges: The Brooklyn Bums, the Miracle Mets and the Extraordinary Life of a Baseball Legend.* New York: New American Library, 2012.

Dawidoff, Nicholas (ed.). *Baseball: A Literary Anthology.* New York: The Library of America, 2002.

DiClerico, James M. and Barry J. Pavelec. *The Jersey Game: The History of Modern Baseball from Its Birth to the Big Leagues in the Garden State.* New Brunswick, NJ: Rutgers University Press, 1991.

Farber, David. *The Age of Great Dreams: America in the 1960s.* New York: Hill and Wang, 1994.

Farber, David and Beth Bailey. *The Columbia Guide to America in the 1960s.* New York: Columbia University Press, 2001.

Fehler, Gene. *When Baseball Was Still King: Major League Players Remember the 1950s.* Jefferson, N.C.: McFarland & Company, Inc., 2012.

Finoli, David. *Pirates by the Numbers: A Complete Team History of the Bucs by Uniform Number.* New York: Sports Publishing, 2016.

Finoli, David and Bill Ranier. *The Pittsburgh Pirates Encyclopedia (2nd ed.).* New York: Sports Publishing, 2015.

Fitts, Robert K., Bill Nowlin and James Forr (eds.) *Nichibei Yakyu: U.S. Tours of Japan, Volume I: 1907-1958.* Phoenix: Society for American Baseball Research, Inc., 2022.

Friedman, David M. *Wilde in America: Oscar Wilde and the Invention of Modern Celebrity.* New York: W.W. Norton & Company, 2014.

Gould, Stephen J. *Full House: The Spread of Excellence from Plato to Darwin.* New York: Three Rivers Press, 1996.

Grimm, Charlie, with Ed Prell. *Jolly Cholly's Story: Baseball, I Love You!* Chicago: Henry Regnery Company, 1968.

Halberstam, David. *The Coldest Winter: America and the Korean War.* New York: Hyperion, 2017.

Halberstam, David. *The Fifties.* New York: Fawcett Columbine, 1993.

Halberstam, David, *Summer of '49.* New York, William Morrow, 1989.

Hanley, Dean. *The Bubble Gum Card War: The Great Bowman and Topps Sets from 1948 to 1955.* Las Vegas: Mighty Casey Books, 2012.

Harris, Howard. "The Eagle to Watch and the Harp to Tune the Nation: Irish Immigrants, Politics and Early Industrialization in Paterson, New Jersey, 1824-1836." *Journal of Social History,* Vol. 23, No. 3 (Spring, 1990), pp. 575-597.

Hartley, James R. *Washington's Expansion Senators (1961-1971).* Germantown, Md.: Corduroy Press, 1997.

Honig, Donald. *Baseball Between the Lines: Baseball in the '40s and '50s.* New York: Coward, McCann and Geoghegan, Inc., 1976.

Honig, Donald. *Baseball in the '50s: A Decade of Transition.* New York: Crown Publishers, 1987.

Houck, Davis W. and Matthew A. Grindy, *Emmett Till and the Mississippi Press.* Jackson, Miss.: University Press of Mississippi, 2008.

Hwang, Jeff. *The Modern Baseball Card Investor.* Columbia, SC: Dimat Enterprises, 2014.

Jamieson, Dave. *Mint Condition: How Baseball Cards Became an American Obsession.* New York: Grove Press, 2010.

Jones, Tanner. *Confessions of a Baseball Card Addict: The Story of a Man who Acquired Ten Million Cards and Managed to Stay Married.* Middletown, Del.: TanManBaseballFan, 2020.

Kahn, Roger. *The Era: 1947-1957, When the Yankees, the Giants and the Dodgers Ruled the World.* New York: Ticknor & Fields, 1993.

Kahn, Roger. *Rickey and Robinson: The True, Untold Story of the Integration of Baseball.* New York: Rodale Books, 2014.

Kahn, Roger, and Al Helfer (eds.) *The Mutual Baseball Almanac.* New York: Doubleday & Co., 1954.

Klima, John. *Bushville Wins!: The Wild Saga of the 1957 Milwaukee Braves and the Screwballs, Sluggers and Beer Swiggers Who Canned the New York Yankees and Changed Baseball.* New York: Thomas Dunne Books, 2012.

Law, Keith. *Smart Baseball.* New York: Harper Collins, 2017.

Leckie, Robert. *The Wars of America.* New York: Harper & Row, Publishers, 1981.

Levine, Peter. *A.G. Spalding and the Rise of Baseball: The Promise of American Sport.* New York: Oxford University Press, 1985.

Lewis, Michael. *Moneyball.* New York: W.W. Norton & Co., 2003.

Lieb, Frederick G. *The Pittsburgh Pirates.* New York: G.P. Putnam's Sons, 1948.

Lurie, Maxine N. and Richard Veit (eds.). *New Jersey: A History of the Garden State.* New Brunswick, N.J.: Rutgers University Press, 2012.

Marazzi, Rich and Len Fiorito. *Baseball Players of the 1950s: A Biographical Dictionary of All 1,560 Major Leaguers.* Jefferson, NC: McFarland & Company, 2009.

McDermott, Mickey, with Howard Eisenberg. *A Funny Thing Happened on the Way to Cooperstown.* Chicago: Triumph Books, 2003.

Meany, Tom. *Milwaukee's Miracle Braves.* New York: A.S. Barnes & Co., 1954.

Miller, Marvin. *A Whole Different Ball Game: The Inside Story of the Baseball Revolution.* Chicago: Ivan R. Dee, Publisher, 2004.

Minoso, Orestes "Minnie," with Fernando Fernandez and Robert Kleinfelder. *Extra Innings: My Life in Baseball.* Chicago: Regnery Gateway, 1983.

Moffi, Larry. *This Side of Cooperstown: An Oral History of Major League Baseball in the 1950s.* Mineola, NY: Dover Publications, 2010.

Moore, Joseph Thomas. *Larry Doby: The Struggle of the American League's First Black Player.* Mineola, NY: Dover Publications, Inc., 2011.

Murphy, Brian. *San Francisco Giants: 50 Years.* San Rafael, Ca.: Insight Editions, 2008.

O'Keeffe, Michael and Teri Thompson. *The Card: Collectors, Con Men and the True Story of History's Most Desired Baseball Card.* New York: William Morrow, 2007.

Oser, Khyber, Mark Friedland and Ron Oser. *Cardboard Gems: A Century of Baseball Cards and Their Stories, 1869-1969.* Burr Ridge, Ill.: Mastro Auctions, 2006.

O'Toole, Andrew. *Branch Rickey in Pittsburgh.* Jefferson, NC: McFarland & Company, 2000.

Peary, Danny (ed.) *We Played the Game: Memories of Baseball's Greatest Era.* New York: Black Dog & Leventhal Publishers, 2002.

Posnanski, Joe. *The Baseball 100.* New York: Avid Reader Press, 2021.

Povletich, William. *Milwaukee Braves: Heroes and Heartbreak.* Madison, Wisc.: Wisconsin Historical Society Press, 2009.

Powers, Albert Theodore. *The Business of Baseball.* Jefferson, N.C.: McFarland & Company, 2003.

Prager, Joshua. *The Echoing Green: The Untold Story of Bobby Thomson, Ralph Branca and the Shot Heard Round the World.* New York: Vintage Books, 2008.

Quinn, Dermot. *The Irish in New Jersey: Four Centuries of American Life.* New Brunswick, NJ: Rutgers University Press, 2004.

Rosen, Charley. *The Emerald Diamond: How the Irish Transformed America's Greatest Pastime.* New York: Harper Collins, 2012.

Rosenthal, Harold. *The 10 Best Years of Baseball: An Informal History of the 'Fifties.* Chicago: Contemporary Books, 1979.

Roth, Philip. *American Pastoral.* New York: Vintage Books, 1997.

Schoendienst, Red and Rob Rains. *Red: A Baseball Life.* Champaign, Ill.: Sports Publishing, 1998.

Shapiro, Michael. *Bottom of the Ninth: Branch Rickey, Casey Stengel and the Daring Scheme to Save Baseball from Itself.* New York: Times Books, 2009.

Slocum, Frank. *Baseball Cards of the Fifties: The Complete Topps Cards, 1950-1959.* New York: Simon & Schuster, 1994.

Slocum, Frank. *Baseball Cards of the Sixties: The Complete Topps Cards, 1960-1969.* New York: Simon & Schuster, 1994.

Spalding, Albert G. *America's National Game.* Lincoln, Neb.: University of Nebraska Press, 1992.

Thomas, G. Scott. *A Brand New Ballgame: Branch Rickey, Bill Veeck, Walter O'Malley and the Transformation of Baseball, 1945-1962.* Jefferson, NC: McFarland & Co., Inc., 2022.

Thorn, John. *Baseball in the Garden of Eden: The Secret History of the Early Game.* New York: Simon & Schuster, 2011.

Treder, Steven. *Forty Years a Giant: The Life of Horace Stoneham.* Lincoln, Neb.: University of Nebraska Press, 2021.

Tunis, John R. *The Kid from Tompkinsville.* New York: Harcourt Brace Jovanovich, Inc., 1940.

Turbow, Jason, with Michael Duca. *The Baseball Codes: Beanballs, Sign Stealing & Bench-Clearing Brawls.* New York: Anchor Books, 2010.

Vincent, Fay. *We Would Have Played for Nothing: Baseball Stars of the 1950s and 1960s Talk About the Game They Loved.* New York: Simon & Schuster, 2008.

Voigt, David Vincent. *American Baseball, Vol. III: From Postwar Expansion to the Electronic Age.* University Park, PA.: The Pennsylvania State University Press, 1983.

Weintraub, Robert. *The Victory Season: The End of World War II and the Birth of Baseball's Golden Age.* New York: Back Bay Books, 2013.

Whitfield, Stephen J. *A Death in the Delta.* Baltimore: Johns Hopkins University Press, 1991.

Wiegand, Steve. *American Revolution for Dummies.* Hoboken, NJ: John Wiley & Sons, 2020.

Wiegand, Steve. *U.S. History for Dummies (4th ed.).* Hoboken, NJ: John Wiley & Sons, 2019.

Wilker, Josh. *Cardboard Gods: An All-American Tale Told Through Baseball Cards.* New York: Seven-Footer Press, 2010.

Will, George. *Men at Work: The Craft of Baseball.* New York: Macmillan Publishing Company, 1990.

Williams, Pete. *Card Sharks: How Upper Deck Turned a Child's Hobby Into a Billion-Dollar Business.* New York: MacMillan, 1995.

Williams, William Carlos. *Paterson.* New York: New Directions Books, 1992.

Wright, Giles R. *Afro-Americans in New Jersey, a Short History.* Trenton, NJ: New Jersey Historical Commission, 1988.

Ziants, Steve. *100 Things Pirates Fans Should Know & Do Before They Die.* Chicago: Triumph Books, 2014.

Online and Other Sources:

Giamatti Research Center, National Baseball Hall of Fame

Society for American Baseball Research (SABR)

Stathead Baseball

Sports Collectors Digest

Baseball Digest Archives

Baseball-Reference.com

Ancestry.com

Newspapers.com.

The Sporting News Archives

Humanities, the Magazine of the National Endowment for the Humanities. Vol. 15. No. 4 (July/August 1994).

Tuff Stuff presents Topps: 50 Years of Topps, January 2001.

INDEX

Flannery, Tim, 338
Fleer Corporation, 104–105, 290
Food and Drug Administration, U.S., 108
Forbes Field, Pittsburgh, 77, 82–83
Ford, Ed "Whitey," 116, 291
Fort Eustis Wheelers, 126
Fort Myer Colonials, 119, 120–121, 125–126, 127–128
Fortune magazine, 42
Fox, Nellie, 294
Fox, Nelson, 304
Frick, Ford, 50, 185, 250, 263, 278, 301–302
Friend, Bob, 142, 243
Frisch, Frankie, 48–49, 76
Fuchs, Bill, 288
Furillo, Carl, 22, 88, 232

Gaedel, Eddie, 166
Galan, Augie, 188
Galbreath, John, 76–77, 85
Gallagher, Jim, 78
Garagiola, Joe, 124, 125, 138, 139
Gardella, Danny, 44
Gehrig, Lou, 76
Gelman, Woody, 192
G.I. Bill of Rights, 45–46
Gillespie, Betty, 207
Ginsberg, Alan, 28
Ginsberg, Joe, 299
Glenn, John, 116–117
Goldin, Ken, 103
Gomez, Ruben, 13
Goodwin and Co. baseball cards, 99
Gooter, Joe
    on barnstormers (1950), 88
    on Danny, 152
    on Danny after baseball, 322
    on Danny at end of 1959 season, 270
    on Danny buying house for his family, 149
    on Danny in the Army, 121–122
    on Danny's 1956 season, 198
    on Danny's belief in the Senators, 318–319
    on Danny's release by Giants, 272–273
Gordon, Sid, 150
Goudey, Enos G., 105–106

Gould, Stephen Jay, 7
Graham, Frank, 72
Grandstand Managers (Pirates' booster club), 148
Grant, Jim "Mudcat," 183
Gray, Pete, 115
Great Depression, 31, 95
Great Falls, Passaic River, New Jersey, 25, 37
Green Light Letter, 115
Greenberg, Hank, 78–79
Greengrass, Jim, 169
Greenville Spinners, South Carolina, 68–69
Griffith, Clark, 47
Griffith Stadium, 287, 293–294
Grimes, Burleigh "Old Stubblebeard," 9
Grimm, Charlie
    Braves fire, 214
    as Braves manager, 151
    Danny popping off and, 180–181, 186
    Danny's defense by, 173
    Danny's hitting streak and, 145
    on Danny's slump, 170
    on 1954 lineup, 164, 171
    pennant race 1956 and, 212
    racism of, 184
    on second base position, 161, 187, 198, 208
    as too easy going, 198, 209–210
Grissom, Marv, 146
Groat, Dick, 124–125, 128
Gruber, John, 102
Grunwald, Al, 125
gum. *See* bubble gum
guns, Paterson, New Jersey and, 27
Gustine, Frankie, 85

Hack, Stan, 33
Haelan Laboratories, 109, 190
Halberstam, David, 52
Hall, Dan, 47
Halpin, Frank, 331
hamburgers, free, 227
Hamey, Roy, 80, 82
Hamilton, Alexander, 25–26
Hamm's Brewery, San Francisco, 20
Handley, Jack, 271

ACKNOWLEDGEMENTS

F irst and foremost, my gratitude—and love—go to my wife Ceil, who despite not being a big baseball fan would make a great umpire.

I owe a debt of gratitude to Dennis Sesma, an old high school pal who happens to be an ace private investigator. Dennis helped me track down the O'Connell clan and get the book moving. Speaking of whom, I can't begin to thank Danny O'Connell IV and his wife Leslie; John O'Connell; Maureen O'Connell Hurley and her husband John, and Nancy O'Connell Mellin. The "kids" were exceedingly generous with their photos, clips and memories of their mom and dad as well as with their time in answering questions. Danny and Vera would be very proud. It was also a hoot to meet and talk to Danny's brother and sister, Bob and Alice, as well as Bob's wife Dona.

I'm grateful for the assistance of Cassidy Lent, reference services manager at the National Baseball Hall of Fame, for patiently amassing a wealth of material for me from the Hall's archive, and graciously accommodating my vague and obscure requests while visiting the Hall. Likewise to John W. Horne Jr., the Hall's coordinator of rights and reproductions. Thank you to Fawn Meeker at St. Bonaventure Roman Catholic Church in Paterson New Jersey for digging out a copy of Danny's 1946 high school yearbook and filling in some gaps for me about Stony Road.

I'd like to say thanks to George Cecrle, a friend and thoughtful sports memorabilia collector who renewed my acquaintance with *Sports Collectors Digest* and was a welcome early cheerleader for the book's premise. Thanks to Society for American Baseball Research (SABR) members Andy Sharp and Bob Buege for sharing memories about their Washington Senators and Milwaukee Braves memories. And I would be derelict if I neglected to thank SABR itself, which for a half-century has functioned as a temple of statistical analysis, historical reflection and keeper of the flame for America's Grand Old Game.

Speaking of Idaho Falls, the Joneses—Paul, Lorraine and Barry, were exceedingly generous with their time in talking about Paul's world-record card collection and regaling me with tales of Paul's traveling bat boy adventures.

This is my third book with Bancroft Press, and a thank-you is due to

Bancroft boss Bruce Bortz, a thoughtful, tenacious and inventive publisher who cares about both readers and writers—and is also the only guy I have ever heard admit he actually *liked* the gum that came with the baseball cards. Deep thanks to Tracy Copes for her once-again excellent cover design and spiffing up the rest of the book to help cover up the writing deficiencies.

And as usual, I'm in debt to Rob Gunnison, Bobbie Metzger, Steve Capps and Steven and Sue Boudreau. Their recommendations, critiques, corrections, counsel, patience and most of all their friendship has once again helped keep the peanut rolling. Thanks guys.

ABOUT THE AUTHOR

Steve Wiegand is a life-long baseball fan even though his own prowess in the game peaked at age 11, when he hit a real over-the-fence home run for the immortal Robin's Frosties Little League team. It was the only homer of his career and probably an accident. Destined for indoor work, he spent 35 years as a reporter and columnist for the *San Diego Evening Tribune*, the *San Francisco Chronicle* and the *Sacramento Bee*.

He is the author, co-author or contributing author of 10 books, including *1876: Year of the Gun; The Dancer, the Dreamers and the Queen of Romania; U.S. History for Dummies*; the *Mental Floss History of the World; The American Revolution for Dummies* and *Lessons from the Great Depression for Dummies*.

Wiegand is a member of the Society for American Baseball Research (SABR.) When not watching the San Francisco Giants fall short of his completely reasonable expectations, he enjoys playing poker and the harmonica, although usually not at the same time. He lives in Arizona.